MW00891130

Miracles of the Rosary
&
The Rosary of Miracles

Meditations
with
Applications, Stories & Apparitions
Compiled from Various Sources

by

Fr. Edmond Gene Mary Kline

Through the Eyes of Mary Publications

Miracles of the Rosary & The Rosary of Miracles

Cover Photo: Our Lady of the Rosary with Child, Simone Cantarini (1612 to 1648), via Wikipedia Commons, Public Domain

Image: Virgin Mary & Child Jesus painted by Haidyn Lyden (2024)
Commissioned by Fr. Edmond Kline fatheredmondkline@blogspot.com

Image of the Rosary: Painted by Kylee Baldetti (2024)
Commissioned by Fr. Edmond Kline

Back page image: Photo of Our Lady of the Rosary, Wea-Bucyrus, Kansas
by Susan Raleigh Rome. Used with permission of Fr. Jerry Arano-Ponce, pastor

Quotations from the *Diary of Saint Maria Faustina Kowalska, Divine Mercy in My Soul*
Used with permission of the Marian Fathers of the Immaculate Conception of the Blessed Virgin Mary, Stockbridge, MA, USA.

Meditation on the Passion, Compiled From Various Sources with Introduction by Reginald Walsh, O.P., The Newman Press, 1959. Public domain in the USA

St. Louis Marie de Montfort, *The Secret of the Rosary,* (Bay Shore, NY: Montfort Publications, 1954) Public domain in the USA

Saint Alphonsus Liguori, *The Glories of Mary, S*econd American Edition (New York: Edward Dunigan & Brother, 1852) Public domain in the USA

All other copyright permissions and credits are located in end notes
A good faith effort was given to obtain all copyright permissions

Wholesale Orderline: HolyRosaryMiracles@gmail.com
Individual Orders: Amazon.com or a Catholic Book Store Near You

ISBN: 9798344816357
First Hardback Edition
Printed in the USA

THROUGH THE EYES OF MARY PUBLICATIONS

Dedication

Miracles of the Rosary & The Rosary of Miracles is dedicated to
my spiritual mother, the Virgin Mary,
and
my natural mother, Cecilia,
whose birthday is October 7,
Feast of the Holy Rosary,
and
My Holy Mother, the Catholic Church, the Bride of Christ.
I pray all will be honored.

O Queen of the Most Holy Rosary, Our Lady Queen of Peace,
I consecrate this book to Your Immaculate Heart.

O Mary, may it be pleasing to You
and may it bring many souls to Jesus through Your Intercession.
Amen.

*All Profits Go To Crisis Pregnancy Centers
& Catholic Organizations*

Special Thanks

Our Lady of Medjugorje, The Queen of Peace

Bishop Carl Kemme

Fr. Christopher Barak

Fr. Miguel Marie Soeherman, MFVA
(Franciscan Missionaries of the Eternal Word)

The people of Holy Trinity Catholic Church in Little River,
Kansas

The Dominican Sisters of the Perpetual Rosary
at the Monastery of St. Jude, Marbury, Alabama

Mike and Carolyn Armendariz

Wayne and Alicia Scheevel

Photos of Mother & Siblings Praying the Rosary

My mother with three of her brothers praying the Rosary
before a statue of the Virgin Mary outside of their home.
My mother has 8 brothers and 1 sister.

Our Lady of the Rosary with the Child Jesus
by
Haidyn Lyden (2024)

PREFACE

The following is a portion from an article from Bro. John Maria Devaney, O.P., June 4th 2014 in *Dominicana,* a publication of the Dominican student brothers of the St. Joseph Province of the Order of Preachers. The article highlights how the Rosary truly does work miracles today and we pray this book will inspire everyone who reads it to pray as many Rosaries a day as possible, most especially the family Rosary.

In May of 1971, the 15th to be exact, Elvis Aaron Presley recorded a song entitled "The Miracle of the Rosary." It would be released the following year on February 20, 1972 on the album entitled Elvis Now! It's one of the great mysteries of faith why Elvis, raised in the evangelical Christian denomination Assemblies of God, recorded a song devoted to arguably the greatest Catholic sacramental, the Rosary.

The song appears to be about the powerful intercession of Our Blessed Mother in the End Times. The track may be short, running for just over two minutes, but there is still time for Elvis to fully intone the Hail Mary.

The song was written by one of Elvis's childhood friends, Lee Denson. Denson was the son of a Pentecostal minister. Lee Denson, who was the son of a Protestant minister in the Pentecostal Church, was married to a young Catholic named Mary. Because of this, Lee became interested in Catholic dogma. He often witnessed his wife praying the Rosary daily, in response to Our Lady of Fatima's request to the little Portuguese shepherds to whom she appeared in 1917. Gradually, Lee turned to Catholicism and decided to embrace it for good.

One day, when Mary had neglected her prayers for some time, she lost her Rosary that had been given to her by a friend who had visited Fatima. She looked for it everywhere in the house but couldn't find it. Yet, on the night of October 13, 1960,

Lee found the Rosary in its case on the bed! [Note: October 13 is the date of the last apparition in Fatima] At the next day's Mass, Lee and his wife were surprised by the words of the priest who, in his homily, said that Our Lady of Fatima sometimes performs miracles in everyday life, yet people forget to thank her.

So Lee decided to write the song, which he then proposed to his friend Elvis in 1967, the 50th anniversary of the Fatima apparitions.

There is more: Only one female co-star appeared in two of Presley's films: Dolores Hart. To the shock of the movie business, she left Hollywood to enter religious life. In 1970, the then-film star entered the Benedictine Abbey of Regina Laudis, Connecticut, where she remains a cloistered nun to this day. The night before she entered the monastery, Presley unexpectedly called her to wish her well in her vocation. He was one of the few of her former Hollywood circle that did so. Later, long after his death in 1977, she was to say that she had never stopped praying for Elvis.

The name of the Benedictine monastery in Connecticut dedicated to Our Lady, Regina Laudis, in English means "the Queen of Praise." Shortly after Hart's entry there, mysteriously, a "king" was to praise that same Queen by singing Miracle of the Rosary.[1]

One more twist to this story, the author of this book had no idea Elvis Presley's song the *Hail Mary* was actually called *The Miracle Rosary*. And even more strange, the date of the release of the song, February 20th is now the feast of saints Jacinta and Francisco of Fatima and also the birthday of author of *Miracles of the Rosary & Rosary of Miracles* and his mother's birthday is October 7, the feast of the Holy Rosary. See Appendix E, for Elvis Presley's lyrics of "The Miracle of the Rosary."

INTRODUCTION

Thanks to my mother, Cecilia, I learned how to pray the Rosary as a child. My mother had a beautiful statue of Our Lady of Grace she placed on an antique dark brown buffet in the living room.

On occasion, she had us kneel before the statue and pray the Rosary. I was about 5 years old when we began to pray the Rosary together, and though I could not read yet, I learned the Our Father, Hail Mary and the Glory Be by praying the Rosary together with mom and my siblings. After a few years, we discontinued and I now wish we would have continued praying the Rosary.

Many years later, I discovered my grandmother, Sophie, mom's mother, had her children pray the Rosary outdoors before a statue of Mary that was placed on a small table with a cloth. Photos of mom and some of her brothers praying the Rosary are on the Dedication page.

When parents do things with their children, especially spiritual things, it leaves a long lasting impression on them.

Although I no longer knew how to pray the Rosary, minutes before my grandmother died, while at her beside at the hospital, I promised grandma Kline, my dad's mother, I would pray a Rosary for her.

I was greatly inspired by the Rosary all prayed at her funeral vigil. Months later, by watching EWTN, I learned how to pray the Rosary and then began to pray the Rosary daily due to the alleged messages of Our Lady of Medjugorje.

After not going to Confession for twenty years, from 2nd grade until I was 27, Our Lady gently nudged me into the confessional by way of the Rosary. The sorrowful mysteries in particular, touched my heart in such a way that I felt sorrow for my sins and especially sorrow for having hurt Jesus by my sins. I wanted to be reconciled with Him and have them washed away.

9

When my sins were finally absolved, my life changed forever. I became a happy man even in the midst of turmoil and difficulties.

My grandmother, my mother and my spiritual Mother, the Virgin Mary, played an important role in inspiring me to learn and pray the Rosary regularly. I would like to encourage all families to daily pray the Rosary and never give up praying it together.

Not much after I was ordained a priest, I gave a retreat on the Rosary in Detroit. Back then, there were no PowerPoint presentations. I used the old-fashioned overhead projector and created images of the mysteries of the Rosary on transparency paper. My talks were written on notebook paper.

At the retreat, I spoke about each mystery and then applied the mystery to our life today. While I was speaking, retreatants looked at the image of the mystery on the projector screen. I felt more comfortable when they looked at the mystery, rather than me.

Looking back on that retreat, I was honestly surprised how well it went. The power of images can help those who attend have a more fruitful experience.

Over the past several years, I used PowerPoint presentations to give talks on the Rosary and other talks, including Divine Mercy.

When we pray the Rosary, we bring to mind images as we meditate. These meditations can especially be helpful to our spiritual life, and for so many other endless causes as well.

I attended a retreat with a Dominican priest Friar, who gave a priest retreat for the priests of our diocese. I was pleasantly surprised he used the mysteries of the Rosary for his talks while applying them to the life of a priest.

A few months later, I gave a 4 hour presentation on the Rosary at our local retreat center. People were very interested in hearing about the Rosary. All went well, except for a computer glitch that happened on slide 66. Perhaps, St. Maximilian would have said, "the devil caught his tail in it."

I had a meeting with my spiritual director on the 20th anniversary of my ordination, and mentioned the Miracle Mysteries of Jesus, that I was meditating upon while praying the Rosary.

He suggested I write a book on the Rosary. When he said that, I thought my high school and college English teachers would have chuckled.

Not knowing where to begin, I decided I would use the format of the first Rosary retreat in Detroit, by giving meditations for each mystery and applying them (applications) to our life today, and conclude with meditations on the Miracles of Jesus Rosary.

I wondered how St. Dominic preached when he gave sermons on the Rosary. As a result of my curiosity, I contacted the Dominican, who gave our retreat to see if any of St. Dominic's sermons or homilies are in existence today. But, there aren't any.

Surely, St. Dominic preached on the mysteries of the Rosary and on the Rosary itself, but what else? Ah Ha! He would have also preached about the problems of his day, especially the Albigensian heresy. The Albigensian heretics taught only the spiritual is good and everything material is bad. Therefore, the body in and of itself is evil, and every person's soul is imprisoned in that evil body. The only way a person could experience salvation was to be freed from the imprisonment of their flesh.

So this is what I am attempting to do in this book, to preach about the Rosary, it's meditations, and apply them to some of our problems of today.

In the first part of the book are helpful hints about the Rosary. Then I give each mystery in Scripture, followed by the Meditation. After the Mediation are Applications of the mystery, and they are followed by Stories. Then, I chronologically give a church approved apparition that in some way had something to do with the Holy Rosary.

Some meditations came from saints such as St. Alphonsus Liguori's classic, *The Glories of Mary.* Much of the sorrowful mysteries came from, *Meditation on the Passion, compiled by Reginald Walsh, OP.* Other meditations are the result of my personal prayer.

Some may not be familiar with meditations, so when one reads a meditation it may come across as though the person who wrote the meditation is departing from the actual Gospel story and adding to it.

But a meditation is when we allow the event to come alive in our mind and begin to experience and explain what may have happened. For example, later in this book, when reading the Meditation on the Assumption of Mary by St. Alphonsus Liguori, one will read: "She then once more visited the holy places of Jerusalem, tenderly taking leave of them, and especially of Mount Calvary, where Her beloved Son had died. She then retired into Her poor cottage, there to prepare for death. During this time the Angels did not cease their visits to their beloved Queen, consoling themselves with the thought that they would soon see Her crowned in Heaven."

What St. Alphonsus Liguori wrote may or may not have actually happened, but what he is saying doesn't contradict the Catholic faith with regard to Scripture or Tradition. Rather, his meditation helps us to enter into the mystery of the event.

There have been many stories about miracles of the Rosary over the centuries, including the winning of battles, putting out a large fire in the USA, expelling demons, freeing young girls held in captivity, helping trapped miners, etc... Additional stories in the book are from *The Secret of the Rosary* by St. Louis De Montfort.

Many of the Applications after giving the meditation speak about some problems of our day.

The Apparitions of Our Lady, at the end of each of the twenty mysteries, help bring about the voice of our sweet Mother, in what She would say about the Rosary today.

Finally, most everyone knows before the Second Coming of Jesus, the anti-Christ will rule the world and will work false miracles.

It is my hope the meditations on the real Miracles of Jesus, will help counteract that future difficulty caused by the man of iniquity. Only God knows when that will be. However, Our Lord told Saint Faustina that His Second Coming is soon and wanted to use her to prepare for it, by establishing the Feast of Divine Mercy.

To prepare for that battle and to help us with our own spiritual battle, let us take up the Holy Rosary, a superior weapon to combat evil and most especially pray it with your family every night. As Father Peyton said, "The Family that Prays Together, Stays Together."

Pray as many Rosaries per day as you are able and invite others to pray it too. Through the eyes and Heart of Mary, may we be an instrument in the world to bring about the Triumph of Her Immaculate Heart, and allow Her to use us, to crush the serpent's head with the Holy Rosary.

CONTENTS

JOYFUL MYSTERIES MEDITATIONS

LUMINOUS MYSTERIES MEDITATIONS

THE MIRACLE MYSTERIES MEDITATIONS

19

Notes

Prayers of the Rosary

Sign of the Cross
In the name of the Father, and of the Son, and of the Holy Spirit. Amen.

Apostles Creed
I believe in God, the Father Almighty, Creator of Heaven and earth; and in Jesus Christ, His only Son Our Lord, Who was conceived by the Holy Spirit, born of the Virgin Mary, suffered under Pontius Pilate, was crucified, died, and was buried. He descended into Hell; the third day He rose again from the dead; He ascended into Heaven, and seated at the right hand of God, the Father almighty; from thence He shall come to judge the living and the dead. I believe in the Holy Spirit, the holy Catholic Church, the communion of saints, the forgiveness of sins, the resurrection of the body and life everlasting. Amen.

Our Father
Our Father, who art in heaven, hallowed be thy name. Thy kingdom come, thy will be done, on earth, as it is in heaven. Give us this day our daily bread and forgive us our trespasses as we forgive those who trespass against us; and lead us not into temptation, but deliver us from evil. Amen.

Hail Mary
Hail Mary, Full of Grace, The Lord is with thee. Blessed art thou among women, and blessed is the fruit of thy womb, Jesus. Holy Mary, Mother of God, pray for us sinners now, and at the hour of our death. Amen.

Glory Be
Glory be to the Father, and to the Son, and to the Holy Spirit. As it was in the beginning, is now, and ever shall be, world without end. Amen.

Fatima Prayer
O my Jesus, forgive us our sins, save us from the fires of hell; lead all souls to Heaven, especially those who have most need of your mercy.

Hail, Holy Queen
Hail, holy Queen, mother of Mercy. Hail, our life, our sweetness and our hope. To thee do we cry, poor banished children of Eve; to thee do we send up our sighs, mourning and weeping, in this vale of tears. Turn then, most gracious advocate, thine eyes of mercy toward us; and after this our exile, show unto us the blessed fruit of thy womb, Jesus. O clement, O loving, O sweet virgin Mary.

V. Pray for us, O holy Mother of God.
R. That we may be made worthy of the promises of Christ.

Let us pray: O God, whose Only Begotten Son, by his life, Death, and Resurrection, has purchased for us the rewards of eternal life, grant, we beseech thee, that while meditating on these mysteries of the most holy Rosary of the Blessed Virgin Mary, we may imitate what they contain and obtain what they promise, through the same Christ our Lord. Amen.

Conclude by kissing the Crucifix and making the Sign of the Cross.

21

How to Pray the Rosary

by Kylee Baldetti

1. Make the Sign of the Cross holding the Crucifix,
   and say the *Apostles' Creed*.

2. On the first bead, say an *Our Father*.

3. Say one *Hail Mary* on each of the next three beads.

4. Say the *Glory Be,* then pray, *the O My Jesus Prayer*.

5. Before each of the five decades, announce the Mystery (you may choose to read a brief Scripture) then say the *Our Father*.

6. While fingering each of the ten beads of the decade, next say ten *Hail Marys* while meditating on the Mystery.

7. After finishing each decade, then say a *Glory Be,* and the prayer requested by the Blessed Virgin Mary at Fatima:
O my Jesus, forgive us our sins, save us from the fires of hell; lead all souls to Heaven, especially those who have most need of your mercy.

8. Announce the Second Mystery, (you may choose to read a brief Scripture) then say the *Our Father*.

9. After saying all five decades, say the *Hail, Holy Queen*.

Sunday: Glorious Mysteries
Monday: Joyful Mysteries
Tuesday: Sorrowful Mysteries
Wednesday: Glorious Mysteries
Thursday: Luminous Mysteries
Friday: Sorrowful Mysteries
Saturday: Joyful Mysteries

Mysteries of the Rosary

The Joyful Mysteries

1. The Annunciation
Mary learns that she has been chosen to be the mother of Jesus.
2. The Visitation
Mary visits Elizabeth, who tells her that she will always be remembered.
3. The Nativity
Jesus is born in a stable in Bethlehem.
4. The Presentation
Mary and Joseph take the infant Jesus to the Temple to present him to God.
5. The Finding of Jesus in the Temple
Jesus is found in the Temple discussing his faith with the teachers.

The Mysteries of Light

1. The Baptism of Jesus in the River Jordan
God proclaims that Jesus is His beloved Son.
2. The Wedding Feast at Cana
At Mary's request, Jesus performs His first miracle.
3. The Proclamation of the Kingdom of God
Jesus calls all to conversion and service to the Kingdom.
4. The Transfiguration of Jesus
Jesus is revealed in glory to Peter, James, and John
5. The Institution of the Eucharist
Jesus offers His Body and Blood at the Last Supper.

The Sorrowful Mysteries

1. The Agony in the Garden
Jesus prays in the Garden of Gethsemane on the night before He dies.
2. The Scourging at the Pillar
Jesus is lashed with whips.
3. The Crowning With Thorns
Jesus is mocked and crowned with thorns.
4. The Carrying of the Cross
Jesus carries the cross that will be used to crucify him.
5. The Crucifixion
Jesus is nailed to the cross and dies.

The Glorious Mysteries

1. The Resurrection
God the Father raises Jesus from the dead.
2. The Ascension
Jesus returns to his Father in heaven.
3. The Coming of the Holy Spirit
The Holy Spirit comes to bring new life to the disciples.
4. The Assumption of Mary
At the end of her life on earth, Mary is taken body and soul into heaven.
5. The Coronation of Mary
Mary is crowned as Queen of Heaven and Earth.

The Miracle Mysteries

1. Jesus Heals the Paralytic
2. Jesus Multiplies of the Loaves & Fish
3. Jesus Walks on Water & Calms the Storm
4. Jesus Heals Boy with a Mute Spirit
5. Jesus Raises Lazarus from the Dead

Brief History of the Holy Rosary

Most of the Hail Mary prayer is found in Sacred Scripture. From the beginning, after Mary was assumed into heaven, Christians would have known and perhaps prayed the words of the angel Gabriel to Mary and Elizabeth's words to Our Lady. Coming to Her, he said, "Hail Full of Grace, the Lord is with thee…" (Luke 1:26)

At the Council of Ephesus in 431, when the dogma Mother of God was proclaimed, the council fathers added, "Holy Mary, Mother of God, pray for us sinners, now and at the hour of our death, Amen."

In 800 AD, Irish monks prayed the 150 psalms which include veiled prophecies of the life, death and Resurrection of Jesus. And they suggested to the illiterate, who couldn't join them in praying the 150 psalms, to rather pray 150 Our Fathers. They used leather pouches with pebbles to count the prayers. Some used ropes with small knots of either 50 or 150 to count the prayers. Eventually strings with wood beads were created to count the prayers. Instead of praying Our Fathers, some prayed the Angelic Salutation "Hail Mary, full of grace, the Lord is with thee…" 50 times.

Around 1050 AD, the words Saint Elizabeth used to greet Mary during the Visitation were added: "Blessed art thou among women, and blessed is the fruit of thy womb" (Luke 1:42).

In 1098, Cistercian monks prayed the Marian Psalter which consisted of praying 150 Hail Marys divided in groups of ten, separated by one Our Father. Prayer beads were used to keep track of the Hail Marys.

St. Dominic Guzman (1170-1221) traveled into France preaching against the Albigensian heresy, but his efforts gained few conversions and even fewer followers.

However, due to the Virgin Mary appearing to St. Dominic requesting that he add mysteries to the Rosary and preach the Rosary, many Albigensians were converted. (See Apparition after the Annunciation meditation to discover how Mary appeared to St. Dominic, page 68.)

Saint Louis Marie de Montfort said, "Saint Dominic has divided up the lives of Our Lord and Our Lady into fifteen mysteries which stand for their virtues and their most important actions. Our Lady taught Dominic this excellent method of praying and ordered him to preach it far and wide so as to reawaken the fervor of Christians and to revive in their hearts a love for Our Blessed Lord."[2]

In 1261, Pope Urban IV, added the name of Jesus to the Rosary.

St. Thomas Aquinas (1225 to 1274), a follower of St. Dominic, said the name of Mary was added to the Rosary to signify who was full of grace. And he said the name of Jesus was added to signify who was the fruit of Her womb.

Saint Peter Canisius added "Mother of God, pray for us sinners, now and at the hour of our death" in his own catechism in 1555, *The Summary of Christian Doctrine*. St. Peter Canisius then intervened at the Council of Trent to make it officially part of the Rosary. It was then added to the *Council of Trent Catechism* in 1566. Saint Peter's main mission was to counter the Protestant revolt in Germany. He was known for praying many rosaries a day. He asked his congregation to pray the Our Father and Hail Mary with him before he began preaching.

The prayer "Glory Be to the Father and the Son and the Holy Spirit" was added between decades by St. Louis Marie de Montfort (1673-1717).

On June 13, 1917, Our Lady of Fatima asked the "O my Jesus prayer" be added to the Rosary. Mary said, "I want you to come here on the thirteenth of next month. I want you to continue saying the Rosary every day. And after each one of the mysteries, my children, I want you to pray in this way: O my

26

Jesus, forgive us our sins, save us from the fire of hell. Take all souls to heaven, especially those who are most in need."

While Pope John Paul II made the Luminous mysteries known through his Apostolic Letter, *Rosarium Virginis Mariae,* "*Rosary of the Virgin Mary*" in 2002, the actual origin of the Luminous mysteries was not him. Blessed Bartolo Longo (1841 to 1946) wrote about the Luminous mysteries Pope Saint John Paul II included in his letter. In his *Colloquies with God,* Saint George Preca (1880 – 1962) canonized by Pope Benedict XVI in 2007, also mentioned the Luminous mysteries, but included the Raising of Lazarus.

Why is the Holy Rosary called the Rosary?

In the spiritual classic, *The Secret of the Rosary* by St. Louis Marie de Montfort, he explains why the Rosary is called the Rosary.

"Ever since Blessed Alan de la Roche (1428 – 1475) re-established this devotion the voice of the people, which is the voice of God, called it the Rosary. The word Rosary means "Crown of Roses," that is to say that every time people say the Rosary devoutly they place a crown of one hundred and fifty-three red roses and sixteen white roses upon the heads of Jesus and Mary. Being heavenly flowers these roses will never fade or lose their exquisite beauty.

Our Lady has shown Her thorough approval of the name Rosary; She has revealed to several people that each time they say a Hail Mary they are giving Her a beautiful rose and that each complete Rosary makes Her a crown of roses.

The well-known Jesuit, Brother Alphonsus Rodriguez, used to say his Rosary with such fervor that he often saw a red rose come out of his mouth at each Our Father and a white rose at each Hail Mary. The red and white roses were equal in beauty and fragrance, the only difference being in their color.

The chronicles of Saint Francis tell of a young friar who had the praiseworthy habit of saying the Crown of Our Lady (the Rosary) every day before dinner. One day for some reason or other he did not manage to say it. The refectory bell had already been rung when he asked the Superior to allow him to say it before coming to the table, and having obtained the permission he withdrew to his cell to pray.

After he had been gone a long time the Superior sent another Friar to fetch him, and he found him in his room bathed in a heavenly light facing Our Lady who had two Angels with her. Beautiful roses kept issuing from his mouth at each Hail Mary; the Angels took them one by one, placing them on Our Lady's head, and She smilingly accepted them.

Finally two other friars who had been sent to find out what had happened to the first two saw the same lovely scene, and Our Lady did not go away until the whole Rosary had been said.

So the complete Rosary is a large crown of roses and the Rosary of five decades is a little wreath of flowers or a small crown of heavenly roses which we place on the heads of Jesus and Mary. The rose is the queen of flowers, and so the Rosary is the rose of all devotions and it is therefore the most important one."[3]

Benefits of Praying the Rosary

Praying the Rosary benefits our soul. It gradually gives us knowledge of Jesus Christ. It purifies our soul, washing away sin. It gives us victory over our enemies. It makes it easy for us to practice virtue. It sets us on fire with love of Our Blessed Lord. It enriches us with graces and merits. It supplies what is needed to pay our debts to God and our fellow man. It obtains all kinds of graces for us from Almighty God. Through the Rosary hardened sinners are converted, great battles have been won, fires have been halted, pestilences have ended, people find courage to flee temptations, vocations have been wrought, and faith has been re-kindled. And through the Rosary we grow in holiness and virtue by leaps and bounds. For more benefits, see the "15 Promises of the Rosary".

Petitions Before Starting the Rosary

Before praying the Rosary, we should mention our specific intentions and also include the intentions of the Blessed Virgin Mary.

Slow Down When Praying the Rosary

In the early 1990's, I knew a woman who led the Rosary after Mass. The rosary was prayed so fast, she sounded like an auctioneer and would take a loud gasp of air after each "Amen". When she was half way through the Hail Mary, she would exclaim "JESUS!" as though someone won the item being auctioned. Few people talk that fast, let alone pray that fast. Some of us wondered if the parishioner was going to pass out for lack of air and for saying it with such speed.

At St. Charles Seminary in Philadelphia, the seminarians prayed the Rosary before Vespers "Evening Prayer." If a group of seminarians wanted the Rosary to be completed in a quick manner, in less than fifteen minutes, they would ask a certain seminarian to lead it.

The average person prays the Rosary either on their own or in a group almost twice as fast as they should. When praying the Rosary aloud by ourselves or in a group, let us pray it with great reverence, with heartfelt fervor, with undivided focus and with great love to whom we are addressing, Our Blessed Mother, the Queen of Heaven and Earth. To pray the Rosary in less than twenty minutes is praying it too fast and it's not being very reverent to Our Lady.

Praying the Rosary with a Group
Pray 30 Rosaries in 25 minutes! What?

When we pray the Rosary, half of the prayers are to be recited in chorus and the other half in the other chorus. One person who leads the rosary can pray half of the prayer, while the group prays the other half of the prayer. This prevents distractions and is stronger in overcoming the devil.

St. Louis de Montfort said, "Somebody who says his Rosary alone only gains the merit of one Rosary, but if he says it together with thirty other people he gains the merit of thirty Rosaries. This is the law of public prayer. How profitable, how advantageous this is!"[4]

The superior of St. Padre Pio once asked him how many Rosaries he prayed in a day. He responded, thirty-four. He actually prayed thirty-four everyday, because he loved the Rosary and had a special gift to be able to do it.

Suppose thirty-four of his religious Franciscan brothers were to pray the Rosary together as a group, it would be as though each friar prayed thirty-four Rosaries in twenty five minutes.

Padre Pio said, "The Rosary is the weapon for these times." He said, "Some people are so foolish that they think they can go through life without the help of the Blessed Mother. Love the Madonna and pray the rosary, for Her Rosary is the weapon against the evils of the world today. All graces given by God pass through the Blessed Mother."

In pilgrimage places like Fatima, Lourdes and Medjugorje, up to 10,000 or more could be praying the Rosary as a group. According to St. Louis de Montfort, it would be the same as though each person prayed 10,000 rosaries. When we pray the rosary as a group, it's the same as an army attacking the devil.

Imagine how many graces you, your family, and your parish will receive if the Rosary is prayed as a group. Your pastor may choose to have the congregation pray it before or after Mass.

Fr. Patrick Peyton, CSC, (1909 to 1992) had massive Rosary Rallies all over the world. His cause has been opened for his canonization. He also developed *Family Theater Productions* and had Hollywood stars perform the mysteries of the Rosary. These are currently available to watch on the Internet. He is noted for saying, "The Family that prays together, stays together." Before attending the rally, grass root volunteers asked families in parishes to sign a pledge card committing to praying the Rosary together every day.

How powerful then are Rosary Rallies! Let us revive them! Let us use them to conquer the devil and receive a multitude of graces for ourselves, those we pray for and the world.

Ferdinand and Imelda Marcos were dictators of the Philippines, until February of 1986, when Corazon Aquino won the election, but Marcos declared himself the winner.

In response, millions of people came out in protest. Hundreds of thousands of people began to pray the Rosary in the streets. Tanks were ordered into the streets.

But, soldiers saw a beautiful woman encased in a globe, who said to them, "Dear Soldiers, stop! Do not proceed. Do not harm my children. I am the Queen of this land." The soldiers dropped their weapons, withdrew from pressing forward and joined the throngs of crowds to turn and fight with them against the Marco regime. President Marcos and his family fled that night for Hawaii.

Ten years later, in commemoration of the public apparition, a church and shrine called Our Lady Queen of Peace was built with a large statue of the Virgin Mary erected on that spot.[5]

In 2010, thirty-three miners became trapped in a mine in Chile for a month. Being a Catholic country, the minors prayed the Holy Rosary everyday so they could be rescued. On the anniversary of the last apparition of Our Lady of Fatima, when Our Lady referred to Herself as Our Lady of the Rosary, October 13, the miners were freed.

100 feet from the mine, the large drill became stuck and would not budge. But suddenly, on its own it began to drill until it reached the miners. Pope Benedict XVI gave the trapped miners a Rosary after they were freed.

Amy Sigle, a 16 year old girl from St. Rose of Lima Catholic Church, in Council Grove, Kansas died from cancer. During her last months before she died, many of her Catholic friends and relatives would visit her home. Before her friends and relatives departed, Amy always asked the group to pray a Rosary with her. Unbeknownst to anyone, until after her death, she made the request to pray the Rosary with each group of visitors, and therefore would pray seven or more Rosaries a day. Due to her virtuous life, Bishop Michael Jackals of the Diocese of Wichita, gave permission to seek her intercession. This young girl bore witness to her love of the Holy Rosary and the Blessed Virgin Mary, while enduring her last days in this life.

32

St. Louis de Montfort in *The Secrets of the Rosary*, spoke about the power of praying the Rosary in a group. He said a monastery, a parish and a diocese were all transformed due to the recitation of the Holy Rosary.

Please encourage others to pray in a group, especially with their family every day.

Keep Your Rosary on You

In the 1970's Ted Bundy, a serial killer, had just killed several sorority girls in their sorority house. In another room was a young girl who promised her mother she would daily pray the Rosary for protection. That night, after Bundy killed the other two girls, he came to the third girl's room. She was holding the Rosary in her hands when he entered. He had a knife in his hand and was about to approach her, when an unseen force caused him to drop the knife and threw him out of the room. When police arrived the girl was so shocked, she said she didn't want to talk to anyone, except a priest. When the priest arrived, she told him what had happened and the priest said it was through the Rosary she was protected.

Years later, when Ted Bundy was on death row, he asked to see a priest, and it just so happened, by God's providence, the same priest who visited the young girl, came to see Bundy. He explained to the priest what happened and said he couldn't understand how a force caused him to drop the knife and forced him to leave. The priest told him, he saw the girl that same night. She was holding a rosary in her hand. The priest said he believed that force was the Holy Rosary.

We should keep our Rosary on us at all times, to be ready to pray it whenever we need Our Lady's special intercession in a powerful way or when any situation arises when we desire Our heavenly Mother's assistance.

Indulgences & Blessed Rosaries

We gain a Plenary Indulgence when the Rosary is prayed in church, or in a public oratory, in a family (family Rosary), religious community, or pious association, while meditating on the mysteries of five decades. One must also: be in the state of grace, pray one Our Father, Hail Mary and Glory Be for the intentions of the Supreme Pontiff, receive Holy Communion with the intention of gaining an indulgence, receive sacramental Confession twenty days before or after the day one intends to obtain it, and detached from sin. We are permitted to obtain only one Plenary Indulgence per day and can obtain one Plenary Indulgence every day, by following the necessary conditions.

Otherwise, a Partial Indulgence is granted when praying the Rosary by yourself and one must also do the same elements as gaining a Plenary Indulgence.

The recitation of [one set of mysteries] is sufficient for obtaining the Plenary Indulgence, but these five decades must be recited without interruption. Devout meditation on the mysteries is to be added to the vocal prayer. In its public recitation the mysteries must be announced in accord with approved local custom, but in its private recitation it is sufficient for the Christian faithful simply to join meditation on the mysteries to the vocal prayer.

Indulgences can always be applied either to oneself or to a soul of the deceased, but can't be applied to another person, other than oneself, who is living on earth.

At the end of the book are *Rosary of the Miracles* meditations, but this particular *Rosary of the Miracles* has no indulgences attached to it.

Every event in the life of Christ is beneficial for our salvation and by meditating on the events in His life including His miracles, we will receive graces.

It is believed, St. Louis de Montfort said, that the Sorrowful mysteries of the Rosary are the most efficacious for our souls.

By providing the *Miracles Rosary*, it is not the intent of the author to replace any officially Church approved Rosaries: Joyful, Luminous, Sorrowful and Glorious. But rather, provide additional mysteries to meditate and therefore inspire the faithful to pray additional Rosaries and perhaps receive special graces that may come by meditating on Our Lord's miracles.

"A Catholic may gain a plenary indulgence by remaining in Adoration of the Blessed Sacrament for at least a half-hour."[6] So if one were to pray the *Miracles Rosary* during their time of Adoration of the Blessed Sacrament for at least a half-hour, or any other prayers, one could receive a Plenary Indulgence.

The Rosary is not required to be blessed by a priest to gain an indulgence. However, if the Rosary is blessed by a priest, extra graces are given when using it or when coming in contact with it because it is a sacramental.

Ordinarily, Rosaries are not to be worn around the neck as jewelry and definitely not to be used as a symbol of belonging to a gang. However, if the purpose to wear the Rosary around our neck is to give witness to it and wear it as a sacramental, with the hope of praying it, and protecting oneself from evil spirits, then these are good intentions.

It's the intention that is important. For example, if one hangs a Rosary on their rear-view mirror for superstitious purposes, that's not a good reason. However, if one places a Rosary around the mirror to have it easily available to pray when driving and receive protection as a sacramental, then these would be good purposes.

Confraternity of the Holy Rosary

The *Rosary Center and Confraternity* mission is to preach the Good News of Jesus Christ by promoting devotion to the Blessed Virgin Mary, especially through her Rosary, to help the faithful grow in their love of the Lord, the Blessed Mother, the Rosary and the Church. Founded by the Dominican friars, the Rosary Center serves as the local headquarters of the global Rosary Confraternity, providing numerous resources to help the faithful grow in their love of our Lord, the Blessed Mother, the Rosary and the Catholic Church.

Each member strives to pray the fifteen mysteries of the Rosary each week (it does not bind under sin), and must have his/her name inscribed in the register of the Confraternity. There are no meetings and no dues. As members pray, they pray also for the intentions of all the other members of the Rosary Confraternity worldwide, living and deceased. Luminous Mysteries are not yet required, but suggested to pray as well.

The are many benefits of the Rosary Confraternity. For example: The special protection of the Mother of God. A share in the prayer of thousands of members the world over, even after death. A share in the prayers, Masses and apostolic works of the Order of Preachers (Dominicans). The intercession of the entire heavenly court. Various plenary and partial indulgences.

Six times a year the Rosary Center publication *The Rosary, Light and Life* is sent to members who wish it. Its purpose is to provide sound doctrine and spiritual guidance for readers everywhere. To become a member: RosaryCenter.org Portland, Oregon or RosaryConfraternity.org Columbus, Ohio.

Meditate on the Mysteries

The Blessed Virgin meditated on and treasured the events in the life of Her Son. According to St. Alphonsus Liguori, after Jesus ascended into heaven, She repeatedly went to the locations where the events happened: the place where He was born, where He was scourged, Mount Calvary where He was crucified, etc…

St. Luke is not one of the twelve apostles, but an evangelist, who wrote the Gospel of Luke and the Acts of the Apostles. Since only Luke describes the annunciation, the visitation, the birth of Jesus, the presentation in the temple and the finding of Jesus in the temple, most believe he personally spoke to the Virgin Mary and then recorded those events in his Gospel. Luke was not only a physician, he was also an artist.

It's believed four icons of the Virgin Mary he painted are still in existence: Our Lady of Vladimir, Our Lady of Perpetual Help, Our Lady of Czestochowa, and Salus Populi Romani.

Before he painted the icons, he must have meditated on the beauty of Mary, who met in person, and contemplated what He imagined the Child Jesus would have looked like as a baby.

There are several scriptures that indicate Mary pondered events in the life of Jesus. When the shepherds found Mary, Joseph and the Infant lying in the manger, "And seeing, they understood of the word that had been spoken to them concerning this child. And all that heard, wondered; and at those things that were told to them by the shepherds. Mary kept all these things, pondering them in Her Heart." (Luke 2:16-20). Also when Mary and Joseph found Him in the temple, "And he went down with them, and came to Nazareth, and was subject to them. And his mother kept all these words in her heart. And Jesus advanced in wisdom, age, and grace with God and men." (Luke 2:51-52)

These events were so precious to Mary, She must have told Luke She pondered them and treasured them with Her Motherly Heart.

The secret to enter into the mysteries of the Rosary is to do so with the eyes and Heart of Mary. What were Mary's thoughts when the events happened? What did She feel? What did She experience? We want to ponder and treasure the mysteries as She did.

Our Lady of Fatima said She wants the world to have devotion to Her Immaculate Heart. When we ponder the mysteries of the Rosary, we enter into Her Heart and ponder with Her. Repeatedly meditating on the mysteries, we will begin to love Jesus, like Mary loved Jesus. Our heart will sorrow, like Her Heart sorrowed. Our heart will be filled with joy, like Her Heart. We turn to the Heart of Mary to help us to know and love Jesus more. We turn to the Heart of Mary, asking for Her loving intercession as She prays with us when we pray the Rosary.

When a specific mystery is announced at the beginning of each decade, we are to meditate (think about) the mystery. By meditating we come in contact with the saving mystery of Jesus or Mary and our soul is flooded with graces, and all this happens with the backdrop of Our Fathers and Hail Marys. Therefore, the Rosary is a double prayer. It's vocal because we use our lips to say the prayers, but also mental prayer, because we think about the mysteries associated with each decade.

They are called mysteries because their actions were completed by God. The action of any human, no matter how good, has limits in its effect upon us.

We can think about or meditate on an action that we did when we were a child and it can bring us joy or sorrow depending upon what we did. But, since it was a purely human act, it has little effect upon us when we meditate on it.

But the action of God is infinite. The mysteries of the life, death and resurrection of Jesus have an eternal effect on our soul.

"For, in reality, the Rosary said without meditating on the sacred mysteries of our salvation would almost be like a body without a soul: excellent matter but without the form which is meditation—this latter being that which sets it apart from all other devotions."[7]

The mystery becomes present to us. It increases our faith. We become more like Christ. We grow in virtue. God gives us insights into the mystery. We receive grace into our souls. We learn to imitate the virtue associated with the mystery. Our mind is reminded of the truth associated with the mystery. We avoid falling into error because we experience the divine truth.

To recite the Rosary, which can be called a "compendium of the Gospel", Pope St. John Paul II said, "is to contemplate the Face of Christ in union with, and at the school of, His Most Holy Mother…Against the background of the words of the Ave Maria the principal events of the life of Jesus Christ pass before the eyes of the soul. They take shape in the complete series of the joyful, luminous, sorrowful and glorious mysteries, and they put us in living communion with Jesus through–we might say through the heart of his Mother…"[8]

"A mystery is a sacred thing which is difficult to understand. The works of Our Lord Jesus Christ are all sacred and Divine because He is God and man at one and the same time. The works of the Most Blessed Virgin are very holy because She is the most perfect and the most pure of God's creatures. The works of Our Lord and of His Blessed Mother can be rightly called mysteries because they are so full of wonders and all kinds of perfections and deep and sublime truths which the Holy Spirit reveals to the humble and simple souls who honor these mysteries."[9]

Failure to meditate on the mysteries while praying the Rosary runs the risk of babbling, as Jesus said the pagans do. "And when you are praying, do not *babble* on and on *like the pagans*; for they think they will be heard because of their many words." (Matthew 6:7)

In September of 1991, a young man went on a pilgrimage to Medjugorje, Bosnia-Herzegovina with a group. The pilgrimage guide suggested that each person find the time to make a Holy Hour with Jesus in the Adoration Chapel, located near St. James church.

He and another young woman went into the chapel to pray. He had never been to an Adoration Chapel before. About a year previously, he learned to meditate on the mysteries of the Rosary by watching the Rosary on EWTN, the Eternal Word Television Network founded by Mother Angelica, a Poor Clare nun of Perpetual Adoration in Irondale, Alabama.

He states that he has never had a good imagination. And consequently, his meditations are oftentimes simply the event as though it were a motionless picture or painting in his mind.

But, as he began to pray the glorious mysteries of the Rosary, while adoring Jesus in the Most Blessed Sacrament, he said he felt peace come over him. Then in his mind, the mysteries came alive, as though he was watching television or a motion picture. He saw Jesus come out of the tomb and appear to the Apostles. Then during the second mystery, he saw Jesus ascend into heaven on a cloud as the Apostles were looking on, and those in the meditation were alive and moving about.

He said this type of meditation only happened one time and after that event, he continued to meditate as previously with motionless images as he prays the Rosary.

This example shows that to meditate well is a gift from God. Likewise, Jesus in the Holy Eucharist is there to help our soul bear fruit.

Praying the Rosary before Jesus in the Blessed Sacrament is more efficacious then praying at our home or some other place, because we are in the physical presence of Our Lord.

On our part, we just do the best we can to think about the mysteries. If we don't have a beautiful experience, like the young man, know that God is continues to be at work within us, but in a more hidden way, that may take more faith, despite dryness or distractions. It is very virtuous for us to persevere.

When we meditate on the mystery, we go there and are present at mystery when it is taking place. For example, you can be there at the Birth of Jesus and participate in the mystery. You can take the place of Mary or Joseph holding the baby Jesus. Or you can picture Mary handing the baby Jesus to you in your arms to hold and cuddle.

Not everyone has an imagination like that and many have "dryness" when trying to meditate. Others, due to their health or busyness of life find it difficult to focus. But, when we persevere doing our best, it's meritorious because we are practicing virtue. When we pray, even if we don't feel like praying, it shows we love and are not attached to feelings.

Every moment in the life of Jesus is inside and outside of time, and our soul is positively affected by just thinking about any moment in the life of Christ. To just think about God is prayer.

Just think about the difference between television or movies or videos verses meditating on the life of Jesus. The images of the world cause us to lose peace, while the images of God give us peace. Once a worldly thought is in our mind, it can come back to disturb us, and if it's an evil thought, it can tempt us to sin.

But, holy thoughts draw us closer to God and help to purify our mind of thoughts we don't want to have.

Meditations on the mysteries of Jesus can be healing. Our Lord can use those meditations to deliver us from a bad way of life. They can heal our wounded souls, like balm on a wound.

The Rosary Can Bring Healing

When we pray the Rosary, the mysteries we meditate upon can help bring about spiritual and emotional healing.

For example, if we have difficulty with a teen, we can meditate on the Finding of Jesus in the Temple. Or if we lost a child through miscarriage or abortion, when we meditate on the Birth of Jesus, and hold the Divine Child in our arms, Jesus will bring about consolation and healing. Or if we lost a loved one, when meditating on the Assumption of Mary, it gives us hope and encouragement. Meditating on the Passion of Jesus in all five of the mysteries can help us to persevere through our suffering and give us peace in the midst of it and heal the spiritual wound of unforgiveness and the emotional wound of feeling forsaken. The prophet Isaiah said, "By His stripes, we are healed." (Isaiah 53:5)

Saint Bishop Theodoret of Cyr gives us a beautiful example of how Our Lord's sufferings can heal us. He states,

> "Of his own free will Jesus ran to meet those sufferings that were foretold in the Scriptures concerning him. He had forewarned his disciples about them several times; he had rebuked Peter for being reluctant to accept the announcement of his passion, and he had made it clear that it was by means of his suffering that the world's salvation was to be accomplished. This was why he stepped forward and presented himself to those who came in search of him, saying: I am the one you are looking for. For the same reason he made no reply when he was accused, and refused to hide when he could have done so; although in the past he had slipped away on more than one occasion when they had tried to apprehend him.

Jesus also wept over Jerusalem because by her unwillingness to believe she was bent on her own ruin, and upon the temple, once so renowned, he passed sentence of utter destruction. Patiently he put up with being struck in the face by a man who was doubly a slave, in body and in spirit. He allowed himself to be slapped, spat upon, insulted, tortured, scourged and finally crucified. He accepted two robbers as his companions in punishment, on his right and on his left. He endured being reckoned with murderers and criminals. He drank the vinegar and the bitter gall yielded by the unfaithful vineyard of Israel. He submitted to crowning with thorns instead of with vine twigs and grapes; he was ridiculed with the purple cloak, holes were dug in his hands and his feet, and at last he was carried to the grave.

All this he endured in working out our salvation. For since those who were enslaved to sin were liable to the penalties of sin, he himself, exempt from sin though he was and walking in the path of perfect righteousness, underwent the punishment of sinners. By His cross He blotted out the decree of the ancient curse: for, as Paul says: Christ redeemed us from the curse of the law by becoming a curse for us; for it is written: "Cursed be everyone who hangs on a tree." And by his crown of thorns he put an end to that punishment meted out to Adam, who after his sin had heard the sentence: Cursed is the ground because of you; thorns and thistles shall it bring forth for you.

In tasting the gall Jesus took on himself the bitterness and toil of man's mortal, painful life. By drinking the vinegar he made his own the degradation men had suffered, and in the same act gave us the grace to better our condition. By the purple robe he signified his kingship, by the reed he hinted at the weakness and rottenness of the devil's power. By taking the slap in the face, and thus suffering the violence, corrections and blows that were due to us, he proclaimed our freedom.

His side was pierced as Adam's was; yet there came forth not a woman who, being beguiled, was to be the death-bearer, but a fountain of life that regenerates the world by its two streams: the one to renew us in the baptismal font and clothe us with the garment of immortality, the other to feed us, the reborn, at the table of God, just as babes are nourished with milk."[10]

Bishop Fulton Sheen explains how the life of Jesus can help us when we have sufferings such as loneliness. In one of his television programs he said,

"What does God know about loneliness? A babe born in Afghanistan, that has no better home than straw. (Jesus was born in a cave and laid in a manger with straw). Does God know about a family that has to escape a dictator and go half across Africa? (The Holy Family had to escape Herod and flee into Egypt). Does God know about a man who was born on the wrong side of the tracks and isolated socially from people due to his callous hands and his kind of labor? (Jesus was raised in the "hick" town of Nazareth, "Can anything good come from Nazareth?" He was a carpenter). Does God know the loneliness of being deserted by friends? (The Apostles deserted Jesus in the Garden of

44

Gethsemane). Does God know about the feeling of doubts, that God has abandoned me? (Jesus felt abandoned by His Father on the Cross, "My God, My God, why have you forsaken me?") Jesus came into the world, not to immunize Himself from loneliness or cut himself from it. Would He be the only one on the battlefield and not help the wounded? He loved us so much that blood poured out from His body. Suppose someone came into the world in all this loneliness and was not overcome by it but conquered it all. He would not only understand it but lift us up through it. We may be lonely every once in a while, but we will not be overcome by it, because we have a captain, who does not press a button by a hand in heaven from a celestial command, but we have a captain, who stumbled (carrying His Cross) to a throne.[11]

Pray the Rosary with Attention, Avoid Distractions, Pray it Well

It is very difficult for Christians to pray without distractions. *The Catechism of the Catholic Church* speaks about distractions in prayer. "The habitual difficulty in prayer is *distraction*. It can affect words and their meaning in vocal prayer; it can concern, more profoundly, him to whom we are praying, in vocal prayer (liturgical or personal), meditation, and contemplative prayer. To set about hunting down distractions would be to fall into their trap, when all that is necessary is to turn back to our heart: for a distraction reveals to us what we are attached to, and this humble awareness before the Lord should awaken our preferential love for him and lead us resolutely to offer him our heart to be purified. Therein lies the battle, the choice of which master to serve." (CCC #2729)

St. Teresa of Avila suffered from distraction in prayer. She said, "Do not imagine that the important thing is never to be thinking of anything else and that if your mind becomes slightly distracted all is lost." It is still important to keep praying. Praying provides us the "the strength which fits us for service... The Lord leads each of us as He sees we have need."

Some people can focus better than others while doing tasks. For example, one may be able to meditate on the mysteries of the Rosary while driving or cooking, or mowing the yard, while others can't.

It is best to do whatever we can to avoid as many distractions as possible when meditating on the mysteries of the Rosary, such as praying the Rosary with others, or praying silently alone in our room or walking down the street. We should turn off the radio, the television and silence the phone.

Before each meditation read Sacred Scripture for a greater fruitfulness. *Praying the Rosary Without Distractions* is a booklet distributed by the Rosary Center and Confraternity in Portland, Oregon. In the booklet, before praying each Hail Mary, a scripture quote can be read to reduce distractions. Pamphlets or booklets with pictures of each mystery are helpful in paying attention while praying the Rosary.

Televised Rosaries and videos of the Rosary with meditations can help maintain focus on the mysteries. Fr. Peyton's re-enactments of the mysteries in his Rosary videos "Family Theater Productions", EWTN's Rosary programs, Rosary *YouTube* videos or Rosary Apps can do wonders to aid us when praying the Rosary.

Some people begin to pray the Rosary when lying down to sleep, but almost always fall asleep praying it. They may say, "My guardian angel will finish the Rosary for me." While it's good to pray an "extra" Rosary when lying down for sleep, it's most likely an excuse to make it a priority and actually pray it alert, and with as few as distractions as possible. We shouldn't just pray one Rosary a day! No, we should pray as many Rosaries as possible every day, and to pray them well for the benefit of our own soul and souls for whom we are praying. Our soul and the souls of many can be saved.

The greater the reverence, attention, fervor, and with the least distractions is the best way to pray the Rosary. When we go to our judgment, the Lord will show us how the Rosaries we prayed touched the hearts and lives of others and saved some from going to hell.

15 Rosary Promises with Commentary

According to tradition, Alanus de Rupe (1428 – 1475), "Blessed Alan de la Roche" received the following 15 promises to those who pray the Rosary devoutly from the Blessed Virgin Mary Herself through a private revelation.

1. Those who faithfully serve me by the recitation of the Rosary shall receive signal graces.

"A signal grace is a gentle nudge, that seems to be a coincidence, but is actually God's way of encouraging us through Mary. In Suellen Brewster's examples in her article, "Signal Graces, How the Blessed Mother Encourages Her Little Ones."she said, "When someone gives you a bag of hand-me-downs and it contains just exactly what you needed and prayed for, that is a signal grace that being a stay-at-home mother was a well discerned choice. When a sudden unexpected decrease in a fixed expense occurs after you stood firm in your conviction not to work on Sundays, that is a signal grace of a well discerned choice. When you prayed for a simple way to help an elderly neighbor and realized, as you are thinking about her, that you made way too much dinner, that is a signal grace. On their own these small graces are not enough to make great changes in your life, or the lives of those you love. They are not meant to do that. They are more of a fortification, a heavenly hug, a love note, helping you to step back and remember the big picture: you are a beloved child of the King!"[12]

2. I promise my special protection and the greatest graces to all those who shall recite the Rosary.

A seminarian from the Diocese of Mobile, Alabama when traveling in his car was praying the Rosary. He was involved in a sudden accident. His car was totally demolished, but he was completely unharmed. If our Lady will provide physical protection to those who pray Her Rosary, how much more spiritual protection does She provide?

3. The Rosary shall be a powerful armor against hell. It will destroy vice, decrease sin, and defeat heresies.

Saint Louis Marie de Montfort said, "If you say the Rosary faithfully until death, I do assure you that, in spite of the gravity of your sins you shall receive a never fading crown of glory. Even if you are on the brink of damnation, even if you have one foot in hell, even if you have sold your soul to the devil as sorcerers do who practice black magic, and even if you are a heretic as obstinate as a devil, sooner or later you will be converted and will amend your life and will save your soul, if— and mark well what I say—if you say the Holy Rosary devoutly every day until death for the purpose of knowing the truth and obtaining contrition and pardon for your sins."[13]

Blessed Bartolo Longo was a fallen away Catholic, who became a satanic priest. His parents devoutly prayed the Rosary together. After his deceased father told him to "Return to God!"

he went to Confession. A Dominican priest encouraged him to pray the Rosary. Due to the Rosary, he had a conversion and believed God wanted him to promulgate the Rosary. He built the world's largest basilica dedicated to Our Lady of the Rosary, in Pompeii, Italy. He had refurbished a severely worm eaten painting of Our Lady of the Rosary with St. Dominic and St. Catherine of Sienna. Immediate physical miracles and miracles of conversion have occurred when the painting was installed.

St. Louis de Montfort said, "For never will anyone who says his Rosary every day become a formal heretic or be led astray by the devil. This is a statement that I would gladly sign with my blood."[14]

As noted earlier, the Albigensian heresy was rooted out by St. Dominic and the Dominicans when they preached the Rosary.

Our Lady revealed to Blessed Alan that no sooner had St. Dominic begun preaching the Rosary than hardened sinners were touched and wept bitterly over their grievous sins. Young children performed incredible penances and everywhere that he preached the Rosary such fervor arose that sinners changed their lives and edified everyone by their penances and change of heart.

4. The recitation of the Rosary will cause virtue and good works to flourish. It will obtain for souls the abundant mercy of God. It will withdraw the hearts of men from the love of the world and its vanities, and will lift them to the desire of eternal things. Oh, that souls would sanctify themselves by this means.

As far as attaining the abundant mercy of God for souls, during the March for Life, a priest was preparing for Mass at the Basilica of the Immaculate Conception in Washington, DC. He didn't know any priests there and decided to pray the Rosary for the intention of hearing other priest's confessions before Mass. By the time he completed the Rosary, three priests independent of each other, though he hadn't said a word to any of them, asked him to hear their confessions. Perhaps, the sign for the other priests, he was open to hearing their confessions, had to do with them noticing he was praying the Holy Rosary and therefore would trust him to be a good confessor.

Each mystery of the Rosary is known for a specific virtue that can be attained while meditating on it. See Appendix C, "Mysteries of the Rosary Virtues."

5. The soul which recommends itself to me by the recitation of the Rosary shall not perish.

"The devout author of the book in honor of the most holy Rosary, entitled, The Secret of every Grace," relates that St. Vincent Ferrer once said to a man dying in despair: "Why will you ruin yourself when Jesus Christ wishes to save you?" And he answered that in spite of Christ he would be damned. The saint replied: "And you, in spite of yourself, shall be saved." He began to recite the Rosary with the people of the house, and behold, the sick man asked to make his confession, made it weeping, and then died."[15]

6. Those who recite my Rosary devoutly, applying themselves to the consideration of its sacred mysteries, shall never be conquered by misfortune. In His justice, God will not chastise them; nor shall they perish by an unprovided death, i.e., be unprepared for heaven. Sinners shall convert. The just shall persevere in grace and become worthy of eternal life.

"...a poor woman, who was buried by an earthquake under the ruins of a house, was found alive and uninjured, with her children in her arms, by some persons who were employed by a priest to remove the stones. When she was asked what devotion she had practiced, she said she had never failed to say the Rosary and visit a chapel of the most holy Mary."[16]

7. Those who have a true devotion to the Rosary shall not die without the sacraments of the Church.

"Blessed Alan de la Roche and other writers (including Saint Robert Bellarmine) tell the story of how a good confessor advised three of his penitents, who happened to be sisters, to say the Rosary every day without fail for a whole year. This was so that they might make beautiful robes of glory for Our Lady out of their Rosaries. This was a secret that the priest had received from Heaven. So the three sisters said the Rosary faithfully for a year and on the Feast of the Purification the Blessed Virgin appeared to them at night when they had retired. [....] Our Lady, clothed in a magnificent robe and attended by Saint Catherine and Saint Agnes, wearing crowns, appeared to them again in the evening. She said to them: "My daughters, I have come to tell you that you have earned Heaven at last—and you will all have the great joy of going there tomorrow." The three of them cried: "Our hearts are all ready, dearest Queen; our hearts are all ready." Then the vision faded. That same night they became ill and so sent for their confessor who brought them the Last Sacraments and they thanked him for the holy practice that he had taught them. After Compline (Night Prayer) Our Lady appeared with a multitude of virgins and had the three sisters clothed in white gowns. While Angels were singing "Come, spouses of Jesus Christ, receive the crowns which have been prepared for you for all eternity," they departed from this life."[17]

8. Those who faithfully recite the Rosary shall have, during their life and at their death, the light of God and the plenitude of His graces. At the moment of death, they shall participate in the merits of the saints in paradise.

We can surmise that to have the light of God means to have His splendor, His glory, His righteousness, His understanding, His mercy, His love. The plenitude of graces means to have all the graces necessary and more to help us in this life to achieve our salvation and help bring others to salvation. To participate in the merits of the saints means to have accomplished His God's will in our life in a heroic manner.

"After earth's exile, I hope to go and enjoy you in the fatherland, but I do not want to lay up merits for heaven. I want to work for your love alone… In the evening of this life, I shall appear before you with empty hands, for I do not ask you, Lord, to count my works. All for justice is blemished in your eyes. I wish, then, to be clothed in your own justice and to receive from your love the eternal possession of yourself." St. Therese of Lisieux, *Story of A Soul* (1873-1897)

9. I shall deliver from purgatory those who have been devoted to the Rosary.

St. Faustina said, "I saw Our Lady visiting the souls in Purgatory. The souls call her "The Star of the Sea." She brings them refreshment. I wanted to talk with them some more, but my Guardian Angel beckoned me to leave. We went out of that prison of suffering. [I heard an interior voice] which said, "My mercy does not want this, but justice demands it." Since that time, I am in closer communion with the suffering souls."[18] (Diary #20)

10. The faithful children of the Rosary shall merit a high degree of glory in heaven.

Saint Francisco Marto at first did not see Our Lady when She appeared to the three children at Fatima. When Lucia told Mary, "Francisco wants to see you too" the beautiful Lady from heaven replied, "Tell him to say the Rosary, and he will see me." The shepherd boy had said five or six Hail Marys when he saw the Lady from heaven. Our Lady promised Lucia she will go to Heaven. Lucia then asked Mary, "And Jacinta?"

Our Lady answers, "She will go also." Lucia then asks, "And Francisco?" Our Lady answers, "He will go there too, but he must say many Rosaries." Francisco and his sister Jacinta were canonized in 2017.

"So by all means we should eagerly crown ourselves with these roses from Heaven, and recite the entire Rosary every day, that is to say three Rosaries each of five decades which are like three little wreaths or crowns of flowers: and there are two reasons for doing this: First of all to honor the three crowns of Jesus and Mary—Jesus' crown of grace at the time of His incarnation, His crown of thorns during His passion and His crown of glory in Heaven, and of course the three-fold crown which the Most Blessed Trinity gave Mary in Heaven. Secondly, we should do this so that we ourselves may receive three crowns from Jesus and Mary. The first is a crown of merit during our lifetime, the second, a crown of peace at our death, and the third, a crown of glory in Heaven."[19]

11. By the recitation of the Rosary you shall obtain all that you ask of me.

Sister Lucia to Fr. Fuentes, 1957, "Look, Father, the Most Holy Virgin in these last times in which we live has given new efficacy in the recitation of the Holy Rosary. She has given this efficacy to such an extent that there is no problem, no matter how difficult it is, whether temporal or above all spiritual, in the personal life of each one of us, of our families, of the families in the world, or of the religious communities, or even of the life of peoples and nations that cannot be solved by the Rosary. There is no problem, I tell you, no matter how difficult it is, that we cannot solve by the prayer of the Holy Rosary. With the Holy Rosary, we will save ourselves."[20]

Two young women and a young man all in their 20's were at Medjugorje in 1991. They heard there was a priest from Australia, who could allegedly read souls and was in Medjugorje too. They agreed to pray the Rosary together asking the Virgin Mary to send him to the confessionals, where they were waiting, so he would hear their confessions. Just as they finished the Rosary and concluded the Hail Holy Queen, that same priest, for whom they had been praying, entered the Confessional directly in front of them and all three went to Confession to him.

12. Those who propagate the holy Rosary shall be aided by me in their necessities.

Saint Dominic, Blessed Alan de la Roche and Blessed Bartolo Long propagated the Rosary in their lifetime and were so aided in their necessities, that the Church has formally recognized them as examples for others to imitate.

13. I have obtained from my Divine Son that all the advocates of the Rosary shall have for intercessors the entire celestial court during their life and at the hour of their death.

"Few Saints have reached the same heights of prayer as Saint Mary Magdalene who was lifted up to Heaven each day by Angels, and who had had the privilege of learning at the feet of Our Lord Himself and His Blessed Mother. Yet one day when she asked God to show her a sure way of advancing in His love and of arriving at the height of perfection, He sent Saint Michael the Archangel to tell her, on His behalf, that there was no other way for her to arrive at perfection than to meditate on Our Lord's passion. So He placed a Cross in the front of her cave and told her to pray before it, contemplating the Sorrowful Mysteries which she had seen take place with her own eyes."[21]

14. All who recite the Rosary are my beloved children and the brothers and sisters of my only Son, Jesus Christ.

Our Lady blesses not only those who preach her Rosary, but she highly rewards all those who get others to say it by their example.

"Alphonsus, King of Leon and Galicia, very much wanted all his servants to honor the Blessed Virgin by saying the Rosary. So he used to hang a large rosary on his belt and always wore it, but unfortunately never said it himself. Nevertheless his wearing it encouraged his courtiers to say the Rosary very devoutly. One day the King fell seriously ill and when he was given up for dead he found himself, in a vision, before the judgment seat of Our Lord. Many devils were there accusing him of all the sins he had committed and Our Lord as Sovereign Judge was just about to condemn him to Hell when Our Lady appeared to intercede for him. She called for a pair of scales and had his sins placed in one of the balances whereas she put the Rosary that he had always worn on the other scale, together, with all the Rosaries that had been said because of his example. It was found that the Rosaries weighed more than his sins. Looking at him with great kindness Our Lady said: "As a reward for this little honor that you paid me in wearing my Rosary, I have obtained a great grace for you from my Son. Your life will be spared for a few more years. See that you spend these years wisely, and do penance."[22]

15. Devotion for my Rosary is a great sign of predestination.

When the word "predestination" is used here, it doesn't mean the person does not have free will. In fact, St. Louis de Montfort said, "Predestinate souls, you who are of God, cut yourselves adrift from those who are damning themselves by their impious lives, laziness and lack of devotion—and, without delay, recite often your Rosary, with faith, with humility, with confidence and with perseverance."[23] With God's grace, we can choose our destiny and determine our final outcome.

Annunciation of the Angel Gabriel to the Virgin Mary

Fruit of the Mystery: Humility

"In the sixth month, the angel Gabriel was sent from God to a town of Galilee called Nazareth, to a virgin betrothed to a man named Joseph, of the house of David, and the virgin's name was Mary. And coming to her, he said, "Hail, Full of Grace! The Lord is with you." But she was greatly troubled at what was said and pondered what sort of greeting this might be. Then the angel said to her, "Do not be afraid, Mary, for you have found favor with God. Behold, you will conceive in your womb and bear a son, and you shall name him Jesus. He will be great and will be called Son of the Most High, and the Lord God will give him the throne of David, his father, and he will rule over the house of Jacob forever, and of his kingdom there will be no end." But Mary said to the angel, "How can this be, since I have no relations with a man?" And the angel said to her in reply, "The Holy Spirit will come upon you, and the power of the Most High will overshadow you. Therefore the child to be born will be called holy, the Son of God. And behold, Elizabeth, your relative, has also conceived a son in her old age, and this is the sixth month for her who was called barren; for nothing will be impossible for God." Mary said, "Behold, I am the handmaid of the Lord. May it be done to me according to your word." Then the angel departed from her." (Luke 1:26-38)

According to Blessed Anne Catherine Emmerich, while Mary was fourteen and living with Her parents in Nazareth, the angel Gabriel appeared to Her. The Virgin was most likely kneeling in prayer, when Her room was suddenly filled with light. Standing before Her with a radiant glow was a young man, She immediately understood to be an angel.

Out of reverence, the angel lowered his eyes and slowly bowed before Her saying, "Hail Full of Grace, the Lord is with You! Blessed are You among women." She was greatly troubled and didn't understand his greeting.

Before the angel appeared to Her, due to Her humility, the thought never occurred to Her, God wanted Her to be the Mother of Jesus, the Mother of the Messiah. She most assuredly was praying for the coming of the Messiah, as most Jews did in Her time. This humblest of virgins believed Herself unworthy of this greeting.

The greeting is actually a title which meant full of grace from the past and to be continually filled with grace in the future. Today, we understand it to mean She was untouched by original sin, never sinned, nor would ever sin in the future.

She was cautious because She knew an angel came to deceive Eve and She prudently needed to discern if this angel was truly sent by God. In Her mind She waited to see what the angel would say next. When the angel told Her to not fear, and She had found favor with God, deep down She knew it was true. When Her fear vanished, She was ready to hear that God wanted Her to conceive Jesus, a King, whose kingdom would have no end.

And if Her Son would be a King, the Jewish tradition is that the mother of the king would be a queen. And therefore, She immediately came to know She would be a Queen. And if Her Son will be called Son of the Most High, then He would be God. Through Her brilliant intellect untainted (not touched by original sin, nor personal sin), now She understood the angel revealed to Her, She would be the Mother of the Messiah, the Queen of heaven and earth, and the Mother of God.

But, She was willing to forfeit all these for the sake of Her vow of virginity. These things could only come about, if Her promise to God could be kept. She was undaunted in Her commitment to give Herself totally to God, as a gift. If the angel was from God, She believed, due to Her supernatural faith, She would remain a virgin and also become a mother and that God could and would make it happen.

And so, She responded, "How will this be, since I know not man?" The angel replied, "The Holy Spirit will come upon You, and the power of the Most High will overshadow You; therefore the Child to be born will be called holy, the Son of God."

She is the first human who God revealed Himself as a Trinity of persons. To be the Mother of the Father's Son, would make Her Mother of God and the daughter of the Father. And as St. Maximilian said, She would be the spouse of the Holy Spirit.

Imagine how thrilled She must have been to be able to become a mother. Every woman would exceedingly enjoy becoming a mother. Yet, She was willing to make that sacrifice, of not having a child, out of Her undivided love of God. But, She had to give Her consent, Her fiat, Her Yes, to become a mother and remain a virgin.

St. Bernard gave a beautiful sermon on how Gabriel waited for Her response, all humanity waited, all pious ancestors of the Old Testament awaited, because everything hung on Her Yes for the salvation of the world to be accomplished. God the Father was asking Her to give Jesus the body and blood of His Son, to become the instrument of salvation for the entire world. And She responded saying, "Behold, I am the handmaid of the Lord. Be it done unto me, according to thy word." And at that moment, by the power of the Holy Spirit, the Word became flesh coming down from heaven in Her womb.

Did She feel anything at that moment? Did She feel the warmth of God's love penetrate Her whole being? Or did God not permit Her to feel anything, when Jesus came down from heaven, like a drop of dew, and caused Her faith to ever more increase? For Mary, it would make no difference, because Her trust would not need consolation to grow, as we at times do.

She certainly immediately turned to Her womb to adore and pray to the divine Child within Her. Suddenly She became the tabernacle of the Most High and the new Ark of the Covenant. She did not have within Her manna, nor the rod of a shepherd, nor the 10 Commandments, as in the Ark of the Covenant. Now within Her womb is the true Bread from Heaven, the person who is the Good Shepherd and the giver of the new Law, the Eternal Word.

By the power of the Holy Spirit, She gave Jesus His flesh and blood that would someday be given to us in Holy Communion. The Incarnation, in a certain sense, was Her First Holy Communion, but it was a continuous Communion for nine months, until the birth of Jesus.

Our Communion lasts at least fifteen minutes and perhaps up to thirty minutes, according to some saints. As we come to adore Jesus in the tabernacle, our time is limited, and we must go about our work. But not so, with Mary. She, Herself, became a tabernacle and carried Jesus wherever She went for nine months.

What did She first say to Jesus within Her womb? "O Jesus, my Son, I worship, adore and praise You. Who am I, that Thou has deigned to favor me, to be Your Mother?" Or did She first simply say, "O Jesus, I love you!" Undoubtedly, She was in continual prayer as She carried the Son of God within Her.

As She walked about near Her parents, or Joseph, or Her cousins, and friends, She hid the mystery within Her. Not saying a word to anyone, She most likely believed it was up to God to make it known. She knew She needed to pray for all who knew Her, because they would not understand how She came to be pregnant and think She committed adultery. But, She wasn't concerned with the opinion of others, only God's. She trusted and believed God would make everything work out and for

60

those who may never understand, that would be between God and them.

Centuries later, the Holy House of Nazareth, where the Eternal Word became flesh in the womb of Mary to dwell among us, would be so favored by God, the Lord would protect the house of Mary from vandals by angels miraculously transporting it in the air and placing it on a road in Loreto, Italy, where it is today. The miraculous transport of the Holy House is celebrated as a memorial on December 10th.

How small was Jesus when He came down from heaven and took on human nature? She certainly carried Him for nine months, and so, was He merely two cells at the beginning?

It's dehumanizing to refer to a person as two cells. The moment a child is conceived, the child is a person, even if the child has only two cells.

At first, He had no heart, no eyes, no fingers, until the normal time of child development. Yet, within Her was the most sacred and most holy. The divine person of Jesus with two natures, human and divine, dwelt within Her at the moment of His conception and who She carried for nine months.

From the moment when Jesus came into the womb of Mary, She became the Mediatrix of all Grace, because the one mediator between God and man, the source of all grace from the Father's throne of grace, chose to dwell within Her. And Mary is that conduit God has chosen to flow every grace into the world for every person. In other words, the fullness of grace came in the womb of Mary in the person of Jesus, and it is through Her, every grace is given to the world.

"This maternity of Mary in the order of grace began with the consent which she gave in faith at the Annunciation and which she sustained without wavering beneath the cross, and lasts until the eternal fulfillment of all the elect. Taken up to heaven She did not lay aside this salvific duty, but by Her constant intercession continued to bring us the gifts of eternal salvation. By Her maternal charity, She cares for the brethren of her Son, who still journey on earth surrounded by dangers and cultics, until they are led into the happiness of their true home. Therefore the Blessed Virgin is invoked by the Church under the titles of Advocate, Auxiliatrix, Adjutrix, and Mediatrix. This, however, is to be so understood that it neither takes away from nor adds anything to the dignity and efficaciousness of Christ the one Mediator."[24]

Just as She mediated for the wedding couple at Cana, She mediates to Her Son, for every grace we need, even those we don't ask, like the wedding couple didn't ask Her for help, but out of love, She wanted to save them from the embarrassment of running out of wine and continue to enjoy their wedding day.

When, through a dream, Joseph finally understood the Child was conceived by the power of the Holy Spirit, he often prayed to Jesus, through the womb of Mary. After Mary, Joseph was the first adorer of Jesus in Her womb. He would have been first to pray through Mary to Jesus. He adored the Son of God in the tabernacle of His virgin spouse.

The Incarnation, when Jesus, the Eternal Word, became flesh in the womb of Mary happened in time, and at that moment, all humanity and all of creation was elevated because Our Lord took on human nature.

Not only were the souls of Adam and Eve affected by original sin, so were their bodies and they suffered illness and death due to it. All of creation was wounded by the fall of Adam and Eve. But when the Word became flesh and dwelt among us, all of creation was elevated, by creation being united with the divinity of God in the divine person of Jesus.

Saint Proclus of Constantinople said, "Loving man He became a man, not being one before; but remaining God He became man without any change. [....] He became man finally, to make our sufferings His own and thus prepare for us adoption as sons, to win for us that kingdom, into which, I pray, we may all be made worthy to enter by the grace and mercy of the Lord Jesus Christ, who with the Father and the Holy Spirit has glory, honor and power, now and forever. Amen."[25]

Saint Peter Chyrsologus said, "The hand that assumed clay to make our flesh deigned to assume a body for our salvation. That the Creator is in the creature and God is in the flesh brings dignity to man without dishonor to Him who made him. He has made you in His image that you might in your person make the invisible Creator present on earth; He has made you His legate, so that the vast empire of the world might have the Lord's representative. And so, Christ is born that He might restore our nature. He became a child, was fed, and grew that He might inaugurate the one perfect age for ever as He had created it. And the creature, He had formed of earth He now makes heavenly… In this way He fully raised man to God…"[26]

Saint Catherine of Siena said, "What an immeasurable profound love! Your Son went down from the heights of His divinity to the depths of our humanity. Can anyone's heart remain closed and hardened after this? Only Your love could so dignify the flesh of Adam. And so by reason of this immeasurable love I beg, with all my strength of my soul, that You freely extend Your mercy to all Your lowly creatures."[27]

In respect for and as a reminder of the Incarnation, at every solemn Mass, during the recitation of the Nicene Creed, the Church requires all to bow at the words "and by the Holy Spirit was incarnate of the Virgin Mary, and became man."

When the Nicene Creed is recited at Mass, there are two liturgical celebrations (Christmas, December 25, and the Solemnity of the Annunciation, March 25) rather than bowing, the priest and the people are to kneel.

To remind the people of the Incarnation, St. Bonaventure as the superior general of the Franciscan order, required all Franciscan churches to ring their bells and pray the Angelus every day, three times a day. Soon after that, many non-

Franciscan churches began to ring their bells for the Angelus too. The Angelus reminds us that Jesus became flesh and dwelt among us.

The Angelus

The angel of the Lord declared unto Mary: And She conceived the Holy Spirit,
Hail Mary full of Grace, the Lord is with thee, blessed art thou among women, and blessed is the fruit of thy womb, Jesus, Holy Mary Mother of God, pray for us sinners, now and at the hour of our death, Amen.
Behold the handmaid of the Lord: Be it done unto me according to thy word.
Hail Mary…
And the Word was made flesh. (Genuflect) And dwelt among us.
Hail Mary…

Pray for us, O Holy Mother of God, that we may be made worthy of the promises of Christ.

Let us pray:
Pour forth, we beseech Thee, O Lord, Thy grace into our hearts; that we, to whom the Incarnation of Christ, Thy Son, was made known by the message of an angel, may by His Passion and Cross be brought to the glory of His Resurrection, through the same Christ Our Lord.

Application 1: Praying the Angelus Daily

How wonderful and blessed we would be, if homes, churches, Catholic institutions and religious communities once again prayed the Angelus everyday at 6am, Noon, and 6pm. Because, "when the fullness of time had come, God sent his Son, born of a woman, born under the law, to redeem those under the law, so that we might receive adoption as sons." (Galatians 4:4-5) "And the Word became flesh and dwelt among us, full of grace and truth; we have beheld His glory, as the only Son from the Father." (John 1:14)

Though She was a virgin and determined to remain a virgin, Mary was open to a miraculous conception of a child in Her womb, resulting in Her being both Mother and Virgin.

Application 2: Conception vs Contraception

The great and marvelous event of the conception of Jesus in the womb of Mary, contrasts with those who do not want to conceive a child in their womb and resort to contraception (against conception). Contraception is seriously sinful because it prevents the total gift of oneself to their spouse in marriage. It's sinful because it definitively tells God no, in bringing a child into the world. It causes one to view their spouse as an object of pleasure and women feel used. Using birth control, it becomes easy for young people to be tempted to premarital relations, rather than to abstain before marriage. It opens the way to marital infidelity. There is a loss of self-discipline and sacrifice. There is less communication between spouses. And it's seriously sinful because the pill, the patch, the injection, and the IUD causes the death of a newly conceived child and the mother did not even know she was pregnant.

Chemicals from birth control can cause serious side effects including: headaches, nervousness, depression, changes in appetite, weight gain, breast cancer, liver disease, acne, heart attack, loss of hair, and stroke.

Birth control goes against God's natural design and treats the body as if there is something wrong with it, when in fact, there is nothing wrong with the body at all.

God's plan for marriage using Natural Family Planning is a reasonable way to space children, using God's natural design, when there is a serious reason, such as a grave financial difficulty, a serious physical or mental health of a spouse or child, or if the couple has a special needs child causing great sacrifices. It fosters self-sacrifice, abstinence and communication. It is proven that 97% of couples, who use Natural Family Planning, won't divorce, whereas birth control users have a 54% chance of divorcing.

Women who obtain a tubal ligation have a 78% chance of divorce. Sterilization by tubal ligation or vasectomy is a serious sin, because it mutilates the body and permanently tells God He cannot bring a child into the world.

How happy and blessed are couples who live their marriages in the state of grace, following God's plan for marriage, trusting that He wants to be part of family planning. By following the Church's teachings, they discover the beauty of marriage through love which finds its deepest meaning in sacrifice. They are open to conceiving a child even when it may seem we have a different plan, but later discover God's plan is much better.

Application 3: In Vitro Fertilization

In vitro fertilization (IVF) is "morally unacceptable" because it separates the marriage act from procreation and establishes "the domination of technology" over human life. Embryos are treated as raw material rather than human beings.

IVF and the pill have something in common. The user of each makes oneself out to be God. It is very selfish and there is no concern for the children. The view, "I have a right to a child", is not true. Life is a gift, not a right. Persons who use IVF and the pill play God presuming the right over another human being, to bring a child into the world, or prevent a child from coming into the world or not allow some children to live because once created, they are later not wanted.

IVF causes the fertilization of human embryos that are then frozen and stored. Parents of the frozen children can't bring themselves to destroy them. Today, there is over 1 million frozen embryos. Some frozen embryos are donated for research.

Some want to select the sex and eye color of their children. It creates a market for eggs and can cause women to be treated like prize cattle listing their eye and hair color, ethnicity, height and weight and command the best price for their eggs.

Sperm is usually obtained by masturbation, which is seriously sinful. IVF makes it possible for single parents or same-sex couples to have children or women who are beyond the age of childbearing. And therefore, denies the child to be born and raised in a stable family with mother and father.

IVF procedures often result in multiple embryos being transferred to the uterus; it's an expensive process. Doctors want to maximize potential for success and so multiple embryos survive in the mother's womb, leading to the temptation, perhaps under pressure from doctors or spouses or perhaps by the woman's design, to undergo "selective reduction" by aborting unwanted embryos (children).

Story 1: Power of the Name of Mary and Power of the Hail Mary

There are several stories that illustrate the power of the Holy Name of Mary.

Gabriel Castillo was raised by his single mother and was a latchkey child. He said he was raised on MTV and watched bad shows like "Sex in the 90's". He made his first Communion in 8th grade and didn't go back to church.

However, while attending a Catholic college, he was invited to pray a Eucharistic Holy Hour and had a spiritual experience in Adoration. This caused him to spend time in church and he became a Eucharistic Minister, but lived a terribly sinful life. A religious sister noticed his sinful behavior and told him he was on the highway to hell. She requested he give up sin for Lent. And as a result, he decided he wasn't going to sin during Lent, but soon fell into pornography and impurity.

He asked God to help him, but heard an evil spirit's audible voice. The scary event caused him to desire to pray the Rosary. After obtaining a pamphlet on how to pray the Rosary, as he started with the Creed, saying, "I Believe…" an evil force grabbed him by the throat and pinned him down on the bed. He tried to scream for help, but couldn't. He heard an interior voice (he later believed was his guardian angel) to pray the Hail Mary. When he was able to pray the Hail Mary audibly, the presence left his room. Gabriel has since said if anyone wants to break free of porn or impure addictions, they should make the commitment to pray four Rosaries a day and they will be set free.

Fr. Donald Calloway, a priest of the Marians of the Immaculate Conception, tells the story of how the name of Mary helped him.

A former non-Catholic as a teen, he became heavily involved in drugs, sex and played Ouija board, tarot cards, etc. But, when he ran across a book on Medjugorje at his parents home, he knew he needed to change his life.

He said an evil spirit came to his room and manifested. He was terrified and in response, from the depths of his soul, he cried out, "M A R Y!". He said at that moment the evil spirit was annihilated, and he heard a woman say, "Donnie, I am so happy." He knew it was the voice of the Virgin Mary. This led him to become Catholic and then later a priest.

The Hail Mary also has great power. One of the earliest known saints who recommended praying three Hail Marys everyday for purity was St. Anthony of Padua (1195 – 1231). His purpose was "to honor the spotless Virginity of Mary and to preserve a perfect purity of mind, heart and body in the midst of the dangers of the world". The practice of saying three Hail Marys in the evening somewhere about sunset had become general throughout Europe in the first half of the 14th century, and it was recommended and given an indulgence by Pope John XXII in 1318 and 1327.

In 1994, before there were cell phones, there used to be at Dallas, Texas, a Marian and Eucharistic youth summer event in the United States called "Youth 2000."

A 28 year old poor man, contemplating whether or not to become a priest, invited his two teenage sisters to come with him to the retreat. He had an old blue Chevette, with the front driver side floor board with a hole in it. He covered the hole with a rubber mat, so his foot wouldn't fall through and hit the road. He called the car his "Fred Flintstone mobile." While returning from the event, they stopped for fuel at a gas station. When attempting to leave, he repeatedly tried to start the car, but to no avail. Not having money for towing or even repairs, he decided to ask his sisters to pray with him the Hail Mary. They laughed and thought it silly, but went ahead and complied with his wishes. After praying one Hail Mary, the car started and they made it back to western Kansas without any difficulty.

This same young man, sixteen years later in 2009, after having been ordained a priest for five years, returned home to visit his father, who was dying from cancer. After giving his father anointing of the sick and the Apostolic Pardon, he prayed the Rosary for his unconscious father. At 7:21am, he asked his sisters, who were present, to pray three Hail Marys with him. Just as the last Hail Mary was concluded, when they finished the words, "...pray for us sinners, now and at the hour of death. Amen.", his father unexpectedly opened his eyes, looked at one of his daughters, and breathed his last.

Fr. Joe Freedy, a priest of the Diocese of Pittsburgh, Pennsylvania tells the story of a parishioner, John Petrovich who was jogging and noticed an ambulance in his neighborhood. John didn't know the person and wasn't a doctor, and in response, he prayed one Hail Mary for the person in crisis and kept running. A week later, when jogging by the house again, he heard a woman call after him. She said, "Last week when the ambulance was here, I was dying. Jesus appeared to me and held out his hand, and your face was on the palm of His hand. Then Jesus said to me, "You were going to die, but due to the prayer of this man, you will live." It became clear, by Mr. Petrovich praying the Hail Mary, she was saved from death.

The Hail Mary (Ave Maria) can be sung in Latin by way of Gregorian Chant is a favorite for religious communities during Night Prayer, is sung at many weddings and during Masses in honor of the Holy Virgin.

Many who hear Franz Schubert's Ave Maria are often moved to tears especially with singers like Luciano Pavoratti or Andrea Bocelli. The Hail Mary, when sung, has the power to move hearts to a greater love of Jesus and Mary.

Story 2: Ave Maria Sung by an Angel

About a month after a priest received permission from his bishop to have a Chapel with a Tabernacle containing the Eucharistic Jesus in his rectory, one night he woke up, and heard the most beautiful singing of the *Ave Maria*. It was at an extremely high tone, but incredibly beautiful. He wondered which neighbor was playing the hymn, but realized the singing came from the Chapel. He didn't get up to see, but believed it was most likely his guardian angel singing the *Ave Maria* in the Chapel. It was truly celestial and heavenly singing, he told a friend.

Apparition: Our Lady Appears to St. Dominic (France)

There are two stories about the Virgin Mary appearing to St. Dominic. The first story is from *Lives of the Saints*. It states, "It was in 1208, while Dominic knelt in the little chapel of Notre Dame de la Prouille, and implored the great Mother of God to save the Church, that Our Lady appeared to him, gave him the Rosary, and bade him go forth and preach. Beads in hand, he revived the courage of the Catholic troops, led them to victory against overwhelming numbers, and finally crushed heresy."[28]

Second story: St. Dominic Guzman (1170-1221), traveled into France preaching against the Albigensian heresy, but his efforts gained few conversions and even fewer followers. In 1208, he went into a forest near Toulouse, France to pray, asking God to provide what he needed in order to overcome the Albigensian heresy. After three days of prayer and fasting, three angels appeared in the sky along with a ball of fire. When they disappeared, the Virgin Mary spoke, telling the priest that he must preach her Psalter (Rosary) in order to succeed in his struggle to overcome the Albigensians.

The Albigensian heretics taught only the spiritual is good and everything material is bad. Therefore, the body in, and of itself, is evil, and every soul is imprisoned in an evil body. The only way a person could experience salvation was to be freed from the imprisonment of their flesh.

Thanks to preaching the Rosary, as Our Lady had requested, St. Dominic and his religious friars were very successful in bringing back the Albigensian heretics to the one true Catholic faith.

The Visitation of the Virgin Mary

Fruit of the Mystery: Love of Neighbor

"During those days Mary set out and traveled to the hill country in haste to a town of Judah, where she entered the house of Zechariah and greeted Elizabeth. When Elizabeth heard Mary's greeting, the infant leaped in her womb, and Elizabeth, filled with the Holy Spirit, cried out in a loud voice and said, "Most blessed are you among women, and blessed is the fruit of your womb. And how does this happen to me, that the mother of my Lord should come to me? For at the moment the sound of your greeting reached my ears, the infant in my womb leaped for joy. Blessed are you who believed that what was spoken to you by the Lord would be fulfilled." (Luke 1:39-45)

When Mary learned through the angel that Elizabeth, Her cousin, was with child, She believed and went in haste to visit Elizabeth, who was advanced in years and needed help giving birth to John the Baptist.

What are the thoughts of any young woman the moment she first discovers she is pregnant? She has excitement, joy, and happiness because she says to herself, "I am now a mother! I have a baby within me." She wants to share the good news, that a new person created by God is inside her. Then She begins to think of the items she will need, such as a crib, a baby blanket, to make diapers, and sew handmade clothes. And she thinks about what she will do for the baby, such as how to nurse, to hold, and rock the baby.

But, Mary's first thoughts were to quickly go to help her pregnant elderly cousin. She trusted God would provide for all needs of the Divine Infant and Herself. Her only concern was to do what She can, for a pregnant elderly woman.

From Nazareth, where Mary lived, to Ain Karem, the city where Elizabeth lived, was about a five day journey on a donkey or to walk. Though we don't know for sure, we can presume Joseph accompanied Mary to Ain Karem and then he returned to Nazareth to continue his carpentry business.

Did Mary tell Joseph about Her pregnancy? Most likely not. She kept Her secret to Herself. During the journey She would have prayed for Joseph, so that, when he finds out about Her pregnancy, he would accept God's plan for Her and the baby Jesus.

Upon her arrival, when Elizabeth heard Mary's greeting, she was filled with the Holy Spirit and the unborn John the Baptist leapt for joy.

The Holy Spirit revealed to Elizabeth that Mary was pregnant, as she said, "Who am I, that the Mother of my Lord, should come to me?" Mary was not just pregnant with any child, but the Child who is the Lord, who is God. Elizabeth could not have known by looking at Mary's figure. A woman who is pregnant for just five days cannot be showing. The unborn baby Jesus was far too small for anyone to know He was there, except Mary.

After five days from conception, due to His divine personhood, and through His human nature, Jesus blessed John the Baptist through the womb of His Mother Mary and through the womb of Elizabeth, the mother of John.

The two unborn children bear witness to the sacredness, the beauty, and the worthiness of life. At conception, every child is created in God's image and likeness and God has a plan for each and every person. "For I know the plans I have for you," declares the Lord, "plans to prosper you and not to harm you, plans to give you hope and a future." (Jeremiah 29:11)

One Child is the Lord of heaven and earth, and has no hands, no feet, nor a beating heart. Yet, God works through that Child to bless another unborn child six months after conception and bless his mother. John the Baptist will prepare the way of the Lord.

The Virgin Mary is the new Ark of the Covenant, as can be symbolized in Her visitation to Her cousin, Elizabeth. The ark traveled to the house of Obed-edom in the hill country of Judea (2 Samuel 6:1-11). Mary traveled to the house of Elizabeth and Zechariah in the hill country of Judea. (Luke 1:39) Dressed as a priest, David danced and leapt in front of the ark (2 Samuel 6:14). John the Baptist – of priestly lineage – leapt in his mother's womb at the approach of Mary (Luke 1:41). David asks, "How can the ark of the Lord come to me?" (2 Samuel 6:9). Elizabeth asks, "Why is this granted to me, that the mother of my Lord should come to me?" (Luke 1:43). David shouts in the presence of the ark (2 Samuel 6:15). Elizabeth "exclaimed with a loud cry" in the presence of Mary (Luke 1:42). The ark remained in the house of Obed-edom for three months (2 Samuel. 6:11). Mary remained in the house of Elizabeth for three months (Luke 1:56). The house of Obed-edom was blessed by the presence of the ark (2 Samuel 6:11). The word *blessed* is used three times; surely the house was blessed by God (Luke 1:39-45). The ark returns to its home and ends up in Jerusalem, where God's presence and glory is revealed in the temple (2 Samuel 6:12; 1 Kgs. 8:9-11). Mary returns home and eventually ends up in Jerusalem, where she presents God incarnate in the temple (Luke 1:56; 2:21-22).[29]

According to the Pontifical Council for the Pastoral Care of Migrants and Itinerant People, *The Shrine: Memory, Presence and Prophecy of the Living God*, "The Virgin Mary is the living shrine of the Word of God, the Ark of the New and Eternal Covenant. In fact, St. Luke's account of the Annunciation of the angel to Mary nicely incorporates the images of the tent of meeting with God in Sinai and of the temple of Zion. Just as the cloud covered the people of God marching in the desert (cf. Numbers 10:34; Deuteronomy 33:12; Psalm 91:4) and just as the same cloud, as a sign of the divine mystery present in the midst of Israel, hovered over the Ark of the Covenant (cf. Exodus 40:35), so now the shadow of the Most High envelops and penetrates the tabernacle of the New Covenant that is the womb of Mary (cf. Lk 1:35)."[30]

After Elizabeth greeted the Virgin Mary, Our Lady gave Her beautiful Magnificat. Her Magnificat is Her song of thanksgiving. Mary gives voice to the jubilation which fills her heart, because God, her Savior, has looked upon his humble handmaid. The beginning of the Magnificat are the words, "My soul magnifies the Lord and my spirit rejoices in God my Savior." From the moment of Jesus' conception in Her womb, by the power of the Holy Spirit, Her soul magnifies Jesus, such that when we think of Mary and when we pray to Mary, She brings Jesus into greater focus as a magnifying glass magnifies whatever it gazes upon. The viewer, so to speak, gets a closer look at Jesus and comes to know Him better because of Mary. When we pray to Mary, She takes the little prayer or little sacrifice we offer and magnifies them when She presents them to Her divine Son. When She was proclaimed Mother of God, by the Church Council of Ephesus, She brought into greater clarity, who Her Son really is. He is God, who always existed, but She is His Mother, because She gave Him His human nature. Therefore, rightly do we call Her Mother of God. St Ambrose said, "In each one may the soul of Mary praise the Lord and the spirit of Mary exult in God." The words of the Magnificat are as it were the spiritual testament of the Virgin Mother. Therefore they quite rightly constitute the heritage of all who, recognizing themselves as her children, decide to welcome her into their homes as did the Apostle John who, at the foot of the Cross, directly received her as Mother from Jesus. The universal Church joins in Her canticle to praise the wonder of the Incarnation every evening during Vespers (Evening Prayer).

When we pray the Rosary, Mary prays with us and makes our petitions pleasing and perfect and presents them to Jesus. It is as though we hand Mary a platter of vegetables, such as a few peas and a radish and when She presents them to Jesus, they appear to Him as a three course meal with meat, potatoes and dessert. And when pray the Rosary with others, our prayers are magnified by the number of people who pray with us.

Application 1: Birth Control & Abortion

Was Jesus' physical nature just a "blob of tissue" when He blessed John causing him to leap for joy and be sanctified in his mother's womb? No. Everyone who has human nature has DNA given to us at conception and will someday grow into an adult human. We don't grow into a blob of tissue. We grow into a mature person. Does a sapling not grow into a tree? Does not a seed grow into a flower? Can it grow into something not designed by God? As St. Elizabeth said, "blessed is the fruit of thy womb."

Particles of the Sacred Host, even though very small are the whole and entire person of Jesus. And this reminds us a person is a person, no matter how small.

Science tells us, it takes about five days for a newly conceived child to pass through the Fallopian tube and implant in the womb.

How horrible for mothers who use birth control (the pill, the patch, the injection and IUD), that prevents the implantation of a newly conceived child, who traveled five days and yet cannot implant in the womb, and so dies due to irritating the womb caused by chemicals or a device. A child five days from conception lives but five days, because he or she is rejected in his or her mother's womb and the mother will not have had any womanly sign of pregnancy and therefore won't even know, she caused the death of her own baby.

Women who have had an abortion oftentimes suffer from PTSD (post traumatic stress disorder). Some completely block out the memory of the abortion(s). But many have nightmares, anxiety, depression, and self-hatred. Some think God can never forgive them, because they think their sin is too great. Still others don't know how to forgive oneself.

The Rachel's Vineyard weekend retreat has helped many women and men on the road to healing after suffering through the heartache of abortion. The confidential weekend has a priest, professional counselor, and team members who provide support and encouragement.

The Lord can sacramentally touch and heal wounded hearts through Confession, receiving Holy Communion often, and spending quiet time praying before Jesus in Eucharistic Adoration during a weekly Holy Hour, that one can choose to do in their parish.

Blessed Carlo Acutis said, "the Eucharist is the highway to heaven." When people sit in the sun, they become tan, "but when they sit before Eucharistic Jesus, they become saints."

If God can forgive Bernard Nathanson, a notorious abortionist for killing 75,000 unborn babies, He can forgive a confused mother who was pressured into having an abortion and was told the lie, "it's not a baby."

God is infinitely merciful. The following quotes are taken from St. Faustina's Diary: Jesus said to her: "Let the weak, sinful soul have no fear to approach Me, for even if it had more sins than there are grains of sand in the world, all will be drowned in the immeasurable depths of My mercy." (Diary #1059) "The greater the sinner, the greater the right he has to My mercy." (Diary #723) "I am love and mercy itself." Diary (#1074) "Let no soul fear to draw near to Me, even though its sins be as scarlet." (Diary #699) "My mercy is greater than your sins, and those of the entire world." "I let My Sacred Heart be pierced with a lance, thus opening wide the source of mercy for you." (Diary #1485)

Rape is a horrible traumatic event. When a baby is conceived as a result of it, God brings about something very beautiful and good despite the evil action. The new child can help bring healing. Who would kill an innocent victim for a crime his or her father was to blame?

When a child is given up for adoption, the insurance of the adoptive parents will pay for the hospital bill where a child is delivered. There is a long wait list for many couples unable to have children.

Due to lies or false information, a mother may forget her unborn child or not believe it's a child at all. However, not so, with God the Father in heaven, who creates each individual person unique, like no other, and has His constant gaze on us. Before we were formed in our mother's womb He knew us and will never forget us. "Can a mother forget her infant, be without tenderness for the child of her womb? Even should she forget, I will never forget you. See, upon the palms of my hands I have engraved you; your walls are ever before me." (Isaiah 49:15-16)

Story 1: Rosary Novena Helps Infertile Woman to Have Children

A young couple were married for three years and hadn't been able to conceive a child. They prayed a Rosary novena to Our Lady, asking Mary to help them conceive, but when it was completed, decided to adopt a child. About the same time, their pastor introduced the couple to *The Pope Paul VI Institute* in Omaha, Nebraska, known for NaProTechnology. (Natural Procreative Technology). A few months after the young woman had surgery to correct her difficulty in having children, she became pregnant. The couple went on to have four children.

Story 2: Rosary Prevents Disruption Mission

A priest gave a parish mission called "God's Plan for Marriage." Due to a misunderstanding with their pastor and parishioners hosting the weekend, there was a threat the weekend mission could be canceled. The priest giving the mission and those hosting the event, prayed the Rosary, asking the Virgin Mary to intercede. The mission went on and he gave an extensive homily explaining Pope Saint Paul VI's document *Humanae Vitae*, why birth control was sinful, and spoke to them about the joy of God's plan for marriage. A group of women who attended the weekend Masses were originally upset by the message, because they had never heard it before. But when the women prayed together, and talked it out, the entire group chose to give up birth control and began using Natural Family Planning.

Apparition: Seven Sorrows Rosary (Italy)

Our Lady originally appeared in 1233 in Florence, Italy, to seven men asking them to found a religious order. But, it was on Good Friday in 1239, while they were meditating on Our Lord's Passion and Our Lady's sufferings, Our Lady appeared to the seven holy men and revealed Her wish for them to form an Order dedicated to practicing and promoting the devotion to Her Sorrows. These men became the founders of the religious Order of the Servants of Mary (Servites) and are all canonized saints today.

These are the Seven Sorrows mysteries of the Servite Rosary: 1) Presentation in temple 2) Flight into Egypt 3) Loss of Jesus for three days & search for Him 4) Mary meets Jesus on way to Calvary 5) Mary stands at the foot of the Cross 6) Jesus is taken from Cross and laid in Mary's arms 7) Jesus is laid in the tomb.

Seven Hail Marys, rather than ten, are prayed for each mystery.

There are seven promises attached to the practice of daily praying seven Hail Marys while meditating on Our Lady's Tears and Sorrows. Our Sorrowful Mother revealed these seven promises to St. Bridget of Sweden (1303 – 1373): 1) "I will grant peace to their families." 2) "They will be enlightened about the divine Mysteries." 3) "I will console them in their pains and I will accompany them in their work." 4) "I will give them as much as they ask for as long as it does not oppose the adorable will of My divine Son or the sanctification of their souls." 5) "I will defend them in their spiritual battles with the infernal enemy and I will protect them at every instant of their lives." 6) "I will visibly help them at the moment of their death. They will see the face of their Mother." 7) "I have obtained this grace from My divine Son, that those who propagate this devotion to My tears and sorrows will be taken directly from this earthly life to eternal happiness, since all their sins will be forgiven and My Son will be their eternal consolation and joy."

Birth of Jesus

*Fruit of the Mystery: Poverty of Spirit,
Detachment from Things of the World*

"In those days a decree went out from Caesar Augustus that the whole world should be enrolled. This was the first enrollment, when Quirinius was governor of Syria. So all went to be enrolled, each to his own town. And Joseph too went up from Galilee from the town of Nazareth to Judea, to the city of David that is called Bethlehem, because he was of the house and family of David to be enrolled with Mary, his betrothed, who was with Child. While they were there, the time came for Her to have Her Child and She gave birth to Her firstborn Son; and She wrapped Him in swaddling clothes and laid Him in a manger, because there was no room for them in the inn. Now there were shepherds in that region living in the fields and keeping the night watch over their flock. The angel of the Lord appeared to them and the glory of the Lord shone around them, and they were struck with great fear. The angel said to them, "Do not be afraid; for behold, I proclaim to you good news of great joy that will be for all the people. For today in the city of David a savior has been born for you who is Messiah and Lord. And this will be a sign for you: you will find an infant wrapped in swaddling clothes and lying in a manger." And suddenly there was a multitude of the heavenly host with the angel, praising God and saying: "Glory to God in the highest and on earth peace to those on whom his favor rests." (Luke 2:1-14)

Due to the requirement of the census, Joseph and Mary, his nine month pregnant wife, journeyed from Nazareth to Bethlehem. It was a ninety mile journey that probably took four days of walking, eight hours a day. They needed to sleep

83

outdoors for three nights, each time not far from the road. Using their provisions, they ate simple food and fed their mule with grain the animal carried.

Trusting in the goodness of people to help a pregnant woman find shelter, when they were to arrive at the city of David, Joseph had faith all would work out and perhaps thought they would return to Nazareth to have the Child after they completed their census duty.

But, Mary knew the prophet Micah's prophecy that the Messiah was to be born in Bethlehem, in a city whose name means "house of bread." "But you, Bethlehem, in the land of Judah, are by no means least among the rulers of Judah; for out of you will come a ruler who will shepherd my people Israel." (Matthew 2:6) Jesus, the Good shepherd will come as an Infant and angels will lead sheepherders to find the Shepherd in the arms of Mary.

When there was no room in the inns, and no one was willing to give up their spot for a pregnant mother, Joseph was in agony because he wanted to provide a respectable place for his wife to give birth to the Savior.

Finally, they were directed to a stable in a cave with cattle. He helped Mary lie down on the hay, and after he removed animal manure, he went to fetch water. When he returned, Mary told him it was time for the Child to be born and reassured him, it was not due to him, that the Child would be born in such poverty, but it was the will of the Almighty. But Joseph was in pain and secretly wept, but trusted the Lord. When Joseph fell asleep, the miracle birth happened. God did not want him to see it.

All women, who suffer from original sin have labor pains, but not so for Mary, who was conceived without sin. Just as Eve came from the side of Adam, Jesus may have come forth from the side of Mary. Dr. Scott Hahn said, "Mary's virginity keeps the physical sign of an interior reality intact. Doing that took a miracle, but no more of a miracle than it took for Jesus, after his resurrection, to enter the room where His disciples awaited Him even though the door was locked (John 20:19). That's also one of the reasons why Mary and Joseph refrained from normal marital relations. Her virginity was too central to her identity to do otherwise."[31]

Saint Proclus of Constantinople said, "She is both virgin and mother, for She gave birth to the Word incarnate without knowledge of man; and yet She retained Her virginity because of the miraculous way He chose to be born."[32]

An immense light filled the cave, when suddenly the Infant Jesus appeared on the blanket beneath Mary. The Virgin Mother who had just been rapt in ecstasy, came out of it, picked up the baby Jesus, and wrapped Him in Her mantle. Tears of joy gave way, as She was first to gaze upon the face of God in His human nature. She kissed His face, then grasping His tiny hands held Him to Her bosom. She then wrapped Him in swaddling clothes to warm His little body.

Joseph was awakened to see the silhouette of Mother and Child reflected from the flames of the nearby fire, he kindled before taking a nap. He knelt down and then prostrated in adoration before the newborn King. Mary touched Joseph causing him to once again kneel and then handed the Child to him. As his heart was moved with deep love, he embraced the little boy and kissed His face. Mary pointed to the manger and Joseph laid the Child on the straw within it.

A manger used to feed animals became symbolic of Jesus, the Bread of Life, who will give Himself to feed His sheep, as spiritual food by His future presence in the Eucharist, the Bread from Heaven.

The poverty of His birth is a reminder Jesus wants us to be detached from material things, be content with the necessities of life, give support and courage to the poor, make Himself one with their poverty, and for us to trust in His Divine Providence.

85

Saint Clare said, "Behold His poverty even as He was laid in the manger and wrapped in swaddling clothes. What wondrous humility, what marvelous poverty! The King of angels, the Lord of heaven and earth resting in a manger! Look more deeply into the mirror and meditate on His humility, or simply on His poverty."[33]

About midnight, in a spectacular sight, the sky lit up as angels were seen by the shepherds guarding their flocks. They saw angels were hovering above the field. The angels were glowing from a light that came forth from their beings which were immensely beautiful. Today the field is called "Shepherd's Field."

Shepherds, who saw the mighty and glorious angel from heaven, were told that the Savior, who is the Messiah and Lord had come and that they would find Him wrapped in swaddling clothes and lying in a manger. They were probably shocked to hear that the Messiah would be born in similarly poor conditions of their birth. Shepherds were outcasts and yet the Lord chose them to first see the newborn babe, the Messiah, Savior and Lord!

In great excitement, they grabbed curds, figs, and bread as gifts, as they quickly departed to find the cave after they heard the glorious song sung by the multitude of angels, "Glory to God in the Highest! And peace to those whom His favor rests!" These beautiful words are sung at every high Mass and on feast days in the Church, to remind us of Christ's birth and that angels were there and are with us singing at Holy Mass.

Some time later, wise men who are Gentiles (non-Jews) came following a star to bow down and worship and give the newborn king gifts of gold, frankincense, and myrrh.

How many children of divorced parents or children of single mothers never had the opportunity to feel the love of a mother and father in their own home and watch the loving interaction of parents? How many children seldom or were never held by their father? When praying the Rosary, by entering into the mystery of the life of the Holy Family, we feel at home and find encouragement by our spiritual parents.

Application 1: "The family who prays the Rosary together, will change the world together."

Do you want to bring back to the Church your fallen away family members and friends? Teach them the Rosary and have them pray it with you. If you want to help a non-Catholic join the Church, teach them the Rosary and pray it with them. If you want to overcome sin, including habitual sin and addictions? Pray the Rosary regularly and often. If you want a war to end, rally Catholics to pray the Rosary. If you want help in making a decision, pray the Rosary. If you want peace in your home and in your family, pray the Rosary together as a family every day.

Men, do you want to be a good husband and father? Take up your true responsibility and be the spiritual leader of the family. It is your duty to help your wife and children get to heaven. As a man, you are the protector of the family. Are you doing that? By leading the Rosary every night, you will protect your family from from "your adversary *the devil* who is *prowling* around like a roaring lion, looking for anyone he can devour." (1 Peter 5:8)
the devil is prowling around like a roaring lion looking for someone to devour." (1 Peter 5:8)

If I may say this...men, stop being sissies! What is a sissy? A sissy is one who cowers to the enemy. He allows the enemy to harm himself and his family. He sits back and does nothing. A man of valor will not be afraid of what others think. He will go into battle with the weapon of the Rosary. And always keep his weapon on him and pull it out and use it whenever it's needed. He is willing to confront the enemy, and say, "Over my dead body will you harm my family!"

Women, do you want to be a good wife and mother? By your very nature, you love. You are an image of the Virgin Mary. Children learn to love by your love for them. Children learn to respect by your love and respect for your husband. Children learn discipline, by your gentle, but firm teaching of values. As children, they turn to you to be consoled and to feel the warmth that comes from a mother's tenderness. A sweet mother is like fresh air, that makes the day brighter and the darkness of gloom disappear, no matter the heartache. When a mother kisses the injury of the child, does the injury get better? No, but it feels better because of mom's love. A mother does all of these for her children, who will instinctively want to please their mother, to honor her, to give her something, such flowers or a hug or a kiss. By teaching your children to pray the Rosary, they will grow in love of Jesus and Mary. Yes, it takes patience when everyone is trying to pray the Rosary, when the little ones are fidgety or scurrying around. It takes patience, when teens would rather be with their friends or on the phone.

And you children, what a joy it is when the family prays in unity. God sees your pure heart and quickly rushes to answer your prayers. The prayers of young people are powerful.

Zachary King, a former satanic priest, said, "What Satan fears the most are the prayers of innocent children, because they move the heart of God to act." When we are young, our motivations can be very simple and purer than adults, because we trust. We just want to please God and to please our parents.

By obeying our parents, it's not for the sole purpose of avoiding punishment, it's to desire to help them and the family, because we love them. We are willing to give up our desires and are ready to make sacrifices for our parents and siblings because of love. We avoid fighting with, or being jealous of, or being excessively competitive towards our brothers and sisters.

Dear families, if we remember God is always first, then our family will honor God first. Family prayer will be more important than sports and other activities. If we keep God first, the family will be a source of power to change the world. Basketball, football, volleyball, baseball, drama, etc. are all good in themselves, but they can't save us. They are worldly activities that can help us become better people, but our end goal should always be heaven.

Dissension, arguments, fights, and pride can all be conquered by a family who prays the Rosary together.

Imagine for a moment, if you were to help a pro-abortion friend or family member to learn the Rosary and pray it regularly. They will be meditating on the annunciation, when Jesus was conceived in His Mother's womb. They will contemplate the Visitation when the unborn John the Baptist leapt for joy, in the presence of the unborn baby Jesus, just five days from conception. They will see with the eyes of Mary the birth of Jesus and the joy of holding Him in Her arms.

Whoever regularly prays the Rosary, will not persist in their errors. They will be pulled from sin. They will grow in love of God and neighbor and will grow in virtue and holiness.

There is a great force ready to be unleashed upon the world, and that force is "The family who prays the Rosary together, will change the world together."

Story 1: Two Sets of Twins Saved by the Rosary

A priest went to pray outside of an abortion clinic to prevent mothers from having an abortion. A parishioner of the local cathedral happened to be at the gates of the clinic and joined the priest in praying two Rosaries, the Litany of Saints and the Chaplet of Divine Mercy. When they concluded, a woman came out of the clinic and as she was passing by the priest and parishioner, said, "I just can't do it. They told me I have twins and want to charge me twice the price, and I can't afford it, so I will keep my twins." After she departed, another woman about the age of thirty, with her daughter, about the age of five and the pregnant woman's mother, were departing the abortion clinic in their car. The woman rolled down her window to receive literature from the parishioner, and said, "I'm pregnant with twins. I'm going to keep them." The priest and parishioner told her they would pray for her and she left. Within twenty minutes, two sets of twins (four unborn children), were saved through the Rosary, the Chaplet of Divine Mercy and the Litany of the Saints.

Apparition: Franciscan Friar James (Italy) – The Franciscan Crown

"Franciscans pray a seven-decade Rosary known as the Franciscan Crown. It dates back to the 15th century when the Blessed Virgin Mary appeared in Assisi to a Franciscan friar named James (1422). As a child, James offered Mary a crown of roses every day as a sign of his love and devotion to her. When he joined the Franciscans, James was distressed that he could no longer make this offering of flowers to Our Lady. But Mary appeared to James and She instructed him to weave for her a crown of prayers instead by reciting a Rosary of seven decades, each one meditating on one of the seven joyful events in her life: the Annunciation, the Visitation, the Birth of Jesus, the Adoration of the Magi, the Finding of the Child Jesus in the Temple, Jesus' Apperance to Mary after the Resurrection, and the Assumption and Coronation of Mary as Queen of Heaven. It consists of seven decades, after which two Hail Marys are added (bringing the number up to 72, the traditional years of Our Lady's life) and a Pater Noster, Ave and Gloria for the Holy Father."[34]

The Presentation of Jesus in the Temple

Fruit of the Mystery: Obedience

"When the days were completed for their purification according to the law of Moses, they took him up to Jerusalem to present him to the Lord, just as it is written in the law of the Lord, "Every male that opens the womb shall be consecrated to the Lord," and to offer the sacrifice of "a pair of turtledoves or two young pigeons," in accordance with the dictate in the law of the Lord. Now there was a man in Jerusalem whose name was Simeon. This man was righteous and devout, awaiting the consolation of Israel, and the Holy Spirit was upon him. It had been revealed to him by the Holy Spirit that he should not see death before he had seen the Messiah of the Lord. He came in the Spirit into the temple; and when the parents brought in the child Jesus to perform the custom of the law in regard to him, he took him into his arms and blessed God, saying: "Now, Master, you may let your servant go in peace, according to your word, for my eyes have seen your salvation, which you prepared in sight of all the peoples, a light for revelation to the Gentiles, and glory for your people Israel." The child's father and mother were amazed at what was said about him; and Simeon blessed them and said to Mary his mother, "Behold, this child is destined for the fall and rise of many in Israel, and to be a sign that will be contradicted (and you yourself a sword will pierce) so that the thoughts of many hearts may be revealed." (Luke 2:22-35)

Jesus, "the light to the nations and the glory of Israel" arrived in the Temple in the arms of His Mother Mary, Our Lady of the Light. According to Jewish law, the first-born male had to be presented to the Lord forty days after his birth.

91

It was also the rite of purification for mothers who just gave birth. After giving birth, women were considered unclean and could not worship in the temple or touch sacred objects until they were first purified by having a lamb or a pair of turtle doves or pigeons sacrificed. Since Mary and Joseph were poor they offered pigeons or turtle doves.

The circumstances of Mary's Immaculate Conception and the miraculous birth of Jesus did not render Her impure, but out of humility, She obediently followed the law and also avoided the appearance of scandal for not doing the Jewish custom.

The presentation of Jesus in the temple was public redemption for any first born son of any other tribe other than the tribe of Levi. The parents would symbolically give their son to God and buy him back by a small monetary offering.

Due to the action of the Holy Spirit, Simeon and Anna are the only ones at the Temple to recognize the Messiah in what appeared to be an ordinary Infant.

Simeon was a devout elderly man, who was inspired by the Holy Spirit to come to the Temple when Mary and Joseph likewise had just arrived. For years, he was expecting to lay his eyes on the promised Messiah before his death. And then the day had come. By an inspiration of God, he immediately recognized the forty day old infant Jesus, as the Redeemer.

Imagine the joy in his heart, when he held the infant in his arms and gazed upon His eyes that penetrated his being. Perhaps he kissed the infant's forehead and grasped one of His tiny hands that rule the world. He finally saw his salvation in the form of a Child who would someday bring about the salvation of all who were longing for it. He saw Jesus as the light to the nations for the glory of the people of Israel.

As a gesture of dedication, he gently raised the Child Jesus in his arms-- to God the Father, to be consecrated (set apart) for the sacred purpose of redeeming mankind. Perhaps, he prayed, "Here, O holy One, O almighty One, O God, our Father in heaven. Here is the promised Messiah, that you brought into the world. Take Him and prepare Him for His mission. I, your servant and priest, present Him to you, as an act of consecration. May You bless Him and be with Him, unto the day, He will return to You from where He came. And now that my eyes have seen Him, take me to the abode of paradise you promised. Amen."

But, God gave Simeon another prophecy, that he will never see, and would cause a gentle tear to fall down his cheek. He thought, "Should I tell this couple what the Lord has just revealed to me?" On this happy occasion, he pondered for a moment, if he should say the prophecy to His parents. He's been faithful to God in his previous inspirations. He knows he must say it to the Child's Mother, even if it breaks Her Immaculate Heart. This is what God wants and he will obey.

Before saying anything, however, he first raised his hand to bless the couple, knowing they will need special graces in the future to embrace the chalice of suffering. Then, in a fatherly way, he gently touched the shoulder of Mary, looked into Her eyes, and said, "Behold, this Child is destined for the fall and rise of many in Israel, and to be a sign that will be contradicted. And You Yourself a sword will pierce, so that the thoughts of many hearts may be revealed." (Luke 2:35-36)

Mary immediately understood something terrible would happen to Jesus and the moment he said it, Her Heart was pierced for the first time, because She knew, that for Her Son to be a sign of contradiction, and for Her soul to be pierced in the future, it would have to refer to Him, whom She loved immensely.

But, did She know He would be crucified? Maybe, since She knew the prophecies of Isaiah, Psalm 22, and Zechariah, better than anyone else, due to Her intellect being untainted by original sin. "They shall look upon Him, whom they pierced."

(Zechariah 12:10). And if Her Son would be physically pierced, it would cause Her Heart to be spiritually pierced.

With His glorious entry into the Temple, the sword of sorrow predicted for Mary announced Christ's perfect and unique oblation on the Cross that will impart the salvation God has "prepared in the presence of all peoples." And so, as the Light came in the world and departed the world, the tears of His Mother fell upon the ground in sorrow. The result of the sword piercing the Virgin Mary, would be the cause of the thoughts of many hearts to be revealed, meaning through Her intercession, many will come to know how their sins hurt Jesus, and at the Last Judgment, all will see each other's sins, through Her mediation.

In the Church of St. Simeon in Zadar, Croatia, the mummified body of Simeon, who received the Child Jesus in the temple, is in a silver plated casket. He was a God-fearing old man who held the child Jesus in his arms.

Just after Simeon spoke his prophecy, God the Father inspired Anna, a wrinkled faced elderly woman and whose hands were worn from years, to immediately come into their presence-- giving Joseph and Mary a consolation in the midst of their having just heard the future sorrow to come.

"Anna was advanced in years, having lived seven years with her husband after her marriage, and then as a widow until she was eighty-four. She never left the temple, but worshiped night and day with fasting and prayer. And coming forward at that very time, she gave thanks to God and spoke about the child to all who were awaiting the redemption of Jerusalem." (Luke 2:36-37)

Anna was known for her fasting and prayer worshiping God night and day. Yet she was eighty-four years old. This old lady puts us to shame.

Mary handed the Child Jesus to Anna, who hugged Him against her chest and squeezed Him with joy. The smile on

Anna's face momentarily took away some pain from the prophecy just uttered by the elderly priest.

Anna gave back the Child to Mary and the Holy Family quickly departed the temple pondering what happened and giving thanks for the amazing events that just transpired.

Application 1: Fasting

As Catholics, we are required to fast and abstain from meat only two days a year, Ash Wednesday and Good Friday. Fasting means limiting food intake. Abstaining means to not eat meat.

Fasting is understood as one meal and *if necessary* two smaller meals that don't equal a meal. Traditionally Catholics have fasted on bread and water, especially on Wednesday, Fridays and Saturdays. The Saturday fast is to honor the Blessed Virgin Mary, because it was the only day She was without Her Son before He rose from the dead.

Did you know Catholics in the USA are required to abstain from meat *every* Friday of the year, unless a Solemnity falls on that Friday? Abstinence is obligatory after reaching the age of 14; fasting becomes obligatory from age 18 until midnight of one's 59th birthday.

It's worth noting that local bishops' conferences have the authority to substitute "other forms of penance" such as exorcises of prayer and works of charity, for abstinence from meat, if they deem it appropriate. However, in the absence of such a directive, Catholics are expected to observe the traditional practice of abstaining from meat on Fridays.

"The purpose of these laws of abstinence is to educate us in the higher spiritual law of charity and self-mastery. This spiritual purpose can also help us to understand the reasons for excluding flesh meat on penitential days. There was a once-widespread belief that flesh meat provoked and excited the baser human passions. Renouncing these foodstuffs was considered an excellent means of conquering the wayward self and orienting one's life toward God. The ascetic and spiritual purpose of fasting and abstinence can also help us to understand why it has always been tied to alms-giving. In this way, it makes little sense to give up steak so as to gorge on lobster and caviar. The idea of abstinence is to prefer a simpler, less sumptuous diet than normal. We thus have something extra to give to those less fortunate than ourselves and also train ourselves in freedom from slavery to material pleasures."[35]

We are all required to do penance for our sins. Jesus said, "...I say to you: but unless you shall do penance, you shall all likewise perish." (Luke 13:3) The prophet Ezekiel said, "But if the wicked do penance for all his sins which he hath committed, and keep all my commandments, and do judgment, and justice, living he shall live, and shall not die." (Ezekiel 18:21)

Application 2: Children's Baptism

Today, some Catholics wrongly take up the idea that a child should not be dedicated to God through baptism, until the child can later determine for himself his own religion. But, that was never the case for Jews. A male child would be circumcised eight days after birth. "When eight days were completed for his circumcision, He was named Jesus, the name given him by the angel before he was conceived in the womb." (Luke 2:21) And forty days after birth, some boys would be presented in the Temple.

Some ancient Jewish fathers thought circumcision would remove original sin. But, later all came to know baptism would definitively remove original sin. The Jews knew that through circumcision, the child would become a member of God's family and a member of the Jewish faith. It was a sign of the covenant between God and Abraham. The parents wanted to guarantee the child would be one of God's children and never belong to a

96

pagan religion that would offend God and risk losing the child's salvation.

Baptism washes away original sin, and if beyond the age of reason, it washes away personal sin and remits all purgatory time. It makes the child a temple of God, a member of God's family, an adoptive child of God the Father, and a member of the Catholic Church, which has been given everything by God for one to obtain eternal salvation. Baptism imparts gifts of faith, hope and charity and is the gateway to the other sacraments.

A baptized child, who dies, before he or she is old enough to commit sin, is guaranteed heaven. Surely, we would want all these gifts for our child. According to ancient writers, baptism of infants is an immemorial tradition from the beginning in the Catholic Church.

Does a child decide on his own, if he will attend school? Or if he will go to the hospital after breaking a leg due to wrecking a bicycle? Or does he decide for himself, if he has a severe infection and should go to a doctor or not? If children would refuse these things, we wouldn't listen to them because they are not old enough to decide for themselves something so important.

If parents decide these things for their children, shouldn't parents also decide for the child, if he is to receive the gift of baptism, be a member of the Catholic Church, and receive all the above gifts? If we decide natural things for them, how much more important should we decide supernatural things for them? Don't we want more than anything else to give them the easiest and safest way to obtain heaven, by being Catholic?

Story 1: Lots of Babies

A priest prepared a young couple for marriage and then presided over their wedding. She was Catholic and he was not. Keeping to the moral way of life, they abstained from sex until

97

after marriage. A few months after they were married, she became pregnant. The doctor gave the parents a specific due date for the child.

Nine months later, on the same day the child was due, they had an appointment with the doctor to see how things were going. Sadly, it was then discovered the child died that same day, the day the child was to be born, after the mother carried the child for nine months. The terrible tragedy devastated the young couple and the mother had to give birth to a fully developed deceased child, a "stillbirth." After the child was born, a funeral was held a few days later at a Catholic Church. They named the child "Emma."

In less than a year, the mother called the priest, and said, "Father, please pray for us. We are scared. I'm pregnant with twins and I'm afraid we will lose our two children." The priest promised to pray for the couple and the two unborn children. Eventually, she carried the twins until they were born and he baptized them at the parish.

Then, a year and half later, the mother called the priest, and said, "Father, I'm pregnant again. We are scared. We're going to have triplets!" The priest, the couple and many others prayed for a safe birth for the triplets and they were born. Soon after being dismissed from the hospital, he baptized the triplets at the parish.

So, in three years, the parents had six children. One deceased and five under the age of two. Praise the Lord! How good God is to a couple, who suffered the loss of their first child and blessed them with five more in less than three years.

Apparition: Our Lady of Las Lajas (Columbia)

In a *Catholic Exchange* website article, Fr. Donald Calloway, MIC spoke about an event in Colombia in 1754 that continues to baffle geologists and other scientists. This event was about the miraculous appearance of the image of Our Lady of Las Lajas on rocks (Our Lady of the Rocks). Our Lady is holding a Rosary and handing it to St. Dominic and the Child Jesus is grasping the cord of St. Francis of Assisi.

The article states, "As the story goes, one day a woman named María Mueses de Quiñones was walking with her deaf and mute daughter, Rosa, through a very treacherous rocky area on their way home. When a storm broke out, Maria and her daughter took shelter in the rocky cliffs of a canyon. All of a sudden, little Rosa spoke for the first time, declaring that she saw a beautiful woman who was calling her. Maria did not see or hear the woman, but was amazed that her daughter could now speak. A few days later, Rosa disappeared from the village. Her mother instinctively knew to return to the rocky canyon where she would find her little girl.

Incredibly, when Maria went to the rocks, she found Rosa playing with a little child whose mother stood nearby. It was an apparition of the Virgin Mary and the Child Jesus! Maria and her daughter decided to keep this event secret, but would frequently return to the rocks to pray and ask Our Lady for her intercession.

After a few months, little Rosa suddenly fell ill and died. Distraught, Maria took her deceased daughter to the rocks to ask Our Lady to intercede with her divine Son to bring Rosa back to life. Miraculously, Rosa came back to life! When Maria returned to the village and the people saw that Rosa was alive, their interest was piqued about this place where little Rosa had miraculously recovered her speech and even come back from death.

The villagers followed Maria and Rosa to the rocks to see the place themselves. While they were there, someone noticed a beautiful image of Our Lady on the rocks. Neither Maria nor Rosa had seen the image there before. No one knew who had painted it or where it had come from. In the beautiful image, Our Lady is holding the Child Jesus and handing St. Dominic a rosary; the Child Jesus is extending a friar's cord to St. Francis of Assisi.

After extensive investigations, civil authorities and scientists determined that the scene was not a painting at all. The image is miraculously part of the rock itself! Geologists have since bored core samples from several places in the rock and discovered that there is no paint, dye, or pigment on the surface of the rock. The colors of the mysterious image are the colors of the rock itself and extend several feet deep inside the rock!

The only man-made aspects of the miraculous image are the crowns above the heads of Jesus and Mary that were later added by local devotees. For more than two centuries, the location has been a place of pilgrimage and devotion. In 1951, the Church authorized devotion to Our Lady under the title of "Our Lady of Las Lajas," and the church built around the image has been declared a minor basilica."[36]

The Finding of Jesus in the Temple

Fruit of the Mystery: Joy of Finding Jesus

"Each year his parents went to Jerusalem for the feast of Passover and when he was twelve years old, they went up according to festival custom. After they had completed its days, as they were returning, the boy Jesus remained behind in Jerusalem, but his parents did not know it. Thinking that he was in the caravan, they journeyed for a day and looked for him among their relatives and acquaintances, but not finding him, they returned to Jerusalem to look for him. After three days they found him in the temple, sitting in the midst of the teachers, listening to them and asking them questions, and all who heard him were astounded at his understanding and his answers. When his parents saw him, they were astonished, and his mother said to him, "Son, why have you done this to us? Your father and I have been looking for you with great anxiety." And he said to them, "Why were you looking for me? Did you not know that I must be in my Father's house?" But they did not understand what he said to them. He went down with them and came to Nazareth, and was obedient to them; and his mother kept all these things in her heart. And Jesus advanced in wisdom and age and favor before God and man." (Luke 2:41-51)

Every year, Jewish parents would go to the Temple for three feasts; the Pasch (Passover), Pentecost and Feast of Tabernacles. While it was only necessary for the man to attend them, most likely the Virgin Mary and the Child Jesus attended them as well. By their faithfulness to their Jewish customs, the Holy Family would give a lesson to all parents as to the practical early teaching of children in the duties of religion. They would have religiously stayed in Jerusalem for the octave days, although not bound to do so.

It is very likely Jesus concealed His design to stay in Jerusalem. He remained not by accident, but by the all-ruling designs of Providence. His parents are not guilty of neglect, because when returning home with their traveling companions, the men formed one company and the women another. Thus, Joseph might have supposed the Divine Boy was with His Mother, while Mary could have supposed He was with Joseph. But, in the evening after the two separated companies gathered together, they realized Jesus was not in the caravan.

Anxiety and fear began to cause sorrow in the hearts of Mary and Joseph. They began to wonder, what could have happened to Jesus? Where is He? Does He have shelter and food? Is He hungry and cold? Is He searching for us in a different caravan? Is He sleeping out in the streets? Did bandits capture Him?

Mary and Joseph began to walk about going through the numerous tents of those traveling in their company looking for Him and asking if anyone had seen Him. As the sun began to set, they chose to wait until dawn to begin their journey back to Jerusalem. They thought He might be beside the road waiting for them to return. Even though they trusted in God's providence, as they laid down for rest, they knew they would not be able to sleep, but rather prayed all night long, and with tears they asked His heavenly Father to bring them back together and take care of Jesus until reunited.

As the sun came up the next day and dew had made the ground moist, they began to walk back to Jerusalem, calling out for Him by the side of the road. When they came upon another company of travelers, they asked them if they had seen Jesus.

Mary and Joseph described His appearance to those whom they questioned: His blue penetrating eyes, light brown hair, His serious nature in speaking, wisdom beyond His age, and His white seamless tunic. But no one could recall seeing their Child. When hearing about His loss, the more pious travelers prayed to God asking Him guide His parents to their Son and they prayed for His welfare and safety.

Although Mary and Joseph did nothing wrong, they felt the pain of losing God, like that of sinners who lose God due to their sins. Though without sin, nevertheless She knew the fears and the loneliness, the darkness and the isolation which every sinner experiences when He loses God. Nothing can satisfy a heart, who does not have God.

Being without original sin, Mary was able to perfectly control Her emotions, but the event caused Her to feel pain to a degree of sensitivity we could not imagine. Original justice is a gift, but with the gift is a tenderness of heart and compassion for others that is intense, and extreme out of love.

But this was not the case for Joseph. He suffered from original sin. His memory, will and intellect were darkened. He had an inclination to sin like all of us. But, God granted Him the grace to be strengthened by manly virtue and not allow his feelings, emotions and imagination to cause despair or to not trust the Lord in this time of great anxiety and fear. Because of his humanness and due to the humanity of Mary, both wept throughout the three days. Their weeping was caused by separation. They just wanted to be together again, out of love for each other.

To comfort Mary, on occasion, Joseph would hug Her, give Her a kiss and whisper words of encouragement to Her, saying, "We will find Him. And He will be okay."

As they entered Jerusalem, both had a simultaneous inspiration, "He must be in the Temple". They asked doctors of the law if they had seen Jesus, and some confirmed they had. They heard of a young boy, who was "listening to the doctors of the law and asking questions."

An old doctor of the law said, "He is the talk of the Temple, because all who heard Him were astonished at His wisdom and His answers." Some have said, "For truly, the Spirit was upon Him." The elderly doctor placed His hand on Mary's shoulder, and said, "He is fine. We have been taking care of Him. Don't worry. He had a place to stay and some food to eat. He's the smartest young man I ever met for His age. His words inspire me to love God and He has helped me to understand the Sacred Scriptures in a way that I never thought possible. This is strange to say, but the thought occurred to me, "Could he be the long awaited Messiah?" "And that's not all, I never felt so comfortable around anyone like Him before. I feel as though I had known Him all my life. But, I have only known Him for three days."

The doctor pointed to one of the courts, and finally, Mary and Joseph could see Him in the distance seated with the doctors causing their hearts to leap with joy. They came towards the boy Jesus and when He saw them, He stood up, walked over to Mary, and hugged Her. He then turned to Joseph and did the same. What was once tears of sadness are now tears of joy.

Out of love, Mary wanted to get to the bottom of this. And now, She understood, He was responsible for staying behind. But, why didn't He say anything to them? Why didn't He ask them to remain with Him? It was surely in God's plan that He would stay without telling them, but why would they have to suffer so grievously? And so, Mary asked, "Why hast thou, done this to us? Behold, your father and I have sought Thee sorrowing." Notice, how out of charity, Mary mentioned Joseph before Herself[37]. She was thinking of his sorrow before Hers. Out of love for Her spouse, She placed Her love for him first, before Her own concern.

Jesus responded, "How is it you sought me? Did you not know, I must be about my Father's business?" These words sound reproachful, but they are not.

104

In other words, Jesus had more lofty duties to His Father, and so was forced to ignore Mary and Joseph for a greater good, even if it meant causing them sorrow and pain they had to endure.

He gave us this example, to show us that at times, parents may oppose their child's entrance into religion (to become a priest or a religious), when their child is clearly called by God to a higher state.

Mary and Joseph did not understand why at His age, He would remain in the Temple with the doctors, but they reverently acquiesced all He said without asking further questions. Perhaps, His staying in the Temple would help the doctors to later accept Him as the Messiah and therefore help others in the future. He was seeking to help the doctors of the law to grow in love of God and understand God ever more perfectly.

Though Mary had perfect charity, She did not have infinite knowledge. God did not always reveal everything to Her. This process of growing in knowledge of things would increase Her merit and holiness.

Jesus was subject to them. He returned with them to Nazareth out of obedience to continue His usual occupation, as a carpenter. Imagine for a moment, what it's like for God to be obedient to human beings. He labored for thirty silent years. He did all Mary and Joseph asked of Him. St. Bernard said, "Who was subject? God. To whom? To men. He, whom the powers of heaven obey, was subject to Mary and not to Mary only; but to Joseph. On both sides, astounding wonder. On both sides, a miracle. That God would obey a woman, is an instance of unexplained humility. That a woman should rule a God, of unequaled sublimity. Blush proud ashes, a God humbles Himself; and dost thou exalt thyself? A God subjects Himself to man, and dost thou anxiously prefer thyself to the Author of thy

105

being? Learn therefore man to obey; learn, O earth, to be subject; and thou, O dust, to submit."[38]

Mary kept all these words in Her Immaculate Heart, by constantly meditating on all the words, actions and events connected to Her Son, whom She knew to be God, which nourished Her piety and acquiring a more certain knowledge of all the mysteries of His life, which She communicated to the Apostles and evangelists,[39] especially Luke, so they could announce them through the world. Isn't that what we do, when we pray the Rosary? We meditate with Mary's Heart on the mysteries of Her Son's life.

The scripture states, "He grew in wisdom and knowledge." Some have erroneously interpreted this to mean that Jesus did not yet understand He was God. But, this false view contradicts the relationship between His divine and human natures. Jesus as God, always knew He was God. *The Catechism of the Catholic Church*, (#474), states, "By its union to the divine wisdom in the person of the Word incarnate, Christ enjoyed in his human knowledge the fullness of understanding of the eternal plans He had come to reveal. What He admitted to not knowing in this area, He elsewhere declared himself not sent to reveal."

After this event, there is no further mention of Joseph. Most likely, he died before Jesus began His public ministry. And there is no doubt, Jesus and Mary were present at his death, which is why Joseph is the patron of a happy death.

Application 1: Obedience to a Higher Calling

Mother Mary Angelica Rizzo, PCPA knew her mother would not approve of her becoming a Poor Clare of Perpetual Adoration, but she chose to respond to her calling from God and leave her mother behind, even if it meant her mother would be hurt and angry. Later, Mother Angelica's mother would join her daughter's religious community and they would become sisters and daughters to God Father in heaven and spouses of Jesus, their groom. Mother Angelica's Poor Clare Nuns of Perpetual Adoration have always prayed the Rosary together as a religious community.

Application 2: Hurting Children & Hurting Families

How many times have we heard and seen photos of missing children in the news? Did they run away from home? Did they get lost when trying to return home? Did they stay at a friend's home without telling their parents? Are they fleeing from an abusive household? Are their parents not feeding them, and in order to survive, they ask neighbors for food. Were they captured by sex traffickers, who promised fake things like being in a movie or taking photos for money? How many children today are being held against their will and are physically, sexually and verbally abused?

The worst type of abuse towards a child is abortion, because abortion kills innocent children. Abortion causes trauma and emotional sufferings for the parents. When a child loses a brother or sister due to abortion, there is a deep wound caused to each sibling, as they wonder how they could be loved, if their parent was willing to kill a brother or sister.

Due to divorce or not being married, single mothers must work and at times leave her children at home unattended because she can't afford childcare. Some children rarely or never see their father and feel abandoned by him.

Fathers abandon their children and don't provide child support to care for them. Some mothers and fathers are addicted to drugs and alcohol.

Some parents raise their children without God. Many children are brought up not knowing who God is, and have rarely or never even attended church. The breakup of the family, the use of contraception and abortions have wrecked families today.

Children become sexually confused and seek excessive affection from someone of the same sex due to a parent not being in the home or due to a parent who is homosexual. This sexual confusion can cause some children to become homosexual or feel they need to change genders. But the root of the problem is really emotional and mental due to the trauma of divorce, abuse, or molestation, etc. they have experienced in their home. What they really need is a stable loving family and truly Catholic mental health experts to help them.

Jesus was home schooled. His parents taught Him to read, write, and Jewish customs and laws. They prayed together as a family and sacrificed themselves for each other.

Parents are the first and best teachers of the faith to their children. *The Catechism of the Catholic Church,* (#2223) states, "Parents have the first responsibility for the education of their children. They bear witness to this responsibility first by creating a home where tenderness, forgiveness, respect, fidelity, and disinterested service are the rule."

Fathers of the family should take their spiritual role seriously and be the spiritual head of the family, just as St. Joseph was the head of the Holy Family. St. Paul told the Ephesians, "Husbands, love your wives, just as Christ loved the church and gave himself up for her..." (Ephesians 5:25) Husbands are to give up their own desires and own will for the sake of their wife and family. The husband is to lay down his life for his family and therefore is the one who is to make the greatest sacrifices.

Fathers should encourage their children by example, but also by words in the practice of the faith. He should show them the importance of reading the bible, praying the Rosary, going to Mass not only on weekends, but during the week when possible. He should set a specific date each month when he and his wife will bring their children to Confession. He is to lead the family in prayers, especially before and after meals and the daily family Rosary. Teaching the children to pray and to get to know Jesus, he will help them to have a strong faith foundation. He should watch over his daughters' friends and help his daughters wear modest clothing.

By teaching his sons to respect young girls, and protecting them from pornography and improper shows on the phone, internet, television, and movie theaters, he will instill the importance of the virtue of chastity.

To listen, to talk, to play games and to work together as a family will bring about unity by sacrificial acts of love.

Mothers should lay aside their aspirations for personal achievements, by first and foremost living out her vocation as mother and wife. Today, many husbands and wives are both forced to work due to economic reasons. But, it is also true many times, the couple is expecting a standard of living beyond what is necessary. Joseph and Mary lived a poor and simple life. If at all possible, mothers should be stay at home moms, to be the primary nurturer of the family.

Otherwise, if both work, the children go to daycare, mom goes to work and after nine hours due to work and driving time, she ends up spending only several waking hours with her children and may not have the ability to even cook a meal for dinner. The children spend more waking time with a stranger, than mom or dad. Many families don't even eat together regularly. The babysitter, who watches the child for the majority of the day, teaches one moral standard and mom and dad teach another. All this disorder can cause confusion among children and cause them to act up when with their parents.

For single mothers and fathers, the burden is great when trying to do everything themselves and so they need support from their family and friends in helping to raise their children. It is all the more important to turn to Jesus, Mary and Joseph for help.

Devotion to the Divine Child can be very helpful in learning to trust with childlike confidence in God and to come to God with humility of heart. The Divine Child Jesus, as a little boy, appeared to St. Faustina, St. Anthony of Padua, St. Rose of Lima, Mother Angelica and many saints and holy men and women.

The Holy Family, Jesus, Mary and Joseph give us an example of how family members should sacrifice for each other, pray together, obey the laws of the Church, worship together, work together, trust in God's providence, and if necessary, live a life of poverty together. The Holy Family was not immune from sufferings and hardships. They show us-- God is first, the family is second and then our work. They show us how the family must be centered on God and our faith.

Application 3: Family Rosary & Rosary Rallies

Pope Pius XI (1922-1939) said, "If you desire peace in your hearts, in your homes, and in your country, assemble each evening to recite the Rosary. Let not even one day pass without saying it, no matter how burdened you may be with many cares and labors."

Fr. Patrick Peyton (1909 – 1992) came as an Irish immigrant with his family to the United States. He became a member of the Holy Cross Fathers religious order. In the 1940's, Fr. Patrick Peyton began preaching parish missions on family prayer and the Rosary, which he called Triduums. With the popularity of radio and television, requests of Father Peyton poured in. He wanted to reach larger audiences, but also wanted his talks to have a lasting appeal in people's lives.

With advice from bishops and his team at *Family Rosary,* he developed a strategy for large scale Rosary rallies. Before he would hold a rally, the bishops would agree to support the event. Teams in every parish would invite people to pray the Rosary as a family. Using this strategy, he held the first diocesan

110

wide Rosary Rally in Ontario, Canada in 1948. Over the course of several months, the team recruited several thousand volunteers. Then a publicity campaign was mounted including a weekly news publication in anticipation of the crusade.

At the Rosary Rallies Fr. Peyton would preach in length about the importance of praying through Mary. The masses would pray that day's mysteries of the Rosary.

The crusade was a success and became a model of hosting crusades around the world. Rosary rallies took place in major cities in every continent. Some rallies grew crowds into the millions. Some suspected prior to Pope John Paul II's world tours, Fr. Peyton held the record for being seen by more people than any other Catholic evangelist. Thanks to Rosary Rallies, the faith of families flourished. The main intention of Rosary rallies was to facilitate the families praying together. The Rosary is vital for family prayer life. Fr. Patrick Peyton said,

"Faith, hope and love are kept active through prayer. What a wonderful way, each member of the family circle enriches the other. And what a wonderful way, each family circle, helps the others to acquire, cultivate, and possess the three powers of a living faith, a firm hope and a burning love. May God and Mary love you and may you raise your voice in the millions and say, the family that prays together stays together." [40]

"What wonderful power for those who believe in the Rosary, who pray for it and for those who use it to make a happy home to live in. To make the home of love, justice and mercy. To make every son and daughter who uses it with love and sincerity, make it a home of tranquility and harmony, and love and joy, and justice to live in."[41]

"Dear men and women who are listening, the first minutes of the day, that God asks of you, (is to pray the Rosary). It is worth more than the wealth of America. Prayer is the most powerful force in the world and it's for your taking. Make it a part of your life. Give it a place in your home. Use it to strengthen your family circle. It is particularly beautiful when you use such prayers as the family Rosary. With its meditations on the life of Christ and Mary, His blessed Mother. When we pray the Rosary, we are asking God for all the blessings we need for our lives, our family, our nation, and our world. May God and Mary love you all. Make it a part of your life, by praying the Rosary."[42]

Jeffery Bruno, an award winning photographer, writer and creative director said, "It's been said that to hold the Rosary beads within one's hand, is to hold Our Lady's hand, as a child trustingly grasps a mother's hand...Trusting in Her who bore forth the Savior of all mankind, Trusting in Her example of what it means to totally and completely trust God, And trusting that she will lead us to her Son."

Story 1: Through the Rosary, a Little Girl Obtains Family Home

A family of three children, expecting their fourth child, wanted to move from their country home. The father was a hired hand for a large cattle feedlot. They wanted to return to be closer to their family and raise their children in the town they grew up in. While looking for a home, the parents were trying to find a house they could afford, but also large enough for their growing family. After visiting a house on Seventh Street, the oldest girl, who was eight years old, decided she wanted their family to move into that particular house, but they couldn't afford it. The child daily prayed the Rosary asking the Virgin Mary for the grace to have that yellow house on Seventh Street for their family. The parents and the banker came to an agreement, resulting in the family moving to their new home, thanks to a young girl who asked the Virgin Mary to answer her request through the Holy Rosary.

Story 2: Rosary & Divorce

A nineteen year old man, with seven siblings found a beautiful Rosary with crystal blue beads in a parking lot. When he was a child his mother taught him and his siblings to pray the Rosary, but over the years he forgot how to pray it. The family was poor and his father was an alcoholic. He often came home drunk late at night and was verbally abusive to everyone. Many nights his mother and father had verbal fights and items were tossed & doors slammed, while the children would hide in the bedrooms and pretend to be sleeping.

One day, his parents asked the young man to go with them for a drive. As he sat in the backseat, he noticed his mother placed the rosary around the rear-view mirror. His parents pulled off into a parking lot and turned toward their son and said, "We are thinking about getting a divorce and would like your opinion?" He was shocked and didn't know what to say.

The sun was setting and was reflecting on the crucifix and shining directly in his eyes. Every time he moved his head, the cross would somehow move and the reflection from the sun would shine in his eyes. He felt like God was trying to tell him how to respond to his parents. Finally, he blurted out, "If you can't get along and if you would have more peace, then maybe you should get a divorce." Later, he regretted his advice, and after reflecting on the event, he believed God wanted him to tell them, pray the Rosary together every night. After coming to know the power of the Rosary, oh, how he wished he had given them that advice.

Story 3: Rosary Ends Boko Haram & Frees Kidnapped Girls

In April 2014, Boko Haram kidnapped more than 200 young girls from a school in Nigeria, Africa. Boko Haram is the notorious radical Muslim group that decapitates or burns non-Muslims alive.

In December 2014, Bishop Oliver Dashe Doeme of the diocese of Maiduguri, Nigeria, went before Our Lord Jesus in Eucharistic Adoration, traumatized and trembling, and began to pray the Rosary. Then suddenly, Jesus appeared to the Bishop in a vision, holding a very long sword in His hands. When he saw Jesus, the Bishop said, "Lord, what is this?" He didn't answer, but He stretched out His arms and put the sword into the hands of Bishop Oliver. But as he took the sword, it turned into a Rosary. Jesus looked at him and said three times, "Boko Haram is gone! Boko Haram is gone! Boko Haram is gone!"

After the vision, the bishop began to promote the Rosary in his diocese and organized Rosary processions in many villages. On October 13, 2016, (The last apparition of Fatima anniversary, when Our Lady referred to Herself as Our Lady of the Rosary), dozens of kidnapped girls were suddenly released by Boko Haram. In May 2017, another 83 girls were released. Then, on July 3, 2017, 700 members of Boko Haram surrendered their weapons and turned themselves in to Nigerian authorities.

Apparition: Our Lady of Lourdes (France)

When the Virgin Mary appeared to Saint Bernadette in Lourdes, France, She held a Rosary in Her hands. On February 11, 1858, Bernadette said, "Without thinking of what I was doing, I took my rosary in my hands and fell on my knees. The Lady made a sign of approval with Her head and took into Her hands a Rosary which hung on Her right arm. When I attempted to begin the Rosary and tried to lift my hand to my forehead, my arm

114

remained paralyzed, and it was only after the Lady had signed Herself that I could do the same. The Lady left me to pray all alone; She passed the beads of Her Rosary between Her fingers, but She said nothing; only at the end of each decade did She say the 'Gloria' with me. "When the recitation of the Rosary was finished, the Lady returned to the interior of the rock and the golden cloud disappeared with her." Bernadette said, "On her right arm she carried a Rosary of white beads on a golden chain, shining like the roses on her feet." But, during the apparitions to St. Bernadette, She never mentioned the Rosary at Lourdes. However, her silent actions with regard to the Rosary, were a witness for all of us to pray the Rosary often.

THE LUMINOUS MYSTERIES MEDITATIONS

Baptism of Jesus by John the Baptist

Fruit of the Mystery: Openness to the Holy Spirit

"In those days John the Baptist came, preaching in the wilderness of Judea and saying, 'Repent, for the kingdom of God is at hand'. This is he who was spoken of through the prophet Isaiah: "A voice of one calling in the wilderness, 'Prepare the way for the Lord, make straight paths for Him.' John wore a garment of camel's hair, with a leather belt around his waist. His food was locusts and wild honey. People went out to him from Jerusalem and all Judea and the whole region around the Jordan. Confessing their sins, they were baptized by him in the Jordan River." (Matthew 1:1-6).

The Jordan River, in the location where it's believed Jesus was baptized, is about fifty feet wide. The river with its lush, sandy shores and steep, rocky banks, is fairly narrow and easy to cross in most places, though the current can be swift and even dangerous in some areas. Beyond the main river flow, however, shallow pools and smaller tributaries are common in the Jordan. On one side of the river, reeds blow in the wind with brush and trees, and on the other side were rocky banks and bare ground with a splattering of small plants that grew through the rocks.

There, in the water was John and hundreds of people standing on the banks of the river waiting to receive baptism. One man in his 20's on the bank cries out, "O God, I am sorry for my sins. I repent of them and desire to truly be a righteous man following the Divine Law given to us by Moses and passed down to us by our ancestors."

John motioned for him to come to the water. The man enters the water and bows his head. John tells the man to close his eyes and hold his breath. Then he placed one hand on his shoulder and with the other grasped his hand. He then gently pushed him below the water in a quick plunge, saying, "O merciful God, forgive this man's transgressions and prepare his heart from the coming of the Messiah." Pulling his hand up and grasping the back of his neck, John helped him to once again stand in the water. Coming out of the water the young man shouts with joy, "O God, how gracious and merciful are you, to me, a sinner!"

When the man returned to the edge of the bank, John noticed Pharisees standing on the shore, and cried out, "You brood of vipers! Who warned you to flee from the wrath to come? Bear fruit that befits repentance, and do not presume to say to yourselves, "We have Abraham as our father, for I tell you, God is able from these stones to raise up children of Abraham." "I baptize you with water of repentance, but He who is coming after me is mightier than I, whose sandals I am not worthy to carry; He will baptize you with the Holy Spirit and with fire." (Matthew 3:7-11)

The people who had gathered on the shore and were baptized gave a collective chuckle at John's rebuke of the Pharisees. And some saying, "See how this man fears no one. He tells the truth that everyone knows, but will not say."

Standing by the shore watching and waiting until the last person was baptized was the cousin of John, Jesus Christ. The two first met at the Visitation when the pregnant Virgin Mary came to visit Her pregnant cousin Elizabeth, John's mother. At that time, John was an unborn babe three months before his birth. At their first meeting, his mother, Elizabeth, was filled with the Holy Spirit and through the action of the Holy Spirit, the unborn Jesus sanctified John, washing away original sin on his soul.

118

Now, John is to baptize Jesus, who sanctified John's soul as an unborn baby through the Holy Spirit. But, the Spirit not visible at the Visitation, will appear in the form of a dove when Jesus is baptized, thus revealing the Blessed Trinity.

Jesus wearing His white seamless garment, entered the water and approached John, who was wearing a garment made of camel's hair. Jesus told John that He wants to be baptized by him. But, when John immediately recognized Our Lord, he said, "I need to be baptized by You, and you come to me?" Jesus answered, "Let it be so now, for thus it is fitting to fulfill all righteousness." (Matthew 3:13-17)

Jesus was baptized by John, and as He came up from beneath the water, the heavens were opened and John saw the Spirit of God descending like a dove.

Through Our Lord's Baptism, the Blessed Trinity is revealed. The Father spoke, "This is my beloved Son, in whom I am well pleased." The Son receives His Father's testimony while He is in His physical body of the Jordan waters. And the Holy Ghost (Spirit) is seen in the visible form of a dove.

Just as a dove was released after the flood as a sign of restoration from man's shipwreck of sin, so now, a dove appears as a sign of God restoring man to Himself, through the opening of the heavens through the sacrament of baptism we receive. In the days of Noah, the dove symbolized a period of peace and deliverance had come.

God is pleased to send His Son to reconcile us to Himself by freeing the world from the sins of men. Through baptism God restores man to the unity of the Trinity that was lost by Adam and Eve. He restores all things in Christ.

The baptism of John was a baptism of repentance from sin to prepare the people for the Gospel message through Jesus and to prepare them for actual baptism later at the hands of the Apostles. The baptism John preached did not wash away sins, but the baptism Jesus taught His Apostles, would not only wash away sins, but also restore the union between man and God lost due to the sin of Adam and Eve. The apostles were given a command, "Go therefore, make disciples of all nations, baptizing them in the name of the Father and of the Son and of the Holy Spirit." (Matthew 28:19-20)

Discipleship is intimately connected with baptism. We become a follower of Jesus through baptism with the mission to make more disciples.

Jesus did not need baptism because He is God. He never suffered from original sin and He never committed sin. But, Our Lord was baptized as an example for us, to do the same. He did it as an act of humility and to show His approval of John's baptism, which was to prepare the way of the Lord.

What would it be like to hear the voice of God the Father? Surely, it was a deep, strong voice that would cause the earth to shiver by its power. "The voice of the Lord is over the waters; the God of glory thunders; the Lord is heard over many waters. The voice of the Lord is powerful; the voice of the Lord is majestic. The voice of the Lord breaks the cedars; the Lord shatters the cedars of Lebanon...." (Psalm 29:3-5) But, it would also be a voice of tenderness, compassion and mercy. "The Lord, the Lord, a God merciful and gracious, slow to anger, and abounding in steadfast love and faithfulness." (Psalm 103:8)

Application 1: Fathers are Images of God the Father

Through baptism we become an adopted child of God. "But when the time had fully come, God sent His Son, born of a woman, born under the law, to redeem those under the law, so that we might receive our adoption as sons. And because you are sons, God sent the Spirit of His Son into our hearts, crying out, "Abba, Father!" So you are no longer a slave, but a son; and since you are a son, you are also an heir through God." (Galatians 4:4-7)

The word "Abba" means "daddy". To call God the Father, daddy, helps us to understand the tender relationship God wants us to have with Him.

Every natural father is an image of God the Father. There is no perfect earthly father and all fall short. But the good characteristics, the virtues practiced, the love shown to us by our natural father, help to reveal God the Father to us.

Jesus came to reveal the Father. He said, "The Father and I are one." (John 10:30) "When you see me, you see the Father." Phillip told Jesus, "Show us the Father." "Jesus answered: "Don't you know me, Philip, even after I have been among you for such a long time? Anyone who has seen me has seen the Father." (John 14:9)

But, we can have a distorted view of God the Father, due to our natural father's mistakes and sins. Sometimes, people can have an inordinate fear of God the Father. They think God the Father is always ready to exact punishment. One of the causes for this unhealthy view of God the Father, can be the way a natural father treated his children. A father who is an excessive disciplinarian, can cause his children to fear punishment from God the Father. A father who is distant and not part of one's life- can cause his children to view God the Father as distant and not part of their life. This is because every father is an image of God the Father. It is innate, meaning God has placed in the hearts of every person, an understanding that when we see the good and holy actions of our natural father, we get a glimpse into God the Father's love for us.

Application 2: Understanding Baptism & Validity

Through baptism we become a member of God's family. God is a family of persons (Father, Son and Holy Spirit). Each gives oneself totally to the other in mutual love. The Father gives

Himself totally to the Son. The Son gives Himself totally to the Father and the love between them is the Holy Spirit.

Marriage is an image of the Blessed Trinity. The natural father gives himself totally to his wife. She gives herself totally to her husband and the love between them can bring forth a child. The analogy is imperfect, but it helps us to understand in a small way the mystery of unity of the persons of the Blessed Trinity and our relationship with the Trinity.

We have an obligation to be baptized. In fact, Jesus said baptism is necessary for salvation. Our Divine Lord said, "Truly, truly, I say to you, unless someone is born of water and the Spirit, he cannot enter the kingdom of God." (John 3:5)

This applies to those who come to know and believe baptism is necessary for salvation. Baptism is the ordinary way God has deigned for us to open the door of salvation. However, those who through no fault of their own, do not know about the necessity of baptism, may still be saved. If one, who is not baptized "seeks God with a sincere heart, and, moved by grace, try in their actions to do His will as they know it through the dictates of their conscience..." (CCC#847) can be saved. God is not bound by the sacraments. Yet, we are bound to follow them, if we come to know the truth of them; and the Church has a duty and obligation to evangelize to bring others to the sacraments.

When a child is baptized, the faith of his parents and godparents supply for the faith of the child and then later when the child is older, and understands his commitment, he will renew his baptismal promises, first made by his parents and godparents and become an active follower of Jesus.

For baptism to be valid, the proper formula must be used. It must be performed with the desire to do it as the Church desires and water must be used. There is to be a triple pouring or immersion when saying the words of baptism. The one baptizing is to say the name of the person, "Name_____, I baptize you, in the name of the Father, and of the Son and of the Holy Spirit."

The only valid formula to baptize is the one Jesus gave to His apostles at their great commission. Just before He ascended into heaven, Jesus said, "Go, therefore, and make disciples of all nations. Baptizing them in the name of the Father, and of the Son and of the Holy Spirit." (Matthew 28:19).

Not well known, is that immediately after the Baptism of a child, the parents can have the child dedicated to the Blessed Virgin Mary. This is done at the end of the Baptism ceremony, whereby the parents, godparents and priest take the child to a statue or image of the Virgin Mary and the priest will offer a prayer dedicating the child to the Virgin Mary.

Today some denominations and at least one mainline Protestant religion (Methodist) do not always validly baptize, because they do not use the proper formula. Some religions such as the Mormons don't baptize validly because they don't believe Jesus is God. Jehovah Witnesses believe Jesus is Michael the Archangel. These religions have invalid baptisms.

When a Methodist minister was asked if they baptize "in the name of the Creator, Redeemer and Sanctifier", and what other formulas they use, a Methodist pastor in April of 2024, said, "United Methodists baptize with a Trinitarian formula in line with the historic tradition of all Christians. Usually that takes the form of "Father, Son, and Holy Spirit." Though a few clergy might use different names for God (Creator, Redeemer and Sanctifier). We are not as rigid on the exact wording of the liturgy as some denominations might be, we are allowed a little creativity."

How tragic when Catholic priests and deacons don't validly baptize. In 2020, Father Zachary Bowman, a priest of the archdiocese of Oklahoma City, discovered he was invalidly baptized as a child by a deacon in Texas, who baptized him saying, "*We* baptize you in the name of the Father and of the Son and of the Holy Spirit." which is invalid. The word "I" must be used, and not "We". Father Bowman was ordained one year, when he discovered his baptism was invalid.

After this was discovered, he was baptized properly, confirmed, and ordained a priest by his archbishop. Due to his invalid baptism, he unknowingly offered invalid Confessions, Masses, and Weddings. What a terrible heart-breaker for him and for the people he served to learn the sacraments he performed were invalid!

The weddings he performed were sanated "healed" and made valid through the archbishop's canonical action. The Masses needed to be re-offered. The baptisms he performed were valid because one does not need to be a priest to baptize, as long as the proper formula is used and there is the proper intention of doing what the Church desires.

Some hospital personnel and ministers at Catholic and non-Catholic hospitals have invalidly baptized newborn children in danger of death for various reasons. At times, lay chaplains and religious sisters failed to call a priest (the primary and ordinary minister of baptism), because they wanted to perform the baptism themselves, and not the priest. Also, when a priest was not available, lay persons, non-Catholic ministers, or religious sisters performed invalid baptisms using invalid formulas.

How sorrowful for parents with children who have medical difficulties resulting in the death of a child, either before or after birth. However, the Church has consoling words, "As regards to children who have died without Baptism, the Church can only entrust them to the mercy of God, as she does in her funeral rites for them. Indeed, the great mercy of God who desires that all men should be saved, and Jesus' tenderness toward children which caused him to say: "Let the children come to me, do not hinder them" allow us to hope that there is a way of salvation for children who have died without Baptism. All the more urgent is the Church's call not to prevent little children coming to Christ through the gift of holy Baptism." (CCC #1261)

All baptisms must be performed as the Church desires and then we know for certain they are valid. For those desiring to become Catholic, if there are doubts, such as the baptism certificate doesn't say what formula was used, one could ask the non-Catholic minister, how he or she performed it.

Some baptism certificates, such as some Lutheran, clearly state the formula used for baptism. When this is the case, a conditional baptism is not necessary.

When someone is validly baptized the first time, it is not necessary to baptize again when becoming Catholic. Once baptized validly, the person is forever baptized.

Persons converting to the Catholic Church from main-line non-Catholic churches, except for some Methodist, do not need conditional baptisms, because the Church has approved these baptisms. The Office of Worship for your local diocese would have a list of approved baptisms by non-Catholic churches.

But due to so many different denominations, we can no longer trust non-Catholic churches if their baptisms are valid, it is most prudent and safest to be conditionally baptized, when a non-Catholic converts to the Catholic faith.

If baptized in a non-Catholic church or if you were baptized in a hospital, by a layperson, or religious, you may wish to speak to your pastor about receiving a conditional baptism.

The times we live in today, should cause us to all the more come to know and love our faith and proclaim it by evangelizing. We should be vigilant and make sure we are receiving valid sacraments. We should have a great desire to help others receive the sacraments, which are the primary means of salvation. And how important it is for the minister of the sacrament to perform it as God desires (as Our Lord's Catholic Church desires).

The baptism of Jesus reminds us of the great wonder and awe that comes with baptism and the duty to faithfully receive it and pass it on to others.

St. Louis de Montfort would say that Consecration to Jesus through Mary is a renewal of one's baptismal promises. He encouraged all to give themselves to Jesus through Mary and developed the consecration prayer to include the renewal of one's baptismal promises.

Story 1: Venerable Mary Agreda Instructed Indians & Gave Rosaries

About the same time pilgrims were at Plymouth Rock, between 1621 and 1631, when she was aged nineteen to twenty-nine years, Sister Mary of Agreda, was a nun at the Franciscan Convent of the Poor Clares of the Immaculate Conception in Spain. She bilocated over five hundred times. It would happen while she was praying. Her body remained in the cloistered convent, but at the same time, she would find herself in the continent of North America, in an area of land stretching across East Texas, New Mexico and Western Arizona. She appeared to the Jumano Indians and other tribes by flying through the sky and proceeded to teach them about the Catholic faith speaking to them in their own language. They described her as "The Lady in Blue." Her spirit carried rosaries from her cell to give to them. She instructed the Indians to get priests to come to their camp.

Thousands of miles away, in a cloistered convent in Spain, Sr. Maria de Agreda was reporting mystical visits that would occur during prayer, often during Mass after receiving Communion, to a tribe of native people in what was called New Spain at the time.

The Jumanos delegation told a Franciscan friar, through an Isletan translator, she had the Indians build a cross and an altar in their villages, taught them how to pray, make a rosary, and other Catholic rituals. The description of the woman, and her

126

clothing, was that of a nun. When the priests arrived, they were greeted by Indians, who had built a large cross and carried it in procession with flowers.

Thanks to Sr. Mary Agreda's appearances and teaching the Catholic faith, the priests baptized 10,000 Indians in the USA.

Story 2: Girl Becomes Carmelite Nun due to Dedication to Mary

A newly baptized child in Mexico at the request of the baby girl's mother was dedicated to Our Lady of Mount Carmel. The mother never told her daughter of the dedication, until 17 years later, when she entered a Carmelite monastery. The young sister eventually became the foundress and superior of a new Carmel foundation in Kansas.

Story 3: Dying Man Baptized

A priest was walking down the corridor of a very large hospital, when he noticed an elderly woman, who seemed to be lost. He stopped to help her and asked who she was seeing at the hospital. She informed him that her husband was dying in the ICU (Intensive Care Unit). After obtaining his name and room number, he went to visit the patient, while the woman departed for home. When he entered the room, he explained that he met his wife and she encouraged the priest to pray with him, despite the fact, he wasn't Catholic. The priest questioned the man and discovered he hadn't been baptized and had always wanted it. The man was baptized and departed from this life just a few days after his baptism.

Apparition: Our Lady of Pontmain (France)

During the devastation of the Franco-Prussian War, Mary appeared on a farm to students at the nearby convent school. Mary's message was written on a banner that unfurled from her feet: "But pray my children. God will hear you in a short time. My Son allows Himself to be moved by compassion."

On November 7, 1871 Eugene Barbedette (12) encountered a beautiful lady suspended in air above a neighboring house. The nearby adults could not see anything but when Francoise Richer (11), Jeanne-Marie Lebosse (9), Eugene Friteau (6) all claimed to see the woman, a nun in the crowd, Sister Marie Edouard, led everyone in prayer.

Also, on that same day, the Prussians halt their advance across France when the Prussian commander encounters an "invisible Madonna barring the way."

Our Lady wore a blue robe embroidered with numerous golden stars. On her head she had a black veil and a gold crown and on her feet blue shoes with gold ribbons. The Lady was tall and beautiful and looked about eighteen; "smiles of ineffable sweetness played about her mouth." When the cross with Christ appeared in her hands, Joseph Barbedette recalled that "her face was marked with a deep sorrow... the trembling of her lips at the corners of her mouth showed deep feeling... But no tears ran down her cheeks."

The apparition was motionless at first for the initial two hours. After the Rosary began to be prayed, a small red cross appeared over Her heart and a blue oval frame with four candles appeared around Her while the stars in Her robe seemed to increase. When the Magnificat was prayed, She elevated Her hands with the palms outward in a protective gesture. The candles in the oval frame were lit by a star, and when the Lady lowered Her hands, two white crosses appeared on Her shoulders. When the parish priest began his prayers, a white veil rose from beneath Her feet and covered Her until she disappeared. Nov 18, 1871 a peace treaty was signed between France and Prussia.

Jesus Changes Water into Wine at Wedding Feast

Fruit of the Mystery: Mary's Intercession

"On the third day there was a wedding in Cana in Galilee, and the mother of Jesus was there. Jesus and his disciples were also invited to the wedding. When the wine ran short, the mother of Jesus said to him, "They have no wine." And Jesus said to her, "Woman, how does your concern affect me? My hour has not yet come." His mother said to the servers, "Do whatever he tells you." Now there were six stone water jars there for Jewish ceremonial washings, each holding twenty to thirty gallons. Jesus told them, "Fill the jars with water." So they filled them to the brim. Then he told them, "Draw some out now and take it to the headwaiter." So they took it. And when the headwaiter tasted the water that had become wine, without knowing where it came from (although the servers who had drawn the water knew), the headwaiter called the bridegroom and said to him, "Everyone serves good wine first, and then when people have drunk freely, an inferior one; but you have kept the good wine until now." Jesus did this as the beginning of his signs in Cana in Galilee and so revealed his glory, and his disciples began to believe in him." (John 2:1-11)

How happy for the young couple to have invited Jesus, Mary, and His disciples. They certainly would have known who they were and were most likely relatives of Jesus and Mary. The Virgin Mary was there in advance and was charitably helping to attend to the feast with all the details that go with preparing for a wedding celebration. She could have helped prepare the meal, set tables with bowls of fruits, set out cups, utensils and dishes for the guests. Most likely they prepared lamb or fish for the meal. It would have taken a number of women to help make the meal to prepare it on time. It's doubtful Mary would have just stood back and watched others prepare for the feast, especially since She immediately went in haste to help of Her cousin Elizabeth.

Jesus had not yet worked any miracles, and therefore, His friends and relatives did not yet know His divine origin because His divinity had not yet been revealed.

During the time of Jesus, Jewish wedding celebrations lasted five to seven days. The following would also take place: The father of the bride would arrange the marriage and choose which man would marry his daughter. The groom would pay a sum of money to the future wife's father; On the day of the wedding ceremony, both bride and groom would wear a crown made out of plants; It is traditional for some communities for the bride to circle the groom seven times and then stand to the groom's right side under the chuppah (canopy).

As the couple were seated next to each other, the groom noticed his new bride was a bit nervous due the crowd, especially since she was gaining so much attention. He gently placed his arm around her, pressed her to his chest, leaned over, and whispered in her ear, "Sweetheart, we have nothing to fear. I will love you forever. Since our friends Jesus and Mary have arrived, I have peace. They are such good people, we can rely on them if we need anything. No matter what happens, everything will be fine."

Can you imagine being friends with Jesus and His Mother? The couple must have surely been righteous and of good character. They would have had ordinary conversations with Jesus and Mary. Perhaps they knew where they lived and the kind of work Jesus was known for as a carpenter.

The young man may have helped Jesus cut down trees and carry large limbs and tree trunks to His workshop for Jesus to cut. We can imagine Jesus carrying wood on His shoulders to His shop, which would later prefigure Him carrying the wood of the tree to Calvary. Most likely, the young woman met Mary at the community water well, where all came to take it to their homes. It could be that Mary showed Her how to sew and knit garments without seams.

The couple did not ask the Virgin Mary for help, but She noticed the problem of running out of wine. She was probably trying to help take care of the guests when She noticed it ran out. It would have been embarrassing for the wedding couple to run out of something so basic and important for guests. The couple was probably poor and didn't have the money to accommodate their guests like they had hoped. And it could also have been that more guests came than expected. Whatever the reason, now the couple had their first marriage crisis.

Mary, knowing Her Son could work a miracle in order to save the couple from embarrassment, simply said to Jesus, "They have no wine." She wasn't expecting Him to go to the local tavern and get more. She was expecting Him to make wine by using His divine power.

Jesus said something to Mary that sounds like a rebuke, but was certainly not at all. If it would have been a rebuke, Jesus would not have immediately worked the miracle. Our divine Lord said, "Woman, how does your concern affect me? My hour has not yet come."

In our day, very few would call out to their mother saying, "woman." I know if I said to my mother, "Woman, what's for supper!", She certainly would be a bit upset that I used such a title that sounds demeaning.

But, during the time of Jesus, using the word "woman" meant to respectfully address women. He would have said it in a tone of tenderness. The word "woman" during that time period, also meant a woman in a position of authority and control. It's like calling His Mother, "My Lady". By using the word woman, He was treating Mary as a true queen, who is to be respected due to Her power and authority.

133

It could have also been a reference to Genesis 3:15, the future woman at enmity with the devil. Jesus will again call His Mother, "Woman", when She is standing at the foot of the Cross. When He was dying, He wanted to show Her the deepest respect possible and refer to Her as the woman fulfilling the role in Genesis. But He also wanted to foreshadow His Mother as the woman of revelation, who, John, the Apostle would say is "clothed with the sun, with the moon under Her feet and crowned with stars." (Revelation 12:1)

"Woman, how does your concern affect me? My hour has not yet come." One translation states, "What is this to you and me?" Our Lord wanted to remind Mary, that once He begins to work miracles, it will eventually lead to His passion "His hour" and once the miracle takes place, Mary will also take on a new role in assisting Her Son to bring about salvation of many.

In other words, it is like Jesus saying to His Mother, "If I work this miracle, things will no longer be the same for You and for Me. My mission will begin and so will yours that will culminate at the Cross. Your intercession will become noticeable in a public way, and You will intercede not only for this wedding couple, but for everyone. You will no longer be only My Mother, because people will come to know You are their spiritual Mother, the Mother of all. You will have a new role. Be ready for the change that will happen in our lives."

When Jesus said, "My hour has not yet come." it was as though He was saying to Mary, "Had you not asked me to do this miracle, I would not have done so, because I would have performed my first miracle at another hour (a later time). But to show everyone, I desire all to turn to You and ask Your intercession, I will work this miracle in view of Your merits, as My Immaculate Mother. They will see, I will refuse You nothing, because You will never ask anything that is not God's will. And, I want to show everyone of all ages the power, importance, and respect You will have in God's plan."

Jesus told the servants to fill six stone water jars used for Jewish ceremonial washings, each holding twenty to thirty gallons. Can you imagine what the servants would have thought?

Perhaps one servant said to another, "Is this guy crazy? What is He going to do with all that water? How many guests are they expecting to come to the wedding? To use that much water for ceremonial washings, we would need nearly 1000 more to show up to the wedding. There aren't that many people who live in this whole city. Most everyone is here now."

They fill up the large jars with water and then Jesus tells them to draw water out of one of the jars and take it to the headwaiter. One servant probably said to the other, "Maybe Jesus saw how thirsty he is from running around waiting on tables all evening."

The servant, not telling the headwaiter of its contents or where it came from, handed the cup to him. The headwaiter, not knowing where it came from or that it came from the jars just filled with water, tasted it, and said to the groom, "Everyone serves good wine first, and then when people have drunk freely, an inferior one; but you have kept the good wine until now."

The servants said, "That isn't wine. We just filled up those jugs with water." The headwaiter said, "Very funny. Taste it yourself." Then the servants, who filled the jugs with water, said, "Jesus just changed the water we filled in those jugs into wine. Wow! How did He do that?" Another servant said, "I saw and heard everything! The Mother of Jesus noticed we ran out of wine and She told Her Son, Jesus, about it. He is the one who told us to fill the large jugs with water and when a cup of water was taken out to give to the headwaiter, it was then everyone noticed the water had changed to wine." "Mary is Her name and She knew He would change it into wine. If anyone needs anything go to Her and She will ask Him and He will do it because His Mother asked." "The man has class. He made the best wine I ever tasted. Have you ever heard a prophet do such a thing? I think only someone who is divine can change water into wine. Is it possible, He is the Messiah, who is God?"

It was the talk of Cana and soon spread to surrounding villages, that Jesus changed water into wine. They never could have imagined He would do it, because He was someone they knew.

Application 1: Meaning of Marriage

When we arrive in heaven, we will be able to meet the wedding couple and talk to them about their relationship with Jesus and Mary and what that was like.

Seated together were Jesus, Mary, His apostles, the wedding couple and their friends. By Jesus attending the wedding celebration, He elevated marriage to a sacrament, whereby He imparts sacramental grace for couples to live out their marital commitment. To be a sacramental marriage, husband and wife must both be baptized.

Marriages between a baptized and a non-baptized person or a marriage between two non-baptized persons are real marriages, but are not sacramental marriages.

With every sacrament, we come in contact with Christ. And through the sacrament of matrimony, Jesus is with every couple during their difficulties, trials and joys. He bestows sacramental graces to couples with sacramental marriages.

While He can assist non-sacramental marriages, the couples don't receive those special sacramental graces to help them live out their commitment.

How blessed couples would be, if they would turn to Jesus in all their needs, remain in the state of grace, and try to live out their marital commitment according to God's plan for marriage.

136

When any couple exchanges their vows, they enter into a covenant, whereby one gives oneself totally to the other. He gives himself totally her and she gives herself totally to him and the two become one flesh.

For a valid marriage it must be free (no obstacles or pressure), faithful (permanent commitment), fruitful (open to life), and total (complete giving of oneself).

Couples living together before marriage may end up helping each other commit the serious sin of fornication, cause scandal, risk pre-marital pregnancy, contract sexual diseases, and use each other for one's own pleasure. Rather than "making love", they end up "making sin" and participate in the wounding of each other's soul.

Cohabitation results in a higher risk of verbal, physical, and sexual abuse and opens the door to infidelity, because there is no permanent commitment.

God is the author of marriage and has decreed that marriage is only between a man and a woman. It is impossible to be a real marriage with a vow exchange between people of the same gender. To attempt to have sex between two of the same gender is unnatural, disordered, intrinsically sinful and physically not possible.

Homosexual actions have long been condemned by God. We can see God's displeasure of rampant homosexual actions in His destruction of Sodom and Gomorrah. Excavations have shown the cities destroyed by fire were a literal event. The word "sodomy" comes from the city of Sodom, known for homosexual activity.

The Catechism of the Catholic Church (#2357) states, "Basing itself on Sacred Scripture, which presents homosexual acts as acts of grave depravity, tradition has always declared that "homosexual acts are intrinsically disordered." They are contrary to the natural law. They close the sexual act to the gift of life. They do not proceed from a genuine affective and sexual

137

complementarity. Under no circumstances can they be approved. The number of men and women who have deep-seated homosexual tendencies is not negligible. They do not choose their homosexual condition; for most of them it is a trial. They must be accepted with respect, compassion, and sensitivity. Every sign of unjust discrimination in their regard should be avoided. These persons are called to fulfill God's will in their lives and, if they are Christians, to unite to the sacrifice of the Lord's Cross the difficulties they may encounter from their condition."

Every person is created in God's image and likeness and God loves them infinitely. If one has the cross of these inclinations, they should embrace their suffering of it, unite the anguish of it to the Cross of Jesus, and to the best of their ability live a life of virtue and chastity. There is a Catholic organization *Courage* for persons with homosexual inclinations and the group *Encourage* for their families and friends.

The month of June has traditionally been the month of the Sacred Heart of Jesus. But the "Pride month" by LGBTQ has taken over the month of June to push their gay agenda. In response, the organization *America Needs Fatima* sponsors 1,000 Rosary Rallies to reclaim June for the Sacred Heart.

In the time of Jesus, there were bath houses that were places of homosexual gatherings. There were also whore houses (brothels) for prostitutes and men driven by lust. There were also immoral plays that mocked Christians. But, they never had pornographic magazines, videos, or images that are a multi-billion dollar industry as they are today. And these are mostly unregulated and easy for children to access, which deeply harms their innocence and corrupts their minds.

Adultery, fornication, impure actions, sexting, pornography, homosexual actions, and lustful thoughts are sins against marriage, as Jesus said, "But I say to you, everyone who looks at a woman with lust has already committed adultery with her in his heart." (Matthew 5:28)

In some places there are bachelor and bachelorette parties where strippers show up and attempt to seduce the groom or bride. Drunkenness and porn videos are sometimes associated with the event. How sad for a couple about to be married to commit such sins just before the wedding. There is unfaithfulness, at a time when a couple is about to vow fidelity to each other for life.

The Virgin Mary wants couples, who are dating and persons with same-sex attraction to daily turn to Her by praying Her Rosary and She will help them to live their life in accord with Her Son and His Church, He founded. She is our sweet Mother, who desires to help Her children be truly happy.

Application 2: Mary Intercedes for Us When We Pray the Rosary

How many times has the Virgin Mary interceded for us without us asking Her, just as She interceded without the couple turning to Her for help? She did not intercede for a spiritual benefit for the couple. But rather for a material benefit, to bring about more wine, which made the guests and the couple happy, who otherwise would have been anxious and worried about it. Rather than relying on Her to intercede for us without asking Her for help, how much greater the likelihood She will answer our prayers if we ask Her to intercede for us?

While praying the Rosary and meditating on this mystery, now is the time to ask Mary for Her Motherly intercession. What shall I ask for? Material needs, yes. But even more important and more beneficial are our spiritual ones for our spouse, our children and our family. Since She is the Virgin Most Powerful, Her prayers are like no others. In fact, Her prayers are more efficacious than all the saints and angels in heaven combined.

Application 3: The Rosary Can Help with Anything

Sister Lucia of Fatima told Father Fuentes in 1937, "The Most Holy Virgin, in these last times in which we live, has given a new efficacy to the recitation of the Rosary to such an extent that there is no problem, no matter how difficult it is, temporal or especially spiritual, in the personal life of each one of us, of our families, of the families of the world or of the religious communities, or even of the life of peoples and nations, that cannot be solved by the Rosary. There is no problem, I tell you, no matter how difficult it is, that we cannot resolve by the prayer of the Holy Rosary. With the Holy Rosary we will save ourselves. We will console Our Lord and obtain the salvation of many souls."

Application 4: Honor Virgin Mary at Weddings

At some Catholic weddings, the Virgin Mary is honored by giving Our Lady and the mothers of the couple flowers. While standing before a statue of Mary, a Marian hymn is sung, quite often Ave Maria. The couple may consecrate their marriage to the Immaculate Heart of Mary asking Her not only to be at their wedding, but to intercede for them until death do they part.

Today, if couples invite Jesus to their wedding and into their marriage, it will be so much better for them. He does not promise that they won't have problems, but He will promise to help them in their every need. Just as John took Mary into his home, everyone should take Mary into their home and ask Her motherly intercession, not only for spiritual needs, but also material needs. As Bishop Fulton Sheen said, "It takes three to get married." If newlyweds begin to daily pray the Rosary together, their entire marriage will be greatly blessed.

Application 5: Wine Used for Mass

The changing of water into wine is a prefigurement of Jesus changing wine into His blood at the Last Supper and at every Holy Sacrifice of the Mass through the priest.

Wine used at Mass is required to be made of grapes, because Jesus used wine made from grapes at the Last Supper.

Today, some priests attempt to save money or want to use wine of their own preference, rather than sacramental wine, and so, they purchase cheap liquor store wine. But, if the wine is not made only of grapes, it could render the Mass invalid.

In the last few years, a parish and a monastery were both using *Carlo Rossi Blush* wine, when they later discovered it is made from strawberries and cherries. Interestingly, the label on the bottle of wine does not indicate the ingredients.

All Masses where the wine was used were invalid. The sacrifice did not happen and so those Masses needed to be re-offered. There is great danger when cutting corners for the Holy Mass. Wine used at Mass should be approved sacramental wine and most worthy for its lofty use.

As Jesus changed water into the best wine for a wedding, so to ensure its quality for its purpose, priests should use, if at all possible, sacramental wine made specifically for the Holy Sacrifice of the Mass. Is there any greater purpose for wine, then to be changed into the true blood of Jesus?

Application 6: The Sinfulness of Drinking Alcohol Excessively
Wine and any alcohol, such as beer and liquor can be misused through immoderate drinking. When the mind is affected by a substance such as alcohol or drugs causing erroneous judgment making, it becomes sinful. It can be seriously sinful, if one gets drunk on purpose and results in placing one's own life or the lives of others in danger.

Jesus did not condemn drinking alcohol. Otherwise, He would not have changed water into wine. However, St. Paul describes drunkenness as a sin that can prevent one from entering the kingdom of God. (1 Corinthians 6:10). *The Catechism of the Catholic Church* states, "The virtue of temperance disposes us to *avoid every kind of excess*: the abuse of food, alcohol, tobacco, or medicine. Those incur grave guilt who, by drunkenness or a love of speed, endanger their own and others' safety on the road, at sea, or in the air." (#2290)

Oh, how sad for parishes when pastors allow drunkenness on parish grounds. If at an annual parish dinner, some pastoral council members, CYO leaders, some from a men's group, who serve alcohol at the dinner, as well as guests became intoxicated, this is a serious moral problem that needs to be addressed. It is also a financial liability for the parish and the diocese.

High school CYO teens who wait tables and other children who attend such events are scandalized to see parishioners, leaders of the church, and especially their CYO leader drunk at a church event. Their bad behavior, when not addressed, gives bad examples, and are condoned by pastors, who fail to protect souls, not provide safety and don't help attendees to avoid sin and practice virtue. If a pastor does nothing, there seems to be no concern for the salvation of souls.

Sadly, a few months after a similar parish event, where there was drunkenness, a couple from a parish was driving out of state and they were instantly killed by a drunk driver not associated with the event. It served as a wake up call to the people of the parish to try to live the Christian way of life.

To protect parishioners and the parish, some priests and pastoral councils have chosen to not permit alcohol on church property in which parishioners and guests have access, except for sacramental wine.

It is certain when Jesus, the all-knowing God, changed water into wine, He would have known how human nature is constantly in battle with His discipleship. He also foresaw that there would be some who would use the miracle of His changing water into wine to justify their immoral drinking.

Yet, He desires us to do our best to follow the way of virtue, expecting, at times, to be misunderstood for trying to help others practice it.

Our Divine Lord said to His apostles, "I have told you these things, so that in me you may have peace. In this world you will have trouble. But take heart! I have overcome the world." (John 16:33)

Story 1: Rosary Helps a Man to Find a Spouse & Preserve His Chastity

"A young man who was left wealthy at the death of his parents, by play and dissipation with his friends, lost all that he had, but always preserved his chastity. An uncle, who found him reduced to such poverty by his vices, exhorted him to say every day a part of the Rosary, promising him that if he would persevere in this devotion he would procure for him a good marriage. The youth persevered, and having amended his life, he was married. On the evening of his nuptials he rose from the table to go and recite his Rosary, and when he had finished it, Mary appeared to him and said: Now I will reward thee for the honor thou hast paid me: I do not wish that thou shouldst lose thy chastity; in three days thou shalt die, and shalt come to me in paradise. And this really happened, for immediately a fever attacked him. He related the vision, and on the third day died in perfect peace."[43]

Story 2: The Virgin Mary Saves a Vocation Through Wine

"A certain parish priest of Asella, named Baldwin, became a Dominican, and when he was in his novitiate there came to him the temptation that he could do greater good in the world in his parish, and he resolved to return. But going to take his leave of the altar of the Rosary, Mary appeared to him with two vessels of wine; she gave him to drink of the first, but the novice had hardly tasted it, when he turned away his mouth, for although the wine was good, yet it was full of dregs; the second he pronounced good, and free from dregs: "Now," said the most holy Virgin, there is the same difference between the life in the world, and the life in religion, which is under obedience." Baldwin persevered, and died a good religious."[44]

Story 3: A Married Couple Daily Prayed the Rosary for 68 Years

Frank and Bertha were married in 1941 in Kansas. They had one daughter, Laura. Every day for sixty-eight years of their marriage, until he died in 2009, they prayed the Rosary together. They prayed at least 24,820 rosaries as a married couple. She continued to pray the rosary every day until her death at the age of 95, two years later.

Story 4: Young Couple Going on a Date

One day, a priest stopped by the parish Perpetual Adoration Chapel to pray his evening prayer. When he entered the chapel, he noticed the regular adorer there and also a young man and young woman sitting next to each other praying the Rosary. After the priest finished praying, he happened to leave at the same time as the young couple and the priest said to them, "Are you brother and sister?" The couple laughed, and said, "No, we are dating. We made a Holy Hour and prayed the Rosary together before we go out. We want Jesus and Mary to be part of our relationship." The priest was humbled by the young couple's own idea to pray together and was encouraged by their inviting Jesus and Mary into their relationship.

Apparition: Our Lady of Gietrzwald (Poland)

The Blessed Virgin Mary visited two young girls over a three month period in the village of Gietrzwald, Poland in the year 1877. This is the only apparition in Poland that the Holy See has approved. In June of 1877, Justyna Szafryńska, who was thirteen, and Barbara Samulowska, who was twelve, were busy preparing for their first Holy Communion. On separate occasions, a woman with long hair greeted them under a maple tree "sitting on a golden throne decorated with pearls". The Infant Jesus sat on Her knee as He held a golden globe on His lap. When they asked the woman who She was, She simply responded by saying: "I am the Blessed Virgin Mary of the Immaculate Conception." The two girls, who were rightfully very inquisitive, also asked what She desired. Our Lady gave a simple, yet very meaningful answer: "I wish you to pray the Rosary every day."

145

Proclamation of the Gospel

Fruit of the Mystery: Trust in God & Call to Conversion

"This is the time of fulfillment. The kingdom of God is at hand. Repent, and believe in the gospel." (Mark 1:15)

"When he saw the crowds, he went up the mountain, and after he had sat down, his disciples came to him. He began to teach them, saying: "Blessed are the poor in spirit, for theirs is the kingdom of heaven. Blessed are they who mourn, for they will be comforted. Blessed are the meek, for they will inherit the land. Blessed are they who hunger and thirst for righteousness, for they will be satisfied. Blessed are the merciful, for they will be shown mercy. Blessed are the clean of heart, for they will see God. Blessed are the peacemakers, for they will be called children of God. Blessed are they who are persecuted for the sake of righteousness, for theirs is the kingdom of heaven. Blessed are you when they insult you and persecute you and utter every kind of evil against you falsely because of me. Rejoice and be glad, for your reward will be great in heaven. Thus they persecuted the prophets who were before you." (Matthew 5:1-12)

When Jesus began His public ministry He proclaimed the Kingdom of God and also called His hearers to repentance.

As He gave His Sermon on the Mount, He said something they never heard before. He said they would be blessed "happy" despite being poor in spirit, persecuted, and sorrowful. His words raised their spirits. As He sat down near the bottom of the mount, which is actually more like a hill overlooking the Sea of Galilee, a vast throng came to listen to what He would say.

At a different location, Jesus wanted everyone to see Him and hear Him. Had He stayed on the edge of the shore near the water and due to the number of people, there was a real potential that He could be inadvertently knocked into the water.

Our Lord sat in a boat offshore to preach to the people. The Gospel of Mark (4:1-2) states, "Again Jesus began to teach beside the sea. And a very large crowd gathered about him, so that he got into a boat and sat in it on the sea; and the whole crowd was beside the sea on the land."

Sitting in the boat afforded visual contact. And due to the natural slope, like that of an amphitheater, if He talked softly, everyone could still hear Him. The exact place He was in the boat, near the water's edge, became a providential location for a natural sound system.

When Holy Land tour guides take pilgrims to the Mount of Beatitudes, they may tell you, it is believed Jesus would have sat near the bottom of the hill by the water and faced the people above Him. They say that spot allows for easy hearing.

When God created the world, He knew His Son would use those specific locations to give His sermon in a way thousands could hear what He said due to the way the land and sea was formed long ago. The grass there is short. The natural slope is easy to move about, and easy for the crowd to sit and hear what Jesus had to say. Even if Our Lord talked softly, everyone could hear His words. No microphone or speaker was needed, because God provided for them naturally. Sound projects upward and is caught up by the amphitheater shape of the land, so that no matter where anyone sat, they could acoustically hear Him.

Sitting in the boat off shore has symbolism. The boat represents the Church and when Jesus spoke to the crowds, it was like Jesus speaking through the Church to the people.

At still another location, Jesus led the people to a deserted place, where there was no food. They were tired and hungry and the disciples asked Jesus to send them home so they could get something to eat, because there was no food in the deserted place.

Our Lord spoke to the crowds, all were able to hear His words and at the same time He worked the miracle of multiplying bread and fish, symbolic of His Eucharistic presence multiplied at every Mass.

Providentially, and as the all-knowing God, Jesus spoke to large crowds in locations that were natural amphitheaters, making it easy for people to hear His preaching.

Before He ascended into heaven, Jesus instructed His apostles, "Go therefore, and make disciples of all nations, baptizing them, in the name of the Father, and of the Son and of the Holy Spirit, teaching them to observe all that I commanded you." (Matthew 28:19:20)

After they heard Jesus say these words, Our Lord ascended into heaven and then they returned to Jerusalem to pray and wait for the coming of the Holy Spirit, who would lead everyone to truth.

When the time of Pentecost came, while the Apostles were hiding in the Upper Room, the Holy Spirit appeared in the form of fire. The Apostles and the Blessed Virgin Mary were filled with the Holy Spirit. The apostles were no longer afraid. And immediately, Peter left the room and standing on the terrace, gave his powerful sermon.

In Acts of the Apostles, it states, "The multitude came together. … Peter lifted up his voice and addressed them. … You who are Israelites, hear these words. Jesus the Nazorean was a man commended to you by God with mighty deeds, wonders, and signs, which God worked through him in your midst, as you yourselves know. This man, delivered up by the set plan and foreknowledge of God, you killed, using lawless men to crucify him. But God raised him up, releasing him from the throes of death, because it was impossible for him to be held by it. Peter then said to them, "Repent and be baptized, every one of you, in the name of Jesus Christ for the forgiveness of your sins; and you will receive the gift of the Holy Spirit. For the promise is made to you and to your children and to all those far off, whomever the Lord our God will call." He testified with many other arguments, and was exhorting them, "Save yourselves from this corrupt generation." Those who accepted his message were baptized, and about three thousand persons were added that day." (cf. Acts 2:1-41)

Peter "made waves" by telling all gathered from different regions of the world that they were responsible for crucifying Jesus and he told them to repent and be baptized. Because of his bold words, thousands became Christian the very day he gave his sermon.

After Pentecost, the apostles went to various countries preaching the Gospel. James went to Spain and then back to Jerusalem. Thomas went to India. Peter went to Antioch and then stayed in Rome, John went to Ephesus and the island of Patmos, Philip went to Greece, Syria and Asia-Minor etc...

Application 1: Proselytizing vs Evangelizing

How many missionaries since the time of Apostles risked their lives and even died preaching the Gospel? St. Francis Xavier, one of the greatest missionaries in the Church, went to Japan, India and China and baptized an estimated 30,000. St. Junipero Serra came from Spain through Mexico and then into California. He catechized and baptized 6,000 American Indians. It is estimated during his 40 years of ministry, St. Peter Claver personally catechized and baptized 300,000 slaves in Columbia.

Yet, today, some say, "Don't proselytize." So, what's the difference between proselytizing and evangelizing? Speaking of the word proselytize, Patrick J. Reilly the president and founder of The Cardinal Newman Society, said, "There is a negative connotation, to mean the promotion of a religion by using means, and for motives, contrary to the spirit of the Gospel; that is, which do not safeguard the freedom and dignity of the human person. So proselytism is seen today by the Church as an abuse of religious freedom, and in the context of education, it is a means of teaching the faith that denies the free use of reason and appeal to conscience. It is nothing that a good catechist or evangelist would do."[45]

Perhaps, "proselytize" originally had a good meaning such as evangelizing, but now it may have a negative connotation which the Vatican document, *Ad Gentes,* warns against. It states, "The Church strictly forbids forcing anyone to embrace the Faith, or alluring or enticing people by worrisome wiles. By the same token, she also strongly insists on this right, that no one be frightened away from the Faith by unjust vexations on the part of others."[46]

True proselytizing is based upon the command of Jesus given to His apostles, "Go into the whole world, preach the Gospel to every creature. He who believes and is baptized shall be saved; but he who does not believe, shall be condemned." (Mark 16:15ff.)

It can be understood in light of Pope Saint Paul VI who said, "Not to preach the Gospel would be my undoing, for Christ himself sent me as his apostle and witness. The more remote, the more difficult the assignment, the more my love of God spurs me on. I am bound to proclaim that Jesus is Christ, the Son of the living God. Because of him we come to know the God we cannot see. He is the firstborn of all creation; in him all things find their being. Man's teacher and redeemer, He was born for us, died for us, and for us He rose from the dead. All things, all history converges in Christ. A man of sorrow and hope, He knows us and loves us. As our friend He stays by us throughout our lives; at the end of time He will come to be our judge; but we also know that He will be the complete fulfillment of our lives and our great happiness for all eternity. I can never cease to speak of

Christ for He is our truth and our light; He is the way, the truth and the life…. Remember it is Jesus Christ I preach day in and day out. His name I see echo and reecho for all time even to the ends of the earth."[47]

In the Decree on Missionary Activity of the Church of the Second Vatican Council, *Ad Gentes,* 4-5, reminds us that everyone has a duty to evangelize. It states, "Whence the duty that lies on the Church of spreading the faith and the salvation of Christ, not only in virtue of the express command which was inherited from the Apostles by the order of bishops, assisted by the priests, together with the successor of Peter and supreme shepherd of the Church, but also in virtue of that life which flows from Christ into His members."

Every member of the Catholic Church has an obligation to preach the Gospel by example and word to help as many possible come to salvation in Jesus Christ. St. Paul said, "Now I make known to you, brothers, the gospel which I proclaimed to you, which you have also received, in which you also stand, by which you are also being saved, if you hold fast to the message I proclaimed to you, unless you believed to no purpose." (1 Corinthians 15:12)

The primary mission of the Church is to proclaim the Gospel by evangelizing to help men share in the divine life of the Blessed Trinity. "Having been divinely sent to the nations that she might be 'the universal sacrament of salvation,' the Church, in obedience to the command of her founder and because it is demanded by her own essential universality, strives to preach the Gospel to all men." (CCC #849). "The ultimate purpose of the mission is none other than to make men share in the communion between the Father and the Son in their Spirit of love." (CCC #850)

St. Maximilian Kolbe said, "It is sad for us to see in our own time that indifferentism in its many forms is spreading like an epidemic not only among the laity but also among the religious. The most resplendent manifestation of God's glory is the salvation of souls, whom Christ redeemed by the shedding of His blood. To work for the salvation and sanctification of as many souls as possible, therefore, is the preeminent purpose of the apostolic life."

For a priest to be an effective preacher, he must first live by what he preaches. Otherwise, he would be a hypocrite. If he exhorts people to help the poor, but lives a life of luxury and ignores the local poor, why would anyone listen to him? St. Francis of Assisi said, "Let all the brothers preach by their works."

Application 2: Preaching Against Heresy: Albigensian & Modernism

St. Paul said, "I charge you in the presence of God and of Christ Jesus who is to judge the living and the dead, and by His appearing and His kingdom: preach the word, be urgent in season and out of season, convince, rebuke, and exhort, be unfailing in patience and in teaching. For the time is coming when people will not endure sound teaching, but having itching ears they will accumulate for themselves teachers to suit their own likings, and will turn away from listening to the truth and wander into myths. As for you, always be steady, endure suffering, do the work of an evangelist, fulfill your ministry." (2 Timothy 4:3-5)

St. Paul warns that preaching is very necessary when the people become confused due to bad preachers, who present false teachings. Canon Law (#751) describes heresy, "Heresy is the obstinate denial or obstinate doubt after the reception of baptism of some truth which is to be believed by divine and Catholic faith."

The Albigensian heretics taught only the spiritual is good, and everything material is bad. Therefore, the body in and of itself is evil, and every person's soul is imprisoned in that evil

153

body. The only way a person could experience salvation was to be freed from the imprisonment of their flesh.

Imagine for a moment, if a Catholic would have fallen into the Albigensian heresy. They would have begun to believe the body is evil and bad. They began to believe the soul is imprisoned in an evil body, and the only way to be released from the prison is to die. That would make euthanasia desirable wouldn't it?

But, if the Catholic who fell into the Albigensian heresy started praying the Rosary, meditating on it mysteries, what would happen to their way of thinking? Even before thinking, their own voice repeating the Hail Mary's would immediately combat the heresy, because the Hail Mary is prayed 53 times in one Rosary. What are we saying when we pray the Hail Mary? "Blessed is the fruit of thy womb."

The fruit of the womb is a body and its blessed. The body of Jesus is blessed, because He is God and His body (human nature) will become an instrument of grace and THE instrument of salvation.

The mysteries of the life of Jesus: His childhood, suffering and glorious mysteries indicate Jesus didn't free us from sinful flesh, but that human flesh is good. When Hail Marys are prayed, we say "blessed is the fruit of thy womb, Jesus" and so, we understand the human and divine natures of Jesus are good. The mysteries show us we will obtain a new glorified body after the resurrection of the dead. The crucified and resurrected body of Jesus brought about our salvation and is not evil, but rather, infinitely good. His flesh & blood are very good! His body is good and our body is good.

At His incarnation, when He became man, His body elevated all human nature to make it good, despite of our human family suffering from original sin. When God created Adam and Eve, He saw that what He created was "very good".

154

Mary gave birth to Jesus and held Him in Her arms. The shepherds and Magi came to adore the newborn babe. When He began His public ministry, through His body, Jesus worked miracles and expelled demons. His body suffered for us, through His passion especially by the nailing of His hands and feet to the Cross. By meditating on the Crucifixion, we see what happens when the body is treated as evil. Our sins nailed Jesus to the Cross. The horror of it all! Then when Jesus rose from the dead, in a new resurrected body, we can see the beauty of the body and that someday, we too will have a resurrected body. O how good is the body!

Modernism is afflicting the Church terribly today. Some of the principal errors of modernism are: Church's dogmas (beliefs) continually evolve over time; external signs of revelation, such as miracles and prophecies, do not prove the divine origin of the Christian religion and are not suited to the intellect of modern man; it is a denial of the supernatural; modernists viewed doctrine not as a means of obtaining supernatural knowledge, but as a symbol of an unknowable ultimate reality or as a symbol of human religious expression; modernism is basing one's religion on one's emotions and feelings and so their beliefs are constantly changing; modernism falsely supposes dogmas can be changed by novel ideas, according to the times. It's a rejection of objective truths. They falsely believe dogmas may change over time, or may be completely rejected, or re-interpreted and given a meaning different than what they originally had. It is a rejection of Divine Revelation. Each person ends up with their own truth, rather than truth that comes from God.

Some example of modernistic ideas include changing the traditional meaning of some scriptures such as the multiplication of loaves and also the Church teaching on homosexual actions. Traditionally, including words from saints and commentaries of Sacred Scripture describe the multiplication of loaves as a real miracle. However, modernism proposes that it wasn't a miracle, but rather those present just shared what they had with others.

St. Jerome (342 to 420) said, "Wherein He calls the apostles to breaking of bread, that the greatness of the miracle might be more evident by their testimony that they [the people] had none [no food]" (Thomas Aquinas, *Catena Aurea*, I.2).

St. Cyril of Alexandria (376 to 444) said, "The feeding of the multitudes in the desert by Christ is worthy of all admiration. But it is also profitable in another way. We can plainly see that these new miracles are in harmony with those of ancient times."

Bishop Athanasius Schneider in an interview, said, "An example of how modernism affects us today, is that some think the Catholic doctrine of homosexuality must change. The Church has always taught homosexual acts are intrinsically in themselves evil. There are some today, who think homosexuality can now be viewed positively, but this is false. Truth does not change."

These relativistic ideas are contrary to the Catholic faith and ignore Scripture, Tradition and the Magisterium. Divine revelation is unchanging and will be passed on until Christ comes again. The fullness of revelation of God is found in Jesus Christ, who is the way, the truth and the life.

So, how do we combat modernism and all heresies? By meditating on the life of Jesus and His supernatural power over created things, it helps prove the divine origin of the Christian religion. While praying the Rosary, we gaze upon the Joyful, Luminous, Sorrowful, and Glorious mysteries, but can also meditate on His miracles, such as His raising of Lazarus, the healing of the paralytic, walking on water, freeing the possessed, multiplying the fish and loaves, etc.

All heresies can be destroyed by the Holy Rosary, because when we pray Hail Marys and mediate on the mysteries of the Rosary, our soul is touched by grace and truth, and truth sets us free. When we gaze upon the mysteries of the Rosary, we contemplate unchanging truths. Truths that bring about our salvation, based on Jesus, who is the Truth. Meditation on the truths of our faith can touch our intellect and our soul with objective supernatural knowledge, that is unchanging.

Application 3: Parish Priests Preaching at Mass

When we come to Mass do we expect the priest to call parishioners to repentance and to preach the Gospel? After all, Jesus began His public ministry, preaching repentance. Yes, of course. But do they? And if not, why not?

You might be surprised as to why he doesn't measure up to what you expect. After ordination many priests start out full of zeal, but over time the zeal becomes tempered due to hard knocks of complaining parishioners and pressure from their pastors to not make waves. Jesus, St. Peter, St. John Vianney and many saints, would have flunked that requirement.

The first several years upon the arrival of St. John Vianney, the people rebelled against his homilies, which dealt with missing Mass on Sunday, working on Sunday, drunkenness, dancing, taking God's name in vain, and cussing. He warned them, that unless they changed their lives they would go to hell.

In response, his parishioners signed a petition to be sent to his bishop asking him to be removed as their pastor. When St. John heard about it, in humility, he signed it too. His bishop supported him and didn't give into the people's complaints.

Imagine, if priests today, only had to preach on the same subjects he did. Today, there are many more serious dangers to the souls of parishioners. Such topics include: contraception, abortion, euthanasia, homosexual marriage, transgenderism, murders, cohabitation, drug problems, pornography viewed by children without parental protection, gang violence, etc…

Seldom are topics like purgatory, heaven, hell, death or judgment mentioned.

Some priests are afraid to preach on these topics, for fear of causing some to discontinue coming to church and fear of losing popularity. Faithful bishops will support the priests when they teach the fullness of truth with love.

In one case, parishioners complained to their bishop about their pastor's homilies. In response, a priest chancery representative and two additional priests read his homilies every week for six months. All his homilies were and continued to be available on the Internet. After the six month homily analysis was concluded none of the priests, including the chancery priest had any problem with the homilies, except the chancery priest thought a twenty minute homily given on a weekend mission was "too long", while the other two priests thought it was appropriate since it was a parish mission.

This shows that sometimes complaints are the result of confused parishioners or parishioners who are at odds with the truth of the Gospel and don't want to changer their life.

How encouraging it is, when bishops support the teachings of the Church and their priests, verses rebel parishioners, who oftentimes are at odds with the truth of the Gospel.

Jesus explained at times the apostles and disciples' preaching will not be accepted. He said, "Do you think I came to bring peace on earth? No, I tell you, but division. From now on there will be five in one family divided against each other, three against two and two against three." (Luke 12:51) "If the world hates you, you know that it has hated Me before it hated you. If you were of the world, the world would love you as its own; but because you are not of the world, but I chose you out of the world, therefore the world hates you" (John 15:18-19) "He who is not with me, is against me." (Luke 11:23) "But woe to you scribes and Pharisees, hypocrites; because you shut the kingdom of heaven against men, for you yourselves do not enter in; and those that are going in, you suffer not to enter." (Matthew 23:13) "Woe to you, scribes and Pharisees, you hypocrites. You are like whitewashed tombs, which appear beautiful on the outside, but inside are full of dead men's bones and every kind of filth." (Matthew 23: 27)

Have you ever heard of a saint telling others to not make waves when preaching? St. John Vianney said, priests should be "a lion in the pulpit, a lamb in the confessional." A lion is not a cute little kitten that tries to rub up against your leg purring to get attention and get along with everyone.

A presenter at a clergy conference once told priests, "Don't preach on hell. You might scare the people." He probably didn't take into consideration that the Virgin Mary showed the children of Fatima a vision of hell at ages seven through ten. Their vision of hell moved the children to sacrifice themselves in a heroic manner to prevent souls from falling into hell. According to *Catholic Answers*, Jesus mentioned hell more than heaven in the Gospels.[48]

St. John Vianney said, "I am going to explain to you, my dear brethren, what is understood by swearing, blasphemy, profanities, imprecations, and curses. Try to sleep well during this period so that when the day of judgment comes, you will be found to have committed this evil without knowing what you were doing-though, of course, you will be damned because your ignorance will all be your own fault! For you to understand the enormity of this sin, my brethren, it would be necessary for you to understand the enormity of the outrage which it does to God's thing which no mortal can ever understand. No, my dear brethren, only the anger, the power and the wrath of God concentrated in the inferno of Hell can bring home to us the enormity of this sin. No, no, my children, let us not run this risk-there must be Hell for all eternity for this sin."[49]

Seminary homiletic professors and also pastors of young priests teach them to not make waves. In fact, seminarians are taught to "stay under the radar" to avoid any kind of attention, thinking once they are ordained they will be able to fully proclaim the truth. But, that turns out to not be the case, because their pastors will teach them to stay under the radar, until they become pastors, and then once they become a pastor, they have learned to go along to get a long and the fullness of the truth is never proclaimed. Topics like abortion, contraception, euthanasia are avoided so as to not upset the people and keep the status quo.

Every year, the USCCB (United States Conference of Catholic Bishops) and many dioceses promote *Natural Family Planning Awareness Week* and priests are expected to preach on the subject on that weekend. But, one pastor of large metro parish with 3,000 families, said he has never mentioned the topic in forty years of his priesthood.

The truth is when most people first hear something that contradicts their lifestyle, they become upset and maybe even angry, because they don't want to be told to change their life. But, when Jesus Christ crucified and the fullness of truth is preached, they eventually come around because they will realize, the priest is right, and he is only trying to help them obtain heaven. If the priest loves them, he is willing to suffer their rebukes, and offer himself on the paten during Mass, as a victim of love, to prevent them from going to hell at the end of their life. He can't be a man who desires to be loved or liked by everyone.

St. John the Baptist called Herod and his wife to repentance to try to save them from hell, but he ended up dying as a martyr for the dignity of marriage.

If priests preach on these topics, those in favor of abortion and birth control users will write letters to the bishop complaining about the homilies. Some may threaten to go to a different parish and discontinue tithing. When bishops support the moral teachings of the Church and their pastors, the people are more apt to follow the narrow road to heaven, as opposed to believing they don't need to follow the teachings of the Church.

Once, a priest exhorted his parishioners a number of times during Lent to go to confession monthly. Some parishioners wrote a letter to their bishop saying he was preaching on confession too often. The bishop wrote a letter back to the parishioners saying, "Although I am always open to receive your letters, before writing me, you should always first visit with your pastor and explain to him your concern. You have a very good pastor and what he is asking of you is commendable. You should do as he is asking."

If a bishop stand ups for the priest and especially stands up for the truth of the Gospel, the unrepentant, obstinate and notorious politicians who support abortion and attempt to enact laws to kill unborn children, may actually have a change of heart. If we love someone, we tell them the truth because we want to help them get to heaven.

The greatest issue today is the right to life, because all other rights are subordinated to it. Since abortion is the greatest evil of our time, it stands to reason, it is necessary to preach about it periodically to prevent parishioners from having an abortion and to motivate parishioners to do something about it, especially to pray.

Whenever preaching about abortion, he should do so with tender mercy, especially since a new analysis from the Guttmacher Institute's Abortion Patient Survey estimates that one in four (24.7%) US women of reproductive age will have an abortion by age 45.[50] When preaching on the subject, the priest must always speak the truth with love, and especially preach in the same homily about God's unfathomable mercy to those who are very much hurting by their sad and terrible choice. If we ask, God will always forgive. There is no sin too big for God to forgive and we can and must forgive our self with God's grace and help.

Have you ever heard of a saint, who walked around the sanctuary preaching throughout the church, asking children or even adults questions during Mass, enlisting responses from them, as though the church suddenly becomes a classroom? Rather than preaching from the lectern (ambo), he walks around trying to gain eye contact with parishioners, which can be very disconcerting to have the priest look directly at you and ask you a question. This style of preaching is certainly an innovation.

Not too many priests can preach substantive homilies off the top of their head without using notes. The average priest, who preaches without notes and walks through the sanctuary, may think he is holding their attention, but is not able to quote scripture, nor the saints, nor even preach on doctrines as effectively as if he had read his homily or at least used notes. To the faithful in the pew, the priest walking around through the church, and even losing sight of the priest when he goes downs the aisle giving his homily, can be head spinning and annoying. It seems better to do as the saints of the Church, who stood in the ambo, and preached successfully for centuries.

There are priests with God given brilliant minds and photographic memories, who have the gift of preaching without notes. They can verbatim give quotes and express Church teaching in a logical, uplifting, and devotional manner. They can give substantive homilies by memorization and move the hearts of parishioners.

One such saint who could do this, was St. Anthony of Padua known for quoting very heavily Sacred Scripture, and was able to proclaim the Gospel effectively by converting thousands. He was known for his tender manner of preaching. The Lord was so pleased with him, that his tongue remains incorrupt, though he died in 1231. Some priests pray to St. Anthony every day, when preparing a homily and just before preaching it.

St. Louis-Marie de Montfort recommended that priests pray one Hail Mary just before giving the homily asking Our Lady to open hearts of the hearers. It is also praiseworthy for priests to pray a Rosary before weekend Masses with the specific intention of touching the hearts of parishioners, who will hear the homily to bring about their conversion.

Before preaching the Rosary, St. Dominic had almost no success in bringing about conversions. That is until, the Virgin Mary told him to preach the Rosary and She gave mysteries for each decade. Then he became enormously successful in converting the Albigensian heretics back to the faith.

The Sunday homily is the primary way people hear about the faith. To preach only a five to ten minute homily at a weekend Mass, the priest loses the opportunity to teach while preaching. As St. Paul said, "Consequently, faith comes from what is heard, and what is heard comes by the preaching of Christ." (Romans 10:17)

Priests, religious and layman please add to your Rosary intentions, prayers for the Pope, Bishops and priests. They need your prayers because the devil attacks them more than laypeople. If a shepherd is struck, the sheep are scattered. But if the shepherd is saintly, the people will become holy.

Application 4: Saints on Preaching

St. Vincent Ferrer, a Dominican, (1315 to 1419) was an eloquent and fiery preacher, who spent the last twenty years of his life spreading the Gospel in Spain, France, Switzerland, the Low Countries and Lombardy, stressing the need of repentance and the fear of coming judgment. He became known as the "Angel of the Judgment."

When giving advice on preaching, he said, "In sermons and talks, use simple language and a homely conversational style to explain each particular point. As far as you can, give plenty of examples; then, whoever has committed that particular sin will have his conscience pricked, as though you were preaching to him alone. But it must be done in such a way that your words do not appear to come from a soul full of pride or scorn. Speak rather out of the depths of love and fatherly care, like a father suffering for his sinful children, as if they were gravely ill, or trapped in a deep pit, whom he is trying to draw out and set free, and look after like a mother. You must be like one who delights in their progress, and in the glory in heaven that they are hoping for. Such a style usually has a good effect on a congregation. For, to speak of virtues and vices in general terms evokes little response from listeners."[51]

Imagine if a bishop were to assign a fervent courageous priest to a community of religious sisters like St. Anthony Zaccaria, who said to some nuns,

"Moreover, my dear Sisters, you make idols when you conform yourselves to worldly people's way of life: you are fastidious, vegetables make you sick, fasting causes you headaches, and early rising spoils your appetite. There is nothing, in fact, that suits you. O you wretches! Do you not know that "those who wear soft raiment are in kings' houses?" Do you not know that the worldly are those who give free rein to every comfort of the body, and hate to suffer any discomfort? Religious life is a cross to be carried one step at a time and in a steady fashion, "for your sake we face death all day long", as the Apostles used to say; and the Lord told us to take up our cross daily. Are you disciples of Christ? Then, carry your cross, mortify your bodies with fasting and toiling, watch in prayer, spend your time helping your neighbor, nail yourselves to holy obedience never withdrawing from it. So, for Christ's sake, do not make any more idols."[52]

A fervent priest today may also add these words, "Dear sisters, please forget the beauty parlor, the pierced ears and designer clothes. Vanity is a sin. True beauty comes from deep

164

within the soul, she's called "virtue." Come to Jesus weekly in Confession and spend an hour every day in Eucharistic Adoration. Pray the Rosary together every day. And never forget, you are a bride of Christ, and are worthy of being treated as one."

Story 1: Monastery is Converted by the Rosary

"The daughter of a certain prince had entered a monastery, where the discipline was so relaxed, that, although she was a young person of good dispositions, she advanced but little in virtue. By the advice of a good confessor, she began to say the Rosary with the mysteries, and became so changed that she was an example to all. The other religious, taking offense at her for withdrawing from them, attacked her on all sides, to induce her to abandon her newly-begun way of life. One day whilst she was repeating the Rosary, and praying to Mary to assist her in that persecution, she saw a letter fall from above. On the outside were written these words: " Mary, mother of God, to her daughter Jane, greeting;" and within: "My dear child, continue to say my Rosary; withdraw from intercourse with those who do not help you to live well; beware of idleness and vanity; take from thy cell two superfluous things, and I will be your protectress with God." The abbot of that monastery soon after visited it, and attempted to reform it, but he did not succeed; and one day he saw a great number of demons entering the cells of all the nuns except that of Jane, for the divine Mother, before whose image he saw her praying, banished them from that. When he heard from her of the devotion of the Rosary which she practiced, and the letter she had received, he ordered all the others to repeat it, and it is related that this monastery became a paradise."[53]

Story 2: Homily on Rosary Saves Wicked Woman

"Father Bavio relates that Ellen, a wicked woman, entered a Church and heard a homily on the Rosary. She bought a pair of rosaries but wore them concealed. She repeated the Hail Mary without devotion, but Our Lady gave her such consolation that she kept repeating the Hail Mary. Filled with horror over her sins, she went to confession and amazed the priest with her sorrow. She then said the Rosary at Our Lady's altar. Our Lady spoke to her, "Ellen, change your life and I will give you a large share in my graces." She promised to spend her life doing penance. She gave away all her goods, and overcame all temptations. She received extraordinary graces of visions and prophecies. The Virgin told her when she would die. On that day Mary came for her with her Son."[54]

Story 3: Preaching on Abortion Before an Election

One weekend, about a month before the General Election, a priest preached on voting in an upcoming election. He said the greatest issue is the right to life and that when we vote we should take into consideration each candidate's stance and vote for the person who is most likely to eliminate or reduce the number of abortions. He said the right to life is more important than the environment and even more important than feeding the poor, though we should always do what we can to help the poor and our community.

When Mass was over an angry parishioner walked up to the priest, and said, "Father, you crossed the line. You talked about politics. You said we can't vote for Democrats." The priest responded saying, "Sir, I never mentioned either political party in the homily, I just said, we should vote to save unborn babies." A short elderly woman, who heard the conversation, took two fingers and banged them into the chest of the man, saying,

"Don't you talk to father like that. He is right." The man walked away humiliated by the elderly woman who defended the unborn and the priest.

It is very important to pray the Rosary for our government leaders, those who will vote in an upcoming election, and pray for the country to bring about respect and love for every human being, especially the most vulnerable.

A 54 day Rosary Novena before an election or any important request can be very beneficial. For the first 27 days a Rosary is prayed in petition, then the second 27 days a Rosary is prayed in thanksgiving for Our Lady answering your prayers.

In the US, Sept. 12th, the feast of the Holy Name of Mary is 54 days before November 5th. What a beautiful day to start a novena for our country!

Apparition: Our Lady of Pompeii (Italy) 54 Day Rosary

The 54 Day novena was composed by Blessed Bartolo Longo in July 1879, which he said himself while he had typhoid fever. The text was inspired by visions of a miraculous portrait of Our Lady of the Rosary, to which the Novena was first dedicated in Pompeii.

"The "54-day Rosary Novena" is an uninterrupted series of Rosaries in honor of Our Lady, revealed to the incurably sick Fortuna Agrelli by Our Lady of Pompeii at Naples in 1884. For thirteen months Fortuna Agrelli had endured dreadful sufferings and torturous cramps; she was given up on by the most celebrated physicians. On February 16, 1884, the afflicted girl and her relatives commenced a novena of Rosaries. The Queen of the Holy Rosary favored her with an apparition on March 3rd. Mary, sitting upon a high throne, surrounded by luminous figures, held the divine Child on her lap, and in her hand a Rosary. The Virgin Mother and the holy Infant were clad in gold-embroidered garments. They were accompanied by St.

167

Dominic and St. Catherine of Siena. The throne was profusely decorated with flowers; the beauty of Our Lady was marvelous. The Blessed Virgin said: "Child, thou has invoked me by various titles and hast always obtained favors from me. Now, since thou hast called me by that title so pleasing to me, 'Queen of the Holy Rosary,' I can no longer refuse the favor thou dost petition; for this name is most precious and dear to me. Make three novenas, and thou shalt obtain all." Once more the Queen of the Holy Rosary appeared to her and said, "Whoever desires to obtain favors from me should make three novenas of the prayers of the Rosary, and three novenas in thanksgiving." Obedient to Our Lady's invitation, Fortuna and her family completed the six novenas whereupon the young girl was restored to perfect health and her family showered with many blessings."[55]

Jesus is Transfigured on Mount Tabor

Fruit of the Mystery: Desire for Holiness

"After six days Jesus took Peter, James, and John his brother, and led them up a high mountain by themselves. And he was transfigured before them; his face shone like the sun and his clothes became white as light. And behold, Moses and Elijah appeared to them, conversing with him. Then Peter said to Jesus in reply, "Lord, it is good that we are here. If you wish, I will make three tents here, one for you, one for Moses, and one for Elijah." While he was still speaking, behold, a bright cloud cast a shadow over them, then from the cloud came a voice that said, "This is my beloved Son, with whom I am well pleased; listen to him." When the disciples heard this, they fell prostrate and were very much afraid. But Jesus came and touched them, saying, "Rise, and do not be afraid." And when the disciples raised their eyes, they saw no one else but Jesus alone." (Matthew 17:1-9)

Jesus, Peter, James and John climbed a very high mountain and when they reached the top, they paused to sit down and rest. The three disciples took a short nap, but were suddenly awakened by a bright light that emanated from Jesus. Our Lord stood transfigured before them glowing brightly and with Him was Moses and Elijah.

But, how did they know who the two men were? Most likely it was a divine intuition from God. The Holy Spirit helped them to immediately recognize who they were. They also heard them speak to Jesus about His upcoming Passion and death and through the conversation they had with Jesus, the three Apostles understood who they were.

Mount Tabor is 1,929 feet from the bottom to the top. It's shaped like a half sphere. Some say it's shaped like a soup bowl.

169

It's above the Jezreel Valley plain in lower Galilee. It's about five miles east of Nazareth and eleven miles southwest of the Sea of Galilee. Scripture states the transfiguration took place six days after Peter's confession of faith, when he declared to Jesus, "You are the Christ, the Son of the Living God." When He called Jesus, "the Christ", he was stating Jesus is the Messiah.

At that time, Jesus also warned them about what was going to happen in the near future, "The Son of Man must suffer many things and be rejected by the elders, the chief priests and the teachers of the law, and He must be killed and on the third day be raised to life." (Luke 9:22)

Tour guides at Mount Tabor will say that on August 6th, the Feast of the Transfiguration, the sun shines directly through the window and onto the apse of the mural of the Transfiguration. On that day the sun will light up the mural, making the image of Lord shine brightly for all to see.

The tour guide pondered if the church was designed and the artwork created in such a way, that they knew the sun would shine directly on the image of the transfiguration, on the Feast of the Transfiguration or was it created through the inspiration of God's Divine Providence without any foreknowledge of the designers. The incredible artistic masterpiece in the apse of the church is described as, "Within the building itself we are immediately struck by the skill of an architect who could seize on the essentials of a site a situation and a mystery, express its meaning in stone, mosaic and bronze, and illumine it all through alabaster with the light of the sun itself."[56]

Most likely, the walk up Mount Tabor caused the four to be tired, thirsty and out of breath. They certainly would need to sit down at the top to get their breath, rest and would have gazed upon the lower valley in awe. Today, it's accessed by a narrow winding road.

In the transfiguration event, we get a glimpse into the divinity of Jesus and also a confirmation that He is the Messiah.

Six days after predicting His death and resurrection, when Peter, James, and John climbed a high mountain, Jesus revealed His glory to them. It wasn't during the night, but during the day, when His face shone like the sun and His clothes became dazzling white.

In a flash, the disciples' eyes are opened. They can see who Jesus really is. He is more than a rabbi, a miraculous healer, or gifted preacher. He is greater than even Moses or Elijah! Jesus is the Messiah. He is God.

During this event, they saw Moses and Elijah talking to Jesus. Moses represents the Law and Elijah represents the prophets. Jesus, as God and Messiah, represents the fulfillment of the law and the prophets.

By revealing His glory, Jesus showed them what it would be like after He rises from the dead. Seeing this gave the disciples strength for the future difficult time of Jesus' suffering and death. By witnessing the transfiguration, they understood Jesus will come back in glory. Our bodies too will be glorified at the resurrection of the dead.

Jesus's disciples didn't fully grasp their mountaintop vision or how they would need to cling to it as Jesus headed toward the Cross. They didn't know how their faith would be tested or how important it was that Jesus was more than a just man. They didn't know what Jesus meant when He said He would die and rise again. But Jesus knew. That's why He told them to keep the revelation to themselves until He had risen from the dead.

In His transfiguration, Jesus was giving His disciples a gift to sustain them for the day of His crucifixion. On that day there would not be three tents, but three crosses. Jesus would not stand between Moses and Elijah, rather He would hang between two thieves on a cross. On that day they would abandon their teacher and Lord to His cruel end. But Jesus' transfiguration not only helped the disciples during His crucifixion. Even more, it foreshadowed a greater revelation of His divinity: the resurrection!

Application 1: Tents (Tabernacles) & the Eucharist

Peter said... "Lord, it is good that we are here. If you wish, I will make three tents here, one for you, one for Moses, and one for Elijah." The three tents Peter suggested that they place on the top of the mountain (for Jesus, Moses and Elijah), were not camping tents. Back then, tents were places where someone could see God face to face.

The feast of the Transfiguration is every year on August 6th. The transfiguration, when linked to the Eucharist, reveals the glory of God and His love for us.

What a grace for Peter, James and John to see Jesus transfigured as His face shone like the sun and his clothes became dazzling white.

Moses and Elijah are the key representatives of the Law and the Prophets. Their coming to talk with Jesus shows Him to be the fulfillment of God's revelation to them. He is therefore the Messiah.

It also reveals the Blessed Trinity. The Father speaks, the Holy Spirit is represented in a cloud and Jesus appears in glory.

Peter also said something that seems strange to us. He is known for his impulsive words and actions. He said, "Lord, it is good that we are here. If you wish, I will make three tents here, one for you, one for Moses and one for Elijah."

Why would Peter want to set up tents? Perhaps he was so thrilled by what he saw, he wanted Moses, Elijah and Jesus to stay there, so others could come to see the glorious event, and to meet God face to face in a tent.

The Jews had what was called the Feast of Tabernacles. It originally began as a festive celebration for the crops of that year after the harvest. The word "tabernacle" was used for the word "tent". During the 40 years in the desert, the Hebrew people lived in tents (tabernacles) and the feast of the tabernacles would commemorate the celebration of reaching the Promised Land. The feast was later celebrated as a result of the erection of the temple, their permanent place of worship, where many animal sacrifices occurred.

When we think of a tent, we think of canvas and poles that are normally used for camping. But, in the Old Testament, some tents were not only used to sleep and rest at night, they were used as a meeting place especially between God and man. One tent contained the Ark of the Covenant.

The book of Exodus states, "The tent, which was called the meeting tent, Moses used to pitch at some distance away, outside the camp. Anyone who wished to consult the Lord would go to this meeting tent outside the camp. Whenever Moses went out to the tent, the people would all rise and stand at the entrance of their own tents, watching Moses until he entered the tent. As Moses entered the tent, the column of cloud would come down and stand at its entrance while the Lord spoke with Moses. On seeing the column of cloud stand at the entrance of the tent, all the people would rise and worship at the entrance of their own tents. The Lord used to speak to Moses face to face, as one man speaks to another." (Exodus 33:7-11)

Today, the tabernacle in every Catholic Church is the meeting place between God and man, because the Eucharistic Jesus is truly present in every tabernacle. The physical church is the new temple. At Mass the one sacrifice of Jesus on the Cross becomes present when bread and wine are changed into the body and blood of Jesus. At Mass, we are in God's presence. We are in the presence of the sacrifice of Calvary and when the Host is elevated, in our mind's eye, we can gaze upon the glory of the face of Christ.

During Holy Communion, our body becomes a tent, where we meet God in our hearts. That meeting with God in our heart, will prepare us for our permanent heavenly home.

When we gaze upon Jesus during Eucharistic Adoration, or when the Host is elevated at Mass above the altar, we are fulfilling on earth what we will do in heaven, as St. Paul states, "All of us, gazing with unveiled face on the glory of the Lord, are being transformed into the same image from glory to glory, as from the Lord who is the Spirit." (2 Corinthians 3:18)

St. Paul said, "Our bodies are like tents that we live in here on earth. But when these tents are destroyed, we know that God will give each of us a place to live. These homes will not be buildings someone has made, but they are in heaven and will last forever. While we are here on earth, we sigh because we want to live in that heavenly home." (2 Corinthians 5:1-2)

Application 2: Jesus is the One and Only True Messiah

During the time of Jesus, many Jews thought the Messiah would heal the sick, the blind, and the lame. They also thought the Messiah would come to bring about lasting peace. However, they were wrong when they thought the Messiah would come to free God's chosen people from the oppression of the Romans. Scriptures do not proclaim Jesus as the leader of an army.

Jesus proves He is the Messiah, by working miracles, forgiving sins and raising the dead, including Himself.

In the future, a false messiah will come. He will claim to be the messiah of the Jews, but will actually be the anti-Christ. The false messiah will be a world leader, who will bring worldly peace, and has answers to worldly problems. He will claim to be God, and want to be worshiped as a god. He will be tyrannical and cause a great persecution of Christians. However, Jews will eventually discover he's false and embrace Jesus as the true Messiah.

There have been false messengers who claim to be from God. Muhammad, Buddha, and Confucius claimed to be messengers of God. But how can we know if there were messengers from God or not?

What if someone would claim to be the Messiah or a messenger from God today? If Jesus claims to be the Messiah, and someone else claims to be the Messiah, then how can we know who the real Messiah is?

Bishop Fulton Sheen indicated there are three ways we know Jesus is the true and only Messiah. The first way is the Messiah will work miracles of physical healing: healing the blind, cleansing lepers, and the deaf will hear.

The second way we know Jesus is the Messiah, is that the morality Jesus declares does not contradict human reason. In other words, the Messiah would never say it's okay to kill an unborn baby or that homosexual actions are acceptable.

The third way we can know Jesus is the Messiah is that He fulfills all the prophecies of the Old Testament. During the time of Jesus, there were 456 known prophecies the Messiah was expected to fulfill.

For example, it was predicted by the prophet Micah that the Messiah would be born in Bethlehem. "But you, Bethlehem-Ephrathah least among the clans of Judah, From you shall come forth for me one who is to be ruler in Israel; Whose origin is from of old, from ancient times." (Micah 5:2).

Jesus predicted He would die in Jerusalem, and be crucified. As the Gospel of Matthew states, "From that time on Jesus began to show His disciples that He must go to Jerusalem and suffer many things from the elders and chief priests and scribes, and be killed, and on the third day be raised." (Matt. 16:21) And (Psalm 22:17-19) prophesied Our Lord's crucifixion, "Dogs surround me; a pack of evildoers closes in on me. They have pierced my hands and my feet. I can count all my bones.

They stare at me and gloat; they divide my garments among them; for my clothing they cast lots."

What is the probability of fulfilling all 456 prophecies? Bishop Sheen said to fulfill 4 of the 456 prophecies is 1 in 100,000. But, Jesus doesn't fulfill 4 prophecies, He fulfills all 456 prophecies. According to Bishop Fulton Sheen, the chance of anyone fulfilling all 456 prophecies is 1 followed by 184 zeros.

It will be impossible for the false messiah to fulfill the prophecies of the Old Testament, because only Jesus did it and only God can do such a thing. The anti-Christ will be human possessed by the devil, whose power is limited.

Did Muhammad or Buddha or Confucius predict in advance where they would be born or predict, in advance, how or where they would die? No. Only Jesus, who is the true Messiah, predicted all these things in Sacred Scripture.

Did Muhammad or Buddha or Confucius ask anyone to have an intimate and personal relationship with them or to love them? No.

But Jesus asked all to have an intimate and personal relationship with Him. Jesus wants all to love Him, remain in His love and be His friends. He said, "As the Father loves me, so I also love you. Remain in my love. This is my commandment: love one another as I love you....You are my friends if you do what I command you." (John 15:9-12)

The anti-Christ will not be sacrificial, and won't be willing to lay down his life for anyone. He will appear to work miracles, but they will not be true miracles. He will claim to raise the dead, but the person he claims to raise from the dead, will not actually be dead. The anti-Christ will not be able to predict where he will be born nor how or where he will die. The anti-Christ will have morality that contradicts human reason. He will not ask anyone to have an intimate union with him.

He will reject the cross and the narrow path of sacrifice that Jesus told His apostles they must do, "Deny yourself, take up your cross and follow me." (Matthew 16:24) He will not do as Jesus, who laid down His life for us. Rather, he will promote worldly honors and pleasures.

So, in the future, if someone were to claim he is the Messiah today, we could easily tell he's not. Rather, Jesus is the Messiah, because He fulfilled all Old Testament prophecies, because He truly raised people from the dead and not just some people, He raised Himself from the dead. Jesus healed the blind, the lame, and the deaf. Jesus predicted His own coming in Bethlehem; His crucifixion in Jerusalem; and that He would rise from the dead. When He comes on the clouds of heaven, only Jesus can and will bring about a lasting peace, when the world will be transformed and made new and all will receive a resurrected body at the end of the world.

But before this happens, the Church must go through Her final passion. "The Church will enter the glory of the kingdom only through this final Passover, when she will follow her Lord in His death and Resurrection." (CCC #677)

Jesus' glory was just as present on the Cross, as it was on the mountaintop. The disciples just couldn't see it. They needed a heavenly perspective and so do we. That's why Jesus invites us to go up to the mountain every day (in prayer) for a glimpse of His glory: to see Jesus, the Son of God, who will be with us always, to the end of time. When you have a difficult time, pray the Luminous mysteries of the Rosary and meditate on the transfiguration and pray the Glorious mysteries of His resurrection from the dead.

Today, we see God face to face in the Sacred Host. In the Eucharist is the face of Christ. When we are in the presence of the Eucharist, all we have to do is listen to the words spoken by God the Father, as He points to His Son at Holy Mass, in tabernacles and monstrances of Catholic churches, "This is my beloved Son, with whom I am well pleased, listen to Him." (Matthew 17:5) Look at Jesus in the Sacred Host with your mind's eye and see

His face. Ask Him to open the eyes of your heart and you will see Him, as He sees you! He will strengthen your faith and fill you with hope!

Story 1: A Child Sees Jesus in an Adoration Chapel

A 12 yr old boy, his grandmother, and his two sisters went through RCIA. His grandmother and her grandchildren became Catholic at the Easter Vigil that year. Shortly after they became Catholic, they signed up for a Holy Hour and were faithful to it.

Just a few months after they became Catholic, as they were making their Holy Hour, the boy said, "As I was looking at the Host, Jesus suddenly came out of the Host and stood before the altar. He was wearing a long white garment, with a gold sash and had a golden crown on His head. He had a scepter in His hand. Jesus spoke and said, "Take off your shoes. And ask the others to do the same. You are on holy ground." The grandmother and his sisters saw him take off his shoes while looking at the Host and they suspected He was seeing something. He told those with him, "Take off your shoes." And they did. Jesus then told the boy, "Tell the priest to ask the people to remove their shoes before entering the chapel. It is up to them if they want to remove them or not." Jesus then told the boy, "I desire you to be a witness and to bring others to me." The boy said Jesus then went back into the Host.

After their Holy Hour, they immediately went to the pastor's office and told him what happened. The priest was astonished and asked the boy, "Are you aware of what God told Moses when he saw the burning bush?" The boy had no idea. He didn't know God told Moses to remove his sandals because he was on holy ground. Since the boy just became Catholic, he had no idea it was a common practice in the Philippines to remove their shoes before entering an Adoration Chapel. All of this seemed to give credence to the boy's story that he really saw Jesus during Eucharistic Adoration.

Story 2: Seeing the Face of Jesus in the Eucharist

One day, a priest asked an elderly woman why she was so faithful in coming to the weekly parish Holy Hour. The woman said, "When I was sixteen, during a Holy Hour, as I was gazing at the Host, I saw the face of Jesus. I have never told anyone that before. But I know He is there."

One week after the woman told the priest she had seen the face of Jesus as a sixteen year old girl, in another parish, about 30 miles from her parish, a sixteen year old girl told the same priest, she saw the face of Jesus in the Host during a Holy Hour that they had that week. The girl and the elderly woman did not know each other and the priest had never told anyone what the elderly woman said.

When praying the Holy Rosary before Jesus in Adoration or before a Tabernacle, we receive many more graces than if we were to pray the Rosary at our home, because we are praying the Rosary in the physical presence of Jesus. And when we do, the Virgin Mary is praying for us and with us to Jesus in the Most Blessed Sacrament.

Apparition: Our Lady of Fatima (Portugal)

Our Lady of Fatima came as Our Lady of the Rosary and mentioned the Rosary at every apparition.

On May 13, 1917 Mary told the children, "Say the Rosary every day, to bring peace to the world and an end to the war." On June 13, She said, "I want you to come here on the 13th of next month. I want you to continue saying the Rosary every day. And after each one of the mysteries, my children, I want you to pray in this way: 'O my Jesus, forgive us our sins, save us from

179

the fire of hell. Take all souls to heaven, especially those who are most in need.' On July 13, Mary said, "I want you to come back here on the 13th of next month. Continue to say the Rosary every day in honor of Our Lady of the Rosary, to obtain the peace of the world and the end of the war, because only She can obtain it." On August 19, She said, "Come again to the Cova da Iria on the 13th of next month, my child, and continue to say the Rosary every day." "I want you [Lucia] to have two ardors [to carry statues] made, for the feast of Our Lady of the Rosary." Sept 13, the Virgin said, "Continue the Rosary, my children. Say it every day that the war may end." On Oct 13, Mary said, "I want a chapel built here in my honor. I want you to continue saying the Rosary every day. The war will end soon, and the soldiers will return to their homes." "I am the Lady of the Rosary, I have come to warn the faithful to amend their lives and ask for pardon for their sins. They must not offend Our Lord any more, for He is already too grievously offended by the sins of men. People must say the Rosary. Let them continue saying it every day."

Jesus Institutes the Holy Eucharist

Fruit of the Mystery: Participation at Mass & Adoration

"For I received from the Lord what I also handed on to you, that the Lord Jesus, on the night He was handed over, took bread, and, after He had given thanks, broke it and said, "This is my body that is for you. Do this in remembrance of me." In the same way also the cup, after supper, saying, "This cup is the new covenant in my blood. Do this, as often as you drink it, in remembrance of me." For as often as you eat this bread and drink the cup, you proclaim the death of the Lord until he comes. Therefore whoever eats the bread or drinks the cup of the Lord unworthily will have to answer for the body and blood of the Lord. A person should examine himself, and so eat the bread and drink the cup." For anyone who eats and drinks without discerning the body, eats and drinks judgment on himself." (1 Corinthians 11:23-32)

It was Thursday morning when Our Lord called Peter and John and told them to prepare the Paschal lamb. In reply to their question where it would be, Jesus mysteriously told them of a man they were to follow to his house, and there prepare the meal.

Tradition says the Upper Room was in Jerusalem in the highest part of the city. It was a large room, twenty yards long and eleven wide, divided in two parts by a couple of pillars. The two apostles prepared tables, utensils, and couches (they didn't use chairs like we do today). The lamb, unleavened bread, bitter herbs, dates, almonds, figs, cinnamon and water and wine were all there.

Jesus knew this would be His Last Supper before He would go through His passion. After all were seated and the meal was near its end, Our Lord said, "With longing I have desired to eat this Pasch with you before I suffer." (Luke 22:15) He gives His long parting discourse, washes their feet as an example of how they are to serve each other in charity, and then warns them He will be betrayed, and all will be scattered this very night.

In silence, awe, reverence and rapt attention and every eye follows their Master. When the moment arrives holding the bread in His Sacred Hands, and looking up to heaven, to His almighty Father, Jesus pronounced the sacred words, "This is My Body which is given up for you." Then He took the metal cup (the chalice), now called the Holy Grail, which has been persevered and is located in the Cathedral of Valencia, Spain, and said, "This is the chalice of my blood, which will be shed for you."

He commanded that we receive His body and blood, when He said, "Take this all of you and eat of it. Take this and drink of it."

The Eucharist is the most glorious sacrament, because it is Christ Himself. It is the Bread of Angels and the Bread of Life for us because Jesus promises, whoever eats His body and drinks His blood will live forever.

Just as He institutes the Holy Mass, the Eucharist, giving us His body and blood, He likewise institutes the Holy Priesthood, when He commanded His Apostles, "Do this in memory of me." Pope Saint John Paul II spoke about the two sacraments being interconnected when he said, "No priesthood, no Eucharist. No Eucharist, no priesthood."

In this Sacrament of the Holy Altar our Lord poured out upon us all the riches of His love. St. Thomas called it the Sacrament of Sacraments. He said, "It is the fulfillment of ancient figures and the greatest of all His miracles while for those who were to experience the sorrow of His departure, it was destined to be a unique and abiding consolation."[57]

O what wonderful miracles. The bread is changed into the whole and entire person of Christ. The Eucharist is truly Jesus. It is Him in His physical resurrected body. The wine is changed into His blood. During Mass angels descend to surround the Altar. At Mass, the sacrifice of Calvary becomes present on the altar. The crucifixion event is re-presented in an unbloody manner. Not representation, but re-representation. At Mass heaven is opened and we join the angels and saints worshiping God. At Mass, Jesus offers Himself to the Father with the bread and wine and with our self and sacrifices. We are to give all our works and sacrifices and ourselves to Him at the offertory, when the bread and wine are brought forward to be given to the priest. At Mass, Jesus, in the priest, speaks with the lips and voice of the priest and makes His divine action take place. At Mass, Jesus speaks to us through the Scriptures and exhorts us through the priest, when he gives the homily beseeching us to live lives of virtue. At Mass Jesus gives Himself to us in Holy Communion, and we give ourselves to Him. The Mass is the new and everlasting covenant, a total giving of oneself to the other.

St. Alphonsus Ligouri tells us Holy Communion lasts for at least 15 minutes. Some saints say Communion lasts up to an hour or longer. St. Thomas Aquinas states Communion lasts until the elements of the Host are assimilated into our body. When we eat food, the food becomes us, but when we eat the Body of Christ, we become Jesus. There is no greater and precious time on earth, than when we are one with Jesus in Holy Communion. We should pour out our hearts to Him who comes inside us, beseeching Him for all our needs and the needs of others, thanking Him for His gifts and just contemplating His presence within us.

After Jesus rose from the dead, ascended into heaven, and after Pentecost, the Apostles, and those whom they made bishops and priests (by the laying on of their hands) offered the Holy Sacrifice of the Mass on the Lord's Day (Sundays).

It is believed due to John taking Mary into his home while at the foot of the Cross, and since She lived with Him until Her Assumption, She would have attended His Masses and received Jesus in Holy Communion. How do you think She received Communion? Most assuredly kneeling and on the tongue!

St. Mark, though not one of the twelve, was captured while offering Mass. A chair was carried around for Peter when he offered Mass. It was called "Peter's chair" and would later be placed in a bronze casing now located in St. Peter's Basilica above the high altar.

The Mass has four ends: atonement for our sins, thanksgiving, adoration, and petition. The saints tell us, it is more efficacious to offer the Mass for the living, than for the dead, though we should offer Masses for both: the dead to reduce their purgatory time, the living to help them obtain salvation.

Our Lord's beloved disciple, John leaned against the chest of Jesus (against His Sacred Heart). Surely, this consoled Jesus. We can console the Heart of Jesus by offering our Holy Communions, especially on the First Fridays, in reparation for sins committed against the Sacred and Eucharistic Heart of Jesus and by spending time in Eucharistic Adoration with Jesus or when we are before Him in the Tabernacle. John was the first lover of the Heart of Jesus and he would see the Heart of Jesus pierced on the Cross.

After Satan entered the heart of Judas, he took the morsel, (the Sacred Host particle), and departed with the purpose of betraying Jesus. Judas was the first to receive the Eucharist sacrilegiously, and the first to leave Mass before it was over. Imagine the sadness in the Heart of Jesus, knowing one of His twelve Apostles (the first bishops), would betray Him. A shocking 8% of His Apostles fell from grace.

For centuries, the Eucharist was not received by the faithful except for a few times a year. They had a holy fear of offending the Lord due to sins on their soul. In many countries, First Holy Communions were not made until the age of twelve. Pope Saint Pius X lowered the age for Holy Communion to the age of reason and promoted frequent Communion, even daily Communion.

Today, the holy fear of receiving Communion is no longer. If 80% of Catholic women, who are of age, use birth control, then how is it all receive Holy Communion? When one is in the state of mortal sin and has no intention of getting out of mortal sin, then one may not receive Jesus in Holy Communion. If one receives Communion in the state of mortal sin, they do so, like Judas, sacrilegiously. It's called a sacrilegious Communion, which deeply offends Our Lord. One then receives no graces whatsoever, and in fact, commits an additional mortal sin.

Short lines for Confession and everyone receives Holy Communion, while 80% of women (who are of age) use birth control. Something is not right.

If in the state of mortal sin, we are not permitted to receive Holy Communion, unless we first go to Confession. Jesus told St. Bridget about the great evil of sacrilegious Communions. He said, "There does not exist on earth a punishment severe enough to punish a sacrilegious Communion." St. Alphonsus Ligouri said that when a person receives Holy Communion unworthily, he attempts to place Jesus on the throne of his heart alongside Satan.

St. Paul exhorted the Corinthians to receive the Eucharist worthily. He said, "For as often as you eat this bread and drink the cup, you proclaim the death of the Lord until He comes. Therefore whoever eats the bread or drinks the cup of the Lord unworthily will have to answer for the body and blood of the Lord. A person should examine himself, and so eat the bread and drink the cup. For anyone who eats and drinks without discerning the body, eats and drinks judgment on himself." (1 Corinthians 11:23-30)

The ordinary and traditional manner the Church desires we receive Communion is on the tongue. Bishops in their own diocese can give an indult (permission) to receive on the hand. But, to receive on the hand can cause one to eventually treat the Eucharist as ordinary bread. If one receives on the hand, after the Host is placed in the mouth, look for particles on your hand and place them in your mouth, lest you drop Jesus on the floor. The Council of Trent has said, each particle is the whole and entire Jesus. There is greater humility to receive on the tongue. Particles and the Sacred Host itself are much less apt to fall to the ground. Communion patens should be used when distributing Communion, so Hosts and particles that fall from the Hosts are captured.

The Congregation for the Divine Worship and the Discipline of the Sacraments, Cardinal Medina has said, "Even where the Congregation has approved of legislation denoting standing as the posture for Holy Communion, in accordance with the adaptations permitted to the Conferences of Bishops by the *Institutio Generalis Missalis Romani* (GIRM 160:2), it has done so with the stipulation that communicants who choose to kneel are not to be denied Holy Communion on these grounds." "The practice of kneeling for Holy Communion has in its favor a centuries-old tradition, and it is a particularly expressive sign of adoration, completely appropriate in light of the true, real, and substantial presence of Our Lord Jesus Christ under the consecrated species."[58]

More and more Communion rails are being restored or kneelers are being used for Masses and people once again can receive Communion on the tongue while kneeling. How wonderful it will be someday, everywhere to give proper reverence, during Holy Communion, due to our Eucharistic King, to whom we genuflect when entering and departing from Church and before whom we kneel during the Consecration!

Oh, how wonderful an entire diocese would begin to love and respect Jesus in the Eucharist. If bishops would give catechesis for a period of time and then remove the indult to receive on the hand. Oh, how wonderful if bishops would teach with their authority love and devotion to Jesus in the Eucharist, the immense good that could come with kneeling and receiving Jesus on the tongue. Vocations would flourish. People would dress up for Mass, wear more modest clothing and discontinue wearing shorts. There would be less profanation and sacrilege. It would lead to less people receiving the Eucharist in mortal sin, because their faith would increase due to how they treat the Lord God with respect and reverence in the Sacred Host!

The most famous painting of the Last Supper was created by Leonardo da Vinci. In the painting, all the apostles and Jesus are seated in chairs and are sitting on the same side of the table. But there is no way the actual table looked like that. Back then, the common way Jews and Romans ate were tables with couches. They would recline laying down when eating. According to Scripture, it seems as though Peter and John were seated next to each other, while John sat next to Jesus. Peter requested that John ask Jesus, who would betray Him. On the other side of Jesus, most likely was Judas, because he took the morsel from the plate in front of Jesus. To offer a morsel of bread was a sign of friendship.

Yet, Jesus told His Apostles, "And as they reclined at table and were eating, Jesus said, "Amen, I say to you, one of you will betray me, one who is eating with me." They began to be distressed and to say to him, one by one, "Surely it is not I?" He said to them, "One of the Twelve, the one who dips with me into the dish. For the Son of Man indeed goes, as it is written of him, but woe to that man by whom the Son of Man is betrayed. It would be better for that man if he had never been born." (Mark 14:18-21)

Some portray Judas as the scapegoat, who innocently tried to help Jesus. They say, "After all, he had to betray Jesus to fulfill the prophecy in scripture." They wrongly say he most likely is not in hell. Really? But, Our Lord's own words state, "...woe to that man by whom the Son of Man is betrayed. It would be better for that man if he had never been born." Sadly, Judas committed suicide by hanging which caused his bowels to burst open. The way he died is in stark contrast to the way the other apostles died, except John, by martyrdom. And even John, they attempted to kill. They died for Jesus, but Judas died unrepentant after he betrayed Our Divine Lord.

Some commit suicide due to circumstances, that may reduce culpability, such as addictions to alcohol or drugs, clinical depression, or mental illness. Yet, those who willfully do so, as in the case of Judas, risk losing heaven for all eternity. When there is less culpability, there is hope for salvation, and the person most likely needs purgatory time.

Jesus knew the heart of Judas, that's why He was able to say, "It would be better for that man if he had never been born." Jesus knows the hearts of each of us. We should never judge the state of another person's soul. But rather entrust them to the mercy of God and pray for them. And we should never look to suicide as an escape from the world and suffering. There is great importance in trusting Jesus and turning to Him asking for forgiveness, which Judas did not.

It is true the Holy Mother Church never officially states if anyone is in hell. The Church leaves that judgment up to the Lord. But the Church, through her divine authority officially proclaims those who are in heaven through the beatification and canonization processes.

Those who say, "Most likely no one is in hell", contradict the words of Jesus in Sacred Scripture and also private revelation such as the children of Fatima, who had a vision of hell and seeing many souls who fall in it. It was so difficult for them that they said had the Virgin Mary not stopped the vision when She did, the children would have died of fright. But this vision was the impetus to move them to make great sacrifices for sinners and prevent them from going to hell.

Jesus states souls go to hell. He said, "I tell you, many will come from east and west and recline at table with Abraham, Isaac, and Jacob in the kingdom of heaven, while the sons of the kingdom will be thrown into the outer darkness. In that place there will be weeping and gnashing of teeth." (Matthew 8:11-12) He also said, "Then he will say to those on his left, 'Depart from me, you who are cursed, into the eternal fire prepared for the devil and his angels. For I was hungry and you gave me nothing to eat, I was thirsty and you gave me nothing to drink, I was a stranger and you did not invite me in, I needed clothes and you did not clothe me, I was sick and in prison and you did not look after me.'" (Matthew 25:41-43)

The goofball theory that no one is in hell, is not found in Scripture, nor Tradition, nor any of the writings of the saints. Most likely that theory came from the depths of hell. Believing in this false doctrine can lead one to believe there is no deterrent for doing evil and one could freely do as they like without consequences. Imagine if there was no penal system, no jails, and no punishment for criminals.

When Jesus consecrated bread and wine into His body and blood for the first time at the Last Supper, the twelve apostles were there and no one else. The Virgin Mary wasn't there and neither was Mary Magdalene, as some suggest. *The Da Vinci Code* novel and the atrocious movie *Mary Magdalene*, by Garth Davis, depict Mary Magdalene and Jesus in a way that is scandalous to Catholics. The movie makes Mary Magdalene, the wife of Jesus. This is blasphemous. Our Divine Lord lived a life of purity, chastity and remained a virgin. May those who created and promoted the book and movie come to repentance, and we pray God will forgive those who promote such lies.

Because the Virgin Mary was not present at the Last Supper and Mary Magdalene was not there, nor any women, this was a sign that the Lord chose only men to be priests. If He wanted women to be priests, most assuredly He would have deigned to have His Mother present at the Last Supper.

Never in the history of the Church has any women been ordained deacons or ordained priests. This is not God's will. Our Lord's bride is His Church. A priest, who is a sacramental Jesus, has for his bride, the Church. A woman can't have a bride, such a thing is gross and unnatural. Women can never be ordained is a dogma of the Catholic Church that must be believed and adhered to, lest one may find themselves outside the Church.

For centuries, and even from the very beginning of Christianity, the Holy Mass was offered "Ad Orientem", meaning "toward the east". This means the priest and the people faced the same direction. Did you know Vatican II never intended for the priest to face the people? Did you know Vatican II documents call for the continued use of Gregorian Chant, and the use of Latin? Sadly, popular songs and even Protestant hymns are now played in Catholic churches and these do not lift the heart and mind to God, as well as traditional Catholic hymns.

Application 1: Loss of Faith in the Eucharist

"On October 15th, 2024, the Real Presence Coalition (RPC) released the results of its massive July 2024 survey seeking to identify causes of a lack of faith in the Eucharist among many self-professed Catholics in the United States. The largest survey of Catholics in the United States ever conducted found that the faithful overwhelmingly say that receiving Holy Communion in the hand has led to loss of faith in the Eucharist and that they want a restoration of traditional liturgical practices. The survey, conducted with assistance from the national polling firm Public Opinion Strategies, received nearly 16,000 responses, including from 14,725 U.S. lay Catholics across every Latin diocese in the country. 780 responses were submitted by attendees of the U.S. bishops' National Eucharistic Congress in Indianapolis. Notably, the RPC survey drew heavily upon practicing Catholics, with 97 percent of respondents saying that they attend Mass at least once a week and believe in the Real Presence of Jesus Christ in the Eucharist. Asked what has contributed most to loss of faith in the Eucharist, respondents overwhelmingly cited reception of Holy Communion in the hand while standing, with nearly 58 percent saying it has had the "greatest" level of impact. They also pointed to the scandal of offering Holy Communion to public sinners who reject Catholic teaching, lack of reverence in the presence of the Eucharist, casual attitudes toward the Eucharist from clergy, failure to catechize the faithful, and moving the tabernacle away from the center of the sanctuary. More than 71 percent of respondents ranked "homosexuality in the priesthood" as having a "major" or "greatest" level of impact on the decline of belief in the Eucharist as well. A majority also said that the use of extraordinary ministers, replacement of sacred music with contemporary music, ending *ad orientem* worship, removing altar rails, failing to hold Eucharistic events like Adoration and processions, the decline of beauty in church architecture and liturgy, loss of silence, and the clerical abuse crisis have had "major" or "greatest" impact. The Real Presence Coalition, a group of prominent Catholic figures that includes Bishop Joseph Strickland, Bishop Athanasius Schneider, Father Donald Calloway, MIC, and LifeSiteNews CEO and co-founder John-Henry Westen, noted that respondents expressed concern about "a general decline in reverence during Mass, including casual dress, loud talking, and treating the Mass as a social event.""[59]

Application 2: Communion on the Tongue Safer than on the Hand

Jules Gomes, a journalist and biblical scholar, said, "A groundbreaking study is smashing the widespread misconception that administering Holy Communion on the hand is safer than dispensing the Sacred Host on the tongue. Contrary to the prevailing consensus among Catholic bishops, receiving Communion on the tongue and in the kneeling position is scientifically the safest and most hygienic method, which is "unlikely to incur a high risk of infection transmission," the new research shows.

Titled "Safety and Reverence: How Roman Catholic Liturgy Can Respond to the COVID-19 Pandemic," the paper published by academic Sergey Budaev, also asks the priest to face the altar and prohibit lay Eucharistic ministers from giving Communion during the pandemic for safety. There is no risk if worshipers remove masks after taking their places, Budaev argues, while insisting on stringently adhering to safety restrictions proposed by health regulators — including social distancing and wearing masks while entering and leaving church.

A researcher in the Department of Biological Sciences at the University of Bergen, Norway, also notes that the World Health Organization's (WHO's) recommendation for ministers to wear disposable gloves were applicable only in the context of burials.

The scientist explains why the traditional manner of Communion is safer: First, the Host used in the Latin rite is nearly dry and hence likely to have low adhesion of outside particles, further reducing the infectious risk. Second, while receiving the Host, the communicant normally extends the tongue forward, requiring holding breath for a while, thus reducing possible respiratory output (since COVID19 is mainly transmitted by small respiratory droplets during close face-to-

192

face contact and airborne transmission via exhaled aerosol). Third, since the faithful is kneeling while receiving the Host, this provides spatial distancing of about 20 inches, and the communicant's face is located at the level of the chest of the priest. Since the communicant says very little, any possible droplets and aerosol are directed at the priest's chest, which poses by far a lower risk than in the face.

In contrast, communicants who received the host standing are in "direct, close, face-to-face interaction" with the priest and any interaction between the priest and communicant would direct the droplets and aerosol directly to the priest's face and the consecrated Host. If the communicant coughs or sneezes, the priest's face and the hosts become "the direct target of both fine and larger ballistic droplets" which "is very unlikely in the kneeling position," according to the study. "It can be argued that the long development of the old traditional Latin rite occurred under continuous health threats in absence of vaccination, efficient pharmacological and other technological interventions that we now take for granted."[60]

In addition to this study, twenty-one doctors in Austria told their bishops Communion on the tongue is 'safer' than in the hand (26 June 2020). The Austrian doctors have authored a letter appealing their country's Bishops' Conference to lift the de facto ban on receiving Holy Communion on the tongue, which has been enforced since Communion in the hand was announced to be the only permitted form of distribution for the consecrated Host.

The twenty-one Catholic doctors of Austria who signed the letter quoted the professional opinion of Professor Filippo Maria Boscia, the president of the Association of Catholic Doctors of Italy who stated that "Communion on the tongue is safer than hand Communion."

Story 1: Eucharistic Miracle Leads to Corpus Christi Feast Day

In 1263, a German priest known as Peter of Prague was struggling with the doctrine of transubstantiation. While he was saying Mass in Bolseno, Italy, blood began to stream out of the Host and onto the corporal at the moment of consecration. This was reported to and investigated by Pope Urban IV, who concluded that the miracle was real. The bloodstained linen is still exhibited at the cathedral in Orvieto, Italy. Many Eucharistic miracles are like the one experienced by Peter of Prague, in which the host turns into flesh and blood.

Pope Urban was already familiar with a Eucharistic miracle. Years earlier, Bl. Juliana of Cornillon, in Belgium, had a vision in which she saw a full moon that was darkened in one spot. A heavenly voice told her that the moon represented the Church at that time, and the dark spot showed that a great feast in honor of Corpus Christi was missing from the liturgical calendar. She reported this vision to a local Church official, the archdeacon of Liège, who later became Pope Urban IV.

Remembering Juliana's vision as he verified the bloody miracle reported by Peter of Prague, Urban commissioned St. Thomas Aquinas to compose the Office for the Mass and Liturgy of the Hours for a new feast dedicated to devotion of the Eucharist. This liturgy of Corpus Christi (more fully defined in 1312) is pretty much how we celebrate it today.

Interestingly, every Eucharistic miracle ever tested by scientists all have the same blood type (AB) and all are living cardiac tissue from a Heart.

Story 2: A Priest's Experience of Offering the Ad Orientem Mass

When giving a talk to retreatants, a priest spoke about his experience of the "Ad Orientem Mass", which faces toward the high altar and away from the people. He said, "I enjoy offering the Novus Ordo Mass facing the Lord, rather than the people. The first time I offered an Ad Orientem Mass I could not believe how much easier it was for me to pray the Mass. There were less distractions, such as people getting up during the Consecration to go to the restroom, children fighting in the pew, a man picking his nose, a boyfriend and girlfriend rubbing shoulders. I gave a series of homilies on switching to Ad Orientem Masses in my parish and was very surprised, that once we started Masses facing God, the majority of the people liked it better than when I faced the people. I have never offered the Traditional Latin Mass, now called the "Extraordinary Form of the Mass." It is the ancient Mass the saints offered for over 1000 years. It is so beautiful! It is so reverent! How mysterious! How many saints either offered the Mass as priests, or laymen and religious who attended the TLM, which helped them to grow in holiness? Unlike the Novus Order (New Order Mass by Vatican II), during TLM Mass the people are required to kneel (if able) and receive Holy Communion on the tongue. When the Ad Orientem Mass is offered with reverence, and as originally intended with Gregorian Chant, Latin and facing the Lord, it raises the heart and mind to God in a way an ordinary English Mass doesn't."

Story 3: Desecration of Sacred Hosts
In 2004, in a Kansas parish, due to Communion in the hand, over a period of 3 months, 14 Hosts were found in missalettes. One Host was found under a back pew and on Christmas Day, a Host was found in the parking lot. At the end of each Mass, the pastor and his two parochial vicars implored the person to stop. But, it continued until they announced the person was excommunicated from the Church and needed to visit with a priest in Confession.

Story 4: Black Mass
A Communion Host was stolen by a satanist due to Communion in the hand, in 2014, at Oklahoma City. He scheduled black mass

at a civic center. The Society of St. Pius X held a Rosary procession, in downtown Oklahoma City. Archbishop Coakley held a Eucharistic procession and Holy Hour with 2,000 attendees. The archbishop took him to court forcing him to hand over the Host because he proved the Host is Church property.

Apparition: The Christ Child & Our Lady of Fatima (Spain)

On December 10, 1925, when Sister Lucia was a postulant nun with the Dorothean Sisters in Pontevedra, Spain, she saw the Divine Child and Our Lady of Fatima. Christ Child: "Have compassion on the heart of your Most Holy Mother, covered with thorns, with which ungrateful men pierce it at every moment, and there is no one to make an act of reparation to remove them." Our Lady: "Look my daughter, at my Heart, surrounded with thorns with which ungrateful men pierce me at every moment by their blasphemies and ingratitude. You at least try to console me. I promise to assist at the hour of death, with the graces necessary for salvation, all those who, on the first Saturday of five consecutive months, shall confess, receive Holy Communion, recite five decades of the Rosary, and keep me company for fifteen minutes while meditating on the fifteen mysteries of the Rosary, with the intention of making reparation to me." Lucia: "But my confessor said in the letter that this devotion is not lacking in the world, because there are many souls who receive You on the First Saturdays, in honor of Our Lady and of the fifteen Mysteries of the Rosary." Christ Child to Lucia: "It is true My daughter, that many souls begin the First Saturdays, but few finish them, and those who do complete them do so in order to receive the graces that are promised thereby. It would please Me more if they did Five with fervor and with the intention of making reparation to the Heart of your heavenly Mother, than if they did Fifteen, in a tepid and indifferent manner...."[61]

Jesus' Agony in the Garden

Fruit of the Mystery: Sorrow for Sin, Union with the Will of God

"Then going out He went, as was His custom, to the Mount of Olives, and the disciples followed Him. When He arrived at the place He said to them, "Pray that you may not undergo the test." After withdrawing about a stone's throw from them and kneeling, He prayed, saying, "Father, if you are willing, take this cup away from Me; still, not My will but yours be done." And to strengthen Him an angel from heaven appeared to Him. He was in such agony and He prayed so fervently that His sweat became like drops of blood falling on the ground. When He rose from prayer and returned to His disciples, He found them sleeping from grief. He said to them, "Why are you sleeping? Get up and pray that you may not undergo the test."

The following was taken taken from: *Meditation on the Passion, Compiled From Various Sources*, with Introduction by Reginald Walsh, O.P., The Newman Press, 1959.[62]

Jesus and the eleven Apostles leaving the Cenacle (Upper Room) went forth singing Jewish hymns to the Mount of Olives. They crossed the Cedron Valley, walked along the left side of the brook and made their way to the Garden of Gethsemane. It was about a mile and half from the Upper Room. It was a large garden surrounded by a hedge, and containing only some fruit-trees and flowers. It was used as a pleasure place and sometimes a place of prayer.

The Garden of Olives was separated by a road from that of Gethsemane, and was open, surrounded only by an earthen wall, and smaller than Gethsemane. There were caverns, terraces, and many olive trees to be seen in this garden and it was easy to find a suitable spot for prayer and meditation.

Olive trees can live up to three thousand years, though most usually live to be about five hundred years old. It's possible the olive trees located in the same place Jesus knelt and prayed could be the same trees who witnessed His agony.

In Aramaic, the word Gethsemane means "olive press". When olives are first crushed in an olive press, the oil that flows out is red, like blood. It becomes symbolic for Jesus who is crushed by the weight of His agony and sweats drops of blood falling to the ground.

The fall of our first parents, Adam and Eve had taken place in the Garden of Eden, and therefore the reparation for the fall was to be made in a garden. Adam could not be found to make reparation after the fall. But Jesus, the second Adam, comes and offers Himself to make full satisfaction. Eventually, His ascension would take Him up in glory on the Mount of Olives. How fitting, it would be the same place where His passion would begin.

"He took with him Peter, James, and John, and began to be troubled and distressed. Then He said to them, 'My soul is sorrowful even to death. Remain here and keep watch.' He advanced a little and fell to the ground and prayed that if it were possible the hour might pass by Him; He said,

'Abba, Father, all things are possible to you. Take this cup away from me, but not what I will, but your will be done.' When He returned He found them asleep. He said to Peter, 'Simon, are you asleep? Could you not keep watch for one hour? Watch and pray that you may not undergo the test. The spirit is willing but the flesh is weak.' Withdrawing again, He prayed, saying the same thing. Then He returned once more and found them asleep, for they could not keep their eyes open and did not know what to answer Him. He returned a third time and said to them, 'Are you still sleeping and taking your rest? It is enough. The hour has come. Behold, the Son of Man is to be handed over to sinners.'" (Mark 14:32-42)

Imagine the distress of Peter, James and John when He asked by Him to pray. They see what is happening to Jesus. They see Him in anguish. They have never seen Jesus like that before and then He says something that shocks them to the core. He said, "My soul is sorrowful even to death. Remain here and keep watch."

They see Our Lord kneel down and pray so intensely, the moonlight cannot hide the sweat and blood falling to the ground. They had a long day, a full meal, three cups of wine, and a long exhortation by Jesus. They witnessed the incredible First Mass. How He washed their feet. He did something new to the Passover and they were trying to ponder what it all meant. Out of human weakness, they are exhausted, overcome with grief and fall asleep while trying to pray.

What caused Jesus so much agony? There are three reasons. First, Jesus, as God and knowing all things, saw His imminent passion about to take place. The second reason for His great anguish is He sees before Him distinctly, every sin and every sinner of the whole human race. The third cause of His terrible agony is the lack of gratitude for what He endured for us. He sees all those who will hate Him and be lost forever, through the many favors He won for them and for those who would be barely saved, not even His generosity, His self-sacrifice would elicit much in return.

The First Reason: His whole passion is vividly before Him. The traitor's kiss, the arrest, the blow to His cheek, the unjust sentence, the blows, kicks, spittle. He sees Himself being placed in a dungeon fastened to the wall. Then in the morning, going before Pilate, His scourging, crowning with thorns, the mocking, the insults, blasphemies, shouts-- "Away with Him Crucify Him! Crucify Him!" Being sent to Herod. Pilate's unjust condemnation. He saw Peter deny Him and the state of his soul afterwards. He saw the state of Judas' soul and His committing suicide. He saw Himself carrying the Cross, falling three times, meeting His Mother, Veronica, Simon and the people along the way. He saw His garments being stripped. His hands and feet nailed to the Cross, then being hoisted above the earth, hanging there for three hours. He saw how difficult it was to breathe, His thirst, and no one to help Him. He saw His last breath. His eyes close and His soul part from His body. He saw His Mother watch, as His Heart was pierced, and then taken down and placed into Her arms. Who could watch their mother suffer so grievously and not prevent it from happening, yet knowing it was His Father's will?

The Second Reason: He sees before Him distinctly, every sin and every sinner of the whole human race. The wars and murders."

"He feels their number, their shame, their malice. And He is to be punished as though He had done all those wicked things. All the penalty, He must bear, all the shame, all the horror. Like a burden, it lay upon Him, yet if He did not carry it, we should die and be lost forever. It was either the Cross for Him or hell for me."[63]

The millions and millions of unborn children who die, the effect that it has on the souls of their mothers and fathers, and all humanity, the abortionists, and all those who support abortion. The corruption of children. He sees addictions to drugs, alcohol, and pornography. He sees sex-trafficking, slavery, adultery, blasphemies, sacrilegious communions, heresies, heretics, terrorism, apostasy, schisms, stolen hosts, child abuse, satanic masses, taking God's name in vain, not keeping the Sabbath on Sundays, etc…

"What a mingled torrent of filth, of sinful filth, of all ages and races now poured upon Jesus as He lay prostrate in agony, and every single drop of it must have filled His sensitive Sacred Heart with unutterable repugnance and horror. And all these sins call for bitter expiation. Once again Jesus cries and prays: "O my Father, if this chalice may not pass away, Thy will be done!" They were His, those sins of ours. He had charged Himself with their payment, and the punishment for each will be scored upon His most Sacred Body-Father! Thy will be done!"[64]

"The Third Reason: Lack of gratitude for what He endured for us and He sees all those who will hate Him and be lost forever, though the many favors He won for them and for those who would be barely saved, not even His generosity, His self-sacrifice would elicit much in return. Even Christians themselves persecute Him, who are full of hatred and become enemies of His doctrine, His sacraments, His representative the Pope. How well He deserves our love and reverence as our Lord and God.

The loss of every soul gave Him infinite pain. He felt the loss of each one acutely. How many will perish. Seeing all this, He mourned and prayed in agony and distress, bathed in perspiration and blood. It seems as if the horrors of hell crowded around Him. There was no one to comfort Him.

There was a last drop in the chalice, one that surpassed in bitterness all that had gone before. His own priests (the Apostles) will desert Him. One will betray Him and hand Him over, another to deny Him and all will forsake Him. His best friends!

Nearly an hour went by. Then He rises and goes to the three Apostles. Still and unconscious, they lie upon the ground, their garments tightly around them, for the night is chilly. They are asleep and don't hear the faltering steps of Jesus approach them. Our Lord looks upon them, who they left alone in His agony. How many times do we show ourselves as unwilling to suffer for Him?

Jesus bends over and says, "Simon, could you not have watched one hour with me?" Jesus is saying to us, suffer with Me and you will be crowned with Me." He then says, "Pray, lest you enter into temptation, the spirit is willing, but the flesh is weak.""[65]

Application 1: Spending an Hour With Jesus in Adoration

It's believed Gabriel appeared to Jesus during His agony to strengthen Him and console Him. He was the archangel, who appeared to the Virgin Mary and Zachariah, the father of John the Baptist. Perhaps, Gabriel showed Our Lord the many souls who would spend an hour with Him in Eucharistic Adoration and the many souls who would die for Him and sacrifice themselves for Him and His Church.

What a great opportunity for us to watch one hour with Jesus every week when we make a Eucharistic Holy Hour. The night hours in Adoration chapels are the special times we keep Jesus company and make reparation for sins committed against His Sacred Heart. Many special graces flow when we spend an hour with Jesus every week. Imagine keeping your hour every week for many years. Fifty-two hours a year or 1040 hours in twenty years. And for those who are committed to a daily Holy Hour, such as priests, religious, and some lay people, pray 365 hours a year keeping Jesus company.

Pope Saint Paul VI said, "Perpetual Adoration extends its influence far beyond the individual adorers, touching their homes and families and reaching out to the parish community and beyond!" Jesus told Blessed Dina Belanger, "A Holy Hour of prayer before the Blessed Sacrament is so important that a multitude of souls go to Heaven who otherwise would have gone to hell!"[66]

Many faithful Catholics, in the wee hours of the night, watch with Jesus in Adoration Chapels. Through Perpetual Adoration, adorers come in the middle of the night to spend time with their best friend. They come to open their heart to a God, who loves them, cares for them, comforts them, and gives them peace. They come to pray in reparation for those who do not watch with Jesus and they come to console the hidden Jesus. Those who spend their time with Him are protecting themselves from falling into temptations that they otherwise would have, if they did not spend time with Our Lord.

At times, we can feel abandoned and unloved and when we do, we feel just a tiny bit of what Jesus endured in the garden and how He must feel in many abandoned tabernacles.

Jesus appeared to St. Margaret Mary asking us to make the First Fridays of the month for nine consecutive months. In June of 1675, Our Divine Lord revealed His Heart to her during Eucharistic Adoration saying, "Behold this Heart which has so loved men that It spared nothing, even going so far as to exhaust and consume Itself, to prove to them Its love. And in return I receive from the greater part of men nothing but ingratitude, by the contempt, irreverence, sacrileges and coldness with which they treat Me in this Sacrament of Love. But what is still more painful to Me is that even souls consecrated to Me are acting in this way."

Notice how Jesus specifically points out priests and religious, who are consecrated to Him. He said His Heart is wounded even more deeply by them and He wants all to make reparation for them.

Jesus gave twelve promises to those who fulfill the first nine Fridays, receiving Holy Communion and to offer Communion in reparation for sins committed against His Sacred Heart. The last and greatest promise of the twelve, states, "I promise you in the excessive mercy of my Heart, that my all-powerful love, will grant to all those who receive Holy

Communion, on the First Fridays, in nine consecutive months, the grace of final perseverance, they shall not die in my disgrace, nor without receiving their sacraments. My Divine Heart shall be their safe refuge in this last moment."

Application 2: Doing God's Will with Love

During the second hour Jesus prayed, red drops of blood stood upon His forehead and trickled down to the ground. The mossy roots of the trees became wet with it, His garments became soaked with His blood. He returns to the Apostles and again finds them sleeping, for their eyes were heavy, and they knew not what to answer Him.

For us, how do we know God's will for us and how will we respond? God's will for us is our daily duty. To be the best parent, grandparent, son or daughter, mother or father, spouse, brother or sister, boss, superior, co-worker or employee we can be is God's will for us.

God's will is at times very difficult, for example, to be there for a sick person, whom we love, but can't stand to see suffer. It is, likewise, difficult for us to endure our own sicknesses.

How hard it is to make sacrifices for a spouse, when it seems like no sacrifices are returned. It is painful to watch a loved one fall away from God and His Church, with our only and greatest hope of prayer.

We know God's will in our ordinary daily duties, through priests, who are our moral and spiritual guides, through the teachings of the Church, by keeping God's commandments, and even by ordinary civil laws that are just.

In our ordinary daily duties, it's God's will we work, and if we are married, we are to be a good spouse and a good parent. It's God's will for children to obey their parents. It's God's will that we be a good brother or sister and a good friend to others.

205

It's God's will that we change the baby's diaper, make sure our children take baths, feed them, take them to school and their activities, to wash clothes, cook food, clean the house, and mow the yard regularly.

For those who have jobs and who volunteer, it's God's will we do our best to obey those over us without grumbling or complaining. We should do our job to the best of our ability and with as much love as possible.

It is God's will volunteers do as priests request of them for they are God's representatives. For example, if a priest asks those who serve Mass as lectors and extraordinary ministers, that they should wear dress clothes and the clothes should be modest, then it is God's will for them to do so. It's God's will we do what the priest asks of us in his homilies and his advice in confession.

We know God's will through the teachings of the Church, such as our obligation to attend Mass on Sundays and Holy Days and follow the disciplines of the Church such as fasting and abstinence. We are to follow all the Church's teachings, such as avoiding illegal drugs, no premarital relations, nor contraception, abortion or euthanasia.

We are to keep God's commandments, by avoiding sin, by practicing virtue, going to Confession regularly, to give alms, and do good deeds. We are to obey ordinary civil laws, that don't contradict God's moral or natural laws such as to pay taxes and to drive the speed limit.

When we are obedient to those over us, we are obedient to Jesus, just as Jesus was obedient to His heavenly Father when He became an unborn baby at the Incarnation and was obedient to the point of death, death on the Cross.

What good is it, if we fast and give alms, yet at work we cause dissension and use foul language, or at home are mean to our family and watch immoral television programs?

If we find ourselves not wanting to do God's will or are lazy in doing it, we can pray for the gift of zeal, turn to the Virgin

Mary to help us, and make a Morning Offering with the desire to do everything we do for the love of Jesus.

Knowing we are to do God's will and yet not having the desire to do it, we can enter into the mystery of the Lord's agony in the garden and unite that suffering to the sufferings of Jesus.

Our greatest suffering will be to accept our upcoming death, and all the pains that go with it. By accepting God's will in the smaller sufferings, it prepares us to accept greater ones.

If, for example, we are diagnosed with cancer, and need chemotherapy, we can see our cross coming and our human will recoil at it. But if we pray, "Not my will, but God's will be done.", then we can accept that chalice of suffering and embrace it for love of God, for the conversion of sinners, and in reparation for our own sins.

We can be tempted to do our will, rather than the Father's will, such as disobeying our boss, parents, superior, or the teachings of the Church. The temptation to flee our cross of obedience can be overcome, as we meditate on the words of Jesus, "Not my will, by thy will be done."

Jesus gave us His Mother as an example, who always did the will of the heavenly Father. "While He was still speaking to the crowds, His mother and His brothers appeared outside, wishing to speak with Him. Someone told Him, "Your mother and your brothers are standing outside, asking to speak with you." But He said in reply to the one who told Him, "Who is my mother? Who are my brothers?" And stretching out his hand toward his disciples, he said, "Here are my mother and my brothers. For whoever does the will of my heavenly Father is my brother, and sister, and mother."(Matthew 12:46-50).

Jesus was not putting Mary down, as some non-Catholics claim. Rather, He did the opposite. He glorified His Mother, because She perfectly did the will of the Father and He used this event as an example to exhort others to do as She always did.

Mary's perfect acceptance of God's will can be seen at the Incarnation, when the angel Gabriel asked Her to be the Mother of Jesus and also at the foot of the Cross, when She endured watching Her Son's Crucifixion and death.

For religious sisters and brothers, who take vows of poverty, chastity and obedience, they know God's will by following the rule of their religious order and by obeying their superior.

Saint Elizabeth Ann Seton said, "And what was the first rule of our dear Savior's life? You know it was to do his Father's will. Well, then, the first end I propose in our daily work is to do the will of God; secondly, to do it in the manner He wills; and thirdly, to do it because it is His will."[67]

In an exhortation to the religious brothers of his order, Saint Maximilian said, "God, who is all-knowing and all-wise, knows best what we should do to increase His glory. Through His representatives on earth He continually reveals His will to us; thus it is obedience and obedience alone that is the sure sign to us of the divine will. A superior may, it is true, make a mistake; but it is impossible for us to be mistaken in obeying a superior's command. The only exception to this rule is the case of a superior commanding something that in even the slightest way would contravene God's law. Such a superior would not be conveying God's will."[68]

Story 1: Sorrowful Mysteries of the Rosary Bring About Conversion

A 27-year-old man hadn't been to confession for 20 yrs., since he was in 3rd grade. He learned how to pray the Holy Rosary and began to pray it daily. He noticed whenever he meditated on the Sorrowful Mysteries, he began to feel sorrow for having hurt Jesus by his sins.

About three months after he learned the Sorrowful Mysteries of the Rosary, he was inspired to return to Confession, but he couldn't remember how to confess. When he finally walked in the confessional, after telling the priest he didn't know how to confess, the priest helped him to feel at ease and walked him through the process.

As a penance, he was told to look at the large Crucifix above the altar in the church for fifteen minutes, a small penance to pray for twenty years of sins and not attending Mass, except on Christmas and Easter.

At the moment of absolution, when his sins were absolved, he felt the Holy Spirit go through him, a weight lifted, and immediate joy. While gazing upon the Crucifix, he realized how much Jesus loved Him and how much Jesus suffered, so that his sins could be forgiven. He was eventually ordained a priest and attributes his conversion to the Virgin Mary, by praying Her Holy Rosary daily. How important it is to confess regularly. Monthly confession of venial sins is very beneficial to the soul and prevents us from falling into mortal sin. St. Padre Pio recommended to all the faithful weekly Confession. Pope St. John Paul II went to Confession daily. Priests and religious have traditionally confessed weekly.

Apparition: Our Lady of Beauraing (Belgium)

On the evening of November 29, 1932, four children walked to a convent school run by the Sisters of Christian Doctrine to meet up with a girl and walk home with her. When they reached the school, Albert pointed to a lady dressed in a long white robe, near a railroad viaduct just past the school. She looked to be around 18-20 years old with deep blue eyes, and a Rosary hung from her arm. When Albert asked, "Are you the Immaculate Virgin?" The Lady smiled and nodded Her head. "What do you want?" he asked.

"Always be good," our Blessed Mother answered. The other children saw Her as well. Over the next several weeks, they saw the Lady 32 more times, generally in the garden of the convent school.

The apparitions continued. For the first few apparitions in the garden, the Lady was already visible when the children got there. Later, She became visible after the children had begun to recite the Rosary. They had formed the habit of saying the Rosary as soon as they arrived in the garden. Each time Our Lady appeared, the children felt themselves drawn to a kneeling position, almost as if they were thrown to their knees.

During the last apparition on January 3, 1933, Our Lady stated: "I will convert sinners. I am the Mother of God, the Queen of heaven." She revealed Her Golden Heart and asked one of the children to sacrifice for Her. Twenty thousand people were present that day.

Three times the Blessed Mother urged the children to pray. In her final apparition she spoke to Fernande Voisin: "Do you love my Son? Do you love me? Then sacrifice yourself for me."

Jesus is Scourged at the Pillar

Fruit of the Mystery: Mortification, Purity

Jesus foresaw His scourging and announced it to His Apostles in secret. "Then He took the Twelve aside and said to them, "Behold, we are going up to Jerusalem and everything written by the prophets about the Son of Man will be fulfilled. He will be handed over to the Gentiles and He will be mocked and insulted and spat upon; and after they have scourged Him they will kill him, but on the third day He will rise." (Luke 18:31-34) "Then Pilate took Jesus and had Him scourged." (John 19:1)

Scourging was so severe a punishment that Jewish law imposed restrictions on its use. "Forty lashes may be given, but no more; or else, if more lashes are added to these many blows, your brother will be degraded in your sight." (Deuteronomy 25:3)

The Romans first stripped the victim and tied His hands to a post above His head.

The hands of Jesus were bound to the pillar by a rope and He was mercilessly scourged much more than Jewish law allowed because it was inflicted by Roman soldiers and their law allowed sixty six. The flogging could be inflicted either in public or in private. Our Lord's occurred in a courtyard.

In a side chapel of the Basilica of St. Praxedes in Rome sits a large fragment of black and white stone. It is claimed to be the Column of Flagellation, a piece of the pillar Jesus was scourged, brought to Rome by St. Helena. The height of the pillar is twenty six inches high and had a ring fastened to the top.[69] Jesus' hands were tied to the ring and He had to bend low so as to present His back to the soldiers.[70] "I gave my back to those who beat me, and my cheeks to those who tore out my beard. I did not hide my face from scorn and spitting." (Isaiah 50:6)

However, in Jerusalem is a side niche in the Chapel of the Apparition (Jesus appeared to His Mother) of the Holy Sepulchre, there stands the portion of a pillar, this one made of red porphyry, also claiming to be the Column of Flagellation. This pillar is believed to have been stained with Our Lord's Blood. No one knows for certain which column is authentic and both stones are venerated as relics.

According to Fr. Tommy Lane, who visited the Shroud of Turin in 1998, he said, "The marks of the scourging at the pillar are clearly visible on the crucified man. The wounds are scattered over the whole body from the shoulders down to the lower part of the legs. Analysis of the scourge marks shows that two soldiers carried out the torture, one on either side of Jesus, one was a little taller than the other. After using one type of whip, they changed and used a different type of whip. The second whip had metal spikes or bones designed to badly damage the skin and cause much bleeding. The whole body is covered with these wounds, but they are particularly evident all over the back, the chest, pelvic area, legs and calves. They are fainter elsewhere. About 120 wounds from the scourging are visible to the naked eye on the shroud but high resolution photography in the year 2000 with image enhancement showed hundreds of scourge wounds. Even with that, not all scourge wounds are on the shroud because it covered only the front and back of the body and we have no way of knowing how many scourge marks were on the sides of the body."[71]

Dr. Truman Davis gave a medical explanation as to how he believes the scourging affected the body of Jesus. He said, "The heavy whip is brought down with full force again and again across Jesus' shoulders, back, and legs. At first the heavy thongs cut through the skin only. Then, as the blows continue, they cut deeper in the subcutaneous tissues, producing first and oozing of blood from the capillaries and veins of the skin, and finally spurting arterial bleeding from vessels in the underlying muscles… Finally the skin of the back is hanging in long ribbons and the entire area is an unrecognizable mass of torn, bleeding tissue."[72]

"As blow follows blow, the virginal flesh of Jesus assumes a livid hue, it swells up and becomes inflamed; red and purple welts appear, the skin breaks—at first in little cracks, the perfect furrows open out, even deeper and longer; the flesh parts asunder—the blows fall upon the very bones. The blood wells forth, first trickles down in little streams, and at last flows in torrents, until the whole body is bathed in it—it is sprinkled upon the pavement and forms pools around the pillar."[73]

Due to the brutality of the Roman soldiers and the number of their scourgings, victims of their scourging seldom survived.

A single drop of the Precious Blood of Jesus would have been sufficient to redeem the whole world, but You O Lord, chose to shed all Your blood to urge us to love You with great fervor.

When St. Bridget of Sweden was a child, she received a vision of Jesus scourged and hanging on the Cross. In sorrow, she asked him who treated Him this way. Our Lord answered,"They who despise me, and spurn my love for them." From that time on, she had a great devotion to the Passion of Christ.

St. Bridget wanted to know how many times the body of Our Lord was struck during the various scenes of his Passion. One day Jesus answered her longing and told her, "I received 5480 blows upon My Body. If you wish to honor them in some way, recite fifteen Our Fathers and fifteen Hail Marys with the following Prayers, which I Myself shall teach you, for an entire year. When the year is finished, you will have honored each of My Wounds."

Jesus then gave St. Bridget 15 prayers to pray every day for a full year, which she would recite along with an Our Father and a Hail Mary for each. Totaled up, these prayers would equal 5475. This could be understood as all the wounds other than the Five Wounds in his hands, feet, and side, which are more commonly honored separately. These 15 Prayers of St. Bridget are also contained in the very popular *Pieta Prayer Book.*

The movie *The Passion of the Christ* by Mel Gibson, starring Jim Caviezel, has a scene of Jesus scourging that is astonishing and heartbreaking to watch. Mr. Gibson used writings from the visions of Blessed Anne Catherine Emmerich and the pious accounts from *Friday of Sorrows* to create the motion picture. It's doubtful one can eat popcorn when watching the movie, as Mr. Caviezel's emotional portrayal of Jesus moves one to tears. In the movie, the soldiers are counting the number of scourgings in Latin and while they are being splattered by blood as they strike Our Lord's body.

"Yet, it was our pain that He bore, our sufferings He endured. We thought of Him as stricken, struck down by God and afflicted. But He was pierced for our sins, crushed for our iniquity. He bore the punishment that makes us whole, by His stripes we were healed." (Isaiah 53:4-5)

Application 1: Respect for the Body

What we do to our body, we do to Jesus. Our body does not belong to us. "Do you not know that your bodies are temples of the Holy Spirit, who is in you, whom you have received from God? You are not your own; you were bought at a price. Therefore honor God with your bodies." (1 Corinthians 6:19-20)

Mutilation of the body can be seriously sinful, such as sterilization (vasectomies, tubal ligations), which tell God no, to permanently not have additional children. Excessive piercings damage the body and can cause infections. According to a recent study, persons with tattoos have a 21% higher risk for lymphoma cancer,[74] than those without them, not to mention infection due to the ink and cutting. Satanic and immoral tattoos are seriously sinful.

Smoking can cause lung cancer. Marijuana and drugs can harm the mind's ability to make good moral choices and therefore are seriously sinful when one can't make proper decisions.

Application 2: Purity

When we pray the Rosary, by meditating on the scourging of the pillar, it will help us attain purity and respect for the body. The bloody mess of the scourging of Jesus, seems to be in part, to make reparation for the sins against purity.

The Virgin Mary told Saint Jacinta Marto, one of the three children who had visions of the Virgin Mary, "More souls go to Hell because of sins of the flesh than for any other reason." She also warned, "Certain fashions will be introduced that will offend Our Lord very much." And she also issued a direct warning to women, saying: "Woe to women lacking in modesty." And also: "Let men avoid greed, lies, envy, blasphemy, impurity."

Women today think nothing of wearing shorts, low cut tops, tight clothing, swimsuits, bikinis at beaches and swimming pools. How horrendous when women wear immodest clothing to Mass and Eucharistic Adoration when in the presence of the King of Heaven and earth, which also causes distractions to those who come to worship the Lord. How scandalous for parents to allow young girls to wear such immodest clothing.

Years ago, never would women have worn such clothing. Men would not have been without shirts. Immodest clothing including sportswear for men and women can lead to the corruption of children, who are being asked to wear such clothing when going out for sports.

Those who view pornography and commit acts of impurity, think no one knows. But God sees and God wants to help.

Our Lady of Good Success, an approved apparition at Quito, Ecuador said, "In those times the atmosphere will be saturated with the spirit of impurity which, like a filthy sea, will engulf the streets and public places with incredible license…" "Innocence will scarcely be found in children, or modesty in women." "There shall be scarcely any virgin souls in the world. The delicate flower of virginity will seek refuge in the cloisters…" "Without virginity, fire from heaven will be needed to purify these lands…" "Sects, having permeated all social classes, will find ways of introducing themselves into the very heart of homes to corrupt the innocence of children."

Parents fail to watch over their children, who at a very young age begin to view pornography on tablets, phones and computers and then become addicted while in high school. Oh, the responsibility of parents!

To regain purity can take a long time, but some saints, like Augustine, by a single act of grace received it immediately and maintained it the rest of their life.

Alessandro Serenelli, a 19-year-old man, made advances toward eleven year old Saint Maria Gorretti and then stabbed her 14 times. She forgave him before she died. Some biographers stated he read a great deal of pornography. He was arrested, put into prison and remained unrepentant for 8 years, until one night he had a dream in which he saw Maria, in a field of flowers, holding out white lilies to him. After his release from prison, he eventually became a Capuchin Franciscan. Lilies represent purity.

Why do some statues of St. Joseph depict him holding a staff in his hand with a lily blossoming out of it? There is a

216

tradition that when it came time for the Blessed Virgin Mary, at the age of 14 to be married, there were several suitors seeking Her hand. Each had their own staff and at the request of the priest, wrote their name on their staff. During the prayer service offered by the priest, Joseph's staff immediately burst into bloom with fragrant white lilies, indicating he was the one chosen by God. St. Joseph is known for his purity. "The just man shall blossom like the lily" is applied to St. Joseph in the liturgy for his feast day, March 19, St. Joseph, Spouse of Mary.

For those who would like to break the habit of pornography and/or impurity, here are some helpful suggestions: Confess your sins once a week. Attend daily Mass and receive Holy Communion as often as possible. Receive Jesus in the Eucharist only in the state of grace. Pray a weekly Holy Hour or daily Holy Hour if you are able. Wear a blessed Scapular, Miraculous Medal and St. Benedict Medal. Every night before retiring, pray three Hail Marys in honor of Mary's purity and ask Mary for the gift of purity. St. Alphonsus Ligouri said those who keep this devotion, will always become pure.   When a lustful thought first enters the mind, or as soon as the idea begins to tempt one to look at pornography, immediately turn your mind on something pleasurable, but non-sinful (such as ice-cream or chocolate cake), and simultaneously pray audibly, an Our Father or Hail Mary. You will see the thought immediately vanish, because most likely it was an evil spirit tempting you.

Regularly avoid eating sweets and drinking pop. Stay away from foods and drinks labeled "sugar free", but actually have alcohol sugars in them. For some men, chocolate can cause impure thoughts.

Deny yourself instant gratification. When a thought for pop or candy first comes to mind, don't have them. When thirsty, make yourself wait a few minutes before drinking water, or wait to turn on the air conditioner when it is hot. Make yourself wait

217

for things. These small non-sinful self-denials can be very helpful in not following through with sinful gratifications.

Fast on bread and water (or however you are able fast) twice a week. By fasting regularly, it is much easier to overcome sinful temptations. Our Lord said, "...this kind can only come out through prayer and fasting." (Matthew 17:21)

The primary motivation for growing in purity is love. First, we love Jesus so much, we want to avoid hurting Him. By meditating on His scourging at the pillar, we can see how we participated in it.

Second, we are to love our neighbor, by seeking what is best for those who have allowed their bodies to be used in an impure way. We should view girls who have allowed themselves to be photographed immodestly as sisters in Christ. We refuse to look at their bodies for our own pleasure, and will pray and fast for them regularly, because we truly love them and want them to be in heaven someday.

Consecrate yourself and your purity to the Hearts of Jesus and Mary and consecrate yourself to St. Joseph, Mary's most chaste spouse. Develop a tender love and devotion to the Blessed Virgin Mary, Virgin Most Pure. Finally, avoid occasions of sin. Get rid of television. Avoid movies with improper content. Install image blockers on your phone and computer. Use *Covenant Eyes* for the protection of yourself and your children.

Daily pray the Holy Rosary as many as you are able in one day, perhaps 3 or 4. The frequent praying of the Rosary, especially the sorrowful mysteries, will lead to greater holiness and leave behind sin and impurity. The Rosary is THE weapon against evil and temptation. Mary will enter the battle for us and crush the head of the serpent.

The Catechism of the Catholic Church speaks of modesty. "Modesty protects the mystery of persons and their love. It encourages patience and moderation in loving relationships; it requires that the conditions for the definitive giving and commitment of man and woman to one another be fulfilled. Modesty is decency. It inspires one's choice of clothing. It keeps silence or reserve where there is evident risk of unhealthy curiosity. It is discreet." (CCC #2522)

Imagine what would happen if a bishop in union with all the priests of his diocese were to promote modesty, especially at the Holy Sacrifice of the Mass and Adoration. If every priest were to lovingly speak to his congregation about dressing up for Mass and Eucharistic Adoration and avoid immodest clothing, like shorts, low cut tops, tight clothing, how quickly they would respond in a positive way. They wouldn't go parish hopping trying to find a priest, who doesn't care about their soul, and who cares nothing about Eucharistic reverence, or perhaps he doesn't want to "make waves."

Our Blessed Lord's flesh is torn from His sacred body, as He is whipped at the pillar. We may be tempted to dress immodestly, or to look upon others as objects of pleasure or be tempted to impurity, and lust. When we meditate on the second mystery of the Rosary, we recall the wounded flesh of Jesus, at the Pillar, which inspires us to flee the temptations of the flesh. The powerful precious blood of Jesus purifies the mind and heart and forces out evil temptations.

St. Bernard said, "Venomous reptiles flee from flowers on vines, and so evil spirits flee from souls when the Virgin Mary is called upon."[75] Therefore, when tempted, let us take into our hands Mary's Rosary and cast our eyes on Her, the beautiful flower on the vine of the Church and call upon Her Holy Name, and by Her power over the enemy, the evil spirits will immediately flee, and through the Virgin Most Pure, we will have triumphed.

Story 1: No Blood on a Crucifix

If Jesus' scourging was as bad as what we are told, why is it that few crucifixes portray the body without scourge markings and not even blood near the wounds of the hands, feet, side, and crown of thorns?

After offering a Sunday Mass, back in 2005, a woman came up to a priest in tears and with a Spanish accent, she said, "It is a disgrace what you have done to Jesus." He said, "Why are you crying, what are you talking about?" She said, "That crucifix hanging above the altar is blasphemous. It's sanitized. There is no blood on that crucifix."

After visiting a bit, he discovered she was from Peru. In South American countries, they portray crucifixes in a lifelike manner, sometimes even attaching real hair on a crucifix and always the body of Jesus on the Crucifix has blood on it. Even though the priest told her, he was not responsible and could do nothing about it, since he was a mere priest associate, and not the pastor, and even though he agreed with her, still she could not be consoled, because the Jesus, whom she loved, was treated disrespectfully, as though He had no pain hanging from the Cross. This woman gave a great witness to her love of Jesus and the importance of acknowledging the wounds of Jesus. They are not only important to her, but especially the wounds are meaningful to Jesus, who went through His sacred passion.

Story 2: The Rosary & Impure Life and Sinful Friendship Delivered

"A person of impure life who had not the courage to quit his sins, began to say the Rosary, and was delivered from his vices. Another person who maintained a sinful friendship was seized with abhorrence of his sin by saying the Rosary. He yielded again to temptation, but by means of the Rosary finally freed himself from it."[76]

Apparition: Our Lady of Banneux (Belgium)

On January 15th, 1933, 11 year old Mariette Beco was in the kitchen when a lady appeared in the garden, beckoning her to come outside. Her mother would not let her.

The child noticed that Our Lady of Banneux had a Rosary, hanging from Her blue sash. The cross was the same color of gold as the rose between her toes. Mariette went to a drawer, and rummaged through it looking for a Rosary that she had found outside on the road. When she found it, she began to pray. The Lady's lips moved, but she didn't say anything that Mariette could hear. After a few decades, the Lady raised Her hand, and motioned with Her finger for Mariette to come outside. The young girl asked permission to leave the house. But, her mother would not permit her to leave.

Three days later, after praying in the garden Mariette went up the road. She saw a bright ball of light that changed into a woman's silhouette. She heard the Lady's voice calling for her. Arriving at a pool of water from a spring, the lady told her to dip her hands into the water. Then the Lady told her "This spring is reserved for me. Goodnight, goodbye."

The next day (January 19, 1933) around the same time, the Virgin appeared again to Mariette, who was surrounded by 17 local people. The girl was the only one to see Mary. She asked the Lady Her identity, and She replied: "I am the Virgin of the Poor." They then went to the spring of water together. Mary declared: "This spring is reserved for all the nations, to bring comfort to the sick." The Virgin Mary asked that a chapel be built there and said She came to alleviate sufferings. She also later said, "I am the Mother of the Savior, the Mother of God. Pray very much."

Crowning of Jesus with Thorns

Fruit of the Mystery: Moral Courage

"Then the soldiers of the governor took Jesus inside the praetorium and gathered the whole cohort around Him. They stripped off his clothes and threw a scarlet military cloak about Him. Weaving a crown out of thorns, they placed it on his head, and a reed in His right hand. And kneeling before Him, they mocked Him, saying, "Hail, King of the Jews!" They spat upon Him and took the reed and kept striking Him on the head. And when they had mocked Him, they stripped Him of the cloak, dressed Him in His own clothes, and led Him off to crucify him." (Matthew 27:27-31)

The following are excerpts taken from, *Meditation on the Passion, Compiled From Various Sources, With Introduction* by Reginald Walsh, O.P., The Newman Press, 1959, pg. 210-213:

"About five hundred men gathered around to make sport of Jesus. Our Lord is seated on a stone bench. An old scarlet cloak was thrown over His shoulders. How is it that they were not satisfied by the scourging He just went through? They could see every time Jesus moved, it caused Him great pain and their hearts had no pity on Him. They were determined to make sport of Jesus by dressing Him up as a king and mocking Him with fake homage.

They had removed His vesture which caused intense pain from the scourging and now

223

they put an old rag as a royal mantle on His shoulders and put a reed in His hand as a scepter. They didn't have a crown for the king, where were they to get one?

They bring a branch of briar covered with hard pointed thorns bristling with sharp points within and without. They put the cap-like crown (helmet of thorns) on His head and beat it down with the reed. The thorns are driven into His temples and nerves. Suddenly tears fall from His eyes due to the intolerable pain. The blood trickles through His hair, disfigures His face, fills and blinds His eyes.

Now they pass before Him, bowing their knees in derision and saluting Him, "Hail, King of the Jews!" One takes the reed from His hands and strikes His head, others pull His beard and buffet Him. Jesus makes no resistance; there is no sign of indignation. He does not turn His face away when they spit upon Him. When they want the reed to strike Him, He gives it to them. When they return it, He takes it again into His trembling hands.

Jesus foresaw what they would do to Him. "Behold, we are going up to Jerusalem, and the Son of Man will be betrayed to the chief priests and to the scribes; and they will condemn Him to death and deliver Him to the Gentiles; and they will mock Him, and scourge Him, and spit on Him, and kill Him. And the third day He will rise again." (Matthew 10:33-34) And yet, He is the "Blessed and only almighty, the King of kings, and the Lord of lords." Yet, see the angels surround Him in adoration and astonishment! How they marvel at it all and try to see what He sees in this human race that is now being redeemed in such a wondrous way, and at such a tremendous cost!

On every side the thorns encircle and pierce His head, wounding the temples, breaking the nerves, and this in expiation of my evil thoughts, my pride, rebellion, contempt of authority, uncharitable interpretations. This is to teach us how to bear headache, anxiety, and worry.

Contemplate His divine Face, defiled by spittle, besmeared with blood, swollen bruised with blows- a fearful sight to look upon. His eyes half-closed have all but lost the power of sight. Dimly through tears and blood, they discerned the long line of mockers, and the hand lifted to snatch the reed and beat the crown still deeper into the head."[77]

The actual Crown of Thorns is preserved in the Louvre Museum at Paris, France. The Crown of Thorns was at the Cathedral of Notre Dame until April 15th 2019, when it was saved during a fire at the Cathedral by fire brigade chaplain Father Jean-Marc Fournier.

"The crown of thorns takes the form of a circle, 8.3 inches in diameter." "In the 13th century, the emperor of Constantinople, Baldwin II, pawned it to bankers in Venice, Italy, because he needed money. After learning this, French King Louis IX, now St. Louis, collected a considerable sum of money, which enabled him to purchase it by compensating the Venetian bankers. In 1239, the king entered Paris carrying the crown himself, barefoot and dressed in a simple tunic."[78]

"At the beginning of the 19th century, once civil and religious peace had been restored (lost by the French Revolution) in France, Emperor Napoleon handed it over to the archbishop of Paris, who had it placed in the Notre Dame Cathedral. Since then, it has been part of its treasury. "Careful checks have been carried out each time it has changed owner and assignee..." "From the fourth century, it has been historically proven that it is the same crown."[79]

Once the Cathedral restoration has taken place the Crown of Thorns will be returned to the Notre Dame Cathedral to once again be venerated by the public.

Before selling the Crown of Thorns to St. Louis, King of France, the Venetians (from Venice) cut off thorns and dispersed them to monasteries and churches throughout the world. The remaining thorns were removed and given to churches by St. Louis and other French monarchs.

It is believed the shrub from which the crown of thorns was taken is known as Ziziphus spina-christi, more popularly known as the jujube tree. It grows about the height of fifteen or twenty feet. It is found growing in abundance by the wayside around Jerusalem. The crooked branches of this shrub are armed with thorns growing in pairs, a straight spine and a curved one commonly occurring together at each point.

The holy Crown of Thorns originally had 70 thorns, each about 4 centimeters in length. Due to examining the Shroud of Turin, believed to be the shroud Jesus was wrapped for burial, researchers found 13 wounds on the forehead and 30 on the back of the head.

Application 1: Crowning of Thorns Causes Us to Flee Bad Thoughts

"This (the Crowning of Thorns) is in atonement for my vanity, my curiosity, my love of display and notice of others. Jesus teaches me self-control when I am hurt. Do I pray for the grace to forgive, when I can't forget? Do I accept the bitterness of speech from others with sweetness? Do I make allowances for mistakes and misunderstandings of others? Am I ready to make an excuse for them? Am I merciful to others, whom I dislike? Do I check my spirit of criticism? Am I ready to make sacrifices for the sake of peace?"[80]

Do I combat negative and judgmental thoughts, with thoughts of understanding and compassion for those who hurt me? Do I flee from lustful thoughts and ask Our Lady to help me have a pure heart to see God in others? When having revengeful thoughts or desiring evil on someone, do I pray for them asking God to help them to live a life of virtue and when they die, to go to heaven, so we can be friends there? When having thoughts of pride, do I counteract those thoughts by viewing myself as less than others? When I have thoughts of jealousy, do I thank God for the gifts He has given them and given me? When I desire the goods of others, do I accept what the Lord has given me, trusting in His Divine Providence will take care of all my needs? When others insult or ridicule me, do I turn the other cheek and ask God to bless them? When it seems as though no one loves me or cares about me and doesn't stand up for me, will I hide myself in the Heart of Jesus, knowing He loves me infinitely and cares about my every need?

Application 2: Moral Courage

Moral Courage (Fortitude) is a cardinal virtue which enables us to endure any hardship or persecution, rather than abandon our duty to God, ourselves and our neighbor.

The Catechism of the Catholic Church tells us, "Fortitude (courage) is the moral virtue that ensures firmness in difficulties and constancy in the pursuit of the good. It strengthens the resolve to resist temptations and to overcome obstacles in the moral life. The virtue of fortitude enables one to conquer fear, even fear of death, and to face trials and persecutions. It disposes one even to renounce and sacrifice his life in defense of a just cause. 'The Lord is my strength and my song.' Jesus said, 'In the world you have tribulation; but be of good cheer, I have overcome the world.'" (CCC #1808)

Story 1: Battle of Muret

On September 12, 1213, about five years after St. Dominic was given the Rosary, Catholic forces with St. Dominic were set to fight the Albigensians in Muret, a small village in France.

The Albigensians wanted to take over France further spreading their heretical beliefs. Catholics were determined to fight for Christ. Unfortunately, Catholic reinforcements failed and they had only 1500 men, while their foe had 30,000. Confident of their hopeful success, the Albigensians spent the night before the battle celebrating in drunkenness. The Catholics spent their night praying the Rosary; and were focused on the Mass and the Sacrament of Reconciliation. St. Dominic went to a church in Muret to pray the Rosary, while they went into battle. Catholics rushed upon the hungover Albigensians, routing the enemy army and declaring a victory for Christ and Our Lady. After the battle, every Catholic in the area attributed the victory to the Rosary.

Story 2: Battle of Vienna, Feast of the Holy Name of Mary

The battle of Vienna in 1683 was the result of the Rosary and the reason for the establishment of the feast of the Holy Name of Mary.

Pope Innocent XI brokered an alliance between the Holy Roman Empire and the Kingdom of Poland, which was also menaced by the Mohammedans. Kara Mustapha, the leader of the army, was overly confident of victory and believed his army would capture not only Vienna but even Rome, where he bragged that he would stable his horses in St. Peter's Basilica.

The Ottoman army crossed the frontier in late June 1683, rampaging and pillaging as they marched.

When it became known that between 100,000 to 300,000 Turks were coming to the capital of Vienna, Pope Innocent ordered Rosaries be recited in the religious houses and churches of Rome. Prayers of supplication were offered throughout the Empire. Special devotions were held at the Capuchin Church in Vienna to Our Lady Help of Christians.

Jan Sobieski, the King of Poland and a devout Catholic raised a relief army. He left Warsaw with an army of 20,000 men, mostly cavalry, on the way to Cracow, where the rest of his troops were ordered to assemble. Along the march, Sobieski stopped to pray at the shrine of Our Lady of Czestochowa. Entrusting the success of his military efforts to the intercession of the Blessed Mother, he began his army's march to Vienna on the Solemnity of the Assumption of the Blessed Virgin Mary, August 15, 1683.

The Polish army hit the numerically superior Turkish force with their surprise attack so hard, the Turks panicked. They did not simply withdraw from the walls of Vienna, they fled. The battle began on September 11 and was over by September 12.

As a result, the pope established the Feast of the Most Holy Name of Mary on September 12, first celebrated in Spain in the sixteenth century and then as a universal memorial for the Church in thanksgiving for the victory at Vienna.

Story 3: St. Bernadette

"Saint Bernadette was persistent in her efforts to return to the grotto even though her parents tried to dissuade her from going there. Bernadette endured relentless interrogations by town elders and the local police who wanted to determine if the visions were a hoax or if she was unbalanced. When Bernadette was instructed by the bishop and local authorities not to return to the grotto, she had the courage to return to the area and stand across the river from the grotto to say her goodbyes to the Blessed Virgin. Bernadette had the fortitude to endure repeated interviews with senior priests at the convent. She displayed remarkable patience even though these interviews were exhausting in her state of failing health. After she left Lourdes, Bernadette endured, with great love, the misunderstanding shown to her regarding the apparitions from Mary."[81]

Story 4: St. Rita of Cascia & the Wound on Her Forehead

Saint Rita was born Margherita Lotti in Roccaporena, Italy in 1381. The day after her baptism, Rita was surrounded by a swarm of white bees, which went in and out of her infant mouth without hurting her. Rather than being alarmed, her family believed she was marked to be virtuous and devoted to God. After her husband and two adult sons died, she became a religious sister. While at the monastery, Rita performed her duties faithfully and received the sacraments frequently. Rita had a great devotion to the Passion of Christ, and one day, when she was sixty-years-old, she asked, "Please let me suffer like you, Divine Savior." After her request, a wound appeared on her forehead, as if a thorn from Christ's crown had pierced her. It left a deep wound, which did not heal, and it caused her to suffer until the day she died. It is said that as she neared the end of her life, Rita was bedridden from tuberculosis and she passed away four months later, on May 22, 1457. Following her death, she was buried at the Basilica of Cascia, and was later discovered to be incorrupt. Her body can be found today in the Saint Rita shrine at Cascia.

Rhoda Wise (1888 – 1948) is the only known visionary, who Jesus appeared asking her to tell the people to pray the Rosary daily and pray it for the conversion of Russia.

The Catholic Diocese of Youngstown website states, "Rhoda Wise was a woman of faith who became interested in Catholicism and the Rosary during a prolonged hospital stay for multiple injuries and cancer. Bishop McFadden confirmed her in Mercy Hospital, Canton, Ohio in March 1939. Her devotion to the Rosary, the Sacred Heart, and the Little Flower continues to inspire thousands."[82]

In the years between Rhoda's cure and her death, she saw Our Lord and St. Therese twenty times. She suffered the visible stigmata every First Friday from 12:00 pm to 3:00 pm for 2 ½ years in 1942 through 1945. Thereafter, she suffered invisible wounds until her death. Our Lord appeared to her the last time on June 28, 1948, just ten days before her death and told her: "Tell the people not nearly enough of them are saying the daily Rosary; they must say the Rosary for the conversion of Russia..." At this time Jesus showed her His Sacred Heart, His bleeding Heart. Declared a servant of God, Rhoda's cause for her canonization has been opened by the Diocese of Youngstown, Ohio.

Jesus Carries His Cross

Fruit of the Mystery: Patience, Self-denial

"So they took Jesus, and He went out, bearing His cross, to a place called the Place of a Skull, which is called in Hebrew, Golgotha." (John 19:17)

When Jesus was an infant, Simeon had prophesied He would be "a sign spoken against" a sign of contradiction. The sign is the Cross. Our Lord told His disciples, they too will need to carry their own cross, lest they can't be one of His disciples, "Whoever does not bear his own cross and come after me, cannot be my disciple." (Luke 14:27). He predicted His crucifixion in a vague way, "...and I, when I am lifted from the earth, will draw all men to myself." (John 12:32) And He explicitly mentioned to His Apostles His Crucifixion before it would happen, "Behold, we are going up to Jerusalem; and the Son of man will be delivered to the chief priests and scribes, and they will condemn Him to death, and deliver Him to the Gentiles to be mocked and scourged and crucified, and He will be raised on the third day." (Matthew 20:18-19)

The place of crucifixion is called the "place of the skull" or Calvary. It got its nickname because the land in the area was shaped like a skull. During the event of the Crucifixion, there were about two million people in and around the city because it was a Jewish Passover feast. Crowds were winding through the dark, narrow streets and gathering in large groups around the place of execution.

"The upright part of the Cross was probably from eight to ten feet long, and to it the traverse part, probably about six feet long, was fastened."[83] After being condemned by Pilate, Jesus, by His own free will took up His Cross. He was not forced, but willingly embraced and carried the Cross for the love of us. "See the love and reverence with which He embraces it—perhaps even kneels to receive it—for He looked beyond the pain, and beheld in the Cross the adorable will of His Father, the instrument of salvation and all our blessings."[84]

"We read St. Andrew (the apostle) that he greeted his cross from afar with the words of heartfelt love and longing: "O holy Cross! O blessed Cross! That will take me to my Master!"[85]

"Contemplate Jesus as He is led forth. The soldiers and officials assemble, the two malefactors (thieves) are led out, and the crosses brought forth. Criminals were executed by day and in public, and had to drag their crosses to the place of execution themselves, in order to increase their pain and disgrace."[86]

"See our dear Lord as He starts on His last and bitterest journey—from the citadel Antonia to the place of execution outside the city. The road is several hundred paces long. A roman centurion rides in front, then followed by the condemned men, each accompanied by four soldiers; after these come the executioners and their assistants with the instruments of death and the title to be hung on the poles; in the rear and on either side of the procession walk countless throngs of people, high and low, especially the Pharisees—both strangers and those of the city."[87]

"Condemned as a false prophet and blasphemer. Crowds of people are awaiting Him. Hear the jeers that reach Him from doors, windows and roofs. The way was long, uneven, and steep too in parts and He falls three times."[88]

It can be disheartening to fall when we carry our cross. We can become discouraged, but discouragement comes from pride. We can be tempted to give up, especially if we repeatedly fall into sin. But, God permits this to happen, that we may all the more turn to Him trusting in His infinite mercy and the fall will help us to grow in humility and avoid pride. We carry our cross well, when we carry it for the love of Jesus.

When He falls, Our Divine Lord is unable to catch Himself, and so His face lands on the stone street causing the Cross to force the Crown of Thorns further into His skull. The Shroud of Turin shows His nose was broken. Was it from a fall or from a soldier who struck Him?

He journeys through the streets carrying His Cross and meeting people along the way including His Mother, Simon the Cyrene, Veronica, and the weeping women.

In what is now known as the fourth station of the cross, Jesus and His Mother meet. Perhaps John was with Mary and guided Her to meet Jesus along the way. Imagine the pain felt in Mary's Heart to see Her Son so abused, hardly able to walk, exhausted, blood over His entire body and running down His face. Our Lord knew their meeting would cause His Mother even more pain, but He didn't prevent it. It was a consolation for Him to see Her, and for Her to see Him, but a deep pain tore through each of their hearts. Oh, how much anguish to look into each other's eyes filled with sorrow. For Jesus to see tears running down Her cheeks, it would have added indescribable sorrow. See them kneel on the stone pavement facing each other, both thinking of the other, before themselves. They teach us to think of others first and to forget our own sufferings for love of others.

Our Lord takes several of His fingers and wipes the tear filled face of His Mother, and then to show His immense love, He kisses His wetted fingers caused by Her tears of sorrow.

When She saw His face, She could hardly recognize it was Him and the words of Isaiah may have come to mind, "As many were astonished at Him—His appearance was so marred, beyond human semblance…" (Isaiah 52:14) But, She recognized His tunic and beneath it was the seamless garment He was wearing. She knitted the garments for Him as a Child and over the years, they miraculously never tore and grew in length to continue to fit Him, according to a pious tradition. The seamless garment was symbolic of priestly robes. The soldiers would not tear it because it was forbidden to tear a priest's robe.

"The sweat and blood in the Garden, which trickled down to the ground, must have saturated His garments. Think how hard and stiff they would have become when dry, what agony they would occasion Him after the scourging and along the Way of the Cross (Via Crucis) or Way of Sorrows (Via Dolorosa), as they rubbed against the raw wounds when they were dragged off, and when He fell. What He suffers now as they are again torn off!"[89]

Simon the Cyrene returning from the country happened to be there when Jesus was carrying His Cross. Because the soldiers noticed the weakness and exhaustion of Jesus, and feared He would die on the way to Calvary, and not be able to carry it Himself, they forced him to help Jesus carry His Cross and at first He was repelled by it. He didn't want to be associated with a criminal. Why should he help carry a condemned man's cross? People will think he is guilty of some crime.

But, as he helped Jesus carry His Cross, he saw His appreciation and noticed how Our Lord was trying to take on the burden Himself. He began to pity Jesus and his heart melted as he watched how cruel He was treated by the soldiers and scoffed by the crowds. Now, he wants to help Our Savior and he begins to become angry at how others are treating Jesus. He learns that to help others when someone is going through terrible suffering is rewarding because the love within us grows and even if it causes us more pain, we know it's the right thing to do. Later, Simon must have shared with others, the day he helped Jesus carry His Cross, was the day he became one of His disciples and would be willing to suffer for Him and even die for Him, if necessary.

Not much later, Jesus met Veronica, also known as Bernice. Her love and pity moved her to be courageous. She pushed her way through the crowd and handed Our Lord her veil to wipe His adorable Face. She didn't know any other way of helping Jesus. She saw the blood and sweat that had flowed down from His Head and from the Crown of Thorns, and how it dripped into His eyes and wanted to relieve Him of that agony. He took her veil, wiped His face with it, and gave it back to her. Then after He departed carrying the Cross and when she reached her home, she noticed the face of Jesus imprinted on her veil. She dropped to her knees and began to weep for joy. Her name Veronica means "true icon" Vere- means "true" and "icon." By consoling Jesus, He consoles her and gives her a treasure that would later be preserved over the centuries and venerated at St. Peter's Basilica every year on the Fifth Sunday of Lent.

Application 1: Embrace Sufferings, Self-Denial, The Power of Suffering

By hiding the pain He suffered on His shoulder, Jesus wanted to teach us to not complain about our sufferings, to not reveal them unnecessarily to others. By keeping them to ourselves, we gain great merit. When we share our sufferings with others, we lose merit and risk losing the graces we obtain for suffering for Jesus and for others.

We learn by the Way of Cross to embrace our sufferings, to unite them to the sufferings of Jesus and to be willing to suffer for others. We learn that if we carry our crosses, and follow Jesus, we are one of His disciples. We deny ourselves, meaning to choose to not do what we want, but rather to do what God wants and what others want. We place ourselves last, deny our sinful inclinations, and our non-sinful pleasures. To deny pleasures, candy, desert, watching television, etc. increases our spiritual strength to overcome sinful pleasures.

At our first moment of pain and suffering, most everyone has an urge to run from it. We are repelled by it. We want the easy way and least painful way. But, we must be willing to suffer in patience. Euthanasia and suicide can be the result of wanting to avoid suffering and escape it, rather than embrace it. And some families can even discontinue hand feeding or tube feeding of a loved one, because they want to run away from watching their loved one suffer and they see suffering as a waste, rather than the beauty and glory of it.

A reporter once asked St. Maximilian Kolbe from where came all the power behind his successful printing press for his magazine "Knight of the Immaculata", which had a monthly circulation of nearly a million. In response, he took the reporter down a long sidewalk and opened the door of a large building. There lying on beds were sick Friars and he pointed to them, and said, "This is where the power comes behind our success. They are offering up their sufferings to the Lord for our apostolate."

Application 2: To be Patient is to be Willing to Suffer for Others

The word patience has as its root "patient." A patient is one who suffers in a hospital. A patient can either suffer well or not. If we suffer well, we are embracing the pain of our cross. Failure to embrace our sufferings causes us to become impatient. We can't stand suffering and don't want to wait until it subsides, that is, if it will subside. An impatient person suffers from undue anger towards others, or themselves or even towards God.

If we consciously accept our sufferings, impatience will naturally fall away. The Virgin Mary asked the three children of Fatima to bear all their sufferings that God would send them. Mary said, "Will you offer yourselves to God and bear all the sufferings he sends you? In atonement for all the sins that offend him? And for the conversion of sinners? The children said, "We will." Mary said, "Then you will have a great deal to suffer, but the grace of God will be with you and will strengthen you."

If we treat every suffering, as though God sent it to us, then we will have peace in our heart. There is God's permitting will and God's ordaining will. Either way, if we view every

238

suffering, as though it comes from God, we will not lose hope, and in fact, will grow in holiness by seeing God's hand in everything we do in our daily life.

God permits sufferings to draw us closer to Him. He uses our sufferings to atone for our own sins and the sins of others. And when our sufferings are united to the sufferings of Jesus on the Cross, they will bring about the conversion of sinners, so they, and we, won't go to hell, but rather enjoy heaven forever with Jesus.

The Virgin Mary also told the children of Fatima, "Make sacrifices for sinners, and say often, especially while making a sacrifice: 'O Jesus, this is for love of thee, for the conversion of sinners, and in reparation for offenses committed against the Immaculate Heart of Mary.'" When we deny ourselves and carry our crosses, we sacrifice ourselves for love of Jesus, for the conversion of sinners and to console the Immaculate Heart of Mary.

Saint Faustina in her diary (Diary #1804), wrote, "If the angels were capable of envy, they would envy us for two things: one is the receiving of Holy Communion, and the other is suffering." And she said, "I united my sufferings with the sufferings of Jesus and offered them for myself and for the conversion of souls who do not trust in God..." (Diary #323)

We should cherish our crosses because through them we gain eternal life. As St. Rose of Lima said, "Apart from the cross there is no other ladder by which we may get to heaven."

"Many, says St. Alphonsus Liguori, love Jesus, as long as the breeze of heavenly consolation refreshes them; but if the clouds of diversity lower, if for their trial, Christ, our dear Lord, withdraws His sensible presence from them, they are sorely tempted to give up prayer, neglect self-denial, sink into despondency and tepidity, and finally turn for comfort to creatures and perishable things. Such souls love themselves more than Jesus Christ. Those who truly love Our Lord are faithful in darkness and trial. Faith tells us that Jesus is sovereignly amiable and good when He afflicts as when He consoles. Oh, how dear to the Heart of Jesus is the soul who suffers with loving submission! Precious, beyond all graces, is the grace to suffer and to love!"[90]

St. Teresa of Avila said, "I would always choose the path of suffering, if only to imitate Our Lord Jesus Christ, if there were no other gain. He who shall courageously present himself to drink our Savior's chalice will never fail in persecutions. I would willingly endure alone all the sufferings of this world to be raised to a higher degree in heaven and to possess the smallest increase of the knowledge of God's greatness. In order to bear our afflictions with patience it is very useful to read the lives of the saints who endured great torments for Jesus Christ."

St Padre Pio said, "I do not love suffering itself; I ask it of God because I desire its fruits: it gives glory to God, saves my brothers in exile, and frees souls from the fires of purgatory. God neither wants, nor is able, to save and sanctify us without the Cross. The more He calls a soul to Himself, the more He sanctifies it by means of the Cross. By suffering we are able to give something to God. The gift of pain, of suffering is a big thing and cannot be accomplished in Paradise. Lean on the Cross as Mary did. She was as if paralyzed before Her crucified Son, but was not abandoned by Him."

St. Louis de Montfort said, "To suffer is not enough: the evil one and the world have their martyrs. We must suffer and carry our cross in the footsteps of Christ. Take advantage of little sufferings even more than great ones. God considers not so much what we suffer as how we suffer… Turn everything as the grocer does in his shop."

St. Margaret Mary said, "The Heart of Jesus is closer to you when you suffer than when you are full of joy."

St. Anthony Mary Claret said, "To suffer contempt in silence is the key to Jesus' Heart and the means of uniting with Him."

Saint Madeleine Sophie Barat said, "Let us go to the foot of the Cross, and there complain—if we have the courage."

Saint John Vianney said, "You must either suffer in this life or give up the hope of seeing God in heaven. Sufferings and persecutions are of the greatest avail to us, because we can find therein a very efficient means to make atonement for our sins, since we are bound to suffer for them either in this world or in the next."

Saint John Bosco said, "Accept afflictions with patience. Silently endure cold and heat, wind and rain, fatigue and all other discomforts that God may deign to send to you."

Let us carry our crosses manfully, keeping our eyes on Jesus, embrace them with love, uniting our sufferings of Jesus on the Cross and making atonement for our sins and the sins of others, and in this way, we will not complain, but will see them as precious gems to help us and others obtain heaven.

Story 1: Jesus' Greatest Suffering – The Wound in His Shoulder

As Jesus carried His Cross, unbeknownst to anyone, the pain in His shoulder would be His greatest. It is believed by many faithful Catholics, Saint Bernard of Clairvaux prayed and asked Christ what was His greatest unknown suffering, and what wound suffered in His Passion was most painful. Christ replied to him: "I had on My Shoulder while I bore My Cross on the Way of Sorrows, a grievous Wound which was more painful than the others, and which is not recorded by men." Jesus asked that Saint Bernard and other members of the faithful keep a devotion to his shoulder wound, and that those who do, will receive God's grace. Our Divine Lord said to Saint Bernard, "Honor this Wound with thy devotion, and I will grant thee whatsoever thou dost ask through its virtue and merit. And in regard to all those who shall venerate this Wound, I will remit to them all their venial sins, and will no longer remember their mortal sins."

241

Story 2: Peter Has Apparition of Jesus Carrying His Cross to Rome

Legend has it that as St. Peter fled Rome to escape persecution under the Emperor Nero, he encountered Jesus along the way, bearing the cross. Peter asked Jesus "Quo vadis, Domine?" or "Where are you going, Lord?" When Jesus answered, "To be crucified again", Peter understood that he must return to Rome to follow in the footsteps of his Savior. He returned, was captured, and then was crucified upside down on Vatican hill because he felt unworthy to be crucified in the same manner of Jesus.

Apparition: Our Lady of Betania (Venezuela)

The Virgin Mary manifested Herself under the title, "Mary, Virgin and Mother Reconciler of all people and nations" to Maria Esperanza.

Throughout her life, Maria had a desire to be a nun, and lived with Franciscan Sisters. However, on October 3 in 1954, two days after her feast day, at the chapel of the convent, Saint Therese of The Child Jesus appeared to Maria Esperanza. She heard the Sacred Heart of Jesus tell her, "Your mission shall not be becoming a nun. You will sanctify yourself in the world as a spouse and family mother spreading my message."

A few days later, on October 7, 1954, (feast day Our Lady of the Rosary), the Virgin Mary gave her the following message, "In addition to daily Communion, fasting, prayer, and penance you must remain in deep reclusion, for I shall come again on October 12th (Feast day of Our Lady of the Pillar of Zaragoza, Spain) so you may prepare your heart to be a spiritual mother of souls, and so I may seal it as such forever. Besides, you shall be the mother of seven children: Six roses and a bud."

The Servant of God, Maria Esperanza once said, "I wish for all of you to get together and pray the Holy Rosary with your family, because then you will see a complete change...Your family will receive special graces, infinite graces from heaven with the kindness of an immense, omnipotent God." She said that, "the Blessed Mother wishes to turn each family that prays together into a paradise." Maria Esperanza said families "should get together at home and pray the holy Rosary, and everyone should sit at table and share bread."

Crucifixion of Jesus

Fruit of the Mystery: Perseverance, Forgiveness, Salvation

"And when they came to a place called Golgotha (which means Place of the Skull), they gave Jesus wine to drink mixed with gall. But when he had tasted it, he refused to drink. After they had crucified him, they divided his garments by casting lots, then they sat down and kept watch over him there. And they placed over his head the written charge against him: This is Jesus, the King of the Jews. Two revolutionaries were crucified with him, one on his right and the other on his left. Those passing by reviled him, shaking their heads and saying, "You who would destroy the temple and rebuild it in three days, save yourself, if you are the Son of God, and come down from the cross!" Likewise the chief priests with the scribes and elders mocked him and said, "He saved others; he cannot save himself. So he is the King of Israel! Let him come down from the cross now, and we will believe in Him. He trusted in God; let him deliver him now if he wants him. For he said, 'I am the Son of God.'" (Matthew 27:33-43)

"The ascent to Mount Calvary was both rough and steep. Soldiers are stationed at different parts of the mount to keep order. See the immense multitude come to witness the Crucifixion. See our dear Lord as He reaches the hill of Calvary—pale, blood-stained, and completely exhausted. Whilst the crosses were pieced together and holes dug to receive them, Our Lord had been confined in the grotto on the north side. The site is still shown in the Church of the Holy Sepulchre."[91]

"Note that Jesus will not drink the wine mixed with myrrh or gall, which was customary to give the condemned, in order to deaden their pain. See His Sacred Body as these men drag off His garments, thus scourging Him a second time, since all the gashes, to which His clothes adhered, were torn open afresh. It is in expiation for our vanity and self-indulgence that Jesus would have His vesture during the whole of His Passion a source of torture for Him!"[92]

"The soldiers now formed a circle around the place of crucifixion, and the executioners entered the ring. Contemplate our dear Jesus. At the bidding of the executioner, Jesus lies down upon the Cross and stretches out His arms. They bind the upper part of the body to the stem of the Cross. One executioner holds His right hand, another places the rough, three-sided nail, filed to a sharp point, in the palm, and drives it with powerful blows, through the tendons in the hollow of the hand and into the hole made for it in the cross. A tremor of exquisite pain passes through our Lord's limbs, the blood spurts up and around about, and the fingers contract convulsively round the nail, the limbs contract, the knees are drawn up, the left hand will not reach the hole prepared for it. They draw a noose around the wrist to stretch the arm till the sinews give way and the joints are dislocated. The blow nails it fast, the chest heaves and the muscles crack. The feet are violently pulled down, and with a spitting crackling sound the nail is driven through the instep into the hole in the place for the feet."[93]

The Cross is hoisted up while the end is dropped into the hole dug in the ground and there is such a forced drop, the onlookers gasp to see the body hanging from the nails.

"Can we not realize the horror and anguish of Our Lord's Blessed Mother, St. John, Magdalene and the holy women, who were close by and heard the strokes of the hammer and the groans of the innocent victim?"[94]

After He had been stripped of His garments, and nailed to the wood of the Cross, Jesus cried out, "Father, forgive them for they know not what they do!" Can you imagine looking down from the Cross and seeing those mocking you? They cried out, "If you are the Son of God, come down from the Cross." Yet, with great love Jesus forgave them, and forgave us, who nailed Him to the tree by our sins. Not only did He forgive our sins, but He also made an excuse. He said, "for they know not what they do."

One of the thieves crucified next to Jesus said, "If you are the Son of God, save yourself and us." But the good thief said, "Lord remember me, when you come into Your kingdom." Jesus responded, "Today, you will be with me in paradise." Today, we pray that when we sin, we too will admit our guilt like the good thief, and with trust, ask Jesus if we may enter His kingdom.

Jesus then said, "My God, my God, why have you forsaken me!" These words came from the depth of Our Lord's heart. Our Lord said these words for three reasons.

The first reason-- was to reveal the mystery of His humanity, which felt abandoned by His Father. Yet, He trusted. He knew His Father was with Him.

The second reason was to give us courage, when we too feel abandoned by God. But, it is only a feeling and not true. God is always with us. He will never leave us alone.

The third reason, why Jesus said, "My God, my God, why have you forsaken me!" caused the Jews to be struck with terror. The Jews prayed the psalms every day. They knew He was quoting the first words from Psalm 22, referring to the suffering Messiah. They knew the rest of the psalm, which said, "I am a worm, not a man, the scorn of men, despised by the people. All who scoff at me; they mock me with parted lips, they wag their heads: "He relied on the Lord; let Him deliver Him, let Him rescue Him, if He Loves them." "My throat is dried up like baked clay, my tongue clings to my mouth. Indeed many dogs surround me, a pack of evildoers closes in upon me; they have pierced my hands and feet. I can count all my bones. They gloat over me; they divide my garments among them, and for my vesture they cast lots."

Can you imagine, being a Jew, knowing this psalm, and gazing upon Jesus, who is fulfilling it. They would have said to themselves, "We are looking at Him, whose hands and feet are pierced. Did we not wag our heads, scoff at Him, and mock Him? Did we not witness the soldiers cast lots for His clothes? O God, Creator the universe, what have we done, are we killing your Son, He who is the Messiah?

From the Cross, Jesus cried out, "I thirst." Yes, He thirsted, because His mouth was parched, for loss of blood. His body was burning from the heat. But, He had a deeper spiritual reason, to say, "I thirst." He thirsts for our love. He thirsts for our souls, that we may come to Him in this life, and be with Him forever in paradise.

How difficult it must have been for Our Lord to look down from the Cross and see the tear filled eyes of His Mother, and see John, the beloved, holding Her close to him. Both were weeping.

And if you were His Mother, can you imagine gazing upon your Son, as He hung from the tree. The same hands and feet the mother kissed when He was an infant are now nailed and bleeding. The same face She kissed every night before going to bed, is dripping blood from the crown of thorns.

When the Mother looked at Her Son, and the Son looked at His Mother, Jesus said, "Woman, behold thy son." And to John, "Behold thy mother." He knew He was about to take His last breath, and after He gave us His very body and blood on the Cross, He had one more gift, the gift of His Mother. When John took Mary into His home, we received our spiritual mother, who would pray for us, and look after us, to lead us to Her Son.

Then Jesus cried out, "Father, into Your hands, I commend My spirit." Moments before His death, He entrusted Himself and His spirit to the Father because He wanted to give us an example of trusting the Father in our agony, despite our intense suffering and feeling of abandonment.

When Jesus said, "It is consummated", He bowed his head and died. With these words, Our Lord accomplished the task He came upon earth. The primary reason why He came down from heaven in the womb of Mary, to take upon human nature, had arrived. His crucifixion, would conquer, sin, death, and the devil. By His death on the Cross, He opened for us the gates of paradise, while at the same time revealed God's infinite love for us.

When the body of Jesus was taken from the Cross, it was placed in the arms of His Mother. The Child She held in Her arms, and rocked as a baby, is returned on Her lap, dead, bloodied, bruised, and marked with wounds all over. The hands that blessed the multitudes, now have holes in them, as a sign of our ingratitude.

Joseph of Arimathea brought a shroud and Mary helped wrap Her Son in it, reminding Her of the first time She wrapped His tiny body in swaddling clothes and laid Him in a manger. Now He is not placed in a feeding trough, but laid on a cold slab and lifeless.

The Church of the Holy Sepulcher houses Mount Calvary and also the tomb where Jesus rose from the dead. There is an altar directly above the spot where it is believed the Cross of Jesus was planted. One can reach down the hole and touch the rock, where the Lord's blood dripped from the Cross into the ground.

Application 1: Cross as a Means of Holiness & Proclaiming it's Power

Have you ever wanted to go to Calvary, but could not afford to go? You can go, and it's free. All you need to do is attend the nearest Catholic Church and attend Mass there.

Every Mass is the re-presentation of Calvary, where the Crucifixion event in an unbloody manner is re-presented. The truth is, at every Holy Sacrifice of the Mass, you are at Calvary.

249

We receive the same graces, as all who were there over 2000 years ago. When you are at Mass, during the consecration (the moment when the bread and wine are changed into the body and blood of Jesus), imagine before your eyes, Jesus hanging from the Cross above the altar and when you receive Holy Communion, you are receiving the true resurrected body of Christ, the whole and entire person of Jesus.

Most Catholic churches have Stations of the Cross on their walls and during Lent most parishes will make the Way of the Cross together on Fridays. However, less and less are coming to make the Stations. Why? Mostly because of the god of sports, which occurs Friday evenings. Fewer and fewer are thinking about the horrific events associated with the Passion of Jesus.

Some Stations of the Cross in churches are truly weird looking. Some have at each station only the head of Jesus in different positions. Others look ghoulish and the characters don't even look like people. How bizarre! Truly a work of the devil to hide the gruesome sufferings of Jesus, for by doing so, one cannot see how much we are loved.

A good set of stations will help all who gaze upon them love Our Divine Savior more by seeing the pain and suffering He went through for love of us.

Some pious Catholics will daily make the "short" Way of the Cross. They begin by saying, "We adore thee, O Christ and we bless thee. Because by thy Holy Cross, thou hast redeemed the world." And then when gazing up at the Station, the person will pray one Hail Mary, and conclude the station saying, "Lord Jesus Crucified, Have Mercy on us!"

St. Helena (248 to 330) did excavations to try to find the true Cross of Jesus and three crosses were discovered where He was crucified. Not knowing which of three was the True Cross, they touched each cross to a sick man, and the last cross caused his immediate healing. Still in order to be certain it was the True Cross, a man, who had just died, and was buried, was then dug up (unearthed). His dead body was then touched to the same third cross and he came back to life.

Other items were also found including the wooden title that hung above Jesus' Head, that read, "Jesus of Nazareth. The King of the Jews" in three languages. Nails were also discovered by St. Helena. One nail is now located in the Basilica of the Holy Cross in Jerusalem located in Rome. A large remaining piece of wood from the true Cross and the Title are located in the Basilica of the Holy Cross in Jerusalem in Rome as well.

Relics of the True Cross are found in many churches. Some have doubts if all are relics of the true Cross, but unknowingly they may quote John Calvin, a Protestant reformer who said, "If all the pieces that could be found were collected together, they would make a big ship-load."

Why presume the worst. It seems better to believe, rather than have the same doubt of a non-Catholic responsible for the loss of faith in many doctrines of the Holy Catholic Church. And besides that, the piece of wood in the reliquary is ordinarily very small.

Today, many Catholic schools, universities, colleges, hospitals, nursing homes, etc... Even religious communities no longer display crucifixes, or if they do, they are either hidden or they use the resurrected Christ on the Cross instead. Has anyone ever heard of Jesus rising from the dead off of a Cross? Rather than appease non-Catholics, it confuses them, as they wonder what kind of ugly cross Catholics now using. They expect us to use real crucifixes and not crosses with the risen Jesus they would never use.

Those who run these organizations desire to make their Catholic institution more non-Catholic friendly, by offending Catholics and denying their own faith. Our Lord said, "Everyone who acknowledges me before others I will acknowledge before my heavenly Father. But whoever denies me before others, I will deny before my heavenly Father." (Matthew 10:32-33)

St. Paul helps us to see the importance of loving the Cross of Jesus and being conformed to it. He said, "May I never boast except in the cross of our Lord Jesus Christ, through which the world has been crucified to me, and I to the world." (Galatians 6:14)

"In His (God's) desire that humanity should know the depravity of sin and the depths of God's love He chose to die on the cross. Displaying a crucifix does not in any way deny the Resurrection of Jesus. After all, do faith communities that display only a cross want to downplay the sufferings of Jesus? Of course not, it is just a different preference of emphasis. In the Catholic Church the crucifix has been the traditional sign and statement of our faith in God's love and mercy. It reminds us that Jesus never promised His followers an easy life (Matt. 16:24) but that if we join our sufferings to His, we too we ultimately triumph as He did."[95]

Meditating on the Crucifixion of Jesus, one will grow in sorrow for their sins, and will strive harder to overcome them. They will grow in love of Jesus, by seeing the depths of His love. During times of suffering, thinking about the crucifixion of Jesus gives us hope, that if Jesus can endure suffering, we can too. The devil flees at the sight of a crucifix, because through the Cross, he was defeated. We will grow in deeper love of our neighbor by our willingness to suffer for others, as Jesus suffered for us. "There is no greater love than this, to lay down one's life for one's friends."(John 15:13)

Once when St. Thomas Aquinas asked his friend St. Bonaventure from whence he drew his great learning, St. Bonaventure pointed to the Crucifix.

St. Thomas Aquinas explains how the cross exemplifies every virtue.

"Why did the Son of God have to suffer for us? There was a great need, and it can be considered in

252

a twofold way: in the first place, as a remedy for sin, and secondly, as an example of how to act.

It is a remedy, for, in the face of all the evils which we incur on account of our sins, we have found relief through the passion of Christ. Yet, it is no less an example, for the passion of Christ completely suffices to fashion our lives. Whoever wishes to live perfectly should do nothing but disdain what Christ disdained on the cross and desire what He desired, for the cross exemplifies every virtue.

If you seek the example of love: Greater love than this no man has, than to lay down his life for his friends. Such a man was Christ on the cross. And if He gave His life for us, then it should not be difficult to bear whatever hardships arise for His sake.

If you seek patience, you will find no better example than the cross. Great patience occurs in two ways: either when one patiently suffers much, or when one suffers things which one is able to avoid and yet does not avoid. Christ endured much on the cross, and did so patiently, because when He suffered He did not threaten; He was led like a sheep to the slaughter and He did not open His mouth. Therefore Christ's patience on the cross was great. In patience let us run for the prize set before us, looking upon Jesus, the author and perfecter of our faith who, for the joy set before him, bore His cross and despised the shame.

If you seek an example of humility, look upon the crucified one, for God wished to be judged by Pontius Pilate and to die.

If you seek an example of obedience, follow Him who became obedient to the Father even unto death. For just as by the disobedience of one man, namely, Adam, many were made sinners, so by the obedience of one man, many were made righteous.

If you seek an example of despising earthly things, follow Him who is the King of kings and the Lord of lords, in whom are hidden all the treasures of wisdom and knowledge. Upon the cross He was stripped, mocked, spat upon, struck, crowned with thorns, and given only vinegar and gall to drink.

Do not be attached, therefore, to clothing and riches, because they divided my garments among themselves. Nor to honors, for He experienced harsh words and scourgings. Nor to greatness of rank, for weaving a crown of thorns they placed it on my head. Nor to anything delightful, for in my thirst they gave me vinegar to drink."[96]

The prophet Zechariah predicted the Messiah would be pierced, "I will pour out on the house of David and on the inhabitants of Jerusalem a spirit of mercy and supplication, so that when they look on Him whom they have thrust through, they will mourn for Him as one mourns for an only child, and they will grieve for Him as one grieves over a firstborn." (Zechariah 12:10)

When gazing upon the wounds of Jesus in His hands, feet and side it reminds us of our redemption and moves our hearts to love. St. Bonaventure said, "The wounds of Jesus are arrows, that wound the hardest hearts, and flames that kindle the coldest souls." Through His wounds and His death, Jesus paid the price to have our sins forgiven and the punishment due to sins washed away, that occurs through Baptism.

254

Through Confession our sins are forgiven, but we need to do penance for them, either in this life or make up for them in the next life in purgatory.

In the history of the Catholic Church, there are mystics who bore the wounds of Christ, including St. Francis of Assisi, St. Rita Cascia, St. Catherine of Sienna, St. Faustina, St. Padre Pio, and servant of God Rhoda Wise. The stigmata is not a punishment for them. But rather a sign of their intimate love and union with Jesus. They had a desire to share in His sufferings, to make reparation for their own sins and the sins of others, for the conversion of sinners and to show their love of Jesus, by sharing His pain.

Application 2: Forgiveness

Our Lord's Passion helps us to forgive. It's not true to say, "I forgive, if I forget". Nobody can choose to forget anything. Our mind is not like a computer, such that, if we hit delete, we won't remember an event in our life anymore.

We can forgive, but still have emotions and feelings from being hurt by others. It is our emotions that also need to be healed. And we can ask Jesus in prayer to heal our wounded emotions.

It's not true we haven't forgiven, if we continue to have unforgiving thoughts. We can't perfectly control our emotions. Only before the fall could Adam and Eve perfectly control their emotions. The Virgin Mary perfectly controlled Her emotions, because She never suffered from original sin and never sinned.

If someone seriously hurt us, sometimes we need to ask God to help us forgive, by saying a simple prayer like this, "O Jesus, I am having difficulty forgiving. Please Lord help me to forgive." Forgiveness is an act of the will. We can choose to forgive, even if our feelings are saying otherwise.

For example, we can say, "In the name of Jesus, I forgive (name)." And when we make the act of forgiveness, then we have truly forgiven.

However, we may still have feelings of unforgiveness and be reminded of the injury done to us. But eventually, if we keep making acts of forgiveness, and if we pray for the person who hurt us, wanting what is best for them, especially to obtain heaven, then eventually our emotions will catch up to our will. And all that hashing and rehashing of the injury will die down.

Forgiveness does not mean we allow others to keep hurting us. We should protect ourselves from repeated serious injury. For example, if a spouse is seriously verbally abusing us or is physically abusing us, or our children, a separation may be needed.

That doesn't mean we don't keep loving them, praying for them and forgiving them. We are to always forgive injuries, but not allow serious injuries to continue. We may choose to visit with a friend or a priest and ask advice on how to deal with the situation.

We should pray for the person who hurt us, as Jesus said, "Pray for those who persecute you."

On the Cross Jesus taught us to make excuses for others, as He made an excuse for us, when He said, "Father forgive them for they know not what they do." We can make an excuse as to why they did the bad behavior, but not excuse the injustice. For example, if someone lost their temper and yelled at us, in prayer we can say, "Lord forgive them. Perhaps they have a bad headache, or maybe they are mentally ill and can't help their behavior or maybe they had a traumatic event happen in their life and for some reason, I remind them of it." We should desire for them to change their life and that they will go to heaven.

We can't hold grudges, desire to get even or wish evil on them. If we do, then we have unforgiveness. If we keep reminding the person who hurt us, of the offense they committed against us, even if they have asked for forgiveness, then we have not forgiven.

If we hold a grudge or if we choose to not forgive, then God will not forgive our sins. We know this because when Jesus gave us the Lord's Prayer, He said, "forgive us our trespasses, as we forgive those who trespass against us". Forgiveness is therefore conditional. We must forgive, or God will not forgive us. By gazing upon a crucifix or by meditating on the Cross, Jesus will give us the grace to forgive and to love our enemies.

A meditation on the Crucifixion can be very helpful in forgiving, especially if someone won't forgive us or if the person has died, or if we are unable to forgive a living person.

Picture the one to forgive standing next to you. You see the person looking up at Jesus on the Cross. He or she says, "Lord forgive me." Jesus responds, "I forgive you." You look up at Jesus and say, "Lord, forgive my unforgiveness." Jesus responds, "I forgive you." The person, who hurt you, looks at you and says, "Please forgive me." You respond, "I accept your forgiveness and I forgive you." Both of you hug each other as a sign of your reconciliation.

The Virgin Mary stood at the foot of the Cross for three hours watching Her Son suffer, bleed, gasp, and die for us. Our Lord gave His Mother to John, when He said to Mary, "Woman, behold thy son." And to John, "Behold thy mother." Then scripture tells us John took Mary into His home. Mary lived with John, until She was assumed into heaven. John's mother is also believed to have been there at the foot of the Cross.

John's act of taking Mary, as his spiritual mother, represented each of us, taking Mary as our mother. We too are to take Mary into our home and take Her as our Mother.

Every Saturday is dedicated to the Virgin Mary, especially under the title of Our Lady of Sorrows, because Holy Saturday was the only day She was without Her Son. On our part, we desire to console Her Immaculate Heart. Many saints, priests and religious communities fast every Saturday in honor of the Blessed Virgin Mary.

Traditionally, in some parts of the world, Catholics would fast three days a week, Wednesdays, Fridays and Saturdays. Will you honor your spiritual Mother, by fasting, doing penance, and praying an extra Rosary on Saturdays? Some saints prayed *The Little Office of the Blessed Virgin Mary* as well.

St. John Chrysostom saw Mary as the new Eve and Jesus as the new Adam. He said, "The symbols of the fall were a virgin, a tree and death. The virgin was Eve (for she had not yet known man); then there was the tree; and death was Adam's penalty. And again the three tokens of our victory. Instead of Eve there was Mary; instead of the tree of knowledge of good and evil, the wood of the cross; instead of Adam's death, the death of Christ. Do you see how the devil was defeated by the very means he used to conquer? By a tree the devil laid Adam low, and by a tree Christ defeated him. The first tree sent men to the world below, the second called back those who had already gone down. The first tree buried man, already naked and a captive; the second revealed the victor naked to all the world... All of this was the glorious result of the cross. The cross is our trophy raised against demons, our sword against sin, and the sword Christ used to pierce the serpent. The cross is the Father's will, the glory of the only begotten, the joy of the Spirit, the pride of angels, the guarantee of the Church, Paul's boast, the bulwark of the saints, and the light to the entire world."[97]

O Mother of God, as Your child, I desire to be held in your Motherly arms. Today and every day, come into my home. Console me in my affliction, comfort me in my sorrows, intercede for me to Your Son, and tenderly embrace me, Your child, who longs to see your beautiful face. Inspire within me a true devotion to you, whereby I truly give myself self to you—trust you-- and walk with you. Meet me on my road to Calvary. Take me by the hand and help me to walk with Your Son, to the gates of heaven. O sweet Mother, as You stood at the foot of the Cross of your Son, during His greatest suffering and death, stand by me when I'm on my cross. Help me to unite my sufferings with His and console me in my hour of need. Please, O Lady, pray for me, now, and at the hour of my death. Keep my soul safe under your mantle-- and hear and answer my prayers, you who are the Mother of God, and our loving Mother. Amen.

Story 1: Rosary Helps to Forgive the Killer of a Family

In 1994, began the Rwandan Massacre. When the genocide began Immaculee Ilibagiza's father gave her a Rosary and hid her in a non-Catholic pastor's 3 by 4 foot restroom with seven other women for 91 days. While in hiding, 1 million Rwandans were killed, including her parents and all her siblings, except one brother. She became overcome with fear and anger, but turned to the Rosary and began to pray it. After the women were freed, she saw face to face the man who killed her family. She said it was the Rosary, who calmed her anger and gave her the grace to forgive him as he stood before her.

Story 2: The Marble Crucifix That Took a Breath at 3pm

At EWTN, the Eternal Word Television Network, founded by Mother Angelica, in Irondale, Alabama, there was an outdoor shrine called the "Holy Cross Shrine." A large marble crucifix was rescued from a church in Chicago and given to Mother Angelica, who created the shrine for the marble corpus and attached it to the wall behind an altar.

At the 3pm hour in memory of Jesus' death on the Cross, some employees and occasionally a religious brother from the Franciscan Missionaries of the Eternal Word, would go before the Cross and pray the Chaplet of Divine Mercy.

One day, as an employee and brother were praying the chaplet before the Cross, and as both were gazing upon it, suddenly the chest of Jesus, made of marble, rose and fell as though He took a breath. Both were astonished and gave thanks and praise to God for witnessing this seemingly miraculous event.

Jesus wants us to daily remember His suffering and death at the 3 o'clock hour. He told St. Faustina, "At three o'clock, implore My mercy, especially for sinners; and if only for a brief moment, immerse yourself in My Passion, particularly in my abandonment at the moment of agony: This is the hour of great mercy for the whole world. I will allow you to enter into my mortal sorrow. In this hour, I will refuse nothing to the soul that makes a request of Me in the virtue of My Passion. (Diary #1320)

Story 3: Eucharistic Miracle of a Crucifix

In 1255, a priest was celebrating the Holy Mass in the little chapel of Regensburg, Germany, when he was struck by doubt regarding the Real Presence of Jesus in the Eucharist. He, therefore, delayed in elevating the chalice and suddenly heard a light noise come from the altar. From the wooden crucifix above the altar, the Lord slowly extended his arms to the priest, took the chalice from his hands and exhibited the Blessed Sacrament for the adoration of the faithful. The priest, repentant, fell to his knees and begged forgiveness for having doubted. The Lord returned the chalice to him as a sign of pardon. The miraculous crucifix is still preserved to this day and many of the faithful go there every year in pilgrimage.[98]

Story 4: The Pope Who Kissed the Crucifix

The holy Pope St. Pius V, who called Christians to pray the Rosary before the Battle of Lepanto, was accustomed to kiss the feet of the crucifix on leaving or entering his room. One day the feet miraculously moved away from his lips. Sorrow filled his heart, and he made acts of contrition, fearing that he must have committed some secret offense, yet he still could not kiss the feet. It was afterwards discovered that the feet of the Crucifix had been poisoned by an enemy.

Apparition: Our Lady of Akita (Japan)

Our Lady of Akita, Japan, is a Church approved apparition approved by a bishop. On October 13, 1973, the Virgin Mary told Sister Sasagawa saying, "As I told you, if men do not repent and better themselves, the Father will inflict a terrible punishment on all humanity. It will be a punishment greater than the deluge, such as one will never seen before. Fire will fall from the sky and will wipe out a great part of humanity, the good as well as the bad, sparing neither priests nor faithful. The survivors will find themselves so desolate that they will envy the dead. The only arms which will remain for you will be the Rosary and the Sign left by My Son. Each day recite the prayers of the Rosary. With the Rosary, pray for the Pope, the bishops and priests." "The work of the devil will infiltrate even into the Church in such a way that one will see cardinals opposing cardinals, bishops against bishops. The priests who venerate me will be scorned and opposed by their confreres... churches and altars sacked; the Church will be full of those who accept compromises and the demon will press many priests and consecrated souls to leave the service of the Lord. "The demon will be especially implacable against souls consecrated to God. The thought of the loss of so many souls is the cause of my sadness. If sins increase in number and gravity, there will be no longer pardon for them." "Pray very much the prayers of the Rosary. I alone am able still to save you from the calamities which approach. Those who place their confidence in me will be saved."

On October 6, 2019, a new message was given to Sr. Sasagawa, which states: "Cover yourself in ashes" (Do acts of penance and reparation for the sins of the world) and please pray the Penitential Rosary every day.

THE GLORIOUS MYSTERIES MEDITATIONS

Resurrection of Jesus

Fruit of the Mystery: Faith

"On the first day of the week, Mary of Magdala came to the tomb early in the morning, while it was still dark, and saw the stone removed from the tomb. So she ran and went to Simon Peter and to the other disciple whom Jesus loved, and told them, "They have taken the Lord from the tomb, and we don't know where they put him." So Peter and the other disciple went out and came to the tomb. They both ran, but the other disciple ran faster than Peter and arrived at the tomb first; he bent down and saw the burial cloths there, but did not go in. When Simon Peter arrived after him, he went into the tomb and saw the burial cloths there, and the cloth that had covered his head, not with the burial cloths but rolled up in a separate place. Then the other disciple also went in, the one who had arrived at the tomb first, and he saw and believed. For they did not yet understand the scripture that he had to rise from the dead. Then the disciples returned home." (John 20:1-18)

There are many resurrection appearances of Jesus, one could meditate upon when praying the Rosary. However, before Jesus appeared to anyone, the amazing moment of the resurrection itself, not spoken of in Sacred Scripture, happened. There are no human witnesses to the Resurrection of Jesus. Nobody was in the tomb. His dead body, marred by His terrible Passion on Good Friday, literally rose from the dead, and was immediately transformed into a glorious body, pre-witnessed by the three Apostles on Mount Tabor at the Transfiguration. When He rose from the dead all wounds and blood disappeared, except for the wounds in His hands, feet and side. Why didn't the Lord allow anyone to see it? Faith. He desires all His followers to believe that by His own power, He rose from the dead.

The Gospel of John explains that the burial cloths were rolled up in a separate place. This suggests that if the body were stolen, no thief would have taken the time to wrap up the burial cloths and placed them in a separate place.

The Shroud of Turin is believed to be the actual shroud that wrapped the dead body of Jesus before it was placed in the tomb. That shroud is a witness to the Resurrection of Jesus because the body of Jesus burst forth through the shroud leaving the imprint of a man who had been crucified. It's called the Shroud of Turin because it is currently located in the city of Turin, Italy. The shroud is rarely made visible for the public to see, usually one time in five years.

The shroud measures 14 feet 3 inches by 3 feet 7 inches. On the shroud is the image of a man with puncture wounds in his wrists and feet. That's right, wrists, not hands.

"In the 1990s, research by Dr. Frederick Zugibe of Columbia University theorized that the nails could have been driven into the palms at an angle, exiting at the wrists. This, he said, would have supported the body's weight and would be consistent with the location where most of the stigmatics had displayed their wounds and with how artists had depicted the Crucifixion throughout the centuries. The Shroud of Turin, considered by many to be the actual burial shroud of Christ, shows a blood print in the location of the bones of the wrist. But it should be noted that the imprint on the shroud is from the back of the hand and could depict only the exit area of the nail and not its entrance."[99]

The shroud has been scientifically examined and scientists discovered there is pollen specific to the area and time period of Jesus on the shroud. There is male human AB type blood on it. The man whose image is on the shroud was crucified, a form of execution by the Romans.

"The image was not formed by dyes, chemicals, vapors or scorching. The only known explanation for the formation of the image is an intense burst of vacuum ultraviolet radiation (equivalent to the output of 14,000 excimer lasers) emitted from every three-dimensional point of the body in the Shroud. The combination of the above evidence is exceedingly difficult to explain in any way other than the burial cloth is that of Jesus of Nazareth. Moreover, the formation of the image by an intense outburst of vacuum ultraviolet radiation is suggestive of a resurrection event similar to that described in the Gospels."[100]

One could imagine the lifeless body of Jesus wrapped in the shroud, lying on a cold slab, when suddenly in a flash, a light so immense and brilliant the naked eye would have been immediately blinded, and the body was suddenly and instantly transformed bursting through the cloth, resulting in Jesus standing immediately next to the slab. Now only the shroud remained on top of the slab.

At the moment of the resurrection, the shroud would not have moved, except to slowly implode, as the body instantly came through the cloth in a micro-burst, and Our Lord stood there in the tomb alive with His resurrected body in divine clothing which materialized immediately on His person.

Jesus desiring to help His Apostles know His body was not stolen, but risen, wrapped up the burial cloth covering His head and placed it in a separate place in the tomb.

The qualities of the risen resurrected body of Jesus included: impassibility, brightness, agility, subtlety. Impassibility means one is no longer subject to pain, disease, death, hunger, thirst, sleep, cold, heat, fatigue, and no more weeping. Brightness means the body shines with great radiance and glory. Agility means the body can pass with the quickness of thought to all parts of the universe. Subtlety means the risen body, although physical, can penetrate material substances, even as Our Lord rose from the tomb and entered the Upper Room, where the Apostles were hiding for fear of the Jews. At the end of the world, all human bodies living and dead will have these qualities at the resurrection of the dead, when our body will be immediately reunited with our soul.

When Jesus rose from the dead, to depart from the tomb, and because of the gift of subtlety, He walked directly through the large stone covering the entrance of the tomb, or the wall, without the stone needing to be rolled away.

"After the Sabbath, as the first day of the week was dawning, Mary Magdalene and the other Mary came to see the tomb. And behold, there was a great earthquake; for an angel of the Lord descended from heaven, approached, rolled back the stone, and sat upon it. His appearance was like lightning and his clothing was white as snow. The guards were shaken with fear of him and became like dead men. Then the angel said to the women in reply, "Do not be afraid! I know that you are seeking Jesus the crucified. He is not here, for he has been raised just as he said. Come and see the place where he lay. Then go quickly and tell his disciples, 'He has been raised from the dead, and he is going before you to Galilee; there you will see him.' Behold, I have told you." Then they went away quickly from the tomb, fearful yet overjoyed, and ran to announce this to his disciples. And behold, Jesus met them on their way and greeted them. They approached, embraced his feet, and did him homage. Then Jesus said to them, "Do not be afraid. Go tell my brothers to go to Galilee, and there they will see me." (Matthew 28:1-10)

This account indicates Jesus was not in the tomb because "there was a great earthquake; for an angel of the Lord descended from heaven, approached, rolled back the stone, and sat upon it." Consequently, Jesus would have departed the tomb prior to the stone being rolled away by the angel, and therefore,

Jesus walked through the wall of the tomb or the large stone before the angel rolled it back.

Due to agility, He would have departed at the speed of thought, and to whom did He first appear?

Sacred Scriptures tell us Jesus first appeared to Mary Magdalene (Mark 16:9). But, there is a pious tradition mentioned by Pope Saint John Paul II, that Jesus appeared to His Mother Mary first. He said, "How could the Blessed Virgin, present in the first community of disciples (Acts 1:14), be excluded from those who met Her divine Son after He had risen from the dead?" "Indeed, it is legitimate to think that the Mother was probably the first person to whom the risen Jesus appeared."[101]

Saint Vincent Ferrer believed Jesus appeared to His Mother first before anyone else.[102] He said, "The first apparition He gave was to the Blessed Virgin Mary, although the gospel does not tell us about this." Saint Ignatius of Loyola, St. Bridget of Sweden and others all believed it.[103]

Unlike Mary Magdalene, who wasn't expecting to find the risen Jesus, the Blessed Virgin Mary knew Her Son Jesus would rise, and so, sorrowfully, but patiently, waited for His resurrection. In a spirit of prayer, Our Lady awaited Her glorified Son.

We can imagine the meeting of Mother and Son when Mary was kneeling in prayer waiting for Her Son to come. Suddenly, Jesus appeared to His Mother, and at that moment, She instantly recognized His glorious body. Her sorrow vanished and Her Heart was filled with joy.

Since She was kneeling, She first saw the wounds in His feet and immediately bent over and kissed them and adored Him. Our Lord reached out His hands to help Her up and then She saw the wounds in His hands and kissed them.

As She beheld His Sacred Wounds, which caused Her immense pain at the Cross, but now are His trophies, proving He is risen, She humbled Herself before God.

As Jesus took His wounded hands and helped Her up from the ground, surely, She embraced Her Son, kissed His face, and hugged Him. What once were tears of sorrow, immediately turned into tears of joy.

What were their first words to each other? Our Lord may have simply said, "Mother!" and She could have responded, "My God, my Son!"

We are reminded of the many appearances of Our Blessed Lord after He rose from the dead. He appeared to Mary Magdalene (John 20:11-18, Mark 16:9-11, Matthew 28:9-10, Luke 24:1-12), the two men on the road to Emmaus (Luke 24:13-32), once to St. Peter (1 Corinthians 15:5), and three times to His apostles, twice in the upper room (Luke 24:36-49, John 20:19-23), and once on the shore of the Sea of Galilee (John 21:1-19). In the first letter to the Corinthians, Jesus appeared to 500 at one time (1 Corinthians 15:6). Scripture also tells us Jesus appeared to James (1 Corinthians 15:7). Our Lord appeared on the Mount of Olives to the eleven giving them His great commission to preach to the whole world (Matthew 28:16, Luke 24:50, Acts 1:12). There is a pious tradition His Mother was on the mountain with them before He ascended into heaven.

With Jesus appearing to so many people, it would be difficult to make up such a story, if it were not true. The Resurrection of Jesus is a historical fact. If Our Lord's resurrection did not happen, why would so many people be willing to lay down their lives, especially in the first three centuries and even up to today? To lay down one's life for something false would be ridiculous.

Mary Magdalene went to the tomb, and much to her amazement, she discovered two angels sitting there. One angel sat at the feet where the body of Jesus was laid and the other at the head. Can you imagine seeing two angels in a tomb? It would be scary to go by yourself inside a tomb early in the morning. No one would expect to see two angels sitting there.

The angels said to her, "Woman, why are you weeping?" She responded, "They have taken away my Lord, and I don't know where they laid Him." Certainly, they would have known why she was weeping. After all, they were sent there by God to help her discover Jesus has risen. Yet, they wanted her to recall that Jesus said He would rise on the third day. However, she had not yet understood that Jesus had risen.

Mary Magdalene turned around and saw Jesus standing there, but she did not recognize Him. Maybe, she failed to recognize our Lord for several reasons. First, she wasn't expecting to see Him alive. Second, her eyes may have been filled with tears—such that it would have been difficult to clearly see who was standing before her. Third, our Lord would have looked different, because now He had a resurrected glorified body.

Our Lord lovingly asked the same question as the angels. He said, "Woman, why are you weeping?" Who are you looking for?" Thinking Jesus was the gardener of the cemetery, she said, "Sir, if you carried him away, tell me where you laid him, and I will take Him."

Imagine for a moment, out of zeal and love for Jesus, Mary Magdalene's heart speaks before she thinks, if what she is saying could even be possible. She said, "Sir, if you carried him away, tell me where you laid him, and I will take Him."

"Based on the shroud, Jesus of Nazareth was a physically commanding person, standing nearly 6 feet tall and weighing 175 to 180 pounds — a large man for that time in history. He had very broad shoulders and well-defined, muscular arms and legs. He had a majestic face and thick, well-groomed hair."[104]

Can an adult woman pick up the dead body of an adult man, who probably weighed between 175 to 180 lbs and carry Him off by herself? No, of course not. But, she was driven by love. It's sort of like a young man speaking to his fiance and pointing to the moon, saying, "Sweetheart, I'm going to own the

269

moon someday. I will buy it for you and throw a lasso around it. I will bring it here for you. Since I know how you dearly love the moonlight, I want you to have it and gaze upon it whenever you want." Of course, this is not possible, but it's reckless and unbounded love, like Mary Magdalene, who was willing to carry off the dead body of Jesus, but was certainly impossible.

Only when Jesus said her name "Mary" did Magdalene immediately recognize who was standing before her. She became the first proclaimer of Christ's resurrection by immediately running to tell the Apostles that He had risen, but they didn't believe her.

"On the evening of that first day of the week, when the doors were locked, where the disciples were, for fear of the Jews, Jesus came and stood in their midst and said to them, "Peace be with you." When he had said this, he showed them his hands and his side. The disciples rejoiced when they saw the Lord. [Jesus] said to them again, "Peace be with you. As the Father has sent me, so I send you." And when he had said this, he breathed on them and said to them, "Receive the Holy Spirit. Whose sins you forgive are forgiven them, and whose sins you retain are retained." (John 20:19-23) "While they were still speaking about this, He stood in their midst and said to them, "Peace be with you." But they were startled and terrified and thought that they were seeing a ghost. Then He said to them, "Why are you troubled? And why do questions arise in your hearts? Look at my hands and My feet, that is I myself. Touch Me and see, because a ghost does not have flesh and bones as you can see I have." And as He said this, He showed them His hands and His feet. While they were still incredulous for joy and were amazed, he asked them, "Have you anything here to eat?" They gave him a piece of baked fish; He took it and ate it in front of them." (Luke 24:36-43)

When Jesus appeared to the Apostles in the Upper Room, He physically walked through walls, despite the fact, He had a real physical resurrected body. In order to remove any doubt that He was not a ghost, and it was truly Him physically standing before them, He ate fish.

And if that was not enough, a week later, when He appeared again to the Apostles, this time with Thomas present, for he wasn't present at Our Lord's first appearance, He asked him to touch His wounds, because Thomas had said He would not believe unless he touched the nail marks and wounds of Jesus. This is where the phrase "doubting Thomas" comes from.

Pope Gregory the Great, said, "Do you really believe that it was by chance that this chosen disciple was absent, then came and heard, heard and doubted, doubted and touched, touched and believed? It was not by chance but in God's providence. In a marvelous way God's mercy arranged that the disbelieving disciple, in touching the wounds of his master's body, should heal our wounds of disbelief. This disbelief of Thomas has done more for our faith than the faith of the other disciples."[105]

By touching the wounds, Thomas cried out, "My Lord and my God!"

Faith is the theological virtue that most expresses the resurrection of Christ. Jesus praises those who believe when He said to Saint Thomas, "Because you have seen me, you have believed; blessed are those who have not seen and yet have believed." (John 20:29)

The Navarre Bible commentary explains the Resurrection of Jesus and its meaning.

> "The resurrection of Christ is one of the basic dogmas of the Catholic faith. In fact, St. Paul says, "If Christ has not been raised, then our preaching is in vain." (1 Corinthians 15"14); and to prove the assertion that Christ rose, he tells us, "that he appeared to Cephas, then to the Twelve. Then He appeared to more than five hundred at one time,

271

most of whom are still alive, though some have fallen asleep. Then He appeared to James, then to all the Apostles. Last of all, as to one untimely born, He appeared to me." (1 Corinthians 15:5-5-8) The creeds state Jesus rose from the dead on the third day (*Nicene Creed*), by His own power (Ninth Council of Toledo, *de Redemptione*), by a true resurrection of the flesh (*Creed* of St. Leo IX), reuniting His soul with His body (Innocent III, *Eius exemplo*), and that this fact of the resurrection is historically proven and provable (St. Pius X, *Lamentabili*)."

By the word "resurrection" we are not merely to understand that Christ was raised from the dead...but that He rose by His own power and virtue, a singular prerogative peculiar to Him alone. Our Lord confirmed this by the divine testimony of His own mouth when He said, 'I lay down my life, that I may take it again [. . .] I have power to lay it down: and I have power to take it up again' (John 10:17-18) [. . .] To the Jews He also said, in corroboration of His doctrine: "Destroy this temple, and in three days I will raise it up' (John 2:19-20) We sometimes, it is true, read in Scripture that He was raised by the Father (cf. Acts 2:24, Romans 8:11); but this refers to Him as man, just as those passages on the other hand, which say that He rose by His own power, relate to Him, as God.

Christ's resurrection was not a return to His previous earthly existence; it was a "glorious" Resurrection, that is to say, attaining the full development of human life—immortal, freed from all limitations of space and time. As a result of the Resurrection, Christ's body now shares in the glory

272

which His soul had from the beginning. Here lies the unique nature of the historical fact of the Resurrection. He could be seen not by anyone but only those to whom He granted that grace, to enable them to be witnesses of this Resurrection, and to enable others to believe in Him by accepting the testimony of the seers.

Christ's Resurrection was something necessary for the completion of the work of redemption. For, Jesus Christ through His death freed us from sins; but by His Resurrection He restored to us all that we had lost through sin and, moreover, opened for us the gates to eternal life (cf. Romans 4:25). Also, the fact that He rose from the dead by His own power is a definitive proof that He is the Son of God, and therefore His Resurrection fully confirms our faith in His divinity. (St. Pius V, *Catechism*, 1, 6, 8)

The Resurrection of Christ, as has been pointed out, is the most sublime truth of our faith. That is why St. Augustine exclaims: "It is no great thing to believe that Christ died; for this is something that is also believed by pagans and Jews and by all the wicked: everyone believes He died. The Christians' faith is in Christ's resurrection; this is what we hold to be a great thing—to believe that He rose." (*Enarrationes in Psalmos*, 120)

The mystery of the Redemption wrought by Christ, which embraces His death and resurrection, is applied to every man and woman through Baptism and the other sacraments, by means of which the believer is as it were immersed in Christ and in His death, that is to say, in a mystical way He becomes part of Christ, He dies and rises with

Christ: "We were buried therefore with Him by baptism raised from the dead by glory of the Father, we too might talk in newness of life." (Romans 6:4)

An ardent desire to seek the things of God and an interior taste for the things that are above (cf. Colossians 3;1-3) are signs of our resurrection with Christ."[106]

"In the first book, Theophilus, I dealt with all that Jesus did and taught until the day He was taken up, after giving instructions through the Holy Spirit to the apostles whom he had chosen He presented himself alive to them by many proofs after he had suffered, appearing to them during forty days and speaking about the kingdom of God." (Acts 1:1-3)

From the time Jesus rose from the dead, until He ascended into heaven, what did He do? Bishop John MacEvilly, Archbishop of Tuam in his *Exposition of the Gospel of Luke,* said, "After having remained with them forty days, proving His Resurrection, and instructing them in everything relating to the government of His Church, both as to faith, morals, and discipline, to the end of time, He led them out of Jerusalem, as far as Bethania."[107]

Pope St. John Paul II in his Ascension homily in 1979, said, "The instructions indicated, above all, that the Apostles were to wait for the Holy Spirit, who was the gift of the Father. From the beginning, it had to be crystal-clear that the source of the Apostles' strength is the Holy Spirit. It is the Holy Spirit who guides the Church in the way of truth; the Gospel is to spread through the power of God, and not by means of human wisdom or strength. The Apostles, moreover, were instructed to teach – to proclaim the Good News to the whole world. And they were to baptize in the name of the Father, and of the Son, and of the Holy Spirit. Like Jesus, they were to speak explicitly about the Kingdom of God and about salvation. The Apostles were to give witness to Christ to the ends of the earth. The early Church clearly understood these instructions and the missionary era began. And everybody knew that this missionary era could never end until the same Jesus, who went up to Heaven, would come back again."

Jimmy Akins writing for *Catholic Answers* states, "At the beginning of Acts, Luke tells us that Jesus essentially did three things during the forty days: (1) "He presented himself alive after His passion," (2) "by many proofs," and (3) "speaking of the kingdom of God. He may well have done other things, too, like spending time with the disciples, sharing table fellowship with them, and even possibly celebrating the Eucharist."[108]

Near the end of the Gospel of John, John states, "Now Jesus did many other signs in the presence of the disciples, which are not written in this book." (John 20:30)

While we may surmise Our Lord may have helped them to know how best to offer the Holy Sacrifice of the Mass, to hear Confessions, and impart other sacraments, and their meaning, etc… we must leave them to the Easter mystery. We can trust everything Jesus did with them during those 40 days was for the good for their souls, the souls of the early Christians and for the future of the Church, that will last until He returns in glory, because the gates of hell shall never prevail against her.

The day Jesus appeared to His Apostles, when He rose from the dead, Our Lord instituted the sacrament of Confession when He said, "Receive the Holy Spirit. Whose sins you forgive are forgiven them, and whose sins you retain are retained." (John 20:23)

God used the Upper Room to institute four sacraments: The Holy Eucharist and Priesthood on Holy Thursday at the Last Supper, Confession on Easter when He appeared to them, and Confirmation with the coming of the Pentecost.

Application 1: Jesus Walks Through Walls & Eucharist

The ability to physically walk through walls by Our Lord's physical body, helps us to understand His physical presence in the Holy Eucharist.

40 days after Jesus rose from the dead, He went to heaven on a cloud. Many erroneously believe Jesus is physically present only in heaven. But this is not true. Yes, Jesus is in heaven, but Jesus is also on earth, in a very unique way. This is a mystery of how He can be in both places at the same time. Yet He is fully present in each sacred Host, so this mystery is not so hard to believe.

The same Jesus, who rose from the dead on Easter Sunday, who ascended into heaven, who has wounds in His hands and feet and side, who appeared to His Mother Mary, to Mary Magdalene, and His apostles, is now really and truly present in the Eucharist, whom we are able to receive today in Holy Communion. We cannot see Jesus, but He is really present in the Eucharist as the Risen Lord. The Host looks like bread, tastes like bread, but is not bread at all. After Mass, He stays with us, in the Tabernacle and He is in Adoration Chapel to adore. The Church uses the following words to describe the presence of Jesus in the Eucharist: We say, "He is present body, blood, soul and divinity in the Eucharist." This does not mean only His body, only His blood, only His soul, and only His divinity. Rather, this is a way to describe His presence, as wholly, entirely, physically and totally present.

Today, many Catholics pray the words of St. Thomas at Holy Mass, when the Sacred Host is elevated above the altar, in the silence of their hearts, they will cry out, "My Lord, and my God!"

Application 2: Raised from the Dead vs Resurrection

When Jesus rose from the dead, Our Lord's body was not resuscitated. Rather, the body which was dead, suddenly came to life and at the same moment by the power of His resurrection, transformed His former body into a glorious body.

There is a big difference between raising a person from the dead and a bodily resurrection. A person raised from the dead, will die again, but a resurrected person will die no more and will have a body transformed and glorified.

Elijah, the prophet raised a man back to life. Our Lord brought back to life Lazarus (John 11:38-44), the boy of the widow being carried out for burial (Luke 7:11-17), and the daughter of Jarius who had died. (Mark 5:21-43) St. Paul is attributed to bringing back to life the young man who fell from the window. (Acts 20:7-12)

When Jesus was crucified, scripture tells us bodies of saints who had fallen asleep were raised and appeared to many. (Matthew 27:52-53)

There have been miracles by saints who brought back to life people who were dead. These saints include St. Anthony of Padua, St. Dominic, St. Ignatius of Loyola, St. John Bosco and St. Patrick, who brought back to life 33 people. All of these incidents are proof of God's power over death.

All who died and were raised back to life, will die again. But at the end of the world, all bodies living and dead will be transformed into a resurrected body that will never die again.

Application 3: The Living Rosary

The Living Rosary can take two forms. The first form is when people gather in person to form a physical Rosary. The other form goes back to 1826, whereby each decade is privately prayed daily, but the Rosary is prayed as a group collectively.

In a Living Rosary, prayed with a group in person, each individual stands in the place of a bead of the rosary (as all gather to form a Rosary on the floor or outside on the ground). Though not necessary, the leader can apply paper circles on the floor, where each person will stand. When it is their turn each person representing a bead will lead the specific prayer (Creed, Our Father or Hail Mary, Glory Be, O my Jesus prayer). The leader begins with the Sign of the Cross, announces each mystery before each decade begins and will lead the group concluding the Hail Holy Queen. At the conclusion of the Living Rosary there can be a crowning of an image of Mary, the Litany of Loreto can be prayed, and a hymn to Our Lady can be sung, such as the "Ave Maria" or "Immaculate Mary." The Living Rosary can take place in a parish hall, gym, or outdoors before a statue of Mary. If there aren't enough persons to do each bead of the Rosary, then a smaller group, who stands in a circle, can pray the Rosary while each person follows the other after a specific prayer is prayed until the Rosary is completed.

What is a Living Rosary prayed collectively, but not in person? Maura Roan McKeegan explains.

"The devotion appears to have begun in France in 1826, when Venerable Pauline-Marie Jaricot formed the Living Rosary Association. She was inspired to pull together groups of fifteen persons who would each be responsible for praying one decade of the Rosary each day, so that the full 15-decade Rosary would be prayed each day by the group.

Over a century later, during the Nazi occupation of Poland, a young layman named Jan Tyranowski formed prayer groups of fifteen men in his parish, representing the fifteen mysteries of the Rosary. One of the group's leaders was the young

278

Karol Wojtyla—the young St. John Paul II (who would later introduce the Luminous Mysteries in his pontificate). Tyranowski met with the men in prayer and guided them in spiritual direction. He called it the Living Rosary prayer group. Wojtyla, the future pope, remained devoted to the Living Rosary prayer group and brought this model into his own parishes after he became a priest.

In some places today, a school or youth group will organize a Living Rosary. They might assemble students into the physical form of a Rosary, where each student represents one prayer bead, and the group recites the prayers together. This is a variation of the original Living Rosary.

In all its variations, the Living Rosary bears in common the practice of a group of people representing the prayers of the Rosary, and sharing in praying the Rosary together.

The Living Rosary has been a great blessing in my life, reminding me that I am not alone in my prayers, and that my small offering can become something much bigger when I join it with the offerings of others. The grace is tangible, and the power is more than we will ever know."[109]

When one prays the Living Rosary at one's own home, rather than meeting in prayer groups (as much as one would like to do), one still feels part of a prayer community. This type of Living Rosary, may be more helpful during times of persecution, when it is difficult to meet in a group.

This form of the Living Rosary is available through *The Living Rosary Apostolate*. www.thelivingrosaryapostolate.com

In the history of the Church, there are about 300 incorrupt bodies. In 2023, the body of Sister Wilhelmina Lancaster, OSB, at the Benedictine Monastery, Queen of the Apostles, was exhumed in order to be placed inside the monastery chapel. To the excitement of many, her body and her habit had not decayed. While the Church has yet to investigate it, eyes can see, she has not decomposed in nearly four years after burial. She left her former religious order, mostly due to her desire to faithfully wear the habit, and truly live an authentic life consecrated to God, as a bride of Christ. She started her own religious community of nuns, which is greatly thriving today. The religious community has always daily prayed the Holy Rosary. Most likely, the Lord in His desire to show His pleasure for her community's faithfulness in wearing the habit and living an authentic life as nuns, would not allow the habit and her body to decay, while at the same time, allowing the coffin cloth to disintegrate. She is not the first nun in the US to be incorrupt.

Saint Rose Philippine Duchesne, Society of the Sacred Heart, ministered to American Indians. Her work at the Sugar Creek Mission near Centerville, Kansas, endeared her to the Pottawatomie Indians who called her "Kwah-kah-kum-ad," the "Woman Who Prays Always." The Rosary was part of her habit and she would have prayed untold Rosaries. She could not speak their language and had health problems that prevented her from interacting with them as she desired, but she prayed much for them and they knew it. Her body, originally found incorrupt, later decomposed.

Interestingly, the bodies of Saint Rose and Sister Wilhelmina, the two nuns who were incorrupt, are only one hour and thirty minute drive from each other. It is also notable that both nuns attended the Traditional Latin Mass and their bodies were not embalmed.

Story 2: Rosary Stops a Plague

In October of 2014, the Ebola virus was causing many deaths in Africa. Liberia was the country hardest-hit with 10,678 people killed in West Africa. Bishop Anthony Fallah Borwah, leading the Diocese of Gbarnga, called on all Catholics to pray to combat Ebola from 5 to 6 pm every day from September 1 through November 30. Bishop Borwah instructed people to use the first ten minutes for education and updates about Ebola and the last 50 minutes to pray the Holy Rosary.

David Dionisi, the founder of a Catholic program in Liberia to care for war orphans, was leading an Ebola quarantine facility. Dionisi was asked to run an Ebola quarantine facility initially by Doctors Without Borders and then by Franciscan Works. Liberia Mission, renamed Franciscan Works in 2009, has served poor children since 2003. By September 2014, the Peace Corps and most non-profits left Liberia.

To combat Ebola David taught the local people how to make chlorine from salt and water because chlorine is effective in killing the virus. He said, "Although I trained people in sterilization processes, I feel that the most effective action we took was praying the Rosary together every day, which gave both children and adults a tangible sense of comfort and peace." Dionisi said, "at the three o'clock hour, during God's hour of grace, (at a time when we should always pray and expect miracles... Acts 3:1), we rang a bell. About 100 or so children and local people gathered together to pray the Rosary and invoke the power of Our Lady to have God save us from the Ebola epidemic. We were asking for a lot, but to what better place could we turn, than to the one, we know in the end, whose Immaculate Heart will triumph? This daily recitation of the Rosary became a powerhouse! Truly, I had hoped for much, but to my utter amazement, none of us who prayed the Rosary became sick. None!

In total about 2000 people in the Blacktom village area were protected by God from the Ebola virus. All around us, people in villages were dying horrible deaths. To put this Holy Rosary miracle in perspective, one of our students, Johnson Moore, went to another village where family members lived and where the Rosary was not prayed. He died from Ebola." David said, "I am convinced that there is no greater protection to save your country, your local government, your home, your family, and your soul, than by praying the Rosary every day. My advice to everyone in these times, and in all times, is to make and take time to pray the daily Rosary." "Jesus says that, "Where two or more are gathered together in My name, I am there with them," (Mat, 18:20). The Church's "Rule of Public Prayer" states, when two pray together, each one has doubled his prayers. When 10 pray a Rosary together, God counts it as 10 Rosaries for each one! So, try often to pray with others to receive more graces! We have learned that with a clock, a call, or a bell, gathering people together at a set time produces great benefits for all."[110]

Note: David is referring to the law of public prayer which St. Louis de Montfort mentioned in his book, *The Secret of the Rosary*, pg 97.

Apparition: Our Lady of Cuapa (Nicaragua)

The following is mostly taken from the Marians of the Immaculate Conception website:

"One evening in April 1980, Bernardo, the sacristan of the local parish in Cuapa, Nicaragua, went to ring the bell to alert the parish to pray the Rosary. Upon entering the church, he noticed a light glowing around the statue of Our Lady emanating from the statue itself.

On May 8, 1980, the Virgin Mary appeared to Bernardo saying, "I come from Heaven. I am the Mother of Jesus." She told

282

Bernardo that she wanted people to pray the Rosary every day at a set hour with no distractions. She wanted people to not rush through it, but recite it while meditating on Scripture. She also encouraged the Five First Saturdays devotion, as She did in Fatima, warning, "If people do not change... they will hasten the arrival of the Third World War."

In his vision on June 8, 1980, Bernardo witnessed the history of the Rosary unfold before him. He saw a procession of saints, whom he later believed to be Dominicans, dressed in white and praying the Rosary while meditating on Scripture.

Then in early September, Our Lady appeared again in the sky, but this time She had the appearance of a very young girl. Bernardo told Her that the townspeople wanted to build a church in Her honor. But She said, "The Lord does not necessarily want a material church. He wants living temples, which are yourselves."

On October 13, Bernardo received the final apparition of Our Lady. Bernardo told her that many of the people did not believe in her. This made Mary cry, so Bernardo asked for Her forgiveness. Again, Our Lady encouraged him to pray the Rosary, and She told him that the people should not just ask for peace, but that they should strive to make it for themselves. Mary also implored Bernardo and all people to accept the suffering of the world and ask for strength to carry their crosses. Though She said that She would no longer be appearing to him, Mary told him, "Do not be troubled. I am with you, even though you can't see Me. I am the Mother of all."[111]

Ascension of Jesus

Fruit of the Mystery: Hope, Desire for Heaven

"Now the eleven disciples went to Galilee, to the mountain to which Jesus directed them. And when they saw Him they worshiped Him; but some doubted." (Matthew 28:16-17)

Before Jesus ascended into heaven, the eleven apostles *with the Virgin Mary* (in accord with a pious tradition, Mary was with them) on the Mount of Olives.

The Apostles adore Jesus and worship Him, as God, and are fully aware He is the Messiah and Son of God. Yet, they must have been so overwhelmed at seeing Him stand before them, they could not believe their eyes, and therefore doubted what they were seeing was real. It shows the humanness of the apostles.

"And Jesus came and said to them, 'All authority in heaven and on earth has been given to me. Go therefore, and make disciples of all nations, baptizing them, in the name of the Father, and of the Son and of the Holy Spirit, teaching them to observe, all that I commanded you, and lo, I am with you always, to the end of the age." (Matthew 28:18:20)

Before ascending, Jesus commanded the apostles to make disciples by baptizing, evangelizing and teaching the new disciples to observe all He commanded them. Jesus wants Christianity to spread throughout the whole world, because He desires as many as possible to believe in Him and become one of His followers, so that they may be saved.

"Then He led them out as far as Bethany, and lifting up His hands He blessed them. While He blessed them, He parted from them, and was carried up to heaven." (Luke 24:50-51)

The last action of Jesus before He ascended was to bless the apostles and His Mother. At the Last Supper, the Apostles were ordained as priests and bishops, and received the power to perform the sacraments and to impart blessings.

Jesus is the eternal high priest, and so, as an act of farewell, gave those present His priestly blessing. Bishop MacEvilly said, "lifting up His hands" is a ceremony commonly used among the ancients in giving benediction... The same ceremony has been constantly in use in the Christian Church, with the addition of the sign of the cross—partly the source of all blessing—which is surely of Apostolic origin." "Some authors—Suarez—St. Jerome, believe that our Lord Himself, on this occasion, made the sign of the cross in the air, while, with uplifted hands, He blessed the Apostles. What wonder if He did so, since it is most likely He carried into heaven, to plead for us, the very scars of His Passion, which He retained after His resurrection."[112]

"Then when He had said this, as they were looking on, He was lifted up, and a cloud took him from their sight." Surely, Our Lord kissed His Mother and embraced Her before He went to heaven. Was She standing beneath Him giving Her Motherly hand wave or blowing Him kisses, or perhaps tears welled up in Her eyes as She just watched knowing She would be unable to gaze upon His face until She sees Her Son in heaven?

What would have been the thoughts of the apostles as they saw Jesus rise heavenward on a cloud. Surely, they were thrilled to see Our Lord ascend to heaven, but sad knowing He was leaving them. They felt abandoned, but they trusted.

St. Paul said, "He who descended is the very one who ascended high above the heavens, that He might fill all men with His gifts." (Ephesians 4:10)

"Our Lord went up body and soul into heaven in the sight of His Apostles, by His own power, to take possession of His glory, and to be our Advocate and Mediator in Heaven with the Father. He ascended as a man, a Head of the redeemed, and

286

has prepared a dwelling in Heaven for all those who follow in His steps."[113]

"The feast of the ascension is forty days after Easter. All power in heaven and on earth has been given to Our Lord. He is the supreme King and Ruler of this world. He governs it invisibly in heaven and on the Last Day will return to visibly, and in glory, to judge the just and the wicked."[114]

"While they were looking intently at the sky as he was going, suddenly two men dressed in white garments stood beside them. They said, "Men of Galilee, why are you standing there looking at the sky? This Jesus who has been taken up from you into heaven will return in the same way as you have seen him going into heaven." Then they returned to Jerusalem from the mount called Olivet, which is near Jerusalem, a Sabbath day's journey away." (Acts 1:10-12)

How wonderful to see two angels. They were probably clothed in white garments. They must have had a joyful and majestic countenance. Their voices would have been pure, strong and heavenly. Since they spoke only the words that God desired them to speak, the words in themselves, would have given peace in the understanding of what God was asking of them. How thankful they must have been to see Jesus one last time and to see angels, who spoke as messengers from God and to know what God desires of them. Their hearts would have rejoiced in being so privileged to behold the event. What an honor, but also what a responsibility.

The apostles' sadness gave way to consolation, because they recall Him saying, "I am with you always, even to the end of the age." (Matthew 28:30) They didn't understand what He meant, but He was always faithful to His words, and so they knew it was true. He will be with them always. They may have recalled His words at the Last Supper, "I will not leave you orphans; I will come to you." (John 14:18)

Jesus rules from His throne in heaven over all creation, angels and men and has put everything under His feet. "...what is the surpassing greatness of his power for us who believe, in accord with the exercise of his great might, which He worked in Christ, raising Him from the dead and seating him at His right hand in the heavens, far above every principality, authority, power, and dominion, and every name that is named not only in this age but also in the one to come. And He put all things beneath His feet and gave Him as head over all things to the church, which is his body, the fullness of the one who fills all things in every way." (Ephesians 1:19-23)

Application 1: Jesus is Always with Us,
Especially through Baptism & the Holy Eucharist

How is Jesus with us always? How does He come to us? He uses physical signs: bread, water, wine, oil, so He can come in contact with us through the sacraments. Through baptism, He dwells within us. He is with us especially at Mass in the Eucharist.

Jesus dwells in us spiritually through baptism. St. Elizabeth of the Trinity said, "It seems to me that I have found my heaven on earth, because my heaven is you, my God, and you are in my soul. You in me and I in you—may this be my motto. What a joyous mystery is your presence within me, in that intimate sanctuary of my soul where I can always find you, even when I do not feel your presence. Perhaps you are all the closer when I feel you less."

A saint once said, she would joyfully kiss the chest of a baby after baptism because in the child's heart, Jesus has come to dwell.

Jesus said, "Where two or more gathered in My name. I am there among them." (Matthew 18:20). When Christians come together in His name to pray, to do His works, to discern His will, He is with us.

288

Our Lord is with us at every Mass because we are gathered in His name when the community prays and sings. Jesus is the Eternal Word and is with us when the Word of God is proclaimed and during preaching.

"We see at the altar the priest, standing in the person of Christ who says "This is my body. This is my blood." In the Eucharistic Prayer, the priest offers the very Body and Blood of Jesus Christ, made present on the altar, as Christ did when he offered himself as a sacrifice for us on the Cross. The priest stands in the person of Christ and does what Christ does in offering the Eucharist."[115] The priest also leads us in prayer to the Father as Christ leads us to the Father. In the person of the priest, we encounter the very presence of Christ. Our divine Lord is in every priest, who exercises His ministry. The priest, therefore, acts in *persona Christi* (in the person of Christ).

We come in contact with Jesus in the sacraments, who sanctifies humanity through them. Jesus helps married couples to live out their vocation of self-gift. Jesus baptizes. Jesus confirms during Confirmation. Jesus absolves sins in Confession. Jesus sacramentally unites baptized couples in matrimony. Jesus, in priests, performs sacramental ministry. Jesus anoints the sick to give them graces to endure their sufferings, to prepare them for their journey home and at times to physically heal.

"And they worshiped Him, and returned to Jerusalem with great joy, and were continually in the temple blessing God." (Luke 24:52-53) Saint Luke tells us they "worshiped" Jesus, which means they prostrated themselves in adoration. "Adoring, falling prostrate, and paying Him, as God, supreme worship, due to the sovereign majesty of God only."[116]

Most especially, far above all other ways, Christ is present in the Most Blessed Sacrament, the Sacrament of Sacraments, because the Eucharist is Jesus Christ Himself in the Tabernacle of every Catholic church. In the Tabernacle, Jesus is there night and day.

Recall Anna, the elderly woman who came to see the Infant Jesus when Mary and Joseph presented Him in the temple, "She never left the temple, but worshiped night and day with fasting and prayer." (Luke 2:36) She was rewarded by seeing Him face to face.

Rather than playing with his friends, Saint Francisco Marto spent hours before the tabernacle consoling the hidden Jesus.

In Perpetual Adoration Chapels and during Eucharistic Holy Hours the faithful gaze upon the real and true presence of Jesus in the Eucharist, adoring, loving, praising, thanking and beseeching Our Savior.

St. Padre Pio said, "A Holy Hour in front of the Blessed Sacrament is worth more than a thousand years of human glory!" Saint Mother Teresa of Calcutta said, "In order to convert America and save the World what we need is for every parish to come before Jesus in the Blessed Sacrament in Holy Hours of prayer!" Pope Saint Paul VI said, "Perpetual Adoration extends its influence far beyond the individual adorers, touching their homes and families and reaching out to the parish community and beyond!" St. John Bosco said, "Do you want the Lord to give you many graces? Visit Him often. Do you want Him to give you few graces? Visit Him rarely. Do you want the devil to attack you? Visit Jesus rarely in the Blessed Sacrament. Do you want him to flee from you? Visit Jesus often!" Blessed Dina Belanger said, "A Holy Hour of prayer before the Blessed Sacrament is so important to Jesus that a multitude of souls go to Heaven who otherwise would have gone to hell!"

In Eucharistic adoration, we gaze upon the Lord God almighty. How many do "face time" to see and talk to someone they love? But, how much more precious it is, to be actually physically and personally with the one you love.

How glorious and joyful, to be in the presence of Jesus, adoring Him, speaking to Him from the heart. To ask Him to

290

console you when you are sad. To give you courage when you are fearful. To help you to forgive those who hurt you. To allow Him to love you, as you love Him in return.

Jesus understands you better than anyone. He knows you better than you know yourself. He loves you and cares about you, infinitely. He wants you to come to Him and show your wounds to Him, so that, by His wounds in His resurrected body in the Eucharist, He can heal you.

Jesus told Peter, James and John, "Can you not spend one hour with me?" The same Jesus whom the Apostles fell down and worshiped as He ascended into heaven, is really truly present in His resurrected body in the Eucharist. O Come, let us worship and adore Him!

Application 2: Priest Blessing

Every priest and bishop today through the power given to them at ordination, also raises their hands to bless and perform the sacraments.

When Saint Philip Neri and Pope St. John Paul II were dying, as a farewell, they raised their hands and blessed those present just before their soul departed from this life to ascend to the throne of Jesus for their judgment.

At the end of every Mass, the priest gives his blessing, as a parting farewell to protect and help those in the congregation to be witnesses of Christ by carrying the good news into the world.

The priestly blessing gives special graces and gifts to those who receive it and can work wonders. For example, St. Maximilian Kolbe's religious order had the world's largest non-commercial printing press for a magazine in honor of Our Lady, *Knight of the Immaculata*. It had a monthly circulation of one million copies. One day, the printing press would not work. In response, St. Maximilian said to one of the friars, "The devil must have his tail caught in it." He then blessed the printing press making the sign of the cross and it immediately began to work.

During a plague, Saint Roch was willing to risk his life. He went to a hospital to take care of the sick and dying and by making the sign of the cross on their foreheads many were cured including a cardinal. He contracted the disease, but survived. His life is a beautiful example for priests and bishops today.

Every year on the Feast of St. Blaise, February 3 at the end of Mass, priests bless throats using blessed candles, saying, "Through the intercession of Saint Blaise, bishop and martyr, may God deliver you free from every disease of the throat, and from every other illness. In the name of the Father and of the Son, + and of the Holy Spirit."

Priests and deacons use *The Book of Blessings* to bless food, cattle, homes, cars, religious articles, families, Mother's Day and Father's Day blessings, etc.

Unborn children can be blessed by a priest or deacon using the United States Conference of Catholics Bishops' *Rite of Blessing of a Child in the Womb*.

While not a sacramental priestly blessing, parents can bless their children before bed or before going on a journey, or to college, or on a date, etc.

We ask God to bless those who sneeze, saying, "God bless you!" But more importantly, St. Paul asked us to bless those who persecute us. "Bless those who persecute you, bless and do not curse them." (Romans 12:14)

Whenever you have the opportunity, when in the presence of a priest, ask for his blessing, for your birthday, or anniversary, or if going on a trip for safety, etc., so the Lord Jesus will give you special graces, or even be healed.

In the 1970's in a small town in the US, parents of a family purchased all sorts of board games to play together as a family. One of the games purchased was the Ouija board. The parents had no idea it was an occult game and through it, demons can enter the home and life of the family. Due to the foreclosure of their local bank and the parent's divorce, the family lost their home. Over the years, the home had numerous owners. The house was known to be haunted and renters would stay but a short time and move out.

One of the boys, whose parents purchased the Ouija board, eventually became a priest. On the weekend of the Ascension, since Jesus blessed the Apostles, before ascending into heaven on a cloud, the priest preached to his congregation about priest's blessings, including homes, individuals, religious articles, etc. That same day, the priest returned to his hometown to visit family. He decided to stop by his boyhood home, and if possible, he hoped, the owners would allow him to see inside the house, which he hadn't seen in 40 years.

When he arrived, he noticed the current occupants were moving out and inquired about looking inside the home. When he entered the house, there was new carpet and the bathroom was remodeled, but otherwise, it looked remarkably the same.

The departing renters, who were moving out, told the priest they were moving out due to weird happenings in the house, such as a doll moving across the floor on its own, religious objects being tossed off of the walls, a dark figure being seen by their children, etc.

The owner of the house lived next door and so the priest asked his permission to bless his boyhood home. After he blessed it and was driving down the road, he realized, on Ascension Sunday, he preached on blessing homes during his weekend

Masses, and on the same day, blessed his former home which became haunted due to the Ouija board played 40 years earlier.

Story 2: Saint Dominic Heals Woman with a Blessing

"Behind the Church of Santa Anastasia lived another recluse named Sister Lucy, whom Sister Cecilia had seen many times before entering the convent. This recluse suffered severe infirmity in one of her arms. It was a disease that so ravaged her flesh and skin that nothing but bone was left from her shoulder to her hand. Since Blessed Dominic passed by her home whenever he journeyed to San Sisto, he frequently stopped in to visit her. One day, as he was visiting her in the company of Brother Bertrand of Spain and some of the other brethren, he made her show him the arm in which she had the infirmity. As she was showing it to him, he made the Sign of the Cross, blessed it and left. Then she discovered that, through the merits of Blessed Dominic, she had received a complete cure."[117]

Story 3: The Rosary Worked Miracles of Conversion
in the Family of Patrick & Nancy

Patrick Latta, a Canadian, said, "I had nothing to do with God, church, marriage, sacraments, school. I had a horrible time in Catholic school." One day, when Patrick was on the football field, the head coach yelled in front of everyone, "Hey, Latta, you can't play because you don't pay to come here." Patrick did not know he did not pay. "That was the end of my school – that was the end in believing in God." "That was the end of my school – that was the end in believing in God." He said, "I quit going to school when I was 16 to go wash cars in a car lot....10 years later I bought the company. I was a super salesman. I bought my own Honda dealership. I bought my own BMW dealership. We were the top gun in Western Canada. Nobody could outsell us."

"I have four children [from two previous marriages]. My children never saw the inside of the church – ever." He used to say to his children, "This is god," and would hold up money. "When you have enough of this, you have all the god you want." Patrick lamented, "That's a father speaking to his children."

He said that one day his youngest son came home from school and announced he had been baptized Anglican. Patrick said to his son, "You're supposed to be Catholic." "Dad, you never took me inside a church." Patrick again lamented, "Wasn't I a great father? And that's how I lived – no God, no prayer, no church. But my business was fantastic, so I have a huge successful business and I don't need God.

After his second divorce, Patrick met Nancy. Within two months they were living together. "No God, no prayer, no church, no marriage, no sacrament – nothing – living in mortal sin. We lived together six years."

One day, Nancy said that they should get married. Patrick agreed, and they got married the next day in a helicopter on top of a mountain. He hired a justice of the peace, and the pilot to be the best man. He didn't even know his name. When he came home from work the next day, Nancy was crying. She said, "I don't feel married." She wanted to get married in a church. Patrick said, "Nancy, do you know how much that helicopter cost?" She said, "I don't care about your helicopter. We have to get married in a church." Patrick reminded her that he had two previous divorces.

Nancy went to see the bishop, who had documentation on Patrick's annulment from his first marriage. Patrick did not even know the marriage was annulled! The second document said that Patrick's second marriage was never valid because he wasn't married in the Catholic Church.

The next day Nancy went to a church called "Immaculate Heart of Mary" to ask the priest to marry them. The priest agreed, but said to Nancy, "You're out of your mind to marry this guy in church. He'll never change. He's the worst case I've ever seen." Patrick agreed to attend marriage preparation classes and he made many promises – go to Mass, Confession, etc. – but admits he is a "professional promiser" since he is a car dealer. They did get married in the church, but he broke every promise he made.

That's how they lived... until one day when Nancy's brother sent them a book of messages of Our Lady of Medjugorje. He opened it and looked for the shortest message in the book. It said, "I call you to conversion for the last time." Then something happened. The tears just started and they wouldn't stop. He asked Nancy, "Why didn't you tell me about these messages? Why didn't you tell me they were true?"

Patrick confessed, "I saw myself for the first time – I'm Catholic and lived in mortal sin for 30 years. And it came back to me in one second – boom! In one minute everything changed in my life." He warned, "The day you see yourself as you live on this earth and you are Catholic and you are living in mortal sin – it's the worst day of your life, because reality hits you so hard and it's the truth." Patrick began to read the messages – they became his whole life.

He said the number one message of Our Lady is to pray the Rosary, because when you do, you'll see miracles in your family. The second message of Our Lady is to go to Mass – minimum of Sunday. Patrick started to say the Rosary and go to Mass. The third message Patrick said is the most difficult. Our Lady said She wants us to fast on Wednesdays and Fridays. Patrick looked up all the messages on fasting, and found that Our lady said, "When you pray and fast you can stop wars." Patrick thought, "What war am I going to stop?" Then the light went on – "I got a war on drugs, I got a war on alcohol, I got a war with divorces, I got a war on immorality you can't even talk about. My house is a war zone!" He repeated, "Fasting stops wars." So they learned to fast every Wednesday and Friday.

296

"When you fast you have no fear of the future." The next message is reading the Bible. They didn't even own a Bible, so Nancy had to buy one. Patrick said the fifth message is the big message of Medjugorje. "You can't start conversion without Confession." Patrick had not been to Confession for 30 years and had lots to confess." You know what the priest did? He said, 'I absolve you.' I broke into tears. 'I absolve you.' Who can say that? Nobody has that power – only a priest. I'm shocked at the mercy of God and I'm shocked at the power the priest has in Confession. 30 years of mortal sin went down the drain in one Confession!"

He asked the youngest son if he'd like to pray a Rosary with them and he declined for months before he finally agreed. Today, 19 years later, that son is a Catholic, married, with two beautiful kids. He is a teacher at a Catholic high school, and one year he even took 52 kids from his school to Medjugorje.

The second son went to Medjugorje once, and Patrick gave him a rosary. He went back to Canada and later called Patrick to tell him he quit drinking, quit rugby, and became a fireman. Patrick said, "How is that possible?" And the son said, "The rosary you gave me in Medjugorje." Today he is married and has two beautiful kids.

For 10 years, Patrick did not hear from his daughter. In February of 2012, he got a phone call from her. She said she was in Canada and wanted to come to Medjugorje."Daddy, I want to start again. Daddy, I don't want to be separated from the family anymore." At this point, she had been through three divorces. She came for two weeks to Medjugorje. She got a healing of her problem with alcohol and went back to the University for a nursing degree. Her life completely changed. "The divorce is gone – the alcohol is gone – the drugs are gone – from someone who started to pray."

Patrick asked for prayers for his oldest son who still lives an immoral lifestyle.

Patrick paraphrased, "Our Lady said if you do this (holding up the rosary), I'll show you miracles in your family." Patrick held up his rosary as he recalled how the priest said their marriage would not work.

Patrick sold his car dealerships, boat, house, cars, and everything to move to Medjugorje without even knowing where it was. Why? He quipped, "The Mother of God lives here and I want to be Her neighbor." He and Nancy built a castle used as a retreat house for priests who come to Medjugorje. He and Nancy gives daily talks to pilgrims. Holding up a rosary, he concluded, "This is the answer to every problem. This is the answer to your marriage. This is the answer to your kids."[118]

Apparition: Our Lady of Medjugorje (Bosnia-Herzegovina)

In Medjugorje, Bosnia-Herzegovina, the Virgin Mary allegedly began to appear to six children in June of 1981. There are five important things Our Lady is asking: 1. Prayer of the Heart & the Rosary daily 2. Attend Mass daily 3. Read the Holy Bible daily 4. Fast on Wednesday and Friday on Bread & Water 5. Monthly Confession.

Currently, monthly messages are given. When the apparitions conclude, there will be ten secrets revealed, including an indestructible permanent sign on apparition hill.

Here are the first three out of a number of messages Our Lady mentioned the Holy Rosary.

"I would like the people to pray along with me these days. And to pray as much as possible! And to fast strictly on Wednesdays and Fridays, and every day to pray at least one Rosary: the joyful, sorrowful and glorious mysteries." (August 14, 1984) "…. I request the families of the parish to pray the family Rosary. Thank you for having responded to my call." (September 27, 1984) "I invite you to call on everyone to pray the Rosary. With the Rosary you shall overcome all the adversities

298

which Satan is trying to inflict on the Catholic Church. All you priests, pray the Rosary! Dedicate your time to the Rosary! " (June 25, 1985) "Dear children! Today I call you especially now to advance against Satan by means of prayer. Satan wants to work still more now that you know he is at work. Dear children, put on the armor for battle and with the Rosary in your hand defeat him! Thank you for having responded to my call. " (August 8, 1985) "Dear children! Today, like never before, I invite you to prayer. Let your prayer be a prayer for peace. Satan is strong and desires to destroy not only human life, but also nature and the planet on which you live. Therefore, dear children, pray that through prayer you can protect yourselves with God's blessing of peace. God has sent me among you so that I may help you. If you so wish, grasp for the rosary. *Even the rosary alone can work miracles in the world and in your lives.* I bless you and I remain with you for as long as it is God's will. Thank you for not betraying my presence here and I thank you because your response is serving the good and the peace. " (January 25, 1991)

In a September 19, 2024 note, the Dicastery for the Doctrine of the Faith (DDF) approved the "spiritual experience connected with Medjugorje" as a place of pilgrimage, while declining to make a judgment about the supernatural character of the alleged private revelations associated with the shrine. The document said, "The uniqueness of the place lies in the large number of such fruits: abundant conversions, a frequent return to the sacraments (particularly, the Eucharist and Reconciliation), many vocations to priestly, religious, and married life, a deepening of the life of faith, a more intense practice of prayer, many reconciliations between spouses, and the renewal of marriage and family life. It should be noted that such experiences occur above all in the context of pilgrimages to the places associated with the original events rather than in meetings with the "visionaries" to be present for the alleged apparitions."

Descent of the Holy Spirit

Fruit of the Mystery: Holy Wisdom and Love of God

"When they entered the city they went to the upper room where they were staying, Peter and John and James and Andrew, Philip and Thomas, Bartholomew and Matthew, James son of Alphaeus, Simon the Zealot, and Judas son of James. All these devoted themselves with one accord to prayer, together with some women, and Mary the Mother of Jesus, and His brothers." (Acts 1:6-14)

Before the descent of the Holy Spirit, by Peter's lead, he requested that the apostles replace Judas. "Then they gave lots to them, and the lot fell upon Matthias, and he was counted with the eleven apostles." (Acts 1:26) Matthias was elected sometime after the Ascension of Jesus and before Pentecost, which would have been in a period of less than nine days.

Praying together in the upper room for nine days from Jesus' Ascension to the day of the coming of the Holy Spirit (Pentecost) was the first novena in the Church. They were still fearful of getting arrested and were in hiding.

It is notable that the Virgin Mary was praying with them. After Jesus ascended, She took part in the early Church. It is quite possible, before Jesus ascended into heaven, He instructed the Apostles to ask Mary to pray for specific intentions and invite Her to pray with them for the coming of the Holy Spirit. Surely, when they met with Her, after Pentecost, She encouraged them, gave them advice and cooked food for them when they were hungry.

"When the time for Pentecost was fulfilled, they were all in one place together. And suddenly there came from the sky a noise like a strong driving wind, and it filled the entire house in which they were. Then there appeared to them tongues as of fire, which parted and came to rest on each one of them. And they were all filled with the holy Spirit and began to speak in different tongues, as the Spirit enabled them to proclaim. Now there were devout Jews from every nation under heaven staying in Jerusalem. At this sound, they gathered in a large crowd, but they were confused because each one heard them speaking in his own language. They were astounded, and in amazement they asked, "Are not all these people who are speaking Galileans? Then how does each of us hear them in his own native language? We are Parthians, Medes, and Elamites, inhabitants of Mesopotamia, Judea and Cappadocia, Pontus and Asia, Phrygia and Pamphylia, Egypt and the districts of Libya near Cyrene, as well as travelers from Rome, both Jews and converts to Judaism, Cretans and Arabs, yet we hear them speaking in our own tongues of the mighty acts of God." They were all astounded and bewildered, and said to one another, "What does this mean?" But others said, scoffing, "They have had too much new wine." (Act 2:1-13)

Imagine for a moment, what it was like in the upper room when they were gathered praying, "O Holy Advocate, Spirit of God, Come! Be with us!" Undoubtedly, they first heard the sound of a strong wind. Most likely, the Holy Spirit first descended upon Mary, then everyone else in the room. They must have been astonished to see the largest of flames above the Mother of Jesus and then above their heads. One of the apostles shouts, "See how His Mother Mary is glowing with love!" It is possible John could have been facing Peter and talking to him, with his back towards everyone else, and then suddenly shouted, "Peter, look, you have flames above your head." And he responded, "John, they are above your head and everyone's in the room." John then turned around and beheld the flames above everyone's head, including his own.

302

Perhaps, they reached above their own head to touch it, only to be surprised by the gentleness and love which came forth from it. The flame didn't hurt, but rather, they felt a sudden pulse inside their heart that gave them courage and strength. An inner joy arose from within. They experienced sweet happiness and unbounded joy mixed with astonishment and praise.

Those gathered outside heard the strong wind, but couldn't see it. Due to the wind, the shutters to the windows and the door suddenly flung open with a bang and crashed against the wall. It was then, the crowd outside noticed something amazing was happening.

Inside the room, the apostles felt God's immense love. "My heart is glad and my soul rejoices!" (Psalm 16:9) "It's like rivers of living water flowing from my heart." (cf. John 7:38) "...courage surged up within me..." (Daniel 10:19) "Its arrows are arrows of fire, flames of the divine. Deep waters cannot quench love, nor rivers sweep it away. Were one to offer all the wealth of his house for love, he would be roundly mocked." (Song of Songs 8:6-7)

Fear immediately vanished from their hearts. They were impelled by the Holy Spirit to witness Jesus and all stepped out on the terrace.

"Then Peter stood up with the Eleven, raised his voice, and proclaimed to them, "You who are Jews, indeed all of you staying in Jerusalem. Let this be known to you, and listen to my words. These people are not drunk, as you suppose, for it is only nine o'clock in the morning. Indeed, upon my servants and my handmaids I will pour out a portion of my spirit in those days, and they shall prophesy." (Acts 2:14-15)

"You who are Israelites, hear these words. Jesus the Nazorean was a man commended to you by God with mighty deeds, wonders, and signs, which God worked through him in your midst, as you yourselves know. This man, delivered up by the set plan and foreknowledge of God, you killed, using lawless

303

men to crucify him. But God raised him up, releasing him from the throes of death, because it was impossible for him to be held by it." "Therefore let the whole house of Israel know for certain that God has made him both Lord and Messiah, this Jesus whom you crucified." Now when they heard this, they were cut to the heart, and they asked Peter and the other apostles, "What are we to do, my brothers?" Peter [said] to them, "Repent and be baptized, every one of you, in the name of Jesus Christ for the forgiveness of your sins; and you will receive the gift of the Holy Spirit. For the promise is made to you and to your children and to all those far off, whomever the Lord our God will call." He testified with many other arguments, and was exhorting them, "Save yourselves from this corrupt generation." Those who accepted his message were baptized, and about three thousand persons were added that day." (cf. Acts 2:22-41)

With great courage, Peter, the first pope, gave a sermon confronting all present with each person's role in the death of Jesus, when he said to them, "whom you crucified". He made it clear everyone without exception was responsible for the crucifixion of Jesus.

Amazingly, through his convicting words by the power of the Holy Spirit, three thousand persons were baptized that day, and the Church was born.

Pentecost was one of the three great Jewish Feasts for which many Israelites went on pilgrimage to the Holy City of Jerusalem to worship God in the temple. It originated as a harvest thanksgiving, with an offering of first fruits. Before Jesus came, the Jewish Pentecost celebration was held fifty days after Passover, when they slaughtered the lambs as sacrifice and ate the Passover meal. When the Holy Spirit came down upon the apostles, it gave a new spiritual meaning to the Jewish Pentecost. It was fifty days after Passover, when Jesus suffered and died on Good Friday, when He "passed over" from this life to the next.

Recall that John took Mary into his home, after the crucifixion. They were together until Mary was assumed into heaven. During the time She lived with Him, She would have attended the Holy Sacrifice of the Mass offered by John and received Her Son Jesus in Holy Communion at the hands of our Lord's beloved apostle. Together, they went to Ephesus and then returned to Jerusalem. No one, other than Joseph, knew the Virgin Mary as well as John. What a tremendous privilege to live with the Mother of God. To eat Her food, to speak to Her about Her relationship with Jesus. How many divine things did She teach Him? Most assuredly She taught him how to pray more intensely and to be a holy priest and bishop. Today in Ephesus, the house in which Mary and John lived, is a shrine many visit.

When the Church was born on Pentecost, so were all the sacraments. After Peter's sermon and the three thousand who were baptized on the day of Pentecost, the Catholic Church began to grow. Recall the method of baptizing new disciples was given to the apostles, just before Jesus ascended into heaven. He said, "Go therefore, and make disciples of all nations, baptizing them, in the name of the Father and of the Son and of the Holy Spirit, teaching them to observe all that I have commanded you." (Matthew 28:19-20)

Pentecost was the Apostles' Sacrament of Confirmation. By the descent of the Holy Spirit upon them, their baptismal graces were strengthened. They became immediate witnesses to Jesus. They became soldiers for Christ, ready to die as a martyr for Him and His Church, if needed. Their mission was to make disciples through baptism and establish the Church by their foundation, with Peter, the first pope, as their leader.

The sacrament of Confirmation was given in the early Church after Baptism through laying on of the hands. "Now when the apostles in Jerusalem heard that Samaria had accepted the word of God, they sent them Peter and John, who went down and prayed for them, that they might receive the Holy Spirit, for

305

it had not yet fallen upon any of them; they had only been baptized in the name of the Lord Jesus. Then they laid hands on them and they received the Holy Spirit. When Simon saw that the Spirit was conferred by the laying on of the apostles' hands..." (Acts 8:14-18)

Application 1: Confirmation

Today, the Sacrament of Confirmation is *erroneously* described to young people and parents, as a moment when a child becomes an adult in the Catholic Church.

It is one of the three sacraments of initiation and so when one receives Baptism, Confirmation and Holy Eucharist, one is fully initiated into the Church, but that does not mean they are adults in the Church.

The sacrament was formerly administered by the bishop before Holy Communion. Now more and more dioceses are reestablishing the practice. Children now more than ever need to receive the Sacrament of Confirmation at an early age to help them make wise choices before their teen years.

By a sacramental outpouring of the Holy Spirit, we receive seven-fold gifts: courage, counsel, knowledge, wisdom, piety, fear of the Lord, and fortitude. We may take on a new saint's name as we befriend them and try to imitate their virtues, asking for their prayers throughout our lives.

The Holy Spirit made all the apostles witnesses for Christ. All but John were martyred, but they attempted to kill him too, by dropping him in boiling oil, but it miraculously had no effect on him. St. Cyprian describes heroic men and women, who died as soldiers for Christ.

"How pleasing did the sworn allegiance and loyalty of his soldiers render the dead in God's sight! In the psalms, where the Holy Spirit speaks to us and

306

counsels us, it is written: Precious in the sight of God is the death of his holy ones. Rightly is that death called "precious," for at the price of blood it purchased immortality and won God's crown through the ultimate act of courage. How happy Christ was to be there, how gladly he fought and conquered in such servants! He protects their faith and gives strength to believers in proportion to the trust that each man who receives that strength is willing to place in him. Christ was there to wage his own battle; He aroused the soldiers who fought for His name; He made them spirited and strong. And He who once for all has conquered death for us, now continually conquers in us. How blessed is this Church of ours, so honored and illuminated by God and ennobled in these our days by the glorious blood of martyrs! In earlier times it shone white with the good deeds of our brethren, and now it is adorned with the red blood of martyrs. It counts both lilies and roses among its garlands. Let each of us, then, strive for the highest degree of glory, whichever be the honor for which he is destined; may all Christians be found worthy of either the pure white crown of a holy life or the royal red crown of martyrdom."[119]

Application 2: Charismatic Movement

Over the past 50 years the Charismatic movement developed, whereby charismatic prayer groups pray to the Holy Spirit. Some are said to experience "praying in tongues" and prophecies or "slain in the spirit" and have a "baptism of the Holy Spirit."

Several popes, Pope Saint John Paul II and Pope Saint Paul VI have given support to the Charismatic movement, but no pope has ever publicly supported "praying in tongues".

The practice of Baptism in the Spirit can cause confusion, because it is not a sacrament, and one undoubtedly receives the Holy Spirit at baptism. But Charismatics describe the experience as stirring up the gifts received at Baptism and Confirmation and thus an increased experience of the Spirit in their lives and thus a fuller activation of the aforementioned gifts.

Pope Benedict in the *Ratzinger Report* said, "In the heart of a world desiccated by rationalistic skepticism a new experience of the Holy Spirit has come about, amounting to a worldwide renewal movement. What the New Testament describes, with reference to the charisms, as visible signs of the coming of the Holy Spirit is no longer merely ancient, past history: this history is becoming a reality today."

When the apostles prayed in tongues (other languages), they knew what they were saying, and so did those who heard them. To be "drunk in the Spirit", as some call it, as they laugh boisterously and holler out loud during Mass, or Eucharistic Adoration cannot be of God. When there is a lack of reverence given to Jesus in the Most Blessed Sacrament and when attention is on an individual and not Jesus in the Sacred Host, something is wrong.

Why is it that these things never happen while attending a Traditional Latin Mass? During the TLM nobody would dare raise their hands and sing spontaneously in tongues, because everyone knows if one were to do such a thing, it would be for the sake of personal attention and cause distractions among attendees of the Holy Sacrifice.

It is disconcerting and not a good sign, when, at times, the movement fails to lead members to the sacraments especially to Confession and the Holy Mass.

Feelings and emotions can fool us, and in fact, evil spirits often use them to attack us and attack others.

Today, the world needs an ever growing love, a more frequent and fervent prayer to the Holy Spirit, to guide us, to speak through us, to strengthen us, to comfort us, to give us wisdom, understanding, knowledge, courage, piety, reverence for God and counsel. We should pray to Our Lady, asking the Virgin Mother to intercede for us, as She prayed for the coming of the Holy Spirit before Pentecost.

The following is a traditional prayer commonly prayed invoking the aid of the Holy Spirit.

> Come, Holy Spirit, fill the hearts of your faithful
> and kindle in them the fire of your love.
> Send forth your Spirit and they shall be created,
> and you shall renew the face of the earth.
> *Let us pray.*
> O God, who have taught the hearts of the faithful
> by the light of the Holy Spirit,
> grant that in the same Spirit we may be truly wise
> and ever rejoice in his consolation.
> Through Christ our Lord. Amen.

Application 3: Mass is Offered in Early Church & Confessions Heard

In the Acts of the Apostles, it speaks about how they came together for the Holy Mass, "And they devoted themselves to the apostle's teaching and fellowship, to the breaking of bread and the prayers." (Acts 2:42) The apostles offered Holy Mass, especially on the Lord's Day. In the New Testament, whenever the words "breaking of the bread" are used, it always refers to the early Christians gathering for the Holy Sacrifice of the Mass.

St. Paul also refers to the Mass as the Lord's Supper, when he said they come to meet to celebrate the Lord's Supper.

When he wrote to the people of Corinth, he spoke about when they came together for the Lord's Supper. "For I received from the Lord what I also handed on to you, that the Lord Jesus, on the night he was handed over, took bread, and, after he had given thanks, broke it and said, "This is my body that is for you. Do this in remembrance of me." In the same way also the cup, after supper, saying, "This cup is the new covenant in my blood. Do this, as often as you drink it, in remembrance of me." For as often as you eat this bread and drink the cup, you proclaim the death of the Lord until he comes." (Corinthians 11:18-26)

The apostles began to exercise the ministry of reconciliation (Confession), after Easter Sunday, when He came to them in the upper room and gave them authority to forgive sins. He said, "Jesus said to them again, "Peace be with you. As the Father has sent me, so I send you." And when he had said this, he breathed on them and said to them, "Receive the Holy Spirit. Whose sins you forgive are forgiven them, and whose sins you retain are retained." (John 20:21-23)

In the words of Paul, the apostles were ministers of reconciliation, "All this is from God, who through Christ reconciled us to himself and gave us the ministry of reconciliation" (2 Corinthians. 5:18). The apostles and their successors are merely ambassadors for Christ (2 Corinthians. 5:20), bringing His forgiveness to the world through the sacraments and the message of the Gospel.

Besides the problem of some priests not making Confession available except for an hour or less on Saturday. Some will tell penitents in Confession or preach in their homilies, that they only need to mention mortal sins in confession. And if a penitent attempts to confess venial sins, the priest may deem the person as scrupulous or has the problem of "navel gazing."

But, the truth is, it is not scrupulous to confess venial sins. It's scrupulous when one thinks every sin they commit is a mortal sin or they perceive something is a sin, but is clearly no sin at all.

The Catechism of the Catholic Church (#1458), states, "Without being strictly necessary, confession of everyday faults (venial sins) is nevertheless strongly recommended by the Church.. Indeed the regular confession of our venial sins helps us form our conscience, fight against evil tendencies, let ourselves be healed by Christ and progress in the life of the Spirit. By receiving more frequently through this sacrament the gift of the Father's mercy, we are spurred to be merciful as He is merciful…"

We should regularly pray for priests and especially the priests to whom we will confess. May Jesus help them to be zealous dispensers of His infinite Mercy, and so, help the souls entrusted to them to grow in holiness.

Pope Saint John Paul II confessed daily. Saint Padre Pio encouraged all his penitents to confess weekly. Priests and religious have traditionally confessed weekly.

This precept or rule of the Church — a violation of which is a sin of disobedience to legitimate authority — is binding on all Catholics over the age of reason. You must go to Confession at least once a year if you're aware of having committed any mortal sin, that is, a grave or serious sin.

While the Church only requires one to confess mortal sins once a year, if one were to fall into mortal sin, one should not delay in going to Confession, in order to continue to receive Holy Communion. When one delays confessing a mortal sin, one is taking the risk of dying unrepentant and going to hell for all eternity.

If we want to give up our sins, avoid mortal sins, grow in holiness and have peace in our heart, regular Confession can be a joyful way to live the Christian life.

The three sacraments Baptism, Confession, Eucharist most especially, help us to see how the Church grew. By making new disciples through Baptism, coming together in "the breaking of the bread" for Holy Mass to receive Holy Communion, and by obtaining forgiveness in Confession. For centuries, these three sacraments were indispensable for Christians in helping them to obtain heaven.

By apostolic succession of ordaining new bishops and priests through the laying on of the hands, once ordained, men became instruments of God's mercy in every age unto today.

St. Paul said to his disciple Timothy: "I remind you to rekindle the gift of God that is within you through the laying on of my hands" (2 Timothy 1:6), and "If any one aspires to the office of bishop, he desires a noble task." (1 Timothy 3:1) To Titus he said: "This is why I left you in Crete, that you amend what was defective, and appoint presbyters in every town, as I directed you" (Titus 1:5).

Application 4: Three Fonts of Mercy & Divine Mercy Feast Day

Due to private revelation in the *Diary of St. Faustina*, these three sacraments (Baptism, Confession, Eucharist) are fonts of mercy and highlighted especially for Divine Mercy Sunday, (the Sunday after Easter) established by Pope St. John Paul II in 2000.

In a 1936 vision to Saint Faustina, Our Lord promised when a baptized Catholic, goes to Confession, and receives Holy Communion on the Sunday after Easter (Divine Mercy Sunday), he or she will have the complete forgiveness of their sins and all the punishment due to them. He said to Saint Faustina, "My daughter, tell the whole world about My inconceivable mercy. I desire that the Feast of Mercy be a refuge and shelter for all souls, and especially for poor sinners. On that day the very depths of My tender mercy are open. I pour out a whole ocean of graces upon those souls who approach the fount of My mercy. The soul that will go to Confession and receive Holy Communion shall obtain complete forgiveness of sins and punishment. On that day all the divine floodgates through which grace flows are opened. Let no soul fear to draw near to Me, even though its sins be as scarlet. My mercy is so great that no mind, be it of man or of angel, will be able to fathom it throughout all eternity. Everything that exists has come forth from the very depths of My most tender mercy. Every soul in its relation to Me will contemplate My love and mercy throughout eternity. The Feast of Mercy emerged from My very depths of tenderness. It is My desire that it be solemnly celebrated on the First Sunday after Easter. Mankind will not have peace until it turns to the Fount of My Mercy." (Diary #699)

For a newly baptized Christian, all sins and the punishment due to their sins are washed away in the ocean of God's infinite mercy no matter the day of the year. We see an amazing example in Dr. Bernard Nathanson, an abortionist, who abandoned his abortion practice and became Catholic, when he was baptized by Cardinal O'Connor in New York's St. Patrick's Cathedral in December of 1996. Before his baptism, he admitted to having killed over 70,000 unborn children. At the moment of his baptism, all his sins and the punishment due to his sins were washed away. And if he would have died immediately after his baptism, without any sin on his soul, he would have gone straight to heaven. Oh, how unfathomable is God's mercy!

Does anyone's sins compare to Dr. Nathanson? Hardly. We merely need to trust that no matter what kind of sin or how many of them, God will forgive.

On the Feast of Divine Mercy, if we go to Confession during the Lenten season, or up to, or on Divine Mercy Sunday, and receive Holy Communion in the state of grace on Divine Mercy Sunday, the Sunday after Easter, then all our sins and the punishment due to them are all washed away. All we have to do is have confidence and trust in God's mercy.

To prepare for the feast of Divine Mercy, there is a nine day novena starting on Good Friday and ending on the Saturday before Divine Mercy Sunday. The feast should be preceded by works of mercy, and on the feast, one should obtain a plenary indulgence, by attending a divine mercy celebration or some other way of obtaining the indulgence on that day, such as, make the Way of the Cross, pray a Holy Rosary in a group, read Sacred Scripture for thirty minutes etc.

The Holy Spirit's action of preparing souls for heaven through the sacraments, that were born on the day of Pentecost, reminds us that, we are not left as orphans, as Jesus promised on the day He ascended into heaven. But rather, Our Lord is with us, unto the end of time and will help us to bear witness to Him under persecution and even unto death.

Application 5: Sacraments are to be Offered as the Church Prescribes

Sadly, in recent years, there have been some priests, who through laxity, or inattentiveness, fail to give absolution in Confession as required by the Church in her *Rite of Penance*.

Every sacrament has form and matter. Form are the words required by the Church to impart the sacrament and matter refers to material such as oil, bread, wine, water, or in the case of Confession, the material is sin.

For example, when anointing with Sacred Chrism (matter), for the sacrament of Confirmation, the bishop or priest delegate uses the words "Name_____ (saint name or baptismal name), be sealed with the gift of the Holy Spirit. Amen." (form)

The proper words used by the priest when absolving sins in Confession are "I absolve you from your sins, in the name of the Father, and of the Son, and of the Holy Spirit. Amen." (form)

Some priests erroneously say, "I absolve you <u>of</u> your sins, Father, Son and Holy Spirit." Notice how the word "from" is substituted with "of." And the words <u>"in the name of the Father, and of the Son, and of the Holy Spirit…"</u> are also not said.

Perhaps priests are confusing the words of absolution with the end of Mass blessing, saying, "May almighty God bless you, the Father, and the Son, and the Holy Spirit." In this particular blessing at the end of Mass, the Church does not have the priest say, "In the name of...."

Some priests have even said, "Jesus forgives you, I forgive you, Father, Son and Holy Spirit forgives you." It is up to proper Church authority to determine if these confessions are valid or not. The point is, the priest should leave no doubt in the mind of the one receiving a sacrament, that what they have received is valid, and therefore, the priest should be exact in following the proper words used when imparting a sacrament.

If you are certain the priest didn't say the words properly, just gently and calmly say, "Father, I'm sure you didn't realize it, but you accidentally said the prayer inaccurately. Would you mind saying the absolution again?" If he refuses or repeats it in the wrong way, just leave the confessional and go to Confession to different priest. If you want, you can later visit with him or send him a charitable note.

Most canon lawyers say the Church does not supply "ecclesia supplet" for invalid sacraments, except for errors that may occur in weddings, and can later be "sanated" or healed.

Please, pray for priests. They are human and can accidentally, either by age, or health, or for some other reason make mistakes.

To be instruments of the Holy Spirit for the sacraments, priests need to strictly adhere to the Church's rites and do as the Church intends. Their life of holiness will allow a greater action of the Holy Spirit to impact those whom they serve. When imparting a sacrament, if a priest himself were to be in mortal sin, the grace of the sacraments are still conveyed. However, less graces will be poured out on those to whom they serve. The holier the priest, the greater graces bestowed, and therefore, the

Holy Spirit is permitted in a greater way to help souls on their journey to heaven.

When we pray the Holy Rosary, it is very important to regularly pray for priests and priests should remember to pray for their brother priests when they pray their daily Rosary.

Application 6: Uneducated Apostles Founded the Church

From a homily on the first letter to the Corinthians by Saint John Chrysostom, bishop.

"It was clear through unlearned men that the cross was persuasive, in fact, it persuaded the whole world. Their discourse was not of unimportant matters but of God and true religion, of the Gospel way of life and future judgment, yet it turned plain, uneducated men into philosophers. How the foolishness of God is wiser than men, and his weakness stronger than men! In what way is it stronger? It made its way throughout the world and overcame all men; countless men sought to eradicate the very name of the Crucified, but that name flourished and grew even mightier. Its enemies lost out and perished; the living who waged war on a dead man proved helpless. Therefore, when a Greek tells me I am dead, he shows only that he is foolish indeed, for I, whom he thinks a fool, turn out to be wiser than those reputed wise. So too, in calling me weak, he but shows that he is weaker still. For the good deeds which tax-collectors and fishermen were able to accomplish by Gods grace, the philosophers, the rulers, the countless multitudes cannot even imagine. Paul had this in mind when he said: The weakness of God is stronger than men. That the preaching of these men was indeed divine is brought home to us in the same way. For how otherwise could twelve uneducated men, who lived on lakes and rivers and wastelands, get the idea for such an immense enterprise? How could men who perhaps had never been in a city or a public square think of setting out to do battle with the whole world? That they were fearful, timid men, the evangelist makes clear; he did not reject the fact or try to hide their weaknesses. Indeed he turned these into a proof of the truth. What did he say of them? That when Christ was arrested, the others fled, despite all the miracles they had seen, while he who was leader of the others denied him!"[120]

Story 1: St. James & Our Lady of the Pillar

Saint James had a tremendous event happen to him. Not only did Jesus appear to His Mother before the other apostles, but James experienced an apparition of the Virgin Mary. Although it was technically a bilocation of Our Lady, because She was living with John the Apostle in Jerusalem at the time, it is still regarded as an apparition by the tradition of the Church.

"The apparition is called Our Lady of the Pillar and is recognized as the first Marian apparition in the history of Christianity. According to tradition, James the Greater, brother of Saint John the Evangelist, traveled with great effort to Roman Hispania (modern-day Spain) to evangelize the local tribes. He not only confronted great difficulties but he also saw very little apostolic fruits of conversion. Tradition says that when he was at his lowest point of discouragement, in A.D. 40, while he was sitting by the banks of the Ebro River in Zaragoza (back then known as Caesaraugusta) Mary appeared to him accompanied by thousands of angels, to console and encourage him. The Virgin Mary, with the Child Jesus in Her arms and standing on a pillar, asked Saint James and his eight disciples to build a church on the site, promising that "it will stand from that moment until the end of time in order that God may work miracles and wonders through My intercession for all those who place themselves under My patronage."[121]

"The church of Our Lady of the Pillar in Zaragoza, is the first church dedicated to Mary in history and it remains standing to this day, having survived invasions and wars. During the Spanish Civil War (1936-1939) the Communists dropped three bombs on the church from an airplane, the bombs tore through the roof and hit the floor, but none of them exploded. The three now deactivated bombs are currently on display in one of the Basilica's walls. Our Lady is also said to have given the small wooden statue of the apparition to Saint James, which now stands on the pillar She arrived on. The wooden statue is about 15 inches high."[122]

Saint James would be the first of the apostles to be martyred. It is no wonder, Our Lord and Our Lady each gave him special appearances.

Story 2: St. Philip Neri & His Experience with the Holy Spirit

Saint Philip Neri is known for a miraculous event with the Holy Spirit. "A few days before Pentecost in 1544, while Saint Philip Neri was with the greatest earnestness asking of the Holy Ghost, His gifts, there appeared to him a globe of fire, which entered into his mouth and lodged in his breast; and thereupon he was suddenly surprised with such a fire of love, that, unable to bear it, he threw himself on the ground, and, like one trying to cool himself, bared his breast to temper in some measure the flame which he felt. When he had remained so for some time, and was a little recovered, he rose up full of unwonted joy, and

318

immediately all his body began to shake with a violent tremor; and putting his hand to his bosom, he felt by the side of his heart, a swelling about as big as a man's fist, but neither then nor afterwards was it attended with the slightest pain or wound." The cause of this swelling was discovered by the doctors who examined his body after death. The saint's heart had been dilated under the sudden impulse of love, and in order that it might have sufficient room to move, two ribs had been broken, and curved in the form of an arch. From the time of the miracle till his death, his heart would palpitate violently whenever he performed any spiritual action."[123]

If the Holy Spirit would come upon the average person, so strongly, it would painfully expand several ribs to break, then that would be a gift of the Holy Spirit! St. Francis of Assisi, St. Catherine of Sienna and St. Padre Pio's wounds could be understood as a gift of the Holy Spirit, ouch! To suffer with pain, is to suffer with love.

Story 3: Rosary Novena Closes Abortion Clinic

The people of the Diocese of Wichita prayed a Seven Sorrows of Mary Rosary Novena from May 16th to May 24th in 2006 to close "Central Women's Services", an abortion clinic. On the last day of the Novena, May 24th, the feast of Our Lady Help of Christians, the clinic permanently closed and later became the home of Operation Rescue. From 1983 until 2006 it is estimated that 50,000 pre-born children died there.

Story 4: The Martyrdom of Saint Eusebius

Maxentius, president of the province, commanded the priest Eusebius to sacrifice to the gods and for refusing, he was sentenced to death by beheading. Eusebius prayed, "I thank Your goodness and praise Your power, O Lord Jesus Christ, that, by calling me to the trial of my fidelity, You have treated me as one of Yours." He heard a voice from heaven say, "If you had not been found worthy to suffer, you could not be admitted into the court of Christ or to the seats of the just." When he came to the place of execution, he knelt down, and his head was struck off.[124]

Apparition: Our Lady of Kibeho (Rawanda)

In the Church-approved apparitions in Kibeho, Rwanda that began November 28, 1981, the Virgin Mary appeared to young girls under the name "Nyina wa Jambo" that is, "Mother of the Word".

In the visions, the Virgin Mary asked for penance and fasting for the conversion of sinners, and the frequent recitation of the Rosary. The girls also saw a prophetic vision of the Rwandan genocide that would occur thirteen years later. During one of Marie-Claire's visions, Our Lady told her that she had come to Rwanda because she was still able to find humble souls who were not attached to wealth. "Pray my Seven Sorrows rosary to find repentance," she said, charging Marie-Claire with the distinctive mission of propagating this Rosary.

On August 15, 1982, another visionary, Alphonsine was shown a river of blood, of decapitated heads, of corpses piled high upon each other, of untold destruction, torture, and hatred. "So much blood!" The horror continued as she saw a million headless bodies piled up in a vast land, and not a single living person to help bury the dead.

Assumption of Mary

Fruit of the Mystery: Grace of a Happy Death

"Arise, O Lord, into your resting place: you and the ark, which you have sanctified" Psalm 131:8 "And a great sign appeared in heaven, a woman clothed with the sun, with the moon under Her feet, and on Her head a crown of twelve stars." (Rev. 12:1)

There is no better way to enter into a meditation on the Assumption of Mary than to read excerpts from St. Alphonsus Liguori's spiritual classic, *The Glories of Mary:*

> "After the ascension of Jesus Christ, Mary remained on earth to attend to the propagation of the faith. Hence the disciples of our Lord had recourse to Her, and She solved their doubts, comforted them in their persecutions, and encouraged them to labor for the Divine glory and the salvation of redeemed souls. She willingly remained on earth, knowing that such was the will of God, for the good of the Church; but She could not but feel the pain of being far from the presence and sight of Her beloved Son, who had ascended to Heaven. [....]
>
> The most holy Virgin consoled Her loving Heart during this painful separation by visiting, as it is related, the holy places of Palestine, where Her Son had been during His life. She frequently visited--at one time the stable at Bethlehem, where Her Son was born; at another, the workshop of Nazareth, where Her Son had lived so many years poor and despised; now the Garden of Gethsemane, where Her Son began His Passion; then the

Prætorium of Pilate, where He was scourged, and the spot on which He was crowned with thorns; but visited most frequently Mount of Calvary, where Her Son expired; and the Holy Sepulchre in which She had finally left Him: thus did the most loving Mother soothe the pains of Her cruel exile."[....]

"...some days before Her death, our Lord sent Her the Archangel Gabriel, the same that announced to Her that She was that blessed woman chosen to be the Mother of God: " My Lady and Queen," said the Angel, " God has already graciously heard thy holy desires, and has sent me to tell thee to prepare thyself to leave the earth: for He wills thee in Heaven. Come, then, to take possession of thy kingdom; for it and all its holy inhabitants await and desire thee.," On this happy annunciation, what else could our most humble and most holy Virgin do, but, with the most profound humility, answer in the same words in which She had answered St. Gabriel when he announced to Her that She was to become the Mother of God: Behold the handmaid of the Lord. May the will of my God and Lord be ever accomplished in Me!"

After receiving this welcome intelligence She imparted it to St. John. We may well imagine with what grief and tender feelings he heard the news; he who for so many years had attended upon Her as a son, and had enjoyed the Heavenly conversation of this most holy Mother. She then once more visited the holy places of Jerusalem, tenderly taking leave of them, and especially of Mount Calvary, where Her beloved Son had died. She then retired into Her poor cottage, there to prepare for death.

During this time the Angels did not cease their visits to their beloved Queen, consoling themselves with the thought that they would soon see Her crowned in Heaven. Many authors, such as Andrew of Crete, St. John Damascene, Euthymius, assert that, before Her death, the Apostles, and also many disciples who were scattered in different parts of the world, were miraculously assembled in Mary's room, and that when She saw all these Her dear children in Her presence, She thus addressed them: "My beloved children, through love for you and to help you my Son left me on this earth. The holy faith is now spread throughout the world, already the fruit of the Divine seed is grown up; hence my Lord, seeing that my assistance on earth is no longer necessary, and compassionating my grief in being separated from Him, has graciously listened to my desire to quit this life and to go and see Him in Heaven. Do you remain, then, to labor for His glory? If I leave you, my heart remains with you; the great love I bear you shall carry with me and always preserve. I go to Paradise to pray for you."

Who can form an idea of the tears and lamentation of the holy disciples at this sad announcement, and the thought that soon they were to be separated from their Mother? All then, weeping, exclaimed, Then, O Mary, thou art already about to leave us. It is true that this world is not a place worthy of or fit for thee; and as for us, we are unworthy to enjoy the society of the Mother of God; but, remember, thou art our Mother, hitherto thou hast enlightened us in our doubts; thou hast consoled us in our afflictions; thou hast been our strength in persecutions; and now, how canst thou abandon us, leaving us alone in the midst of so many enemies and so many conflicts, deprived of thy consolation? We have already lost on earth Jesus, our Master and Father, Who has ascended into Heaven; until now we have found consolation in thee, our Mother; and now, how canst thou also leave us orphans without father or mother? Our own sweet Lady, either remain with us, or take us with thee." Thus St. John Damascene writes: "No, my children" [thus sweetly the loving Queen began to speak], "this is not according to the will of God; be satisfied to do that which He has decreed for me and for you. To you it yet remains to labor on earth for the glory of your Redeemer, and to make up your eternal crown. I do not leave you to abandon you, but to help you still more in Heaven by my intercession with God. Be satisfied. I commend the holy Church to you; I commend redeemed souls to you; let this be my last farewell, and the only remembrance I leave you: execute it if you love me, labor for the good of souls and for the glory of my Son; for one day we shall meet again in Paradise, never more for all eternity to be separated."

She then begged them to give burial to Her body after death; blessed them, and desired St. John, as St. John Damascene relates, to give after Her death two of Her gowns to two virgins who had served Her for some time. She then decently composed Herself on Her poor little bed, where She laid Herself to await death, and with it the meeting with the Divine Spouse, who shortly was to come and take Her with Him to the Kingdom of the blessed. Behold, She already feels in Her heart a great joy, the forerunner of the coming of the Bridegroom, which inundates Her with an unaccustomed and novel sweetness. The holy Apostles, seeing that Mary was already on the point of leaving this world, renewing their tears, all threw themselves on their knees around Her bed; some kissed Her holy feet, some sought a special blessing from Her, some recommended a particular want, and all wept bitterly; for their hearts were pierced with grief at being obliged to separate themselves for the rest of their lives from their beloved Lady. And She, the most loving Mother, compassionated all, and consoled each one; to some promising Her patronage, blessing others with particular affection, and encouraging others to the work of the conversion of the world; especially, She called St. Peter to Her, and as head of the Church and Vicar of Her Son, recommended to him in a particular manner the propagation of the faith, promising him at the same time Her especial protection in Heaven. But more particularly did She call St. John to Her, who more than any other was grieved at this moment when he had to part with his holy Mother [....] said: "My own John, I thank thee for all the assistance that thou hast afforded my Son, be assured of it, I shall not be ungrateful. If I now leave thee, I go to pray for thee. Remain in peace in this life until we meet again in Heaven, where I await thee. Never forget me. In all thy wants call me to aid; for I will never forget thee, my beloved son. So bless thee, I leave thee my blessing. Remain in peace. Farewell!"

But already the death of Mary is at hand; [....] Then the host of Angels come in choirs to meet

Her, as if to be ready for the great triumph with which they were to accompany Her to Paradise. Mary was indeed consoled at the sight of these holy spirits, but was not fully consoled; for She did not yet see Her beloved Jesus, Who was the whole love of Her heart. [….]

But, behold, Jesus is now come to take his Mother to the kingdom of the blessed. It was revealed to St. Elizabeth that Her Son appeared to Mary before She expired with His Cross in His hands, to show the special glory He had obtained by the Redemption; having, by His death, made acquisition of that great creature, who for all eternity was to honor Him more than all men and Angels. St. John Damascene relates that our Lord himself gave Her the Viaticum, saying with tender love, "Receive, O My Mother, from My hands that same Body that thou gavest to Me." And the Mother, having received with the greatest love that last Communion, with Her last breath said, "My Son, into Thy hands do I commend my spirit. I commend to Thee this soul, which from the beginning Thou didst create rich in so many graces, and by a singular privilege didst preserve from the stain of Original Sin. I commend to Thee my body, from which Thou didst deign to take Thy flesh and blood. I also commend to Thee these my beloved children [speaking of the holy disciples, who surrounded Her]; they are grieved at my departure. Do Thou, Who lovest them more than I do, console them; bless them, and give them strength to do great things for Thy glory."

The life of Mary being now at its close, the most delicious music, as St. Jerome relates, was heard in the apartment where She lay; and, according to a revelation of St. Bridget, the room was also filled with a brilliant light. The sweet music, and the unaccustomed splendor, warned the holy Apostles that Mary was departing. This caused them again to burst forth in tears and prayers; and raising their hands, with voice they exclaimed, "O, Mother, thou already goest to Heaven; thou leavest us; give us thy last blessing and never forget us miserable creatures."

Mary, turning Her eyes around upon all, as if to bid the last farewell, said, " Adieu, my children; I bless you, fear not, I will never forget you." And now death came; not indeed clothed in mourning and grief, as it does to others, but adorned with light and gladness. But what do we say? Why speak of death? Let us rather say that Divine love came, and cut the thread of that noble life. And as a light, before going out, gives a last and brighter flash than ever, so did this beautiful creature, on hearing Her Son's invitation to follow him, wrapped in the flames of love, and in the midst of Her amorous sighs, gave a last sigh of still more ardent love, and breathing forth Her soul, expired. Thus was that great soul, that beautiful dove of the Lord, loosened from the bands of this life; thus did She enter into glory of the blessed, where She is now seated, and will be seated, Queen of Paradise, for all eternity."[125]

"The Apostles took up Her body on a bier and placed it in a tomb; and they guarded it, expecting the Lord to come. And behold, again the Lord stood by them; and the holy body having been received, He commanded that it be taken in a cloud into paradise: where now, rejoined to the soul, [Mary] rejoices with the Lord's chosen ones..." (*Gregory of Tours, Eight Books of Miracles*, 1:4; 575-593 A.D.)

Another tradition concerning Mary's assumption is that Her burial robe was left in the tomb. When the tomb was opened at the request of St. Thomas the Apostle, it was filled with roses and lilies.

The Church has never formally defined whether the Blessed Virgin Mary died or not, and the integrity of the doctrine of the Assumption would not be impaired if She did not in fact die, but the almost universal consensus is that She did die.

Pope Pius XII, in Munificentissimus Deus (1950), defined that Mary, "after the completion of her earthly life" (note the silence regarding her death), "was assumed body and soul into the glory of heaven."

Eastern Catholics are more apt to believe Mary didn't die when She was assumed into heaven. After all, Adam and Eve would not have died if they had not eaten the forbidden fruit. When it would have been time for them to go to heaven, they would have been assumed without dying.

Catholics from the west, like St. Alphonsus Liguori and St. John Damacene believe Mary died. Some have as their opinion that, Mary wanted to experience death like Her Son.

"St. John Damascene (d. 749) said, "St. Juvenal, Bishop of Jerusalem, at the Council of Chalcedon (451), made known to the Emperor Marcian and Pulcheria, who wished to possess the body of the Mother of God, that Mary died in the presence of all the Apostles, but that Her tomb, when opened upon the request of St. Thomas, was found empty; where from the Apostles concluded that the body was taken up to heaven. In all, the Patristic Fathers defended the Assumption on two counts: Since Mary was sinless and a perpetual virgin, She could not suffer bodily deterioration, the result of Original Sin, after Her death. Also, if Mary bore Christ and played an intimate role as His mother in the redemption of man, then She must likewise share body and soul in His resurrection and glorification."[126]

Since, one of the punishments for Adam and Eve's original sin was death, why do some saints believe Mary died? After all, She was conceived without sin and never sinned in Her life, so She would not have had the need to experience death. Perhaps, the reason why She may have died was because She wanted to experience death like Jesus, Her Son, to be as perfectly conformed to Our Lord as possible. In other words, She wanted to die, like Her Son, out of love for Him.

"Mary, then, has left this world; She is now in Heaven. Thence does this compassionate Mother look down upon us who are still in this valley of tears. She pities us, and, if we wish it, promises to help us. Let us always beseech Her by the merits of Her blessed death to obtain us a happy death; and should such be the good pleasure of God, let us beg Her to obtain us grace to die on a Saturday, which is a day dedicated in Her honor, or on a day of a novena, or within the octave of one of Her feasts; for this She has obtained for so many of Her clients, and especially for St. Stanislaus Kostka, for whom She obtained that he should die on the feast of Her Assumption..."[127]

This meditation helps us to think about the grace of a happy death. A happy death does not mean when a person dies, suddenly large snowflakes fall from the sky at the moment the soul departs from the body.

Application 1: The Grace of a Happy Death

What is the grace of a happy death? A happy death means that one died in good moral and religious circumstances. To have died as a friend of Jesus. It means that you didn't die in some morally compromised situation, you didn't die alienated from your church, you didn't die bitter or angry at your family, and, you didn't die with a mortal sin on your soul. A happy death is

329

to have lived our life for others by doing good deeds, forgiving injuries, practicing virtue and being ready for our personal judgment, where we will must give an account of our entire life.

One freely embraced their sufferings and upcoming death; were detached from this world in such a way, that they trust God will take care of their family and concerns of their life; are looking forward to departing this world to be with Jesus forever in our heavenly home. They forgave all those who have hurt them. They are reconciled with everyone. They thanked the Lord for all He has done in their life. To the best of their ability has apologized to all those whom they have hurt. We should much rather be in heaven, then on earth, or at least indifferent to God's will one way or the other.

The Last Rites help souls who fall short of the above to receive the grace of a happy death and it includes: Confession, Anointing of the Sick, Viaticum (Holy Communion one last time with the Apostolic Pardon) resulting in their soul being in the state of grace. They us to be reconciled with God and with others.

Anointing of the Sick can impart three effects. To absolve sins from a dying person unable to confess, to give graces to persevere through suffering, and if beneficial for their soul, the Lord could grant physical healing.

"The Church encourages us to prepare ourselves for the hour of our death. In the litany of the saints, for instance, she has us pray: 'From a sudden and unforeseen death, deliver us, O Lord'; to ask the Mother of God to intercede for us 'at the hour of our death' in the Hail Mary; and to entrust ourselves to St. Joseph, the patron of a happy death" (Catechism of the Catholic Church, 1014).

We should daily pray for the grace of a happy death, such as one Our Father, one Hail Mary and one Glory Be.

Today, family members wait too long before obtaining the Sacrament of the Sick for a dying person. It's imprudent to wait until just before death to call a priest, which could deprive the person from making a good Confession, receiving Holy Communion as Viaticum (remitting punishment due to sin), being granted spiritual gifts to persevere through their suffering and may not live to receive Anointing of the Sick...

Some may erroneously believe when a priest anoints a sick person, it's only for those who are immediately dying, and will wait to call the priest until the person is unconscious, depriving the dying person of much needed graces before death.

When dying or seriously ill, the sick person or a family member should call a priest at once, so they can receive spiritual gifts such as Confession to have their sins forgiven, Anointing of the Sick which will give graces to endure their last hours, and may even result in being physically healed; and receiving Jesus in Holy Communion. Wouldn't everyone want to receive Jesus inside their heart when they are deathly ill?

A patient gave the following testimony to a diocesan priest about the physical effects of Anointing of the Sick.

The man said while in ICU at a hospital in Florida, his heart suddenly stopped beating and the monitor flat lined. Nurses called a "Code Blue" and a doctor began to administer CPR. A priest responded to the Code Blue and immediately anointed the patient. At the moment the priest gave the anointing, the patient opened his eyes, looked around, and his heart began to beat. The priest was so shocked, he jumped back and hit the wall. The doctor cried out, "You were dead! You were dead! But now, you came back to life!"

St. Joseph is the patron of a happy death, because when he was dying, it is believed Jesus and the Blessed Mother were at his bedside.

We hope our very last thoughts will be on God and our last words be such that we desire heavenly things, or to help others by our passing. How beautiful to die with "Jesus! and Mary!" on our lips, or to die praying the Hail Mary.

331

To die alone, without any family or friends, could be considered a gift, because then we feel how Jesus felt abandoned by His Father on the Cross.

But how precious and how much needed it is, when family and friends are gathered around a dying person praying the Holy Rosary.

It may be that when dying, we are unable to speak or even to pray, but if we hear others praying Hail Marys for us, we are consoled, and it keeps at bay the enemy who tries one last time to steal our soul.

Those who are present with the dying should regularly sprinkle Holy Water on the dying soul and on their bed because at times the enemy will come to tempt them.

When St. Martin of Tours was dying, he saw the devil standing near, and said, "Why do you stand there, you bloodthirsty brute? Murderer, you will not have me for your prey. Abraham is welcoming me into his embrace."

Saints tell us it is much more efficacious to offer Masses for the living than for the dead. When we first discover that we or someone we know will die, Masses should be offered before death.

"Mary not only consoles and relieves Her clients in purgatory, but She delivers them by Her prayers. Gerson says, "that on the day of Her assumption into heaven, purgatory was entirely emptied." Novarinus confirms this, saying, "that it is maintained by many grave authors, that when Mary was going to heaven, She asked as a favor from Her Son to take all the souls then in purgatory with Her. "And from that time forward", says Gerson, "Mary had the privilege of delivering Her servants. A woman named Marozia appeared after her death to her godmother. She said that, on the feast of the Assumption, Mary set free from purgatory more souls than Rome's population. "On Christmas and Easter, Mary visits purgatory and sets many souls free" says Denis the Carthusian.[128]

332

If we want to prepare for death with the help of our glorious Mother in heaven, we need to wear Her brown scapular. The Virgin Mary has given us the brown scapular as a means of not only preventing us from suffering eternal fire, but also from helping us to get out of purgatory quickly.

In the year 1251, in the town of Aylesford in England, Our Lady appeared to St. Simon Stock, a Carmelite. She handed him a brown woolen scapular and said, "This shall be a privilege for you and all Carmelites, that anyone dying in this habit shall not suffer eternal fire." In time, the Church extended this magnificent privilege to all the laity who are willing to be invested in the Brown Scapular of the Carmelites and who perpetually wear it.

The conditions for gaining the promise of the scapular one is to observe exactly what has been prescribed regarding the material, color, and shape of the Scapular, that is it must be 100% brown wool in a rectangular shape. The person is to be enrolled in the Scapular by a priest and to wear it continually. There are no special prayers or good works that are necessary to receive the promise. The Scapular is a silent prayer that shows one's complete consecration and dedication to the Blessed Virgin Mary. The Scapular is a devotion whereby we venerate, love, and trust in Her protection. We tell Her these things every moment of the day by simply wearing the Brown Scapular.

The Sabbatine (Saturday) Privilege came about when Pope John XXII had a vision, in which Mary said She will deliver Her faithful children who have worn the Scapular devoutly from purgatory soon after their death, notably the first Saturday after death. "As a tender Mother, I will descend into purgatory on the Saturday after their death, and will deliver them into the heavenly mansions of life everlasting."

The requirements for obtaining the First Saturday Privilege are: to wear the Brown Scapular continuously, to observe chastity according to one's state in life, to daily recite the *Little Office of the Blessed Virgin Mary* OR to abstain from meat on

Wednesdays and Saturdays OR with the permission of a priest say five decades of the Holy Rosary daily.

The Virgin Mary appeared with the Child Jesus as Our Lady of Mount Carmel during the Fatima apparition on Oct. 13th, 1917, as reminder for us to wear Her scapular.

St. Peter Claver baptized 300,000 slaves and gave every one of them a scapular. St. Alphonsus Liguori's scapular was found incorrupt in his tomb and the scapular of Pope Gregory X, who died in 1275, was found incorrupt in 1830 when his body was exhumed. It is the oldest known scapular in existence today.

St. Elizabeth of the Trinity helps us to understand every moment of our life should be lived out of love for God and neighbor. She said, "In light of eternity, the soul sees things as they really are. Oh how empty is all that has not been done for God and with God. I beg you, mark everything with the seal of love. It alone endures. How serious life is. Each moment is given to us in order to root us deeper in God."

The Imitation of Christ, Chapter 23, says, "Very quickly there will be an end of you here: look what will become of you in another world. Today the man is here; tomorrow he is gone. And when he is out of sight, he is also quickly out of mind. Oh the stupidity and hardness of man's heart, which thinks only about the present, and does not instead care about what is to come! You ought to order yourself in all your thoughts and actions, as if you were about to die today. If you had a good conscience, you would not greatly fear death. It would be better to avoid sin than to fly death. If you are not prepared today, then how will you be prepared tomorrow? Tomorrow is uncertain, and how do you know that you will live until tomorrow? What does it avail to live long, when there is so small an amendment in our practice? Alas! The length of our days more often makes our sins greater than to make our lives better. Oh that we had spent just one day in this world thoroughly well! There are many who count how long it is since their conversion, and yet often the fruit of the amendment of their life is so slender. If dying is considered dreadful, then to live long may perhaps prove more dangerous. Happy is the man who always has the hour of his death before his eyes, and daily prepares himself to die. If at any time you have seen another man die, take note that you must also pass the same way.[129]

Just before the moment of death, some have given witness by their actions that Jesus comes to take them to their judgment.

Not much after the death of John Cardinal Krol of the Archdiocese of Philadelphia, on March 6, 1996, seminarians at St. Charles Seminary were told the story of how he died. They were told, "Moments before he died, his room was filled with light. Although he had been unconscious for sometime, he opened his eyes, sat up in bed, reached out his arms as though wanting to embrace someone, saying, "Jesus!" He immediately fell back and died." What a beautiful witness!

Jesus speaks about how the Chaplet of Divine Mercy will affect those who pray it before death and use it to pray for the dying. He told Saint Faustina, "At the hour of their death, I defend as My own glory every soul that will say this chaplet; or when others say it for a dying person, the indulgence is the same. When this chaplet is said by the bedside of a dying person, God's anger is placated, unfathomable mercy envelops the soul, and the very depths of My tender mercy are moved for the sake of the sorrowful Passion of My Son." (Diary, 811) "Write that when they say this chaplet in the presence of the dying, I will stand between My Father and the dying person, not as the just Judge but as the merciful Savior." (Diary, 1541)

When we are dying, Jesus wants us to trust. He said to Saint Faustina, "Pray as much as you can for the dying. By your entreaties, obtain for them trust in My mercy, because they have most need of trust, and have it the least. Be assured that the grace of eternal salvation for certain souls in their final moment depends on your prayer." (Diary, 1777)

When we pray the Hail Mary and especially the Holy Rosary which has 53 Hail Marys, we ask the Blessed Virgin Mary to "pray for us, now and at the hour of our death." Because of the Hail Mary prayer, we know for certain, the Virgin Mary prays for the dying, who constantly invoke Her Motherly intercession when praying Her Rosary. Just as She prayed for Her Son while She stood at the foot of His Cross, during His last three hours until death, She stands beside the bed of the dying, praying for them, comforting them, consoling them and protecting them from evil spirits, until their soul departs. And surely, She stands at their judgment, asking for leniency from Her Son, who is the just judge. There is no better advocate than the Virgin Mary, especially when we pray Her Rosary.

Application 2: Brain Death

At a large metro hospital, a woman was declared brain dead. The doctor encouraged her fiance to permit the hospital to remove all medical equipment and allow her to die. The man decided to wait and pray about it. A priest anointed the woman and the day after she received it, she came out of her coma and was dismissed two days later.

Organ harvesting in many hospitals can be a serious cause for concern, especially since many hospitals remove the organs before death, which is unethical.

A Catholic man's mother was declared brain dead and was asked permission from the doctor, if they could harvest her organs. After giving permission, he was horrified to discover she was still alive when they removed her organs.

There is also great controversy in 2024 over whether or not brain death constitutes death. According to *LifesiteNews*, "On April 11, 2024, the *National Catholic Bioethics Center* (NCBC) issued a landmark position statement, acknowledging that at least half of patients diagnosed as "brain dead" still have partial brain function." For more information read Appendix A, "Brain Death and Organ Donation".

At times, difficult decisions need to be made with regard to end of life issues. See Appendix B, "Question and Answer regarding Nutrition and Hydration".

Story 1: The Rosary & Scapular Saves the Soul of a Dying Man

"Father Crasset relates, that a certain military officer told him, that after a battle he found a soldier on the battle-ground who held in his hand a Rosary and the scapular of Mary, and asked for a confessor. His forehead had been pierced by a musket-ball, which had passed through the head and came out behind, so that the brain was visible and protruded through each opening, and he could not live without a miracle. He however raised himself, made his confession to the chaplain with great compunction, and after receiving absolution, expired."[130]

Story 2: The Scapular Helps Man Receive Baptism

The following story is from Fr. Scott A. Haynes. "An old man was rushed to the St. Simon Stock Hospital in New York City, unconscious and dying. The nurse, seeing the Brown Scapular on the patient, called the priest. As the prayers were being said for the dying man, he became conscious and spoke up: "Father, I am not a Catholic." "Then why are you wearing the Brown Scapular?" asked the priest. "I promised my friends to wear it," the patient explained, "and say one Hail Mary a day." "You are dying," the priest told him. "Do you want to become a Catholic?" "All my life I wanted to be one," the dying man replied. He was baptized, received the Last Rites, and died in peace. Our Lady took another soul under Her mantle through Her Scapular!"[131]

Apparition: Our Lady of San Nicholas (Argentina)

The apparitions began on September 25, 1983 when Mary appeared to Gladys Quiroga de Motta, a housewife, while she was praying the Rosary in her bedroom. The Mother of God is said to have been dressed in blue, held the Infant Jesus in Her arms and a Rosary in Her hand. According to the History of Mary of the Rosary of San Nicholas, the Virgin Mary appeared again on the 7th and 12th of October and began to speak to her on October 13th. Our Lady told the seer: "You have done well. Do not be afraid. Come to see me. I will take you by the hand and you will travel many paths. Rebels are unjust and humble the servants of the Lord. Seek help and you will receive it. Do not fear. Nothing will happen to you. The Lord leaves nothing at random." On another occasion, "The Holy Rosary is the most feared weapon of the enemy," Mary said during one apparition. Jesus also appeared to Gladys numerous times saying, "Previously the world was saved with Noah's Ark. Today the Ark is My Mother. By means of Her, the souls will be saved because it will bring them towards Me. Whoever rejects My Mother, rejects Me." Gladys was also instructed to have a medal struck with the invocation of Mary of the Rosary of San Nicholas, and the Most Holy Trinity on the reverse with seven stars. "My daughter, the meaning of seven stars is seven graces that my Son Jesus Christ will grant to whoever has it on their chest. Praised be the Lord," Mary instructed.

Mary is Crowned Queen of Heaven & Earth

Fruit of the Mystery: Trust in Mary's Intercession
& True Devotion to Mary

"God's temple in heaven was opened, and the ark of his covenant could be seen in the temple." "A great sign appeared in the sky, a woman clothed with the sun, with the moon under her feet, and on her head a crown of twelve stars." (Revelations 11:19, 12:1)

Here we can picture the event of Mary entering heaven. Upon entering the gates of heaven, Her own body became suddenly glorified as She received a transformed and resurrected body. Her clothes became dazzling and with an immense glow, Her veil, mantle and dress are arrayed in gold, sparkling like the sun.

Though She knew the Trinity better than any human being, and perhaps, at times, had a tiny glimpse of heaven in one of Her ecstasies, She was immediately enamored and overcome by the beauty, the glory, the power and the majesty of God in heaven. Her eyes welled up in tears as She gazed upon the multitude of angels and saints, and, to Her shock and amazement, they all bow down in humble reverence to Her, the Queen.

There next to Our Lord Jesus Christ, the King of heaven, is Her faithful spouse St. Joseph, whose glory shines for all to see. He appears in bodily form. Just as St. Francis de Sales suspected, his body did not undergo corruption and was assumed body and soul into paradise.

Jesus takes Mary's hand and walks Her to the throne of God the Father. Upon arrival, She kneels before Him and bows. He takes Her left hand and lifts Her up. There, before Her, are three large golden thrones. On the left is the throne of God the

Father, next to His is the throne of Jesus and to his left is the throne of Mary. The three take their seats and the Holy Spirit, in the form of a dove, hovers above the three thrones. There is total silence in heaven, as all know the Father is about to speak.

Jesus and God the Father stand. Between the two, a royal crown studded with gems suddenly appears and is placed on the head of the Virgin. At the moment the crown is set, a burst of light comes forth from above and twelve stars appear and glisten like that of a giant halo.

The twelve stars above Her head apply to both the twelve patriarchs of the tribes of Israel (original people of God), and the twelve apostles (renewed people of God). The twelve stars also represent Her Queenly dignity and Her rule over angels and saints.

She is clothed with the sun, meaning She is surrounded by God's power and protection and shines with grace as the Mother of God. The moon under Her feet represents Her Virginity, Immaculate Conception, and Her power over created things.

The Father spoke and said, "Behold, O creatures of heaven, is the handmaid of the Lord. The Queen of heaven and earth. She is my daughter, in whom I am well pleased. Listen to Her and do whatever She says. In Her hand I place the scepter, in which I have bestowed my entire ocean of Mercy, from now unto eternity. Those who love, honor and ask for Her intercession will find a loving and caring Mother. She is the image and model of the Church founded by my Son. She is my daughter. She is the Mother of the Redeemer and the Spouse of the Holy Spirit. What I say, I decree, unto eternity."

The host of angels and saints sing the most beautiful and elegant hymns praising and giving thanks to God and the Virgin Mary. Exceedingly high notes are mixed with tones that correspond in perfect harmony. To those on earth, if the singing could be heard, it would cause ecstasies of rapture. "Praise to the

Virgin! Praise to the Queen! Praise to the Blessed Trinity for whom She was created and has exalted above heaven and earth!"

When the angel Gabriel requested that Mary become the Mother of Jesus, it was at that moment She gave Her fiat, "Behold the handmaid of the Lord, be it done unto me, according to thy word.", She became the Queen of heaven and earth. If Jesus is the King of heaven and earth and of the whole universe, then Mary, as His Mother is the Queen of the Universe.

Saint Alphonsus Liguori said, "As the glorious Virgin Mary has been raised to the dignity of Mother of the King of Kings, it is not without reason that the Church honors Her, and wishes Her to be honored by all, with the glorious title of Queen. Saint Athanasius said, "If the Son is a King, the Mother who begot Him is a Queen and Sovereign.""

St. Bernadine of Siena said, "as many creatures as there are who serve God, so many they are who serve Mary: for as angels and men, and all things that are in heaven and on earth, are subject to the empire of God, so are they also under the dominion of Mary."

Mary is called: Queen of Angels, Queen of Patriarchs, Queen of Prophets, Queen of Martyrs, Queen of Apostles, Queen of Virgins, Queen of All Saints, Queen conceived without original sin, Queen of the Most Holy Rosary, Queen Assumed into heaven, Queen of Families, Queen of Peace, Queen of the Clergy, Queen of Heaven and Earth, Queen of Mercy, Queen of the Universe, and Queen of All Hearts.

"The queen stands at your right hand, arrayed in gold." "All glorious is the king's daughter as she enters, her raiment threaded with gold; In embroidered apparel she is led to the king. The maids of her train are presented to the king. They are led in with glad and joyous acclaim; they enter the palace of the king." (Psalm 45:14-16)

St. Augustine said, "This venerable day has dawned, the day that surpasses all the festivals of the saints, this most exalted and most solemn day on which the Blessed Virgin was assumed body and soul into heavenly glory. On this day the queenly Virgin was exalted to the very throne of God the Father, and elevated to such a height that the angelic spirits are in admiration."

What does a queen do, but intercede for her subjects. She has authority over the subjects of Her Son's kingdom, which is God's kingdom on earth, as it is in heaven. If a subject finds himself or herself in trouble, and if the King refuses clemency, he has recourse to the Queen. This is the reason why Mary has the title Mother of Mercy and Queen of Mercy. If our prayer is not answered when asking the King, go to the Queen. Our Lord Himself desires this of us, so that we may grow in love of His Mother and that He may be glorified through Her intercessory prayers. He desires to honor Her, by showing us, He refuses nothing through Her intercession. One learns to first approach the Queen before approaching the King.

There are ways we can approach the Queen. One way is a simple heartfelt prayer, asking Her to pray for our needs and present them to Her Son.

Another way is hand over the problem or difficulty to Her, such as placing the intention in a prayer box or an intention prayer book at the foot of Her statue, giving Her dominion over it, and consecrating the intention to Her Immaculate Heart.

A third way is to wear Her Miraculous Medal, clinging to it, trusting if we wear it, She will protect us and even work miracles by carrying it on our person. The Queen has wrought conversions of notorious sinners, such as former Satanist high wizard Zachary King and Alphonse Ratisbonne, a Jewish man who persecuted Catholics.

The medal given to Saint Catherine Laboure was originally called the Medal of the Immaculate Conception, but due to the many miracles, it became known as the Miraculous

Medal. When we wear Mary's medal, as Queen, She works miracles in our life, especially the miracle of conversion.

A fourth way is to ask the Queen of the Most Holy Rosary to pray for a specific intention by praying Rosaries and novenas.

A fifth way is the most radical, whereby one consecrates not only problems, difficulties, but oneself, one's life, to Her, as a slave, body and soul, all our possessions, all our goods both interior and exterior and the value of all our good actions past, present, and future and all merits and glory in heaven to the Queen, leaving Her the full right of disposing of all, according Her good pleasure, for the greater and honor of God, in time and in eternity.

Slaves are forced to be attached to their master and are required to do everything they ask. But, not this kind of slavery. Rather, it is an attachment by desire. Because we love Her and want to do whatever She asks, knowing it is best for our soul, we are joyfully "shackled" to Her Immaculate Heart, because She is the Queen of All Hearts.

The sixth way comes from St. Louis Marie de Montfort in his book, *True Devotion to Mary*. Within the book and also sold separate is his "Preparation for Total Consecration to Jesus through Mary" by thirty-three days of preliminary prayers and readings. A special feast day of Our Lady is selected. One prepares for that feast day by Confession and then attends Mass receiving Holy Communion on that day. Then once a year, the person renews their thirty-three days and does the consecration again. They begin to live their life in imitation of Mary's virtues, and over time, they become more and more transformed into an image of Mary.

The Queenship of Mary is a reminder to seek heaven and that heaven is our final goal. It is also a reminder that we have a Queen Mother in heaven, who can intercede for us and help us on our journey home. We should think of heaven often and do everything we possibly can, to go there at the end of our life.

The end of our life comes much quicker than we think and before long our life is over. We should live every day, as though it were our last, because no one knows the day nor the hour when we will depart from it. The Virgin Mary received the glorious crown as Queen. And little as ours may be, everyone who goes to heaven will receive a crown.

Acknowledging Mary as Queen is not only about obtaining heaven and receiving the greatest crown of glory that God destined for us, no! Its also about honoring the Queen by giving Her flowers, carrying Her image in procession, doting over Her, praising Her, bringing others to Her, so that they too may love, honor, and ask for Her queenly intercession.

These scripture quotes are reminders that we have a crown awaiting us. "I am coming soon; Hold fast to what you have, so that no one may seize your crown." (Revelation 3:11) "And when the Chief Shepherd appears, you will receive the unfading crown of glory." (1 Peter 5:4) "Every athlete exercises discipline in every way. They do it to win a perishable crown, but we an imperishable one. Thus I do not run aimlessly; I do not fight as if I were shadowboxing. No, I drive my body and train it, for fear that, after having preached to others, I myself should be disqualified." (1 Corinthians 9:25-27)

Jesus reminds us, at the end of our life, we are not to be afraid, but rather trust that He will come to take us. "Do not let your hearts be troubled. You have faith in God; have faith also in me. In my Father's house there are many dwelling places. If there were not, would I have told you that I am going to prepare a place for you? And if I go and prepare a place for you, I will come back again and take you to myself, so that where I am you also may be." (John 14:1-3)

But, do you think when Jesus comes to take us, Mary will not be there? Surely, She is at our bedside and prays for us when we are dying, since throughout our life or just before we die, if we pray the Rosary or even just simple Hail Marys, She will be praying for us now and at the hour of our death.

Application 1: Judgment, Purgatory, Hell, Heaven

When we depart from this life, we will go to our judgment. Don't we want to have the Queen Advocate at our side? When we are judged, our entire life will be brought before us. Then, we will go to one of three places, heaven, hell or purgatory, and if we go to purgatory, we will eventually go to heaven. We should not settle for wanting to go to purgatory, because as St. Augustine said, "This fire of Purgatory will be more severe than any pain that can be felt, seen or conceived in this world." Imagine burning to death by fire, being tortured on a rack, lions attacking and killing us. All of these are not as bad as purgatory! We should rather suffer in this life and do penance, so as to avoid purgatory.

The Virgin Mary at Fatima showed the three children a vision of hell. Lucia describes what they saw. "The rays [of light] appeared to penetrate the earth, and we saw, as it were, a vast sea of fire. Plunged in this fire, we saw the demons and the souls [of the damned]. The latter were like transparent burning embers, all blackened or burnished bronze, having human forms. They were floating about in that conflagration, now raised into the air by the flames which issued from within themselves, together with great clouds of smoke. Now they fell back on every side like sparks in huge fires, without weight or equilibrium, amid shrieks and groans of pain and despair, which horrified us and made us tremble with fright (it must have been this sight which caused me to cry out, as people say they heard me). The demons were distinguished [from the souls of the damned] by their terrifying and repellent likeness to frightful and unknown animals, black and transparent like burning coals. That vision only lasted for a moment, thanks to our good Heavenly Mother,

Who at the first apparition had promised to take us to Heaven. Without that, I think that we would have died of terror and fear."

Our Lady told the children, "Each time you say the Rosary, My children, say after each decade, 'O my Jesus, forgive us our sins, save us from the fire of Hell, lead all souls to heaven, especially those most in need."

What is Heaven Like? There is no old age, no suffering, no pain, no tears, no heartaches, no cancer, no mourning, no war, no disagreements, no disunity, no physical ailments, no arthritis and no death. Rather, there is joy, peace, love, unity and happiness. In heaven our tears are wiped away. Our imperfect relationships on earth become perfect in heaven. We come to know each other and love each other in a way beyond our imagining. Every question we have, will be answered in heaven. Everything we want to do in this life will be fulfilled, and not just fulfilled, but in the most profound and incomprehensible way. As God said, "As the heavens are higher than the earth, so are my ways higher than your ways and my thoughts than your thoughts." (Isaiah 55:9) On earth, we suffer, we go through difficulties, and by doing so, we learn to love, to forgive and to grow in virtue. God dwells in our heart through baptism, and so, He is in us, and feels what we feel. In heaven we can pray for those on earth. We will see myriads and myriads of angels as they worship God singing, "Holy, Holy, Holy, Lord God of Hosts, heaven and earth are filled with your glory!"

On earth we learn to become like God, by imitating Jesus and by praying to God. In heaven, we worship, adore, and praise God in a perfect and harmonious way. The God, whose friend we became on earth, will be our greatest joy in heaven. The God we adored on earth, we will adore and be one with in heaven. On earth, when we talk to Jesus from our heart, telling Him about our needs, our struggles, our desires and thanking Him and loving Him, it is very pleasing to Him. But, in heaven we do it face to face.

When we get to heaven we will meet our guardian angel for the first time and learn how he protected us. We will see all the angels and saints and come to know how they helped us by their prayers. And we will see the beauty and glory of the Virgin Mary and understand more fully Her motherly concern and love for us. And we will get to know our great grandparents and their parents, their grandparents and we will learn about their life, their struggles, and how they made it to heaven.

Application 2: Bucket List

What's on your bucket list? What do you want to do before you die? It's good to have desires and dreams and accomplish things in this life, but if our life is cut short, we should in no way be disappointed if we were unable to fulfill our "bucket list." Why? Because every dream, every desire, everything we want to accomplish in this life will be fulfilled in heaven and greater than we ever could have imagined.

Once we depart from this life, we are no longer able to do any good deeds. Nor make acts of faith, hope and love. We can no longer suffer for God or for others out of love. We can no longer ask God for forgiveness. The good deeds we do, the love we shared, the sufferings we endured, our prayers, the times we went to church, the Rosaries we prayed, the Masses we attended, the Communions we received, all these and more, we will take with us to our judgment, as the Book of Revelation says, "Our good deeds go with us." (Revelation 14:13)

St. John of the Cross helps us to know what our judgment will be like. He said, "In the end, we will be judged on love." We will be judged on our spiritual and corporal works of mercy, which is love in action. When we share God's gifts He has given us, with others, that is love.

347

For example, mowing yards for those who can't, sewing for others, using our voice to sing, or to smile at someone who needs cheering up, or to make greeting cards.

To compliment co-workers. To financially help a single mother. To bake cookies or make meals for a neighbor. To help our neighbor move cattle or harvest wheat. To donate vegetables from your garden. To send a sympathy card. To give words of encouragement to the discouraged. All of these, and more, are works of mercy, which are acts of love.

We can create a new and different kind of "bucket". Let's make it the biggest invisible bucket we can and fill it with acts of love, mercy, good deeds, and kind words, so when we go to our judgment, and when Jesus says to us, "How much did you love?", we can hand Him a giant bucket filled of overflowing with love, and He will say to us, "Well done, good and faithful servant.... Come share your master's joy." (Matthew 25:23)

We can't earn our salvation. It's a free gift from God, but we cooperate in obtaining it. God inspires us to do charitable deeds. He inspires us to love and He performs acts of love through us for others.

Let us keep our eyes on heaven, our only true home, and remember "Eye has not seen, nor ear heard, neither has it entered the heart of man, what things God has prepared for those who love Him." (1 Corinthians 2:9)

We should consecrate our self to the Queen of Heaven and Earth, wear Her Miraculous Medal and Scapular, and daily pray Her Rosary as often as possible. If we do these things, we can be assured She will help us to truly love and make our judgment go well by interceding for us before the King of Heaven and Earth. She will quickly get us out of purgatory and hopefully even skip it, thanks to Her intercession.

St. Cajetan was born in 1480 at Vicenza in 1480 of noble parents who dedicated him to the Blessed Virgin Mary. From childhood he was known as a saint and in his later years as "the hunter of souls."

He went to Rome and was forced to accept office at the court of Pope Julius II. When the pope died, he returned to his hometown of Vicenza and joined the Confraternity of St. Jerome, whose members were drawn from the lowest classes.

He spent his fortune building hospitals and devoted himself to nursing the plague-stricken. To renew the lives of the clergy, he instituted the first community of Regular Clerics, known as the Theatines. They devoted themselves to preaching, administering the sacraments, and the careful performance of the Church's rites and ceremonies.

He was the first to introduce the 40 hours devotion of the Blessed Sacrament as an antidote to the heresy of Calvin. Forty hours devotion is continuous Adoration for 40 hours with special sermons on the Eucharist and Mass each day.

He had a tender love of our Blessed Lady, and his piety was rewarded; for one Christmas Eve She placed the Infant Jesus in his arms.

When the Germans sacked Rome, St. Cajetan was barbarously scourged to exhort from him riches which he had long before given away and securely stored in heaven.

When he was on his death-bed, resigned to the will of God, eager for pain to satisfy his love, and for death to attain life, he beheld the Mother of God, radiant with splendor and surrounded by ministering seraphim. In profound veneration, he said, "Lady, bless me!" Mary replied, "Cajetan, receive the blessing of my Son, and know that I am here as a reward for the sincerity of your love, and to lead you to paradise." She then exhorted him to be patient in fighting an evil spirit who troubled him, and gave orders to the choirs of angels to escort his soul in triumph to heaven. Then, turning Her countenance full of majesty and sweetness upon him, She said, "Cajetan, my Son calls thee. Let us go in peace." Worn out with toil and sickness, he went to his reward in 1547.

Story 2: Family Rosary for Dying Mother

An elderly mother of a family was dying in a nursing home. The priest was called and when he arrived at her room, he anointed her and gave the Apostolic Pardon. Because she was unconscious, she was unable to receive Holy Communion. As the priest was visiting with her family, it just so happens more and more of her children and grandchildren came at the same time. The priest told the family members to say their last goodbyes and one by one, each came forward and said something to their mother. After all had finished, the priest asked the family if they would like to pray the Rosary together for her. When he began to lead the Rosary, he was surprised to notice each had their own Rosary on their person. When the Rosary was completed, and immediately after they prayed the Hail Holy Queen, the woman breathed her last and departed from this life. What a beautiful death! She was surrounded by her family, who prayed the Rosary for their mother and grandmother and just when it was completed, the Blessed Virgin Mary, must have surely assisted the woman to her judgment. As the priest was departing, he noticed the deceased woman was wearing a scapular and had a Rosary in one of her hands. She must have been praying it before she became unconscious. One of her sons said, "Mom taught us to pray the Rosary."

Story 3: In the USA Rosary Saves Catholics from Large Fire

On October 8 of 1871, was the great Peshtigo fire in Wisconsin and Michigan. It was the greatest fire tragedy in the history of the United States killing between 1,200-2,400 people and burning 1.2 million acres. Due to the high winds and dry grounds, the fire quickly became a storm of fire and roared towards the convent, chapel, and school near Champion.

Desperate for help, people from the surrounding countryside fled to the Chapel where Sister Adele Brise and her companions were praying for Mary's protection. Lifting the statue of Mary, they processed around the sanctuary, praying the Rosary and singing hymns to Jesus and the Blessed Mother. Early the next morning, a steady rain came and extinguished the flames. Everything around the property was completely charred. But the fire came only to the fence of the land consecrated to the Blessed Virgin Mary, containing the chapel, school and convent, where they were praying and halted. Twelve years earlier on that exact date, October 8, 1859, the Virgin Mary appeared to Sr. Adele Brise. Our Lady told Adele, "I am the Queen of Heaven who prays for the conversion of sinners, and I wish you to do the same. You received Holy Communion this morning and that is well. But you must do more. Make a general confession and offer Communion for the conversion of sinners. If they do not convert and do penance, my Son will be obliged to punish them." Our Lady of Good Help is a Church approved apparition in Champion, Wisconsin. If the Rosary can save us from a natural fire, how much more can it save us from the fires of hell?

Apparition: Apparition: Our Lady of Guadalupe, Mexico
& Our Lady of Las Lajas, Columbia

There are two miraculous images of the Virgin Mary associated with the Book of Revelation, "A great sign appeared in the sky, a woman clothed with the sun, with the moon under her feet, and on her head a crown of twelve stars." (Revelation 12:1)

In 1531, on Tepeyac Hill, near Mexico City, the Blessed Mother appeared four times to St. Juan Diego asking for a church to be built in Her honor. The last time She appeared to him, on December 12th, 1531, She arranged roses in his tilma, which he then took to the bishop. When he opened his cloak, the image of Our Lady of Guadalupe miraculously became present on the tilma. The image shows the Virgin clothed with the sun, standing on a crescent moon; Her blue mantel was imprinted with stars; Her head is bowed in prayer; Her hands folded; an angel is holding up Her mantle; and She wears a black sash indicating She is pregnant.

At that time Aztec Indians were performing thousands of human sacrifices. But, the image caused millions to convert to the Catholic faith. They came to understand they were worshiping a false goddess, and false gods of the sun, moon and stars, not the only one true God and not honoring Mary, as Mother of God.

In Guadalupe, Mary revealed She is the "true Mother of the true God." In the first apparition to Saint Juan Diego, on December 9, Mary said, "Know and understand well, you my most humble son, that I am the ever-virgin Holy Mary, Mother of the True God for whom we live, of the Creator of all things, Lord of heaven and the earth."

She desired a temple or shrine to be built on the spot in Her honor, which in former times had been sacred to the goddess Theotenantzin ("the mother of the gods").

The image very closely describes the Book of Revelation image of a woman clothed with the sun, the moon under Her feet.

In the Guadalupe image, Mary is not crowned with stars. However, the Church does not hesitate to perform canonical coronations, and so, Pope Leo XIII granted the image a decree of canonical coronation on February 8, 1887, and it was pontifically crowned on October 12, 1895.

The second miraculous image that depicts a woman clothed with the sun, etc. as in the Book of Revelation, Chapter 12, is Our Lady of Las Lajas (Our Lady of the Rocks). Our Lady is holding a Rosary and handing it to St. Dominic and the Child Jesus is grasping the cord of St. Francis of Assisi. The image miraculously appeared on rock from the side of a cliff and depicts the Virgin Mary clothed with the sun and with the moon under Her feet.

There are now man-made crowns on the images of Jesus and Mary. Pope Pius XII granted the venerated Marian image of the shrine a canonical coronation on September 16, 1952 by a decree on May 31, 1951.

Sung or Prayed after Night Prayer or just before retiring.

Salve Regina
Hail, Holy Queen, Mother of Mercy,
our life, our sweetness and our hope.
To thee do we cry,
poor banished children of Eve.
To thee do we send up our sighs,
mourning and weeping in this valley of tears.
Turn then, most gracious advocate,
thine eyes of mercy toward us,
and after this our exile
show unto us the blessed fruit of thy womb, Jesus.
O clement, O loving,
O sweet Virgin Mary
Pray for us, o Holy Mother of God,
that we may be made worthy of the promises of Christ. Amen.

See Latin "Other Forms of Salve Regina" in Appendix D

THE ROSARY OF MIRACLES EXPLANATION

The Lord wants us to remember His miracles, because through His miracles He is glorified and He reveals His love for us. The Lord God worked miracles in the Old Testament, such as: the healing of Naaman, the leper (2 Kings 5:1-19), the burning bush that doesn't burn (Exodus 3:2-5), the ten plagues (Exodus 7-10), the staff that turns into a snake (Exodus 7:8-13), water from the rock (Numbers 20:11), manna and quail in the desert (Exodus 16), the crossing of the Red Sea (Exodus 14:10-31), etc. to reveal His power and glory.

He wanted the Hebrew people to recall His works of wonder, so they would not lose hope and not worship idols. He wanted them to know He cares for them, loves them and wanted them to meditate on and appreciate His miracles. Cassiodorus said, "We praise God by recalling His marvelous deeds."

In the book of Joshua it states, "Far be it from us to forsake the Lord, our God, who brought us and our fathers up out of the land of Egypt, out of the state of slavery. He performed those great *miracles* before our very peoples through whom we passed. Therefore we also will serve the Lord, for He is our God." (Joshua 24:16-17)

Psalm 145 explains God's works speak of His glory and majesty and how they should be meditated upon, "One generation shall laud thy works to another, and shall declare thy mighty acts. On the glorious splendor of thy majesty, and on thy wondrous works, I will *meditate*." (Psalm 145:4-5)

God desires that we remember every good thing He has done for us, because by remembering them, we are reminded of His power, glory, divinity, and love.

The ordinary Christian faithful to Jesus, regularly meditates on the Gospels.

Jesus, as God, worked miracles so we may believe in Him.

Some of Our Lord's miracles include: healing the blind man (Mark 10:46-52), the man who was deaf with a speech impediment (Mark 7:31-37), the woman with a hemorrhage (Mark 5:25-34), the ten lepers (Luke 17:11-19), the raising of the dead girl (Mark 5:21-43), the raising of the dead young man (Mark 7:11-17), and the raising of Lazarus (John 11:1-44), the expelling of demons from the demoniac (Mark 5:1-20), the walking on water (Matthew 14:22-33), the calming of the storm (Mark 4:35-41), the multiplication of loaves and fish (Mark 6:30-44), the healing of the paralytic (Matthew 9:1-8), etc.

How good it would be to meditate on some miracles of Jesus, with the eyes and heart of Mary, when we pray the Holy Rosary. Though She may not have been present at these miraculous events, She can help us to meditate upon them, because She would have heard about Her Son's miracles and meditated upon them.

It is believed St. Louis de Montfort said the Sorrowful mysteries of the Rosary are the most efficacious for our souls.

By providing *The Rosary of Miracles*, it is not the intent of the author to replace any officially Church approved Rosaries: Joyful, Luminous, Sorrowful and Glorious. But rather, provide additional mysteries to meditate and therefore inspire the faithful to pray additional Rosaries and perhaps even receive special graces that may come by meditating on Our Lord's miracles. Every event in the life of Christ is beneficial for our salvation and by meditating on His miracles, we will receive graces.

There are no indulgences directly attached to the *Miracles Rosary*. However, "A Catholic may gain a plenary indulgence by remaining in Adoration of the Blessed Sacrament for at least a half-hour."[132] Therefore, if one were to pray *The Miracles Rosary* during their time of Adoration of the Blessed Sacrament for at least a half-hour, or any other prayers, one could receive a Plenary Indulgence.

Jesus Heals the Paralytic

Fruit of the Mystery: Help the Infirm Obtain Physical
& Spiritual Healing

"When Jesus returned to Capernaum after some days, it became known that He was at home. Many gathered together so that there was no longer room for them, not even around the door, and He preached the word to them. They came bringing to Him a paralytic carried by four men. Unable to get near Jesus because of the crowd, they opened up the roof above Him. After they had broken through, they let down the mat on which the paralytic was lying. When Jesus saw their faith, He said to the paralytic, "Child, your sins are forgiven." Now some of the scribes were sitting there asking themselves, "Why does this man speak that way? He is blaspheming. Who but God alone can forgive sins?" Jesus immediately knew in His mind what they were thinking to themselves, so He said, "Why are you thinking such things in your hearts? Which is easier, to say to the paralytic, 'Your sins are forgiven,' or to say, 'Rise, pick up your mat and walk'? But that you may know that the Son of Man has authority to forgive sins on earth" — He said to the paralytic, "I say to you, rise, pick up your mat, and go home." He rose, picked up his mat at once, and went away in the sight of everyone. They were all astounded and glorified God, saying, "We have never seen anything like this."

"So many gathered at the house Jesus was staying in Capernaum, there was no room for anyone to enter, not even at the door." (Mark 2:1-12)

The friends of the paralytic made a very noble effort to bring their handicapped friend to Jesus. Unable to get near to Our Divine Lord because of the crowd, and in an act of faith, they broke through the roof to let him down.

Using ropes attached to the four corners of the pallet the paralytic was lying on, they slowly lowered him until he was laid directly in front of Jesus. Our Lord must have been pleased with their ingenuity and especially their faith.

In those days, many houses had terraced roofs, which were accessible by steps at the back of the house. It was a matter of just removing tiles, in order for the roof to be opened.

The house was most likely the home of St. Peter, who lived in Capernaum. Surely, Peter wasn't happy they tore part of the roof off of his home.

Jesus saw the faith of the men, who brought the paralytic, and said to the paralyzed man, "Child, your sins are forgiven." Bishop Fulton Sheen said the paralytic was a teenager, which is why Jesus called him, "child."

Jesus first healed the paralyzed man's soul, and then His body. He teaches us that He first came to cure and save souls, and that the soul is more important than the body.

The friends of the paralytic, realizing the young man could not go to Jesus by himself, took their friend to Our Lord, to discover there was no way to get in the front door. Due to their faith, the men wouldn't give up and found a way to bring him to Jesus.

After Jesus said to the paralytic that his sins were forgiven, some of the scribes accused Our Lord of blasphemy, stating, "Who, but God alone can forgive sins?" Jesus responded, "Which is easier, to say to the paralytic, 'Your sins are forgiven' or to say, 'Rise, pick up your mat and walk.' But that you may know that the Son of Man has authority to forgive sins on earth —"He said to the paralytic, "I say to rise, pick up your mat, and go home." He rose, picked up his mat and went away in the sight of everyone.

In His confrontation with the scribes, Jesus revealed His divinity. Anyone can say, "your sins are forgiven", but how could it be proven—that the sins were forgiven? That is why Our Blessed Lord healed the paralytic, it was proof, He, as God, could forgive sins.

St. Jerome states, the man's physical paralysis was a type or figure of spiritual paralysis. The crippled young man was unable to return to God by his own efforts. And Jesus, who is God, cured both the physical and spiritual paralysis of the man.

Perhaps Our Lord also wanted to show us, if one lacks repentance, He may choose to not physically heal the person. Therefore, if we desire to be healed physically, or desire someone to whom we are wanting to be healed, it is important to first receive forgiveness of sins. How can we expect God to do something for us, if we fail to be reconciled with Him?

Even though the paralytic didn't express sorrow for his sins, Our Lord, who is God, knows our hearts, and knew the paralytic was repentant. Otherwise, Jesus would not have said, "Child, Your sins are forgiven."

Since the paralytic was unable to come to Jesus on his own, with great faith his friends wanted to obtain the two-fold gift of a spiritual healing (forgiving his sins) and the physical healing of his body.

Our Lord uses the example of the paralytic's friends, to show us that when we ask the Lord to heal someone, He sees our faith and responds to it.

Application 1: We Bring Spiritually Paralyzed to Jesus in Adoration

24 hours a day, 7 days a week, men, women, teenagers, and children, come to adore Jesus in Eucharistic Adoration Chapels night and day.

359

Many who are spiritually or emotionally paralyzed, come to Jesus, not through the roof, but through the door of an Adoration Chapel to be healed. They can come and pray using the words of the psalm, "Lord, heal my soul, for I have sinned against you." (Psalm 41:1)

Many come to Jesus to give Him their fears, their worries, their distresses, their sufferings. They come for consolation and peace and to receive our Lord's tender love. They come to pray for their family, for peace in the world, for the poor, homeless, hungry, the sick, the abandoned, and abused. They come to pray for the forgotten of society and the poor souls in purgatory. And they come with an open heart, knowing they also need graces and strength to live out their daily lives.

In a video called *"I am the Living Bread"*, there is a testimony to the power of coming to Jesus in the Eucharist, that involves several Catholic teens, who live in San Antonio, Texas.

One of the teenagers became pregnant. Her boyfriend wanted her to have an abortion, but she didn't. However, out of fear of losing her boyfriend, she made an appointment at the local abortion clinic. She confided to her teenage Catholic friend that the next day, she was going to have an abortion. The Catholic teen tried to convince her to not go through with it.

The next day, the young Catholic friend went to pray at an Adoration Chapel begging Jesus to change her friend's mind. She didn't know what to pray. And she told Jesus, "Please Lord, if necessary scare her out it so she won't go through with it."

The spiritually paralyzed young girl went to the abortion clinic. But when the doctor pulled out the long needle, she became frightened and left. She later gave birth to a little boy.

The teenage girl who went to the abortion clinic was like the paralytic. It was her good friend, who spiritually placed her before Our Lord in the Eucharist. With great faith she prayed, and God used her as a friend to save the life of the little boy.

Those who have had an abortion and have sought forgiveness in the sacrament of confession, the words of the prophet Isaiah are comforting, "It is I, who wipe out, for my own sake, your offenses; your sins I remember no more." (Isaiah 43:25)

After confessing the sin of abortion, some may continue to feel guilty. However, confession forgives all sin and wipes away all real guilt. In Our Lord's tender mercy, He remembers our sins no more. We need to have confidence in His mercy, that He has truly forgiven us and we need to forgive ourselves too.

Coming to an Adoration Chapel can make a difference in a teen's life. Teens can save lives, as they place before Jesus, those suffering from the spiritual paralysis of sin. With great faith, they believe Our Lord can heal others.

There was an unfortunate tragedy at an abortion facility, when a teenage girl came from out of state to have an abortion. Not only did the baby die, but the young teenager developed complications from the abortion and was taken by ambulance to a local hospital, where she also died.

Perhaps, if one person, perhaps a teen, would have come to the Adoration Chapel and prayed for an end to abortion, maybe the abortion would not have happened, and the child and mother would still be alive.

During the anniversary of Roe vs. Wade large groups of teens travel to Washington for the March for Life. There were also many who prayed at their local abortion clinics giving great witness to their faith.

May each and every one of us come to Jesus in the Eucharist and bring someone, whom we know is spiritually paralyzed, first our selves, but also others, especially mothers, contemplating an abortion and with Jesus, we can change the world.

May Our Lady, Refuge of Sinners and Help of the Sick, help us to examine our conscience, cultivate a deep contrition,

361

and like the paralytic, cast our eyes down, asking for pardon. And hear the words of Jesus, speak to us, "Child, your sins are forgiven."

Application 2: Visible Miracles Help Us to Believe in His Doctrine

From the beginning of a sermon on the beatitudes by Saint Leo the Great, pope.

> "Dearly beloved, when our Lord Jesus Christ was preaching the Gospel of the kingdom and healing various illnesses throughout the whole of Galilee, the fame of his mighty works spread into all of Syria, and great crowds from all parts of Judea flocked to the heavenly physician. Because human ignorance is slow to believe what it does not see, and equally slow to hope for what it does not know, those who were to be instructed in the divine teaching had first to be aroused by bodily benefits and visible miracles so that, once they had experienced his gracious power, they would no longer doubt the wholesome effect of his doctrine."[133]

Story 1: Healing at Lourdes During Eucharistic Procession

"On August 22, 1888, at 4 o'clock in the afternoon, there took place for the first time at Lourdes the procession together with the benediction of the sick with the Blessed Sacrament. It was a priest who proposed this pious practice and it has not been abandoned since that time. Once, on August 22, 1888, when the Benediction with the Blessed Sacrament was imparted to the sick gathered in front of the grotto of the apparitions, Pierre Delanoy, who had been suffering for years from ataraxy (an illness which impedes the coordination of voluntary movements, and leads to certain death), was healed instantly as the Monstrance passed by him. It was the first Eucharistic Miracle that took place at Lourdes. From that day on, the sick who make their way to Lourdes on pilgrimage are blessed with the Blessed Sacrament, and the miraculous healings that have been confirmed through the Blessed Sacrament passing by are innumerable. The Shrine of Lourdes is a shining example of faith in the Real Presence of Jesus in the Eucharist."[134]

Jesus Multiplies Loaves & Fish

Fruit of the Mystery: Gratitude for God's Providence,
Deeper Understanding of the Holy Mass

"When He disembarked and saw the vast crowd, His heart was moved with pity for them, for they were like sheep without a shepherd; and He began to teach them many things. By now it was already late and His disciples approached Him and said, "This is a deserted place and it is already very late. Dismiss them so that they can go to the surrounding farms and villages and buy themselves something to eat." He said to them in reply, "Give them some food yourselves." But they said to Him, "Are we to buy two hundred days' wages worth of food and give it to them to eat?" He asked them, "How many loaves do you have? Go and see." And when they had found out they said, "Five loaves and two fish." So He gave orders to have them sit down in groups on the green grass. The people took their places in rows by hundreds and by fifties. Then, taking the five loaves and the two fish and looking up to heaven, He said the blessing, broke the loaves, and gave them to His disciples to set before the people; he also divided the two fish among them all. They all ate and were satisfied. And they picked up twelve wicker baskets full of fragments and what was left of the fish. Those who ate of the loaves were five thousand men." (Mark 6:30-44)

The Apostles had good intentions, and asked Jesus to dismiss the crowds, so everyone could get something to eat. They knew the people were hungry and had empathy for them. They must have been shocked to hear Jesus say to feed them, themselves. Where could they get enough food to feed all those people? Even if a place near had food, they didn't have enough money to feed everyone.

Imagine the Apostles looking through the crowd trying to find someone with bread and fish. "One of His disciples, Andrew, Simon Peter's brother, said to Him, "Here is a boy with five small barley loaves and two small fish, but how far will they go among so many?" The young boy, due to his innocent and trusting heart and love for others was happy to share his food.

Jesus then told them to tell the people to sit down in groups of fifty and a hundred. Can you imagine counting the immense crowd or asking others to help them count the people in groups of fifty and hundred? The people must have wondered why they were supposed to sit in groups. How long would it have taken to divide 5000 men into groups, not counting women and children?

Jesus then gave the apostles an example. He first prayed. He looked up to heaven. He blessed the food. Then broke the loaves. And then gave them to the disciples to distribute. Amazingly, the bread and fish kept multiplying until everyone was able to eat.

Doesn't it make you wonder how they ate the fish? Did people carry around fish in a leather bag? Obviously, the fish wasn't raw and wet. Most likely, some carried baked or smoked fish and would eat it when traveling.

The people and the Apostles would have been astonished all could be fed. What were they thinking when they realized all that food was coming from the same baskets and no one was refilling them? They must have rejoiced and filled with gratitude to have their appetite satisfied.

Application 1: Multiplication of Loaves & The Holy Mass

This is one of the few Gospels that specifically mentions the Heart of Jesus. When Our Lord saw the vast crowd, "...His Heart was moved with pity for them, for they were like sheep without a shepherd." First, Jesus began to feed them spiritually. He began to teach them many things. At Mass, we hear the Word of God and listen to the homily during the Liturgy of the Word. During the Liturgy of the Eucharist, we are fed with the true body and blood of Jesus.

First, they are hungry. They hadn't eaten. Jesus teaches them and then gives them food. Isn't that what happens at Mass? Jesus permitted them to feel hunger, so they would have a deeper appreciation and a longing for eternal food.

This is one of the reasons before Mass, we are to fast at least one hour before Holy Communion. It used to be that the Church required people to fast after midnight. You can see how being hungry and receiving the Eucharist on an empty stomach creates a greater desire to receive receive Jesus in Holy Communion and appreciate our union with Him. We develop a longing to have spiritual food that satisfies our heart.

When the Apostles asked Jesus to send them home because they had no food and especially since they were in a deserted place, Our Divine Lord told them to give them food themselves.

Obviously, at that time, they couldn't give the people spiritual food, but in the future they will. At the Last Supper, they will be ordained priests and bishops and will have power and authority given to them by Jesus to change bread and wine into His Body and Blood at Mass.

Our Lord is preparing the apostles to give their future sheep, whom they will serve, spiritual food, by proclaiming the Word of God and by teaching them. Then they will give them food that is eternal, His body and blood, because as priests, they will do as Jesus.

But, today, when the vast crowd is with Him, He wants to first help them understand He can provide ordinary food to sustain them, just as He did their ancestors in the desert.

He is the true Bread of Life, who has come down from heaven. Their ancestors were given bread from heaven in the form of manna.

While He is seated with them and teaching them, they do not understand God is present physically before them in the divine person of Jesus.

At this time, He is unable to give them His physical presence as food in the Eucharist, because He had not yet given His flesh and blood on the Cross, so they could eat His flesh and blood for spiritual food during Holy Mass.

Their ancestors complained by grumbling before Moses interceded for them. They failed to trust that God would provide their food as they were journeying through the desert to the Promised Land. God sent quail and gave them manna "hoarfrost" for them to eat. The food that they had in the desert would feed their bellies, but all would eventually perish, because it was earthly food and not heavenly food.

After Jesus worked the miracle of the multiplication of the loaves and fish, the people grumbled saying, "What sign can you do? Our ancestors ate manna in the desert, as it is written: He gave them bread from heaven to eat." Jesus responded, "Amen, Amen, I say to you, it was not Moses who gave you the bread from heaven; my Father gives you the true bread from heaven and gives life to the world." They then told Jesus, "Sir, give us this bread always." Jesus responded, "I am the bread of life; whoever comes to me will never hunger, and whoever believes in me will never thirst." "Amen, amen, I say to you, you are looking for me not because you saw signs but because you ate the loaves and were filled. Do not work for food that perishes but for the food that endures for eternal life, which the Son of Man will give you." "Your ancestors ate the manna in the desert, but they died; this is the bread that comes down from heaven so that one may eat it and not die. I am the living bread that came down from heaven; whoever eats this bread will live forever; and the bread that I will give is my flesh for the life of the world." (cf. John 6:30-51)

Our Blessed Lord wanted to point out He is the sign which is infinitely greater than the multiplication of the bread and fish. He will multiply His presence in the Eucharist, so that all who receive the Eucharist will have eternal life.

The bread given to their ancestors through Moses-- kept them alive in this life, but He who is the Bread from Heaven, will give them something much greater, eternal life. It is the Holy Sacrifice of the Mass, where we receive the flesh of Jesus, the true bread from heaven, which gives eternal life.

In the future, when His apostles, bishops and priests through apostolic succession offer Mass, the re-enactment of the Lord's Supper, they will not be giving their sheep perishable food, but food that is eternal.

During the Holy Mass, Jesus comes down from heaven on the altar as the Bread of Life. He said, "I am the Bread of Life" and said, "Truly, truly, I tell you, unless you eat the flesh and drink the blood of the Son of Man, you have no life in you. Whoever eats My flesh and drinks My blood has eternal life, and I will raise Him up on the last day. For My flesh is real food, and My blood is real drink. For my flesh is true food, and my blood is true drink. Whoever feeds on my flesh and drinks my blood abides in me, and I in him." (John 6:52-56)

During Holy Communion He abides in us and we abide in Him. His Heart, that was moved with pity for the crowd is now united to our heart during Communion. The two hearts (our heart and the Heart of Jesus) are united and beat for love of the other. He pours His love into our hearts and we pour our feeble love into His Heart.

St. Peter Julian Eymard said, "Why separate the Heart of Jesus from His body and Divinity? Is it not through His Heart that He lives in the Blessed Sacrament, and that His body is alive and animated? Having risen from the dead, Jesus dies no more;

why separate His Heart from His Person and try to make Him die, so to speak, in our mind? No, no! This Divine Heart is living and palpitating in the Eucharist, no longer of a passable and mortal life, subject to sadness, agony, and pain, but of a life risen and consummated in blessedness. This impossibility to suffer and die diminishes in no way the reality of His life; on the contrary, it makes that life more perfect. God has never known death, and still He is the source of perfect and eternal life. The Heart of Jesus therefore lives in the Eucharist, since His body is alive there."

St. John Vianney said, "if we knew the value of the Mass, we would die for joy." Pope Benedict the XV said,"The Holy Mass would be of greater profit if people had it offered in their lifetime, rather than having it celebrated for the relief of their souls after death." Once St. Teresa of Avila was overwhelmed with God's goodness and asked Our Lord: "How can I thank you?" Our Lord replied, "Attend one Mass."

He told the apostles to have them be seated in the green grass. Amazingly, they are separated into groups of fifties and hundreds. Why would Jesus have them do that? He wanted to be sure it was done in an orderly fashion. So the bread and fish could be distributed, not only in a timely manner, but so that the people won't be anxious, as to whether or not they would receive food. They were hungry, and if they saw food being distributed, many of them would have attempted to grab the food and there may have be shoving and pushing.

Again, here is another symbol of the Mass and how its celebration is done in an orderly manner.

Then Our Lord uses the similar language He would use at the Last Supper and then at every Mass thereafter. The multiplication of the loaves and fish is a foreshadowing of the Mass. Before multiplying the loaves and fish, "He said the blessing, broke the loaves, and gave them to His disciples to set before the people."

Jesus then makes the miracle happen. The five loaves and two fish kept multiplying and multiplying until over 5,000 men, not counting women and children were fed. Imagine the astonishment of the Apostles and the people.

What do you think the people would have done when they witnessed the miracle? Truly, they would have thanked God for the food, because they knew it was Him, who provided it.

The word "Eucharist" means "thanksgiving." While in the desert, the Israelites grumbled rather than thanking God.

But, here during the multiplication of the loaves and fish, the people rejoiced and thanked God for His divine providence for feeding them in a deserted place. Do we thank Jesus, after every Holy Communion we receive?

Some theologians and priests erroneously say the multiplication of the loaves and fish wasn't a miracle. But rather, all just shared their own loaves and fish with each other.

However, the Church has always taught through Sacred Tradition and writings of saints, that the multiplication of the loaves was a real miracle. In fact, the Gospel says, "they filled the wicker baskets with fragments from the five barley loaves…" In other words, the loaves and the extra fragments came from the five barley loaves.

"Then Jesus called his disciples to Him and said, 'I have compassion on the crowd, because they have been with me now three days, and have nothing to eat; and I am unwilling to send them away hungry, lest they faint on the way.'" (cf. Mark 8:2-4)

Jesus states clearly that the people had been with him in the deserted area for three days. Even if they originally brought hidden food, they would have eaten it during the three days in the wilderness. Jesus clearly stated they had "nothing to eat."

The Gospel of John, states, "When the people saw the sign that Jesus had performed, they began to say, "Truly this is the Prophet who is to come into the world." Then Jesus, realizing that they were about to come and make Him king by force, withdrew again to a mountain by Himself." (John 6:14-15) Why would they want to make Him King, if they just shared food with each other?

At Holy Sacrifice of the Mass, the Eucharist is a multiplication of the real physical presence of Jesus. It's a miracle that every person who attends Mass is able to receive the real physical body of Christ in Holy Communion.

When Jesus broke the bread during the multiplication of loaves, it foreshadowed the sacrificing of Our Lord's body on the Cross. When the bread is distributed by the Apostles during the multiplication of the loaves, it also foreshadowed His body, the Bread of Life, being distributed during Holy Mass.

The bread is broken at the multiplication of the loaves, but His body is not broken on the Cross, but rather pierced. The Eucharist is not a symbol. It's His real flesh.

This sacrifice becomes present on the altar when the bread and wine are consecrated into His body and blood. The Holy Mass is a sacrifice.

Although there is one Jesus, He multiplies His presence in the Eucharist, so He can be united to each person's heart. He wants to give them His love and graces to endure their sufferings, to help them persevere through life's difficulties, and give them the gift of eternal life.

The Holy Eucharist is a double miracle. One miracle is that the bread and wine are changed into the body and blood of Jesus. The other miracle is the bread and wine continue to appear and taste like bread and wine, but they are in fact, the real body and blood of Jesus. At the Last Supper, Jesus took bread and said, "This is my body." and took the wine and said, "This is my blood." Through the sacrament of Holy Orders, Jesus uses the mouth of the priest to speak His words and his hands to work His miracle at Mass.

St. Thomas Aquinas states the Mass is the greatest of all His miracles. He said, "O precious and wonderful banquet, that brings us salvation and contains all sweetness! Could anything be of more intrinsic value? Under the old law it was the flesh of calves and goats that was offered, but here Christ Himself, the true God, is set before us as our food. What could be more wonderful than this? No other sacrament has greater healing power; through it sins are purged away, virtues are increased, and the soul is enriched with an abundance of every spiritual gift. It is offered in the Church for the living and the dead, so that what was instituted for the salvation of all may be for the benefit of all. Yet, in the end, no one can fully express the sweetness of this sacrament, in which spiritual delight is tasted at its very source, and in which we renew the memory of that surpassing love for us which Christ revealed in His passion. It was to impress the vastness of this love more firmly upon the hearts of the faithful that our Lord instituted this sacrament at the Last Supper. As He was on the point of leaving the world to go to the Father, after celebrating the Passover with his disciples, He left it as a perpetual memorial of His passion. It was the fulfillment of ancient figures and the greatest of all His miracles, while for those who were to experience the sorrow of His departure, it was destined to be a unique and abiding consolation."[135]

If Jesus was concerned about the fragments left over from the multiplication of the loaves, how much more is He concerned about fragments from His real and true presence in the Eucharist? Each particle is the whole and entire person of Jesus. *The Catechism of the Council of Trent* states: "Nor should it be forgotten that Christ, whole and entire, is contained not only under either species, but also in each Particle of either species. Each, says St. Augustine, receives Christ the Lord, and He is entire in each portion. He is not diminished by being given to many, but gives Himself whole and entire to each."[136]

When extraordinary ministers of Holy Communion are finished giving Communion, they dip their fingers in an ablution bowl of water located near the tabernacle to remove Particles that may remain on their fingers. They then dry their fingers on a finger towel that will later be purified before being washed. The priest also washes Sacred Particles from his hands after distributing Holy Communion by pouring water over his fingers in the chalice.

Linen purificators and corporals used during Mass are usually soaked overnight before washing to allow small Particles of the Hosts to dissolve. The water used to dissolve the Sacred Particles are then poured into the ground or a sacrarium in the sacristy, rather than a drain that goes into the sewer, out of respect for the Sacred Species.

Server patens are not only used to catch a Host that may fall during distribution of Communion, they are also used to catch small Particles that may fall during distribution. We pay attention to every Particle is the whole and entire person of Jesus. The patens are also purified (wiped with a purificator) during Mass, so no Particle falls to the floor, which would be disrespectful to the true presence of Jesus.

Story 1: Multiplication of Hosts During Mass

In 2004, during a Sunday Mass, there was a priest and extraordinary ministers of Holy Communion distributing Holy Communion at a parish in the United States. While distributing the Hosts, the priest noticed he had only about ten Hosts left, but there were at least fifty communicants standing in his line. He walked over to the nearest extraordinary minister to obtain Hosts from her ciborium. But she was almost out as well, so he didn't take any. As he was about to break Hosts into smaller pieces, he noticed there were still about the same number of Hosts left. Then as he kept distributing, the Hosts multiplied one by one, so

374

when he finished giving out Communion to the fifty, there were five Hosts left. And the extraordinary minister never ran out of Hosts either. After Mass, they both talked about it and realized, the Lord must have worked the miracle of the multiplication of Hosts. Astonished by it all, they didn't know what to do, except give thanks and praise to God, who was looking after His sheep to be sure they were all fed spiritually with His true and real body. And perhaps, Jesus didn't want Hosts broken into smaller pieces during Mass.

Story 2: St. Dominic and the Multiplication of the Bread

"Saint Dominic was at the Friary of Saint Sixtus, as was the general custom, he sent two friars to the city to beg alms for the community. Poverty was the general rule with the friars and it often happened that they were forced to do without their meals for days at a time. They had no regular income and lived on alms collected by the friars each day. On that day, the two friars who were sent to beg alms, were returning empty handed to the friary when a pious woman took pity on them and gave them a loaf of bread. However, before they could reach the friary, they met a young man who seemed in greater need and happily gave the bread to him. When they reached the friary, they narrated what had happened to Saint Dominic who was very pleased with their generosity and believed it was a test from God.

At supper time, Saint Dominic trusted in the Divine Providence and summoned all the brethren to the refectory. The table was prepared, dishes and cups placed and all the friars sat down. They bowed their heads in prayer. St. Dominic with his hands on the table too bowed his head in prayer. As they were praying, suddenly, two beautiful young men appeared in the midst of the refectory, carrying loaves of bread in two white cloths which hung from their shoulders before and behind. They began to distribute the bread, beginning at the lower rows, placing before each brother one whole loaf of bread. Then, when they came to St. Dominic, they placed an entire loaf of bread, bowed and disappeared. No one knew where they came from and where they went."[137]

Story 3: Eucharistic Miracle of Bleeding Host on Corporal

"In 1405 Our Lord appeared to John of Huldenberg in the tiny village of Bois Signeur Isaac about fifteen miles south of Brussels. He showed himself covered with His wounds. He appeared to John twice and then on a third time He spoke, ordering John "Go into the Chapel of Isaac, you will find Me there." At the same time, the parish priest, Peter Ost, heard a voice instructing him to offer the Mass of the Holy Cross in the Chapel of Isaac. The priest knew nothing of John's visions at this time.

The following day the pastor summoned all the faithful to assist at Mass at the Chapel of Isaac. As the priest began to celebrate Mass he noticed that the priest Host was actually bleeding, and was thoroughly mystified. John Huldenberg, who was present at the Mass, assured the priest that he should not be alarmed. John then revealed his visions to the priest to reassure him that this was all in God's plan.

The Host bled on the corporal for almost a week, until the entire corporal was soaked in blood. Then it slowly began to dry up and coagulate. The Bishop decided to launch his own investigation and gathered testimony from the many people who had witnessed the event. The Bishop had the corporal in his possession for about two years.

On June 16, 1410, the Bishop granted an indulgence of 40 days to those who visited the Chapel at Bois-Seigneur-Isaac. On May 3, 1413, he allowed the corporal to be venerated as a relic and established a solemn procession in honor of the miracle, along with public exposition of the Blessed Sacrament."[138]

Jesus Walks on Water & Calms the Storm

Fruit of the Mystery: Trust During Storms of Life and in the Church,
& Recognize Jesus is God.

"Then He made the disciples get into the boat and precede Him to the other side, while He dismissed the crowds. After doing so, He went up on the mountain by Himself to pray. When it was evening He was there alone. Meanwhile the boat, already a few miles offshore, was being tossed about by the waves, for the wind was against it. During the fourth watch of the night, He came toward them, walking on the sea. When the disciples saw Him walking on the sea they were terrified. "It is a ghost," they said, and they cried out in fear. At once Jesus spoke to them, "Take courage, it is I; do not be afraid." Peter said to Him in reply, "Lord, if it is you, command me to come to you on the water." He said, "Come." Peter got out of the boat and began to walk on the water toward Jesus. But when he saw how strong the wind was he became frightened; and, beginning to sink, he cried out, "Lord, save me!" Immediately Jesus stretched out His hand and caught him, and said to him, "O you of little faith, why did you doubt?" After they got into the boat, the wind died down. Those in the boat paid him homage, saying, "Truly, you are the Son of God." (Matthew 14:22-43)

It had been a long day for Jesus, who through His compassion healed the sick and multiplied the loaves. He then ordered His disciples to cross the lake, and then He journeyed up the mountain to pray to His Father. Our Blessed Lord gives us an awesome example to take time during our busy day in order to pray to Our Heavenly Father alone.

Due to the storm, the disciples boat was tossed about by the wind, which caused the waves to nearly tip it over. Spending

377

hours on the boat, unable to reach the other side, they battled the wind and waves, and must have been exhausted.

They feared the boat would capsize in the dark night. This fear was increased by terror, when they saw what appeared to be a ghost walking on the water. The Gospel states, "they cried out in fear". It's not often we hear about full-grown men crying out in fear. They must have been afraid they would die, as they most certainly were afraid of the ghostly figure that came toward them in the darkness of the night.

With regard to seeing Jesus during the night, how could they have seen Him in darkness? As the wind was blowing and the waves were high, was Jesus illuminated? Or perhaps the moon was shining, and so reflected His clothing. Whatever the case, they were relieved to hear, "Courage it is I; do not be afraid".

Peter had great faith, and trusting that Jesus would help him walk on water, he said, "Lord, if it is you, command me to come to you on the water." He said, "Come." But unfortunately, he saw how strong the wind was, took his eyes off of Jesus, and began to sink. But, our tenderhearted Lord, rescued him, by reaching out and grasping the hand of Peter, bringing both into the boat, and by His divine power, He immediately calmed the storm.

Jesus wanted to help Peter understand that he needed to grow in faith, and said to Peter, "O you of little faith, why did you doubt?" Peter had faith. He had enough faith to step out of the boat and start walking on water. But his faith needed to be strengthened, because after Our Lord would die, rise from the dead, and ascend into heaven, it will be Peter's duty to strengthen the faith of the apostles and tend the sheep with sound doctrine.

The apostles made an act of faith in Jesus as God. They did him homage (worshiped Him), saying, "Truly, you are the Son of God."

Some Fathers of the Church have said that Peter's boat represents the Church on the rough seas. Despite the many obstacles and struggles, the Lord's help and protection will never be lacking in assisting the Church. Christ's Church will never be overcome.

Application 1: Jesus Calms the Waters of Our Heart

God wants to calm the waters of our heart and to trust Him. No matter what ghostly fears may seem to haunt us during the day, whether it be sickness, fears of surgery, fear of dying, fear of old age, financial fears, fears at work, fears for loved ones, fear of what is going on in the world or in the Church, or whether it be wars, natural disasters, tornadoes, earthquakes, tsunamis, or terrorism, we should ask Our Lord to come into the boat of our lives. We can trust that if we are in the boat of the Church, we will be safe despite any turmoil as it comes and goes.

Our Savior may ask us to step out of our boat in faith, trusting that He will calm the waves of our fears. With great faith we should humble ourselves before Him in adoration and worship Him crying out, "Lord save me!" knowing He will have compassion on us. And "He will stretch out His hand", grasp us with His love, and take away all our fears as He speaks in the silence of our heart, "Courage it is I; do not be afraid."

Whether it be literal storms of weather or personal storms raging in our hearts through our feelings and emotions Jesus is always with us to bring calm and peace.

Story 1: St. Christopher

St. Christopher lived from the 200's to 251. He became a hermit and built a hut near a river. As an act of charity, he helped people cross the river. One day, a small child approached him wanting safe passage across the water. He hoisted the boy on his shoulders, and with his trusty staff, began the journey walking through the river. As the river deepened, the child began to grow heavier with waters quickly rising. The weight of the child continued to weigh Christopher down. As he reached the banks of the river, he said, "Child, you have put me in great peril; you weigh almost as if I had all the world upon me..."

The little boy said, "You have not only borne all the world upon yourself, but you have borne Him that created and made all the world, upon your shoulders."

It was then he realized he had carried the Christ Child. Christopher's name means "Christ-bearer." St. Christopher is the patron of travelers and many wear the St. Christopher medal or have it in their vehicle for safe travel.

Story 2: St. Anthony of Padua Prayer Against Storms

The prayer against storms attributed to St. Anthony paused a rainstorm on Palm Sunday, March 24, 2024. The city located in the USA had just completed its 40 Days for Life Prayer and fasting campaign to close Planned Parenthood, where many abortions take place.

A priest was asked to do a Eucharistic procession on Palm Sunday around Planned Parenthood, but the forecast was rain throughout the day. The night before the event, due to the rain forecast, he emailed Catholics the *Prayer Against Storms* by St. Anthony of Padua.

The next day, even though it had been raining all morning and was still raining, just before the procession was to begin, all who came to participate trusted Jesus would cause the rain to stop for the procession.

After nearly 100 people arrived, it was still raining. But just as it was time to start, the rain stopped and the Eucharistic procession began. When the procession concluded, just as everyone returned to their vehicles, it started to rain again. The

Prayer Against Storms by St. Anthony worked. Jesus paused the rain storm, so all could process His Eucharistic presence around Planned Parenthood, where unborn babies die from abortion.

Story 3: Battle of Lepanto, Feast of Our Lady of the Rosary

On October 7 of 1571 was the Battle of Lepanto off the Italian coast. Before departing for the battle, not one of the 81,000 soldiers and sailors had failed to confess and receive Holy Communion.

From the Ottoman Empire 274 Muslim ships greatly outnumbered the 208 Christian war ships, and were about to attack Christian Europe.

The Turks had ravaged Corfu, Greece the month before and left their usual calling cards: burned-out churches, broken crucifixes, and mangled bodies of priests, women, and children. In response, Pope Saint Pius V initiated the Holy League to unite Christian powers to fight in battle against the Muslims and asked all Catholics to pray the Holy Rosary.

In the morning of October 7, 1571, the commander, Don Juan of Austria, ordered the celebration of Mass on all Christian vessels.

As the battle began, the wind shifted in favor of the Christians causing the defeat of the Muslim invaders. The Muslim Turks lost 230 galleys and up to 30,000 Turks were killed. The League suffered a trifling 13 galleys sunk; 7,600 men were killed.

At the time the battle was won, Saint Pius V was studying financial sheets with the papal treasurer. Suddenly, the pontiff stopped, opened a window, and stared at the sky. "This is no time for business," he told his interlocutors. "Go and give thanks to God, for our fleet is about to meet the Turks, and God will give us the victory!" Then the Pope knelt in prayer before a crucifix. Several weeks after the battle, word came that what the pope said was true.

In response to winning the battle, Pope Pius V declared October 7 as the Feast of Our Lady of Victory "Our Lady of the Rosary." Historians have said, had the Christians lost the battle, all of Europe would have been invaded.

Story 4: Eucharist Halts Tsunami

On January 31, 1906, on the small island of Tumaco off the coast of Columbia at 10 o'clock in the morning, the earth shook violently for almost ten minutes. Due to a tsunami, all the inhabitants of the village ran to the church and begged the pastor, Fr. Gerardo Larrondo, to lead a procession with the Blessed Sacrament. The sea plunged inland more than a half a mile and a mountainous wall of water was building up threatening to drown everyone and everything in one gigantic wave.

Fearing the church would be destroyed by water, Fr. Gerardo consumed the small Hosts in the ciborium and placed the large Host in a monstrance. The priest and the people began their march, weeping and crying out to God. Fr. Larrondo reached the beach with the monstrance in hand when he advanced courageously to the water's edge and as the waves came rushing in-- he calmly raised the Sacred Host in the monstrance and with it made the Sign of the Cross. The wave hesitated, paused and backed off. The people cried out "Miracle, miracle!" The mighty wall of water that threatened to wipe the village of Tumaco off the face of the earth was halted and began to recede, and then the sea resumed its normal level. The inhabitants of Tumaco were overcome with joy at having been saved from death by Jesus in the Blessed Sacrament. Prayers of fervent thanks poured out. All buildings in the area were destroyed, except for the island of Tumaco where the miracle occurred.

Story 5: St. Hyacinth Walks on Water

"When St. Hyacinth (1257) was at Kiev, the Tarters sacked the town, but it was only as he finished Mass that the saint heard of the danger. Without waiting to unvest (remove his priestly vestment) he took the ciborium (a metal container with lid in which consecrated Hosts are placed and stored in the tabernacle) in his hands, and was leaving the church. As he passed by an image of Mary a voice said: "Hyacinth, my son, why dost thou leave me behind? Take me with thee, and leave me not to mine enemies." The statue was of heavy alabaster; but when Hyacinth took it in his arms, it was light as a reed. With the Blessed Sacrament and the image he came to the river Dnieper, and walked dryshod (feet didn't get wet) over the surface of the waters."[139]

Story 6: Miracle of the Tabernacle Saved in the Peshtigo Fire

During the great Peshtigo Fire on October 8 of 1871, in Wisconsin and Michigan, St. Mary's Church was destroyed. However, before it was destroyed, Father Pernin was able to carry the church's wooden Tabernacle, containing the Blessed Sacrament, to the river on his wagon. He pushed the wagon partially into the river and abandoned it to save his own life. The next day, a parishioner who had also survived found Father Pernin and asked if he knew what had happened to the Tabernacle. The priest said, "This wagon had been blown over on its side by the storm; whilst the Tabernacle itself had been caught up by the wind and cast on one of the logs floating on the water. Everything in the immediate vicinity of this spot had been blackened or charred by the flames. But, the Tabernacle was saved when the wind tossed it on a log floating on water."

Story 7: St. Bosco Dream

St. John Bosco was known for his many dreams which foretold future events. One such dream dealt with the Church going through a storm. He relates the following about his dream.

"In the midst of this endless sea, two solid columns, a short distance apart, soar high into the sky. One is surmounted by a statue of the Immaculate Virgin, at whose feet a large inscription reads: 'Auxilium Christianorum' ('Help of Christians'). The other, far loftier and sturdier, supports a Host of proportionate size, and bears beneath it the inscription: 'Salus credentium' ('Salvation of believers'). "The flagship commander – the Roman Pontiff – standing at the helm, strains every muscle to steer his ship between the two columns, from whose summits hang many anchors and strong hooks linked to chains. The entire enemy fleet closes in to intercept and sink the flagship at all costs. They bombard it with everything they have: books and pamphlets, incendiary bombs, firearms, cannons. The battle rages ever more furious. Beaked prows ram the flagship again and again, but to no avail, as, unscathed and undaunted, it keeps on it course. At times, a formidable ram splinters a gaping hole in its hull, but immediately, a breeze from the two columns instantly seals the gash. "Meanwhile, enemy cannons blow up; firearms and beaks fall to pieces; ships crack up and sink to the bottom. In blind fury, the enemy takes to hand-to-hand combat, cursing and blaspheming. Suddenly the Pope falls, seriously wounded. He is instantly helped up, but struck a second time, dies. A shout of victory rises from the enemy, and wild rejoicing seeps their ships. But no sooner is the Pope dead than another takes his place. The captains of the auxiliary ships elected him so quickly that the news of the Pope's death coincides with that of his

successor's election. The enemy's self-assurance wanes.
"Breaking through all resistance, the new Pope steers his ship
safely between the two columns; first, to the one surmounted by
the Host, and then the other, topped by the statue of the Virgin.
At this point, something unexpected happens. The enemy ships
panic and disperse, colliding with and scuttling each other.
"Some auxiliary ships, which had gallantly fought alongside
their flagship, are the first to tie up at the two columns. Many
others, which had fearfully kept far away from the fight, stand
still, cautiously waiting until the wrecked enemy ships vanish
under the waves. Then they too head for the two columns, tie up
at the swinging hooks and ride safe and tranquil beside their
flagship. A great calm now covers the sea."[140]

Jesus Heals Boy with a Mute Spirit

Fruit of the Mystery: Overcome Evil by Faith, Prayer & Fasting

"And when they came to the disciples, they saw a great crowd about them, and scribes arguing with them. And immediately all the crowd, when they saw Him, were greatly amazed, and ran up to Him and greeted Him. And He asked them, "What are you discussing with them?" And one of the crowd answered Him, "Teacher, I brought my son to you, for he has a mute spirit; and wherever it seizes him, it dashes him down; and he foams and grinds his teeth, and becomes rigid; and I asked your disciples to cast it out, and they were not able. And He answered them, "O faithless generation, how long am I to be with you? Bring him to me." And they brought the boy to Him; and when they spirit saw Him, and immediately it convulsed the boy, and he fell on the ground and rolled about, foaming at the mouth. And Jesus asked the Father, "How long has he had this?" And he said, "From childhood. And it has often cast him into the fire and into the water, to destroy him; but if you can do anything, have pity on us and help us." And Jesus said to him, "If I can! All things are possible to him who believes." Immediately the father of the child cried out and said, "I believe; help my unbelief!" And when Jesus saw that a crowd came running together, he rebuked the unclean spirit, saying to it, "You mute and deaf spirit, I command you, come out of him, and never enter him again." And after crying out and convulsing him terribly, it came out, and the boy was like a corpse; so that most of them said, "He is dead." But Jesus took him by the hand and lifted him up, and he rose. And when he had entered the house, his disciples asked him privately, "Why could we not cast it out?" And He said to them, "This kind cannot be driven out by anything but prayer and fasting." (Mark 9:14-29)

387

The father of the possessed boy came to Jesus for help. Imagine the anguish in the father's heart to see his son possessed and tormented by an evil spirit, and yet feeling helpless in his inability to help him. The man told Our Lord that the disciples could not free his son from the demon. Our Blessed Lord responded stating, "O faithless generation, how long will I be with you?" He said these words to help all present understand the need for greater faith.

As the father brought his boy to Jesus, the devil threw him into convulsions. He fell to the ground, and began to roll and foam at the mouth. The father of the boy said, "If you can do anything, have compassion on us and help us." When he had said this, it revealed the man did not have full confidence in the Lord.

However, Our Blessed Lord helped the boy's father come to a deeper faith. That is why Jesus said, "If you can!" "Everything is possible if one has faith." This caused the man to recognize that he needed more faith, and so, he said, "I do believe; help my unbelief."

Jesus then commanded the demon to leave the boy. The demon shouted and threw the boy into convulsions and then it left him. The boy became like a corpse, and some thought he had died. But Jesus took him by the hand and raised him up.

All of us in some way-- are like the father of the boy. We do believe and trust the Lord, but not as we ought. Sometimes it takes difficult circumstances in our life to come to understand we need more faith.

For example, when God does not answer our prayers, we may feel as though He is not listening, or perhaps what we are asking is not His will, and so we give up asking the Lord in prayer.

It takes prayer, faith and sometimes fasting, to undo the work of the devil. We also need to ask that our faith be increased, as the man asked Jesus, when he said, "I do believe, help my unbelief. We trust "Everything is possible to one who has faith."

Some may not consider Jesus delivering the possessed from evil spirits as a miracle. A miracle is defined as an extraordinary sensible effect wrought by God that surpasses the power and order of created nature. But the *The Catholic Encyclopedia* describes miracles as, "Wonders performed by supernatural power as signs of some special mission or gift and explicitly ascribed to God." It also describes expelling demons as a miracle, "In many of the miracles faith is not required, and is in fact absent; this is shown, in the miracles of power, by the expressed fear of the Apostles, e.g., at Christ stilling the tempest (Mark, iv, 40), at Christ on the waters (Mark, vi, 51), at the draught of fishes (Luke, v 8), and in the miracles of expelling demons. In some miracles Christ requires faith, but the faith is not the cause of the miracle, only the condition of His exercising the power."[141]

In his great *Summa Theologiae*, St. Thomas wrote that "the miracle of the restoration and salvation of a soul is, in God's eyes, a greater miracle than the creation of the universe itself. For the material universe is something that is brought into being for a time, but then one day will pass away. A soul that is saved, however, is saved for eternal life."

Whether or not Jesus expelling a demon is considered a miracle of nature, this mystery was added to *The Miracle Mysteries* to show that Jesus, as God, can deliver us not only spiritually (through the washing away of sins), but also physically deliver his creation from evil.

Application 1: Prayer and Fasting

It takes prayer, faith and sometimes fasting to undo the work of
the devil. We also need to ask that our faith be increased, as the
man asked Jesus, when he said, "I do believe, help my unbelief.
We trust "Everything is possible to one who has faith."

In an article by Rev. Daniel Merz, "A Reflection on Lenten
Fasting," he lists seven reasons for fasting in the Christian
tradition: 1. From the beginning, God commanded some fasting,
and sin entered into the world because Adam and Eve broke the
fast (eating the forbidden fruit). 2. For the Christian, fasting is
ultimately about fasting from sin. 3. Fasting reveals our
dependence on God and not the resources of this world. 4.
Fasting is an ancient way of preparing for the Eucharist (today,
one hour before receiving Communion). 5. Fasting is preparation
for baptism (and all the sacraments)—for the reception of grace.
6. Fasting is a means of saving resources to give to the poor. 7.
Fasting is a means of self-discipline, chastity, and the restraining
of the appetites.[142]

It's important to pray when fasting, so that fasting will
develop wings. Ask the Lord to help you fast. We should not fast
on Sundays because every Sunday we celebrate the Resurrection
of Jesus.

In addition to fasting; pray the Rosary everyday; go to
Confession often (fasting from sin); make a Holy Hour every
week; pray the Chaplet of Divine Mercy; attend daily Mass; wear
a Scapular.

Here are some ideas for fasting from Alice Schoenhofer and Celia
Chin:[143]
 1. We can fast or abstain in a number of ways with regard to
food and drink.
For example: We can fast twice a week on Wednesday and
Friday using the Lent Fasting regulations. "When fasting, a

person is permitted to eat one full meal, as well as two smaller meals that together are not equal to a full meal." --USCCB. Fast twice a week such as Wednesday and Friday on Bread and Water. If one has good health and is not diabetic or hypoglycemic and/ or if it does not adversely affect your temperament or mood or physical activity, then one could fast on bread and water. Skip one meal a week, like breakfast or lunch. Abstain from meat continuously for 40 days. The Church requires all from age 14 until death to abstain from meat every Friday of the year, unless a solemnity falls on a Friday. However, the United States Conference of Catholic Bishops has determined that Catholics can choose a different penance outside of Lent. But during Lent, they must abstain from meat on Fridays.

2. Deny yourself dessert on set days.

Fast from candy such as chocolate. Most of us eat too much sugar anyway. Skip salt or pepper on your food. Fast from soda. It's terrible for you! Skip beer or other alcoholic drinks when going out to eat.

3. Don't eat between meals.

This sounds easy, but try it. You'll find it's quite difficult since most of us snack frequently and don't even realize it. Fast (one main meal with two small snacks) one day a week. Drink only water (abstain from coffee, tea, pop, milk, juice, alcohol). Eat foods you don't like. Eat your favorite food on your plate last and your least favorite first. Avoid ketchup or mustard.

4. Include fasting from things other than food and drink.

For example, we should do our daily duties to the best of our ability and accept sufferings for the love of Jesus. We can fast from all technology one day a week, such as Television, except EWTN. Limit the amount of time you spend per day on the Internet. Fast from your favorite television program or fast from watching or listening to the news. Fast from your favorite websites. Fast from texting while walking or driving. Avoid radio music that doesn't lift up the soul. Give an anonymous charitable donation to someone or an organization. Don't hit the snooze and immediately get out of bed. If you are lacking sleep, go to bed early every night.

5. Most especially we should fast from sin.

For example: Fast from gossip and lying. Fast from complaining. Fast from interrupting others who are speaking. Listen more, talk less. Make it a point to compliment one person per day. Fasting helps overcome addictions and sins. It can deliver us from demons who try to influence us and tempt us. We can offer our fast to help another person who is struggling with specific sins, addictions, temptations or demonic influences.

6. Beware of pride.

With any kind of self-discipline, penance, or fasting comes a temptation to pride. We face the danger of believing we are superior to others because we fast, or can think fasting is an end in itself. But fasting itself is never the goal, nor does it make us better than others. Rather, fasting is an aid, a training tool in our ascent toward perfection, which is found in a pure, self-giving love of God and neighbor. "Be on your guard when you begin to mortify your body by abstinence and fasting," says St. Jerome, "lest you imagine yourself to be perfect and a saint; for perfection does not consist in this virtue. It is only a help; a disposition; a means though a fitting one, for the attainment of true perfection."

Story 1: Man Possessed with 15,000 Evil Spirits

The following true story is from St. Louis de Montfort's *The Secret of the Rosary:*

"When Saint Dominic was preaching the Rosary near Carcassone an Albigensian was brought to him who was possessed by the devil. Saint Dominic exorcised him in the presence of a great crowd of people; it appears that over twelve

392

thousand had come to hear him preach. The devils who were in possession of this wretched man were forced to answer Saint Dominic's questions in spite of themselves. They said that:

1. There were fifteen thousand of them in the body of this poor man, because he had attacked the fifteen mysteries of the Rosary;

2. They went on to testify that by preaching the Rosary he put fear and horror into the very depths of Hell and that he was the man they hated most throughout the whole world, because of the souls which he snatched from them through devotion to the Holy Rosary;

3. They then revealed several other things.

Saint Dominic put his Rosary around the Albigensian's neck and asked the devils to tell him who, of all the Saints in Heaven, was the one they feared the most, and who should therefore be the most loved and revered by men. At this they let out such unearthly screams that most of the people fell to the ground, faint from fear. Then, using all their cunning, so as not to answer, the devils wept and wailed in such a pitiful way that many of the people wept also, out of purely natural pity. The devils spoke through the mouth of the Albigensian, pleading in a heartrending voice:

"Dominic, Dominic, have mercy on us—we promise you that we will never hurt you. You have always had compassion for sinners and those in distress; have pity on us, for we are in grievous straits. We are suffering so very much already, so why do you delight in heightening our pains? Can't you be satisfied with our suffering without adding to it? Have pity on us! Have pity on us!"

Saint Dominic was not one whit moved by the pathos of these wretched spirits and told them that he would not let them alone until they had answered his question. Then they said they would whisper the answer in such a way that only Saint Dominic would be able to hear. The latter firmly insisted upon their

393

answering clearly and out loud. Then the devils kept quiet and refused to say another word, completely disregarding Saint Dominic's orders—so he knelt down and prayed thus to Our Lady: "Oh, all powerful and wonderful Virgin Mary, I implore you by the power of the Most Holy Rosary, order these enemies of the human race to answer me."

No sooner had he made this prayer than a glowing flame leaped out of the ears, nostrils and mouth of the Albigensian. Everyone shook with fear, but the fire did not hurt anyone. Then the devils cried:

"Dominic, we beseech you, by the passion of Jesus Christ and by the merits of His Holy Mother and of all the Saints, let us leave the body of this man without speaking further—for the Angels will answer your question whenever you wish. After all, are we not liars? So why should you want to believe us? Please don't torture us any more; have pity on us."

"Woe unto you wretched spirits, who do not deserve to be heard," Saint Dominic said, and kneeling down he prayed to Our Lady:

"Oh most worthy Mother of Wisdom, I am praying for the people assembled here who have already learned how to say the Angelic Salutation properly. Please, I beg of you, force your enemies to proclaim the whole truth and nothing but the truth about this, here and now, before the multitude."

Saint Dominic had hardly finished this prayer when he saw the Blessed Virgin near at hand, surrounded by a multitude of Angels. She struck the possessed man with a golden rod that She held and said: "Answer my servant Dominic at once." (Remember, the people neither saw nor heard Our Lady, but only Saint Dominic.) Then the devils started screaming:

"Oh you who are our enemy, our downfall and our destruction, why have you come from Heaven just to torture us so grievously? O Advocate of sinners, you who snatch them from the very jaws of Hell, you who are the very sure path to Heaven, must we, in spite of ourselves, tell the whole truth and confess before everyone who it is who is the cause of our shame and our ruin? Oh woe unto us, princes of darkness:

Then listen well, you Christians: the Mother of Jesus Christ is all-powerful and She can save Her servants from falling into Hell. She is the Sun which destroys the darkness of our wiles and subtlety. It is She who uncovers our hidden plots, breaks our snares and makes our temptations useless and ineffectual.

We have to say, however reluctantly, that not a single soul who has really persevered in Her service has ever been damned with us; one single sigh that She offers to the Blessed Trinity is worth far more than all the prayers, desires and aspirations of all the Saints.

We fear Her more than all the other Saints in Heaven together and we have no success with Her faithful servants.

Many Christians who call upon her when they are at the hour of death and who really ought to be damned according to our ordinary standards are saved by Her intercession.

Oh if only that Mary (it is thus in their fury that they called Her) had not pitted Her strength against ours and had not upset our plans, we should have conquered the Church and should have destroyed it long before this; and we would have seen to it that all the Orders in the Church fell into error and disorder.

Now that we are forced to speak we must also tell you this: nobody who perseveres in saying the Rosary will be damned, because She obtains for Her servants the grace of true contrition for their sins and by means of this they obtain God's forgiveness and mercy."

Then Saint Dominic had them all say the Rosary very slowly and with great devotion, and a wonderful thing happened: at each Hail Mary that he and the people said together a large group of devils issued forth from the wretched man's body under the guise of red-hot coals.

When the devils had all been expelled and the heretic was at last entirely free of them, Our Lady (who was still invisible) gave Her blessing to the assembled company, and they were filled with joy because of this. A large number of heretics were converted because of this miracle and joined the Confraternity of the Most Holy Rosary."[144]

Jesus Raises Lazarus from the Dead

Fruit of the Mystery: Faith in Jesus' Power over Death
& in the Resurrection of the Dead,
Friend of Jesus

"Now a man was ill, Lazarus from Bethany, the village of Mary
and her sister Martha. Mary was the one who had anointed the
Lord with perfumed oil and dried his feet with her hair; it was
her brother Lazarus who was ill. So the sisters sent word to Him,
saying, "Master, the one you love is ill." When Jesus heard this
He said, "This illness is not to end in death, but is for the glory of
God, that the Son of God may be glorified through it." Now Jesus
loved Martha and her sister and Lazarus. So when He heard that
He was ill, he remained for two days in the place where He was.
Then after this He said to His disciples, "Let us go back to
Judea." The disciples said to him, "Rabbi, the Jews were just
trying to stone you, and you want to go back there?" Jesus
answered, "Are there not twelve hours in a day? If one walks
during the day, He does not stumble, because He sees the light of
this world. But if one walks at night, He stumbles, because the
light is not in Him." He said this, and then told them, "Our
friend Lazarus is asleep, but I am going to awaken him." So the
disciples said to Him, "Master, if he is asleep, he will be saved."
But Jesus was talking about his death, while they thought that
He meant ordinary sleep. So then Jesus said to them clearly,
"Lazarus has died. And I am glad for you that I was not there,
that you may believe. Let us go to him." So Thomas, called
Didymus, said to his fellow disciples, "Let us also go to die with
him." When Jesus arrived, He found that Lazarus had already
been in the tomb for four days. Now Bethany was near
Jerusalem, only about two miles away. And many of the Jews
had come to Martha and Mary to comfort them about their

brother. When Martha heard that Jesus was coming, she went to meet Him; but Mary sat at home. Martha said to Jesus, "Lord, if You had been here, my brother would not have died. [But] even now I know that whatever you ask of God, God will give you." Jesus said to her, "Your brother will rise." Martha said to him, "I know he will rise, in the resurrection on the last day." Jesus told her, "I am the resurrection and the life; whoever believes in Me, even if he dies, will live, and everyone who lives and believes in Me will never die. Do you believe this?" She said to him, "Yes, Lord. I have come to believe that You are the Messiah, the Son of God, the one who is coming into the world." When she had said this, she went and called her sister Mary secretly, saying, "The teacher is here and is asking for you." As soon as she heard this, she rose quickly and went to Him. For Jesus had not yet come into the village, but was still where Martha had met Him. So when the Jews who were with her in the house comforting her saw Mary get up quickly and go out, they followed her, presuming that she was going to the tomb to weep there. When Mary came to where Jesus was and saw him, she fell at His feet and said to Him, "Lord, if you had been here, my brother would not have died." When Jesus saw her weeping and the Jews who had come with her weeping, He became perturbed and deeply troubled, and said, "Where have you laid him?" They said to Him, "Sir, come and see." And Jesus wept. So the Jews said, "See how He loved him." But some of them said, "Could not the one who opened the eyes of the blind man have done something so that this man would not have died?" So Jesus, perturbed again, came to the tomb. It was a cave, and a stone lay across it. Jesus said, "Take away the stone." Martha, the dead man's sister, said to Him, "Lord, by now there will be a stench; he has been dead for four days." Jesus said to her, "Did I not tell you that if you believe you will see the glory of God?" So they took away the stone. And Jesus raised His eyes and said, "Father, I thank you for hearing Me. I know that You always hear Me; but because of the crowd here I have said this, that they may believe that You sent Me." And when He had said this, He cried out in a loud voice, "Lazarus, come out!" The dead man came out, tied hand and foot with burial bands, and his face was wrapped in a cloth. So Jesus said to them, "Untie him and let him go." (John 11:1-44)

Martha, Mary and Lazarus were friends of Jesus. He stayed at their home in Bethany and visited them periodically. Imagine having Jesus as a friend. He comes to your home to eat with you and have friendly conversations. In this Gospel it mentions that Jesus loved Lazarus. If we love someone, we will spend time with them and speak to them as our friend. Shouldn't we spend time with Jesus and speak to Him as our friend? Jesus loves each of us infinitely. But, do we really know and believe it's true? Lazarus did.

Jesus wept! Wow! Our Lord has two natures, human and divine. His human nature had feelings of sorrow just like us. He wept because Our Lord felt great empathy for Lazarus and grief for his family and friends. Just think about that for a moment. Jesus feels empathy for us and grief for our family and friends when we go through the loss of a loved one. Because Jesus is inside us through baptism, He feels what we feel: sadness, anger, confusion, and when we weep, He weeps with us. Despite the fact, Jesus knew He was going to raise Lazarus back to life, He still felt these feelings. Isn't one a good friend, who feels what we feel? The word compassion means to "suffer with." Jesus has compassion on us and suffers with us.

Martha made four acts of faith believing the Lord could have worked a miracle to heal her brother, Lazarus, she said, "Lord if You had been here, my brother would not have died." Her faith was imperfect, because she didn't realize it was unnecessary that Our Divine Lord be present to work a miracle, as was the case of the centurion's servant.

She then made her second act of faith believing Jesus could raise the dead to life. She said, "But even now I know that whatever You ask of God, God will give You."

When Jesus said, "Your brother will rise", she makes a third act of faith, as she says, "I know he will rise, in the resurrection on the last day." Her act of faith indicates she believes in the resurrection at the end of the world, which the Sadducees did not believe.

The tender love of Jesus for Martha is revealed in His conversation with her. Our Blessed Lord aimed at increasing her faith in Him, by His declaration, "I am the resurrection and the life and whoever believes in me, even if he dies, will live, and anyone who lives, and believes in Me will never die."

She then responded with her fourth and greatest act of faith, "I have come to believe that You are the Christ, the Son of God, the one who is coming into the world."

Bishop McEvilly, in his *Commentary on the Gospel of John* states, 'She believes Jesus to be the natural Son of God, God Himself and all that He has taught is true, and that He is the Resurrection and the life. She also believes Him to be the promised Messiah, and even more than the Messiah, "the Son of the living God" who has come to save mankind.'

Recall the precious event where Jesus came to their home. Martha was busy preparing food for Jesus and she asked Him to tell her sister, Mary, who was sitting at His feet listening to Him, to help her. But Our Lord responded saying, "Martha, Martha, you are worried about many things. Mary has chosen the better part." Mary chose the better part, because in heaven no one rushes around doing good works like Martha was doing. Rather, we will do as Mary who sat and adored Jesus at His feet.

Mary is the one who sat in silence and bathed His feet with her tears. Some believe this is Mary Magdalene, who was a prostitute and whom Jesus cast out seven demons. She was also at the foot of the Cross with Mary, the Mother of Jesus and it was

Magdalene, whom Jesus appeared after He rose from the dead and told her to tell His Apostles, He had risen. It's believed after Jesus ascended into heaven, Mary Magdalene lived as a hermit in a cave for thirty years.

When in the future, we think of Martha and the words of Jesus echo in our heart, "Martha Martha, you are worried about many things." --- may we rather think, "Martha, Martha, what great faith you had. Increase my faith, that it may be as strong as yours."

The most important part of this story is that Jesus, as God, has power over death. Not only did He raise Lazarus from the dead, but He raised Himself from the dead with a new resurrected body. Lazarus will die again, but through Our Lord's resurrection, Jesus will never die again.

The raising of Lazarus also points to the General Resurrection of the dead at the end of the world. The event of raising Lazarus from the dead gives us confidence in Jesus' power over death and great hope in our own resurrection at the end of the world. And Jesus uses His three friends, Lazarus, Martha, and Mary to help us to believe and understand that He is truly the Christ "Messiah", the Son of the living God, who has come into the world to save us, and bring us to our eternal home in heaven to be with Him forever.

Application 1: Saints Who Raised the Dead

Fr. Albert Hebert wrote a book called *Saints Who Raised the Dead, 400 True Stories*. Some saints while they were living on earth, raised the dead include: St. Francis Xavier, St. Dominic, St. Patrick, St. Don Bosco, St. Elizabeth of Hungary, St. Rose of Lima, St. Teresa of Avila, St. Margaret of Castello, etc...

"When Blessed Dominic and the three cardinals took their seats and the abbess, with her nuns, stood before them, a man rode up pulling his hair and yelling: "Alas! Alas!" When he was asked what the trouble was, he answered: "Cardinal Stephen's nephew fell from his horse and is dead." The nephew's name was Napoleon. When his uncle, the Cardinal, heard this, he fell backwards against Blessed Dominic prostrate with grief. Then, as the others supported him, Blessed Dominic arose and blessed him with holy water. Leaving them, he went to the scene, where he found the dead young man horribly crushed and badly lacerated. He had him carried to a house nearby, with instructions to leave him there. Dominic told Brother Tancred and the others present to prepare themselves for Mass. Present were Blessed Dominic, the cardinals and their retinue, and the abbess with her nuns. Blessed Dominic and the cardinals held her in high esteem for her sanctity.

Then, with tears, Blessed Dominic started to say Mass. Coming to the elevation, he held the Body of the Lord in his hands and was elevating it according to custom, when all were astonished to see Blessed Dominic raised to a height of one foot above the ground. When Mass was over, he and the cardinals with their companions, together with the abbess and her nuns, returned to the body of the dead young man. With his blessed hands he arranged all the crushed and lacerated members from the head to the feet. Then with much groaning, he knelt down to pray near the coffin. For a second and third time, he repeated the process of arranging the lacerated face and body and then kneeling down to pray.

Then arising, he made a Sign of the Cross over the body and, standing at the head of the corpse, he raised his hands to heaven and, being himself raised more than a foot from the ground, he shouted with a loud voice: "Young man, Napoleon, in the name of our Lord Jesus Christ, I say to thee arise." At once, before the eyes of those who had come to this great spectacle, he arose sound and healthy and said to Blessed Dominic "Father, give me something to eat." Then Blessed Dominic gave him food and drink and returned him in gay spirits to his uncle with not even the slightest mark of injury. The young man had been dead from morning to three o'clock in the afternoon."[145]

Story 2: Stillborn Baby Boy Raised from the Dead

In the United States there was a miracle of raising a child from the dead in 2011. A stillborn boy from Goodfield, Illinois was dead for 61 minutes and without any heartbeat. His mother kept praying to Bishop Fulton Sheen and suddenly the boy's heart began to beat. This miracle of raising the boy from the dead through Fulton Sheen's intercession has been approved by the Vatican and will lead to his beatification.

The Rosary of Miracles

The First Rosary of Miracles
Jesus Heals the Paralytic

Frank Zimmerman (1900)

"And they came bringing a paralytic by four men. And when they could not get near Him because of the crowd, they removed the roof above Him,… and let down the pallet on which the paralytic lay, and when Jesus saw their faith, He said to the paralytic, "Child, your sins are forgiven." The scribes sitting there were questioning in their hearts, "Why does this man speak like this? It is blasphemy! Who can forgive, but God alone?" Jesus said to them.., "Which is easier, to say to the paralytic, 'Your sins are forgiven' or say, 'Rise, take up your pallet and walk?" But that you may know the Son of Man has authority on earth to forgive sins", He said to the paralytic, "I say to rise, take up your pallet and go home." And he rose, and immediately took up the pallet and went out before them all…" (Mark 2:1-12)

The Second Rosary of Miracles
Jesus Multiplies the Loaves & Fish

Ambrosius Franken I (Flemish, 1544–1618)

"His disciples came to Jesus and said, "This is a lonely place, and the hour is now late; send them away, to go into the country and villages round about and buy themselves something to eat." But, He answered them, "You give them something to eat." And they said to Him, "Shall we go and buy two hundred denari worth of bread, and give it to them to eat?" And He said to them, "How many loaves have you? Go and see."…" They said, "Five, and two fish." Then He commanded them to all sit down...So they sat down in groups… And taking the five loaves and the two fish, He looked up to heaven, and blessed, and broke the loaves, and gave them to the disciples to set before the people; and divided the two fish among them all. And they all ate and were satisfied. And they took up twelve baskets full of broken pieces and of the fish. And those who who ate the loaves were five thousand men." (Mark 6:30-44)

The Third Rosary of Miracles
Jesus Walks on Water & Calms the Sea

Philipp Otto Runge (1777 to 1810)

When evening came, He was there alone, but the boat by this time was many furlongs distant from land, beaten by the waves; for the wind was against them. And in the fourth watch of the night He came to them, walking on the sea, they were terrified, saying, "It is a ghost! And they cried out for fear. But immediately, He spoke to them, saying, "Take heart, it is I; have no fear."... Peter got out of the boat and walked on the water, and came to Jesus; but when he saw the wind, he was afraid, and beginning to sink he cried out, "Lord, save me." Jesus immediately reached out His hand and caught him,...And when they got into the boat, the wind ceased. And those in the boat worshiped Him saying, "Truly you are the Son of God." (Matthew 14:22-32)

The Fourth Rosary of Miracles
Jesus Heals Boy with Mute Spirit

James Tissot (1836 - 1902)

"Teacher, I brought my son to you, for he has a mute spirit; and wherever it seizes him, it dashes him down; and he foams and grinds his teeth and becomes rigid; and I asked your disciples to cast it out, and they were not able. And it has often cast him into fire and into water, to destroy him, but, if you can do anything, have pity on us.... Jesus said to him, "If you can! All things are possible with him who believes." The father cried out, "I believe, help my unbelief!" He rebuked the unclean spirit. ...after crying out and convulsing him terribly, it came out..." ...His disciples asked Him privately, "Why could we not cast it out?" And He said to them, "This kind cannot be driven out by anything but prayer and fasting." (Mark 9:14-29)

The Fifth Rosary of Miracles
Jesus Raises Lazarus from the Dead

Carl Bloch (1834-1890)

"Lord," Martha said to Jesus, "if you had been here, my brother would not have
died. But I know that even now God will give you whatever you ask." Jesus
said to her, "Your brother will rise again." Martha answered, "I know he will rise
again in the resurrection at the last day." Jesus said to her, "I am the resurrection
and the life. He who believes in me will live, even though he dies; and whoever
lives and believes in me will never die. Do you believe this?" "Yes, Lord," she
told him, "I believe that you are the Christ, the Son of God, who was to come
into the world." Jesus, once more deeply moved, came to the tomb. It was a
cave with a stone laid across the entrance. "Take away the stone," he said. "But,
Lord," said Martha, the sister of the dead man, "by this time there is a bad odor,
for he has been there four days." Then Jesus said, "Did I not tell you that if you
believed, you would see the glory of God?" So they took away the stone....
Jesus called in a loud voice, "Lazarus, come forth!" And presently he that had
been dead came forth, bound feet and hands with winding bands; and his face
was bound about with a napkin. Jesus said to them: "Loose him, and let him go.
(cf. John 11:1-56)

408

APPENDIX A

Brain Death & Organ Donation

"While some Catholics hold that the person is dead when there is complete and irreversible cessation of all brain activity ("whole brain death"), a growing number of Catholics agree that whole brain death cannot be used to diagnose the death of the person. Crucially, though, on a pragmatic level, this difference of opinion is irrelevant because the medical criteria to diagnose brain death establishes only partial loss of brain function ("partial brain death").[146]

All Catholics agree that patients with partial brain death are alive, and the Catholic Church forbids removing vital organs when this act would kill the patient.[147]

"More than 150 prominent Catholic clergy and laity have added their names to a document urging action against current standards of "brain death" because they are resulting in organ harvesting from persons who are still alive. Current standards for brain death 'do not provide moral (prudential) certainty of death' and often categorize persons who are not fully brain dead as being legally dead, the authors warn. "Catholics United on Brain Death and Organ Donation: A Call to Action" was released February 27, 2024. The statement is co-authored by Dr. Joseph M. Eble, Dr. John Di Camillo, and Professor Peter Colosi. The statement further observes that "since the current brain death criteria do not provide moral certainty of death" and "since it is morally wrong to remove vital organs when this would kill the patient, it is therefore wrong to remove organs from patients declared dead using these inadequate criteria." "As Catholics, we have an obligation to defend the sacredness of human life from conception to natural death. Given the facts above, even as there remains disagreement about whether and how the criteria could be improved, we call on our fellow Catholics to unite against utilization of the current brain death criteria, especially when determining death before vital organ transplantation."[148]

"Within the Church there have been points of disagreement between scholars on organ donation and whether brain death fulfills the requirements for actual death, i.e. when the soul leaves the body. In the year 2000, John Paul II delivered an address to the International Congress of the Transplantation Society. At the time, he said that brain death could potentially offer moral certainty of death only if there were "complete and irreversible cessation of all brain activity." (cf. March 5, 2024 LifesiteNews "More than 150 Catholic clergy, laity sign statement calling for changes to 'brain death' criteria".)[149]

"On April 11, 2024, the National Catholic Bioethics Center (NCBC) issued a landmark position statement, acknowledging that at least half of patients diagnosed as "brain dead" still have partial brain function. The NCBC statement was prompted by the 2023 updated guideline for the diagnosis of "brain death" published by the American Academy of Neurology (AAN) together with the American Academy of Pediatrics, the Child Neurology Society, and the Society of Critical Care Medicine. See article entitled, "Bioethics group admits most people declared 'brain dead' actually have brain function", *LifesiteNews,* April 22, 2024). [150]

Feeding Tubes and IVs

Question:

I spoke to a hospice representative about my Aunt Emma. She's 81 and a week ago suffered a stroke. When she arrived at the hospital she received an IV and a feeding tube three days later. She's no longer in ICU but in a regular room at the hospital. Her mind is good, but due to the stroke she is unable to swallow. She is able to walk, but needs a walker. She said she does not want to be put on a ventilator and wants to be DNR (Do Not Resuscitate). She has indicated that the IV and feeding tube isn't very painful but doesn't want to "live like a vegetable strung up with tubes." The hospital doctor said she could live for several weeks without any oral intake and without any IV or feeding tube and would die due to a lack of food and water and not from the stroke because her body can continue to assimilate food and water. He also said she could live years with a feeding tube and IV, but that there is a risk of infection at the feeding tube site. The hospice representative said they never have feeding tubes and IV's at their hospice, and that they could put her on "Comfort Care", and the staff would wet her mouth with a sponge and give her morphine shots to relieve her pain until she dies. They said the IV and feeding tube would need to be removed before she leaves the hospital and comes to their hospice. She is still able to talk. In fact, she said, she just wants to die, since she won't have a good quality of life. The Catholic doctor has said it would go against his conscience to remove the feeding tube and IV because a lack of food and water would be the cause of her death. Should Emma have a feeding tube and an IV? Can she morally be put on hospice? Can the Catholic hospital force the Catholic doctor to remove the feeding tube?

Answer:

Aunt Emma is responsible for her own decisions since her mind is good. She should seek advice from a priest about her decisions. The ventilator would be considered extraordinary medical care. However, if the use of a ventilator would be temporary with a good possibility of recovery and return to her normal life, then even a ventilator might be a choice she should make. What needs to be established is the purpose of the ventilator and whether there will be a reasonable hope for benefit or if the burdens are disproportionate to the good to be gained. With regard to the DNR, if there's no hope for a reasonable benefit in any form of treatment or care, then she could be placed on DNR.

The CDF document *Good Samaritan - On the Care of Persons in the Critical and Terminal Phases of Life* states, "Medicine today can artificially delay death, often without real benefit to the patient. When death is imminent, and without interruption of the normal care the patient requires in such cases, it is lawful according to science and conscience to renounce treatments that provide only a precarious or painful extension of life. However, it is not lawful to suspend treatments that are required to maintain essential physiological functions, as long as the body can benefit from them (such as hydration, nutrition, thermoregulation, proportionate respiratory support, and the other types of assistance needed to maintain bodily homeostasis and manage systemic and organic pain). The suspension of futile treatments must not involve the withdrawal of therapeutic care. This clarification is now indispensable in light of the numerous court cases in recent years that have led to the withdrawal of care from – and to the early death of–critically but not terminally ill patients, for whom it was decided to suspend life-sustaining care which would not improve the quality of life. In the specific case of aggressive medical treatment, it should be repeated that the renunciation of extraordinary and/or disproportionate means "is not the equivalent of suicide or euthanasia; it rather expresses acceptance of the human condition in the face of death" or a deliberate decision to waive disproportionate medical treatments which have little hope of positive results. The renunciation of treatments that would only provide a precarious and painful prolongation of life can also mean respect for the will of the dying person as expressed in advanced directives for treatment, excluding however every act of a euthanistic or suicidal nature."[151]

If Aunt Emma's decision to not have an IV and feeding tube is based solely upon giving up on life, due to not having the quality of life she desires, then her choice to end the IV and feeding tube is unethical. The provision of removal or withholding of assisted nutrition and hydration has to be considered in accord with the benefits and burdens of its use.

If Emma can receive the feeding tube food and fluids (IV) and it will nourish her body, then it likely should be given. If she would have an inability to assimilate food or was imminently dying (such that her death would not be caused by a lack of food or water, rather than the illness), or they would be excessively burdensome to her, and if she would not benefit from them, then a feeding tube and IV would not be morally obliged.

Good Samaritan states, "The principle of proportionality refers to the overall well-being of the sick person. To choose among values (for example, life versus quality of life) involves an erroneous moral judgment when it excludes from consideration the safeguarding of personal integrity, the good life, and the true moral object of the act undertaken. Every medical action must always have as its object—intended by the moral agent—the promotion of life and never the pursuit of death."

"A fundamental and inescapable principle of the assistance of the critically or terminally ill person is the continuity of care for the essential physiological functions. In particular, required basic care for each person includes the administration of the nourishment and fluids needed to maintain

413

bodily homeostasis, insofar as and until this demonstrably attains the purpose of providing hydration and nutrition for the patient. When the provision of nutrition and hydration no longer benefits the patient, because the patient's organism either cannot absorb them or cannot metabolize them, their administration should be suspended. In this way, one does not unlawfully hasten death through the deprivation of the hydration and nutrition vital for bodily function, but nonetheless respects the natural course of the critical or terminal illness. The withdrawal of this sustenance is an unjust action that can cause great suffering to the one who has to endure it. Nutrition and hydration do not constitute medical therapy in a proper sense, which is intended to counteract the pathology that afflicts the patient. They are instead forms of obligatory care of the patient, representing both a primary clinical and an unavoidable human response to the sick person. Obligatory nutrition and hydration can at times be administered artificially, provided that it does not cause harm or intolerable suffering to the patient."[152]

The doctor has the right to refuse to do something that is unethical and the Catholic hospital has a moral obligation to support the doctor and to prevent anything that would be immoral at the facility.

Good Samaritan states, "The physician is never a mere executor of the will of patients or their legal representatives, but retains the right and obligation to withdraw at will from any course of action contrary to the moral good discerned by conscience."[153]

"Catholic healthcare institutions are called to witness faithfully to the inalienable commitment to ethics and to the fundamental human and Christian values that constitute their identity. This witness requires that they abstain from plainly immoral conduct and that they affirm their formal adherence to the teachings of the ecclesial Magisterium. Any action that does not correspond to the purpose and values which inspire Catholic

414

healthcare institutions is not morally acceptable and endangers the identification of the institution itself as "Catholic."'[154]

Therefore, Aunt Emma cannot morally refuse an IV and feeding tube if they would not be unduly burdensome to her. She cannot morally choose to go on hospice because she can tolerate an IV and feeding tube. PEG tubes are easily placed with minimal burdens. They have the benefit of providing nutrition and fluids that will nourish the person without excessive difficulty. If a person can still benefit from nutrition and hydration and is not expected to die in the next two to three days (imminently), they should not enter a hospice facility or hospice program that refuses to provide IV hydration or nourishment through a feeding tube. If they did, the foreseen unacceptable outcome would be the person dying of dehydration and malnutrition rather than from their underlying disease or condition.

In fact, when a person who can no longer take food or water orally and yet continues to live for multiple days, it is a sign the person could benefit from an IV and feeding tube. A person should not die from a lack of food or water, but from the disease or illness.

It would be good if a Catholic priest could help Aunt Emma understand the dignity and beauty of life and that it's not based upon usefulness, but rather being created in the image and likeness of God. He could also tell her about how suffering is redemptive for her own soul and the souls of others when it's united to the sufferings of Jesus on the Cross. He should encourage her to hope and be prepared for her upcoming judgment and the joy of heaven. He should also be sure she is able to regularly receive the sacraments of Confession, the Holy Eucharist (a tiny particle of the Host could be given, if she would be able to swallow sips of water) and Anointing of the Sick. The priest should also accompany her through her suffering with his prayers and pastoral visits.

415

The National Catholic Bioethics Center can answer ethical questions by calling their hot line day or night. (215)-877-2660. Authored by Fr. Edmond Kline. Examined and approved by Dr. Joseph Meaney, PhD, KM, the president of the National Catholic Bioethics Center. Reviewed by Fr. Donald Henke, professor of Moral Theology and Bioethics, Kenrick Seminary.

APPENDIX C

Virtues of the Mysteries of the Rosary

The Joyful Mysteries
(Mondays, Saturdays, Sundays in Advent and Christmas)
1. The Annunciation: Humility
2. The Visitation: Love of Neighbor
3. The Nativity: Poverty of Spirit,
      & Detachment from Things of the World
4. The Presentation of Jesus at the Temple: Obedience
5. The Finding of Jesus in the Temple: Joy of Finding Jesus

The Luminous Mysteries
(Thursdays, Sundays in Ordinary Time after Theophany to Lent)
1. The Baptism of Jesus in the Jordan: Openness to the Holy Spirit
2. The Wedding at Cana: Mary's Intercession
3. Jesus' Proclamation of the Gospel: Trust in God
      & Call to Conversion
4. The Transfiguration. Desire for Holiness
5. The Institution of the Eucharist: Participation at Mass
      & Adoration

The Sorrowful Mysteries
(Tuesdays, Fridays, Sundays in Lent)
1. The Agony in the Garden:
      Sorrow for Sin, Union with the will of God
2. The Scourging at the Pillar: Mortification, Purity
3. The Crowning with Thorns: Moral Courage
4. The Carrying of the Cross: Patience, Self-denial
5. The Crucifixion: Perseverance, Forgiveness, Salvation

The Glorious Mysteries
(Wednesdays, Sundays during Easter, and Sundays in Ordinary Time after Easter until Advent)
1. The Resurrection: Faith
2. The Ascension: Hope, Desire for Heaven
3. The Descent of the Holy Spirit: Holy Wisdom and Love of God
4. The Assumption of Mary: Grace of a Happy Death
5. The Coronation of Mary: Trust in Mary's Intercession
      &True Devotion to Mary

The Miracle Mysteries
1. Jesus Heals a Paralytic:
      Help the Infirm Obtain Physical & Spiritual Healing
2. Jesus Heals Boy with a Mute Spirit:
      Overcome Evil by Faith, Prayer & Fasting
3. Jesus Walks on Water & Calms the Storm:
      Trust During Storms of Life & in the Church,
      & Recognize Jesus is God.
4. Multiplication of Loaves & Fish:
      Gratitude for God's Providence
      & Deeper Understanding of the Holy Mass
5. Jesus Raises Lazarus from the Dead:
      Faith in Jesus' Power over Death & the Resurrection of
      the Dead, Friend of Jesus

The Seven Sorrows Mysteries
Rosary of 7 Hail Marys for each of Her 7 mysteries of Her Sorrows.
1. Presentation in Temple
2. Flight into Egypt
3. Loss of Jesus for three days & search for Him.
4. Mary Meets Jesus on Way to Calvary.
5. Mary Stands at the Foot of the Cross
6. Jesus Taken from Cross Laid in Mary's Arms
7. Jesus is Laid in the Tomb. Seven Hail Marys, rather than ten,
      are prayed for each mystery.

The Franciscan Crown

Rosary of seven decades (10 Hail Marys),
       meditate on Mary's 7 joyful events.

1. Annunciation
2. Visitation
3. Birth of Jesus
4. Adoration of the Magi
5. Finding of the Child Jesus in the Temple
6. Appearance of Jesus to Mary after His Resurrection
7. Assumption and Coronation of Mary as Queen of Heaven.

Our Father between each decade, Glory Be, O My Jesus....

When the Rosary is completed, pray 2 additional Hail Marys, bringing the number of Hail Marys to 72, the traditional number of years of Our Lady's life.

APPENDIX D

Other Forms of Salve Regina

Salve Regina

Salve, Regina, Mater misericordiae,
vita, dulcedo, et spes nostra, salve.
ad te clamamus
exsules filii Evae,
ad te suspiramus, gementes et flentes
in hac lacrimarum valle.
Eia, ergo, advocata nostra, illos tuos
misericordes oculos ad nos converte;
et Iesum, benedictum fructum ventris tui,
nobis post hoc exsilium ostende.
O clemens, O pia, O dulcis Virgo Maria.

Ave, Regina Caelorum

From Presentation of Jesus, Feb 2 to Wed before Easter

Hail, O Queen of Heaven

Welcome, O Queen of Heaven.
Welcome, O Lady of Angels
Hail! thou root, hail! thou gate
From whom unto the world, a light has arisen:
Rejoice, O glorious Virgin,
Lovely beyond all others,
Farewell, most beautiful maiden,
And pray for us to Christ.

V. Allow me to praise thee, O sacred Virgin.
R. Against thy enemies give me strength.

Grant unto us, O merciful God, a defense against our weakness, that we who remember the holy Mother of God, by the help of her intercession, may rise from our iniquities, through the same Christ our Lord. Amen.

Ave Regina Caelorum

Ave, Regina caelorum,
Ave, Domina Angelorum:
Salve, radix, salve, porta
Ex qua mundo lux est orta:
Gaude, Virgo gloriosa,
Super omnes speciosa,
Vale, o valde decora,
Et pro nobis Christum exora.
V. Dignare me laudare te, Virgo sacrata.
R. Da mihi virtutem contra hostes tuos.

Oremus. Concede, misericors Deus, fragilitati nostrae praesidium: ut, qui sanctae Dei Genitricis memoriam agimus; intercessionis eius auxilio, a nostris iniquitatibus resurgamus. Per eundem Christum Dominum nostrum. Amen.

Regina Caeli

It is sung or said throughout Eastertide. From Easter Day through Pentecost, the seventh Sunday after Easter.

Queen of Heaven

V. Queen of Heaven, rejoice, alleluia.
R. For He whom you did merit to bear, alleluia.
V. Has risen, as he said, alleluia.
R. Pray for us to God, alleluia.
V. Rejoice and be glad, O Virgin Mary, alleluia.
R. For the Lord has truly risen, alleluia.

Let us pray. O God, who gave joy to the world through the resurrection of Thy Son, our Lord Jesus Christ, grant we beseech Thee, that through the intercession of the Virgin Mary, His Mother, we may obtain the joys of everlasting life. Through the same Christ our Lord. Amen.

Regina Caeli

V. Regina caeli, laetare, alleluia.

R. Quia quem meruisti portare, alleluia.

V. Resurrexit, sicut dixit, alleluia.

R. Ora pro nobis Deum, alleluia.

V. Gaude et laetare, Virgo Maria, alleluia.

R. Quia surrexit Dominus vere, alleluia.

Oremus. Deus, qui per resurrectionem Filii tui, Domini nostri Iesu Christi, mundum laetificare dignatus es: praesta, quaesumus; ut per eius Genetricem Virginem Mariam, perpetuae capiamus gaudia vitae. Per eundem Christum Dominum nostrum. Amen.

APPENDIX E

"The Miracle of the Rosary" lyrics
by Elvis Presley

Oh Blessed Mother we pray to Thee
Thanks for the Miracle of Your Rosary
Only You can hold back
Your Holy Son's hand
Long enough for the whole world to understand
Hail Mary full of grace
The Lord is with Thee
Blessed are thou among women
And blessed is the fruit of thy womb, Jesus
Oh Holy Mary dear Mother of God
Please pray for us sinners
Now and at the hour of our death
And give thanks once again
For the Miracle of Your Rosary

Notes

1   Fr. John Maria Devaney, O.P. "Elvis & the Rosary", *Dominicana, June 4, 2014.*

2   St. Louis Marie de Montfort, *The Secret of the Rosary*, (Bay Shore, NY: Montfort Publications, 1954), 54.

3   St. Louis Marie de Montfort, *The Secret of the Rosary*, (Bay Shore, NY: Montfort Publications, 1954), 26-27.

4   St. Louis Marie de Montfort, *The Secret of the Rosary*, (Bay Shore, NY: Montfort Publications, 1954), 97.

5   John Carpenter, "Divine Mysteries and Miracles",www. Divinemysteries.info/manila-philippines-1986

6   United States Conference of Catholic Bishops, *Manuel of Indulgences*, Norms and Grants (grant 7 §1, 1°), *Apostolic Penitentiary Translated into English from the fourth edition (1999) of Enchiridion Indulgentiarum:Normae et Concessiones* (Washington, DC)

7   St. Louis Marie de Montfort, *The Secret of the Rosary*, (Bay Shore, NY: Montfort Publications, 1954), 55.

8   Pope Saint John Paul II, *Rosarium Virginis Mariae*, Apostolic Letter, (Vatican City: Libreria Editrice Vaticana, 2002), #2

9   St. Louis Marie de Montfort, *The Secret of the Rosary*, (Bay Shore, NY: Montfort Publications, 1954), 54.

10 Saint Theodoret of Cyr, "From a treatise On the Incarnation of the Lord by Theodoret of Cyr, Bishop. *The Liturgy of Hours Vol. IV,* (New York: Catholic Book Publishing Corp., 1975), 94.

11 Bishop Fulton Sheen, "Life is Worth Living", Loneliness, Episode 7, Youtube.com Vision Video. (Rochester, NY: St. Bernard's School of Theology & Ministry)

12 "Suellen Brewster, "Signal Graces, How the Blessed Mother Encourages Her Little Ones." *Catholic Stand, May 27, 2018.*

13 St. Louis Marie de Montfort, *The Secret of the Rosary*, (Bay Shore, NY: Montfort Publications, 1954), 12.

14 Ibid, 62.

15 Saint Alphonsus Liguori, *The Glories of Mary*, Second American Edition (New York: Edward Dunigan & Brother, 1852), 716.

16 Ibid.

17 St. Louis Marie de Montfort, *The Secret of the Rosary*, (Bay Shore, NY: Montfort Publications, 1954), 93, 94

18 Saint Maria Faustina Kowalska, *Divine Mercy in My Soul, Diary of Saint Maria Faustina Kowalska*, (Stockbridge, MA: Marian Press, 2010), 11.

19 St. Louis Marie de Montfort, *The Secret of the Rosary*, (Bay Shore, NY: Montfort Publications, 1954), 11-12.

20 Father Fuentes interviewed Sister Lucia, December 26, 1957.

21 St. Louis Marie de Montfort, *The Secret of the Rosary*, (Bay Shore, NY: Montfort Publications, 1954), 64.

22 Ibid. 28-29.

23 Ibid, 99.

24 Vatican II, *Lumen Gentium*, Nov 21st, 1964, #62.

25 Saint Proclus, "From a sermon by Saint Proclus of Constantinople, bishop", *The Liturgy of Hours Vol. III*, (New York: Catholic Book Publishing Corp., 1975), 1643.

26 St. Peter Chrysologus, "From a sermon by Saint Peter Chrysologus, bishop", *The Liturgy of Hours*, Vol. III (New York, Catholic Book Publishing Corp., 1975), 1563.

27 St. Catherine of Sienna, "From a dialogue on Divine Providence by Saint Catherine of Siena, Virgin, *Liturgy of Hours* Vol III, (New York: Catholic Book Publishing Corp., 1975), 90-91.

28 *Pictorial Lives the Saints with Reflections for Every Day of the Year*, (New York, Cincinnati, St. Louis, Benziger Brothers, 1883, Eighth Edition), 341-342.

29 Steve Ray, "Mary the Ark of the New Covenant" (San Diego, Catholic Answers, 2019)

30 Archbishop Stephen Fumio Hamao, *"The Shrine: Memory, Presence and Prophecy of the Living God"*, Pontifical   Council for the Pastoral Care of Migrants and Itinerant People, May 8, 1999.

31 Scott Hahn, "Understanding Mary's Perpetual Virginity", November 21, 2018, St. Paul's Center,
www. stpaulcenter.com

32 Saint Proclus, "From a sermon by Saint Proclus of Constantinople, bishop", *The Liturgy of Hours Vol III*, (New York: Catholic Book Publishing Corp., 1975), 1643.

33 St. Clare, "From a letter by Blessed Agnes of Prague by Saint Clare, virgin." *The Liturgy of the Hours, Vol. 4*, (New York: Catholic Book Publishing Corp. 1975), 1311.

34 Ordo Franciscanus Saecularis, Consilium Internationale OFS (CIOFS) | (Rome: Italy, Secular Franciscan Order), www. ciofs.info

35 Father Edward McNamara, *"Why Abstinence from Meat"*, Daily Dispatch, Zenit.org, March 21, 2016 (Alpharetta: GA, Innovative Media Inc.)

36 Fr. Donald Calloway, "The Miraculous Image of Our Lady of Las Lajas", *Catholic Exchange* www.catholicexchange. com March 29, 2017

37 The Most Rev. Dr. MacEvilly, Archbishop of Tuam, *An Exposition of the Gospel of Luke, Consisting of An Analysis of Each Chapter and A Commentary, Critical, Exegetical, Doctrinal, and Moral*, Second Edition. (Dublin: Gill & Son, Upper O'Connell Street, 1887), 70.

38 St. Bernard of Clairvaux, "Sermon on the Feast of the Holy Family"

39 The Most Rev. Dr. MacEvilly, Archbishop of Tuam, *An Exposition of the Gospel of Luke, Consisting of An Analysis of Each Chapter and A Commentary, Critical, Exegetical, Doctrinal, and Moral*, Second Edition. (Dublin: Gill & Son, Upper O'Connell Street, 1887), 71.

40 Venerable Patrick Peyton, "The Family Rosary Crusade, Golden Gate Park San Francisco", October 1961, YouTube, Sensus Fidelium

41 Ibid.

42 Ibid.

43 Saint Alphonsus Liguori, *The Glories of Mary,* Second American Edition (New York: Edward Dunigan & Brother, 1852), 715-716.

44 Saint Alphonsus Liguori, *The Glories of Mary,* Second American Edition (New York: Edward Dunigan & Brother, 1852), 712.

45 Patrick Reilly, "Did Pope Francis Say, Don't Proselytize?" in *National Catholic Register,* Blog, Nov. 25, 2015. (Reprinted with permission)

46 Vatican II document, Ad Gentes, Chapter 2, Article 2, #13

47 Pope St. Paul VI's homily, Nov 29, 1970.

48 Catholic Answers, "Q.A., Where is Hell Mentioned in the Bible?" (San Diego: Catholic Answers, 2024)

49 St. Jean Baptiste Marie Vianney, "*Sermons of the Blessed Cure of Ars,* (New York: Joseph F. Wagner, 1901)

50 Guttmacher Institute, "One in Four US Women, Expected to Have an Abortion in Their Life Time" News Release, April 17th, 2024

51 Saint Vincent Ferrer, "A reading from the treatise of St Vincent Ferrer" *On the Spiritual Life.* (Rome: Pontifical University Saint Thomas Aquinas).

52 Saint Anthony Zaccaria, *Appendix to Sermon 1*, (Bethlehem, PA: Barnabites, Clerics of St. Paul)

53 Saint Alphonsus Liguori, *The Glories of Mary,* Second American Edition (New York: Edward Dunigan & Brother, 1852), 683-684.

54 Saint Alphonsus Liguori, *The Glories of Mary,* Second American Edition (New York: Edward Dunigan & Brother, 1852), 87-88.

55 Kathleen Heckenkamp, "Let us begin the Miraculous 54 Day Rosary Novena to Our Lady of Pompeii", Feb 14, 2020. www.OurLadyofGoodSuccess. com

56 Israel Tours, "Transfiguration on Mount Tabor", May 3, 2011. Israel-tourguide.info

57 Saint Thomas Aquinas, "From a work by Saint Thomas Aquinas, priest", *The Liturgy of the Hours Vol. I,* (New York: Catholic Book Publishing Corp. 1975), 610-611.

58 Jorge A. Card. Medina Estevez, November/December 2002 issue of *Notitiae, the Journal of the Congregation for Divine Worship and the Discipline of the Sacraments*, Prot. n. 1322/02/L, July 1, Rome 2002.

59 Peter Martin, "Largest ever survey of US Catholics shows faithful want an end to Communion in the hand", LifeSiteNews, Oct 15, 2024

60 Sergey Budgaey, "Safety and Reverence: How Roman Catholic Liturgy Can Respond to the COVID-19 Pandemic", Department of Biological Sciences, University of Bergen, Postboks 7803, 5020 Bergen, Norway

61 George Pollard, "The Revelation of the Immaculate Heart at Fatima in 1917, The Revelation Of The Two Hearts in Modern Times", (Irondale, Alabama, Eternal Word Television Network, Inc., 2024)

62 Reginald Walsh, O.P., *Meditation on the Passion, Complied From Various Sources, with an Introduction by Reginald Walsh, O.P.,* (Westminster, Maryland: The Newman Press, 1959), cf. 87 to 103.

63 Ibid., 99.

64 Ibid., 99 to 100.

65 Ibid.

66 Attributed to Blessed Dina Belanger, but unable to locate source.

67 Saint Elizabeth Ann Seton, "From a Conference to her spiritual daughters by Elizabeth Ann Seton", *Liturgy of Hours* Vol. I (New York: Catholic Book Publishing Corp, 1975), 1689 to 1691

68 Saint Maximilian Kolbe, *"From the Letters of Maximilian Mary Kolbe", The Liturgy Hours Supplement: New Feasts and Memorials for the Roman Calendar for the Dioceses of the United States of America* (New York: Catholic Book Publishing Corp, 1992), 11-13.

69 Reginald Walsh, O.P., *Meditation on the Passion, Compiled From Various Sources, with an Introduction by Reginald Walsh, O.P.,* (Westminster, Maryland: The Newman Press, 1959), 206.

70 Ibid.

71 Fr. Tommy Lane, "Jesus' Love for us as Revealed by the Shroud of Turin, 2013" from a homily,
www. Frtommylane.com

72   C. Truman Davis, M.D. M.S. "The Crucifixion of Jesus. The Passion of Christ from a Medical Point of View," Arizona Medicine Association, *Arizona's Medicine* 22, no. 3 [March 1965], 185.

73 Reginald Walsh, O.P., *Meditation on the Passion, Complied From Various Sources, with an Introduction by Reginald Walsh, O.P.,* (Westminster, Maryland: The Newman Press, 1959), 206.

74 Hannah Flynn, "Tattoos may increase blood cancer risk by 21%", *Medical News Today,* May 31st, 2024

75 Saint Alphonsus Liguori, *The Glories of Mary,* Second American Edition (New York: Edward Dunigan & Brother, 1852), 158-159.

76 Saint Alphonsus Liguori, *The Glories of Mary,* Second American Edition (New York: Edward Dunigan & Brother, 1852), 717.

77 Reginald Walsh, O.P., *Meditation on the Passion, Complied From Various Sources, with an Introduction by Reginald Walsh, O.P.,* (Westminster, Maryland: The Newman Press, 1959), 210-211.

78 Caroline de Sury, "The Astonishing History of Jesus' Crown of Thorns", *Our Sunday Visitor,* March 28, 2024

79 Ibid.

80 cf. Reginald Walsh, O.P., *Meditation on the Passion, Complied From Various Sources, with an Introduction by Reginald Walsh, O.P.,* (Westminster, Maryland: The Newman Press, 1959), 210-211.

81 "Virtue of the Month Fortitude", Offices of Catechesis and Evangelization and Catholic Schools in the Diocese of La Crosse, WI. www. diolc.org

82 Catholic Diocese of Youngstown, "Rhoda Wise Canton Woman Servant of God."www. doy.org/rhoda-wise

83 cf. Reginald Walsh, O.P., *Meditation on the Passion, Complied From Various Sources, with an Introduction by Reginald Walsh, O.P.,* (Westminster, Maryland: The Newman Press, 1959), 224.

84 Ibid.

85 Ibid.

86 Ibid.

87 cf. Ibid, 225

88 cf. Ibid.

89 Reginald Walsh, O.P., *Meditation on the Passion, Compiled From Various Sources, with an Introduction by Reginald Walsh, O.P.,* (Westminster, Maryland: The Newman Press, 1959), 237.

90 cf. Reginald Walsh, O.P., *Meditation on the Passion, Compiled From Various Sources, with an Introduction by Reginald Walsh, O.P.,* (Westminster, Maryland: The Newman Press, 1959), 229.

91 Ibid, 236.

92 Ibid, 237.

93 Ibid, 239.

94 Ibid, 240.

95 Fr. Charles Grondin, "Why Do Churches Have Crucifixes If Jesus Is Risen?" (San Diego, Catholic Answers, 1996-2024)

96 St. Thomas Aquinas, "From a conference by St. Thomas Aquinas, priest" *The Liturgy of the Hours*, Vol III, (New York: Catholic Book Publishing Corp. 1975), 1335-1336.

97 Saint John Chrysostom, "From a homily by Saint John Chrysostom, bishop", *The Liturgy of the Hours, Vol III*, (New York: Catholic Book Publishing Corp., 1975), 1646.

98 Saint Carlo Acutis, *The Eucharistic Miracles of the World*, (Regensburg, Germany, 1255).

99 Father Kenneth Doyle, "Nailed Through Wrists or Hands?", *The Arlington Catholic Herald*, 08/28/13, © Catholic News Service / U.S Conference of Catholic Bishops

100 Father Robert Spitzer, "Shroud of Turin: Evidence of Jesus' Resurrection?", (Garden Grove, California: Magis Center of Reason and Faith), 2015

101 Pope Saint John Paul II, "General Audience", May 21st, 1997.

102 Joseph Pronechen, "After His Resurrection, Jesus Appeared First to His Mother Mary, Say the Saints", in *National Catholic Register*, Blog, April 06, 2021. (Reprinted with permission)

103 Ibid.

104 Jim Graves, "Clues on the Shroud of Turin Tell Us What Christ Endured on Good Friday", Commentary in *National Catholic Register*, April 22, 2021 (Reprinted with permission)

105 Saint Gregory the Great. "From a homily on the Gospels by Saint Gregory the Great, pope." Feast of Thomas, Apostle. *The Liturgy of Hours Vol. III*, (New York: Catholic Book Publishing Corp., 1975), 1516.

106 *The Navarre Bible, Reader's Edition, The Gospels and Acts of the Apostles*, (Dublin: Four Courts Press, Scepter Press), Princeton, NJ.,) cf 182-184. (Dublin, Ireland: Four Courts Press, 2005)

107 The Most Rev. Dr. MacEvilly, Archbishop of Tuam, *An Exposition of the Gospel of Luke, Consisting of An Analysis of Each Chapter and A Commentary, Critical, Exegetical, Doctrinal, and Moral*, Second Edition. (Dublin: Gill & Son, Upper O'Connell Street, 1887), 245-246.

108 Jimmy Akin, "What did Jesus do for 40 days?", *Catholic Answers*, April 2nd, 2024. www.Catholic.com

109 Maura Roan McKeegan, "The Living Rosary: An Old Devotion for the New Year", December 21, 2016, www. catholicexchange.com

110 David Dionisi, "It Stopped Ebola", by 101 Foundation, Summer of 2016 Newsletter Number 105, pg 2.

111 "Who Was Our Lady of Cuapa?" "This is the seventh article in a series on approved apparitions of the Blessed Virgin Mary". www.TheDivineMercy.org, June 15, 2018.

112 cf. The Most Rev. Dr. MacEvilly, Archbishop of Tuam, *An Exposition of the Gospel of Luke, Consisting of An Analysis of Each Chapter and A Commentary, Critical, Exegetical, Doctrinal, and Moral,* Second Edition. (Dublin: Gill & Son, Upper O'Connell Street, 1887), 246.

113 Bishop Frederick Justus Knecht, D.D, *A Practical Commentary on Holy Scripture from the 16th German Edition*, (Charlotte, North Carolina: Tan Books, 2013), 820.

114 Ibid.

115 Josh Perry, "The Presence of Christ at Mass", *The Inland See*, March 19, 2023, The Roman Catholic Diocese of Burlington.

116 The Most Rev. Dr. MacEvilly, Archbishop of Tuam, *An Exposition of the Gospel of Luke, Consisting of An Analysis of Each Chapter and A Commentary, Critical, Exegetical, Doctrinal, and Moral,* Second Edition. (Dublin: Gill & Son, Upper O'Connell Street, 1887), 246.

117 *The Miracles of Saint Dominic, Narrated by Sister Cecilia*, Chapter 6, (Washington, DC: The Thomist Press), April 29, 1964.

118 June Klins, "The Fruit of Faithful Prayer of Two Mothers", (Erie, Pennsylvania: The Spirit of Medjugorje Online, Vol 26, #5 , May 5, 2013)

119 St. Cyprian, "From a letter by Saint Cyprian, bishop and martyr" from Saints Pontian and Hippolytus Memorial, *The Liturgy of Hours Vol. IV*, (New York: Catholic Book Publishing Corp., 1975), 1314.

120 St. John Chyrostom, "From a homily on the first letter to the Corinthians. Feast of St. Bartholomew, Apostle, *The Liturgy of Hours, Vol. IV*, (New York: Catholic Book Publishing Corp., 1975), 1344.

121 Alejandro Bermudez, "Why Our Lady of the Pillar is the patroness of Spain and the Americas", *Catholic News Agency*, Oct 12, 2021.

122 Ibid.

123 St. Philip Romolo Neri, *Catholic Encyclopedia*, (New York: Robert Appleton Company, 1911) www. newadvent.org

124 *Pictorial Lives the Saints with Reflections for Every Day of the Year*, (New York, Cincinnati, St. Louis: Benziger Brothers, 1883, Eighth Edition), 353-354.

125 cf. Saint Alphonsus Liguori, *The Glories of Mary*, ed Rev. Eugene Grimm, (St. Louis, Brooklyn, Toronto: Redemptorist Fathers, P.J. Kennedy and Sons, 1931), 407-423.

126 Fr. William Saunders, Mary's Assumption, "Please explain our Catholic belief in the Assumption of Our Blessed Mother", *Arlington Catholic Herald*

127 Saint Alphonsus Liguori, *The Glories of Mary, ed* Rev. Eugene Grimm, (St. Louis, Brooklyn, Toronto: Redemptorist Fathers, P.J. Kennedy and Sons, 1931), 420-421.

128 St. Alphonsus Liguori, *The Glories of Mary*, ed Rev. Eugene Grimm, (St. Louis, Brooklyn, Toronto: Redemptorist Fathers, P.J. Kennedy and Sons, 1931), 233-234.

129 Thomas a Kempis, *The Imitation of Christ*, (Introduction by William J. Peterson), Public Domain, Chapter 23

130 Saint Alphonsus Liguori, *Glories of Mary*, "Various Additional Examples Appertaining to the Most Holy Mary", (New York: P.J. Kennedy and Sons, 1888), #23.

131 Rev. Scott A. Haynes, "Stories of the Brown Scapular" in Mystical Theology, www.mysticaltheologyofthemass.com

132 *Manuel of Indulgences*, Norms and Grants (grant 7 §1, 1°), *Apostolic Penitentiary Translated into English from the fourth edition (1999) of Enchiridion Indulgentiarum: Normae et Concessiones*

133 Pope St. Leo the Great, "From the beginning of a sermon on the beatitudes by Saint Leo the Great, pope" *Liturgy of the Hours*, Vol. IV (New York: Catholic Book Publishing Corp. 1975) 206.

134 "Eucharistic Miracles at Lourdes, France 1888" in *The Real Presence*, www. therealpresence.org

135 Saint Thomas Aquinas, "From a work by Saint Thomas Aquinas, priest", *The Liturgy of the Hours Vol. I*, (New York: Catholic Book Publishing Corp. 1975), 610-611.

136 *The Roman Catechism, The Catechism of the Council of Trent for Parish Priests*, (Charlotte, North Carolina: Tan Books, 2017), 249.

137 "Mystical Church - Gift of Multiplication of food - Saint Dominic", *Anointing Fire Catholic Media*, https://afcmmedia.org/index.html

138 Saint Carlo Acutis, "The Eucharistic Miracles of the World. An International Exhibition Eucharistic Miracle Display", Bois-Seigneur-Isaac, Belgium.

139 *Pictorial Lives the Saints with Reflections for Every Day of the Year*, (New York, Cincinnati, St. Louis: Benziger Brothers, 1883, Eighth Edition), 357.

140 St. John Bosco, (Memoirs, Vol. VII. Pages 107-108), May 30, 1862.

141 John T. Driscoll. "Wonders performed by supernatural power as signs of some special mission or gift and explicitly ascribed to God", *Catholic Encyclopedia*, (New York: Robert Appleton Company, 1911) by way of *Catholic Answers*, www. catholic.com

142 Rev. Daniel Merz, In writings of Alexander Schmemann, "Notes in Liturgical Theology", *St. Vladimir's Seminary Quarterly*, Vol. 3, No. 1, Winter 1959, pp. 2-9.

143 Alice Schoenhofer and Celia Chin, Apostolate of Perpetual Adoration, Wichita, Kansas. They required parishes to fast 40 days prior to starting Perpetual Eucharistic Adoration Chapels. Together they started over 100 Perpetual Adoration chapels in the United States.

144 St. Louis Marie de Montfort, *The Secret of the Rosary*, (Bay Shore, NY: Montfort Publications, 1991), 76-79.

145 *The Miracles of Saint Dominic, Narrated by Sister Cecilia*, Chapter 6, (Washington, DC: The Thomist Press), April 29, 1964.

146 Joseph Eble, M.D, Opinion: "Catholics Should Not Be 'Brain Death' Organ Donors". Commentary: The April 11 statement by The National Catholic Bioethics Center affirms that 'a partial brain death standard can never be acceptable to Catholics.' *National Catholic Register*, April 29, 2024. www.ncregister.com

147 Pope Saint John Paul, "Address of the Holy Father John Paul II to the 18th International Congress of the Transplantation Society", Aug 29, 2000.

148 Stephen Kokx, "More than 150 Catholic clergy, laity sign statement calling for changes to 'brain death' criteria," *LifesiteNews,* March 5, 2024.

149 Ibid.

150 Heidi, Klessig, M.D., "Bioethics group admits most people declared 'brain dead' actually have brain function", *LifesiteNews*, April 22, 2024.

151 Luis F. Card. Ladaria, S.I. *Samaritanus bonu*, "On the care of persons in the critical and terminal phases of life", V. The Teaching of the Magisterium, #2, July 14, 2020, Offices of the Congregation for the Doctrine of the Faith.

152 Ibid, V. The Teaching of the Magisterium, #3

153 Ibid, V. The Teaching of the Magisterium, #2
154 Ibid, V. The Teaching of the Magisterium, #9